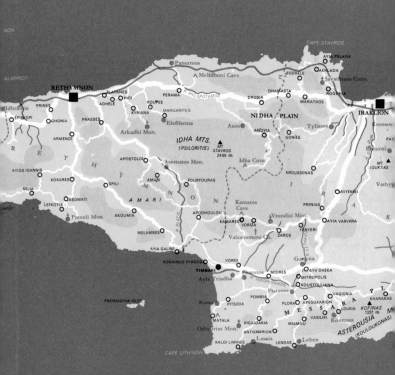

SEA OF CRETE

CAPE STAVROS

AYIA PELAYIA

Panormos

Melidhoni Cave   FODHELE
                                    Savathiana Conv.
ALMYROS   AKHLADA
                                                      ROGDHIA
RETHYMNON   PLATANES   DHAMASTA
                        PERAMA   DROSIA   IRAKLION
Idhramia   PRINES   ADHELE   PIGI   MARATHOS
    EPISKOPI   ROUPES   NI DHA PLAIN   Knossos
        GHONIA   PRASSES   KYRIANA   MARGARITES   Fourni
            ARMENOI   Eleftherna   Axos   ANOYIA   Tylissos   MT.
R   Arkadhi Mon.   GONIES   IOUKTAS
    AYIOS IOANNIS   E   IDHA MTS.   Vathys
                    T   (PSILORITIS)   MT.   KROUSSENAS
        KOXARES   H   APOSTOLOI   STAVROS   I   AVYENIKI
    SELIA   Y   Asomatos Mon.   2456 m   Idha Cave   R
        LEFKOYIA   M   SPILI   AMARI   FOURFOURAS   PRINIAS   A
    castle   ASOMATI   A M A R I   N   Kamares   Vrondisi Mon.   K
            Preveli Mon.   AKOUMIA   APODHOULOU   Cave   VORIZA   AYIA VARVARA
                        MELAMBES   KAMARES   YERYERI
                                    Valsamonero Ch.   ZAROS
                    AYIA GALINI   Gortyna
            KOKHINOS PYRGOS   VOROI
                        TIMBAKI   Phaestos   MOIRES   AYII DHEKA
                            Ayia Triadha   MITROPOLIS
    PAXIMADHIA ISLES   Platanos   KOUSTOULIANA   VAGIONIA
                        Komo   PITSIDIA   POMBIA   PLORA APESOKARION   KHARAKAS
                            MATALA   M E S S A R A   LOUKIA   KOFINAS
                        Odiyitrias Mon.   PIGAIDAKIA   VASILIKI   MIAMOU   Koumasa   1231 m
                                ANTISKARION   ASTEROUSIA
                    KALOI LIMINES   Lasaia   LENDAS   Leben   (KOULOUKONAS)
            CAPE LITHINON

LIBYAN SEA

Crete

Crete

Travellers' Guide

Crete

by John Bowman

Jonathan Cape London

By the same author:

Early Civilizations
The Quest for Atlantis
Imperial Greece
Treasures of Ancient Greece

First published 1962
Second edition 1969
Reprinted 1970, 1972, 1973
Third edition 1974
Fourth edition 1978
Fifth edition 1981
Sixth edition 1985
Reprinted with corrections 1987
Seventh edition 1990

Maps drawn by Janet Landau and John Hunt
General Editors: Judith Greene and June Gordon-Walker

Jonathan Cape Ltd
20 Vauxhall Bridge Road, London SW1V 2SA

A CIP catalogue record for this book is available from the British Library

Cover photograph of 'Bull Leaping' Fresco, Minoan Royal Palace, Knossos (Travel Photo International)

ISBN 0-224-02638-0

Typeset by Computape (Pickering) Ltd, North Yorkshire and printed in Great Britain by Thomson Litho Ltd, East Kilbride

CONTENTS

MAPS AND CHARTS

Note on pronunciation Although there are a number of minor differences between the Greek spoken on Crete and on the mainland (see p. 116), the main challenge to foreigners who attempt to use Greek – apart from the alphabet – is to place the stress on the right syllable. Native Greek speakers must hear the correct stress before they recognize the word. To help with this, the Index lists all Greek names and words with an acute accent to mark the stress.

Meanwhile, the question of transliterating Greek words into English, always a vexing problem, has been compounded by the Greeks' desire to use a system more in keeping (or so they feel) with the modern language. Thus Psykhro is now Psihro (just as Athens is Athine): this may be 'purer' but it doesn't always help the English-speaker pronounce the Greek. The best advice is to remain alert and open to various possibilities.

Acknowledgments

Since the first edition of this guide appeared, many individuals have inevitably helped to contribute to it in many ways. For instance, any book like this depends on numerous authorities and sources – the works of archaeologists, the authors of other books, those professionally engaged in tourism – not to mention the many Cretans who have provided information along the way. To single out but two, all who write about Crete's history are indebted to the researches of Sterghios Spanakis, just as all who come to know Khania and its nome are indebted to Anestis Makridakis. And we especially want to acknowledge the work of Hanni Guanella – not just for help in the revisions but in revealing Crete through her own writings. Since translating the first edition of this guide into German, Hanni Guanella has become one of that select band of foreigners who have wholly embraced Crete. We remain indebted to the instigator and inspirer of the guide, Andreas Vlahakis, and now we are especially indebted to his successor at the National Tourist Organization in Iraklion, Evangelos Smaryanakis: both true Cretans, who give of themselves beyond the call of duty. In particular, Mr Smaryanakis has given special help for revisions in recent years. We would also like to repeat our thanks to Robert Grantham, one of the first to discover and introduce to some of us the Crete that so many have since come to enjoy. Here, too, we thank Kathryn Thompkins, lecturer at Manchester University, for her contributions to various specialized sections; Dr. N. C. Flemming, of the British Institute of Oceanographic Sciences, for his guidance on geological matters; Kostas Pallierakis, the extraordinary operator of the tourist information office in Rethymnon; John Richmond, for help in revising; and Dorothy Andrews and the Hogans, three legendary residents of Khania, for their insights and kindnesses. For aid in producing the recent editions, I should like to thank the National Tourist Organization of Greece, Olympic Airways, Hertz Corporation and Mikhalis Karapiperis of Hertz of Iraklion. And to Professor Joseph Shaw, chief of excavations at Kommos, special thanks for his extraordinary cooperation with the account and plan of this fascinating and emerging new site.

The author is always pleased to hear from users of the guide c/o the publisher.

INTRODUCTION

Mention Crete to many people and they will retort with something such as '... one of those Greek islands ... with the Minoans, isn't it?' Although it is obvious why people might think this, the fact is that Crete is not just another Greek island. Its independent history goes back a very long way – Crete did not even join the Greek nation officially until 1913 – and the islanders often think of themselves as Cretans first and Greeks second. This is nothing to worry about, but the visitor might be aware of it. Beyond this, the casual tourist might also be informed that all who come to know Crete really well – lured though they may have been by the Minoan sites – end by becoming involved with another Crete, an island with many other layers of culture, a realm of nature, a living people.

And because of the island's intense variety, with its rich history, dramatic landscapes and proud traditions, we can understand the self-sufficiency of its inhabitants and their feelings that Crete has everything to offer the visitor. One of the biggest islands in the Mediterranean, it seems still larger, owing to the configuration of mountains and valleys which can make a journey of even a few miles into an exciting expedition (an effect sometimes reinforced by the condition of certain minor roads).

Since the early 1960s, when this guide first took shape, tremendous changes have occurred on Crete, not all to everyone's liking but most of them inevitable as part of the times – and many of them attributable to each and every tourist who has set foot on the island. Some of the changes seem superficial – literally: new shop-fronts, for instance, or a luxury hotel on a bare stretch of coast, a straight highway imposed on the rough terrain. Other developments are deeper and more pervasive: the growing chic and cosmopolitanism in the major tourist centres; the prosperity that transforms many towns and villages; new industrial and touristic enterprises that affect employment and work habits. These in turn lead to more subtle but no less crucial changes: a more blasé attitude in the cities, a certain wariness in the villages, as more and more Cretans become accustomed to the stream of foreigners; a homogenization and 'bourgeoisization' of a people leaving its rural roots and becoming a consumer society.

But it is more than futile to spend one's time criticizing the disappearance of the more traditional, even naive, Crete: who is to deny each Cretan the right to take a share of the modern world? And

CHART OF EXCURSIONS

Centre	Iraklion	Rethymnon
Town sights	*Major* Archaeological Museum Harbour, Venetian Castle and Wall Fountain Square, Market Cathedral of Ayios Menas Historical and Ethnographic Museum *Minor* Basilica of St Mark Church of Ayios Titos Venetian Loggia Liberty Square Church of St Katherine	*Major* Loggia and Museum Venetian Fort *Minor* Arimondi Fountain Churches Minarets
Major excursions	*Half day* Knossos (5 km.) Mallia (39 km.) *Full day* Arkhanes (Phourni), Mount Iouktas and Vathypetro (21 km.) Gortyna, Phaestos and Ayia Triadha (65 km.), Kommos (75 km.) Mallia, Ayios Nikolaos and Gournia (90 km.) Lasithi Plain and Dhiktaion Cave (69 km.) Arkadhi Monastery and Rethymnon (112 km.) Kato Zakros (185 km.)	*Half day* Arkadhi Monastery (22 km.) *Full day* Iraklion and Knossos (83 km.) Khania (72 km.)
Minor excursions	*Half day* Fodhele (34 km.) Tylissos (14 km.) Eileithyia Cave, Amnisos, Nirou Khani and Limin Khersonisou (31 km.) Melidhoni Cave (60 km.) *Full day* Ano Viannos and Arvi (85 km.) Kommos (75 km.) and Matala (80 km.)	*Half day* Preveli Monastery (38 km.) Melidhoni Cave (30 km.) Margarites (27 km.) *Full day* Fourfouras for Amari Province (43 km.) Ayia Galini (64 km.) Khora Sfakion (80 km.)
Overnight excursions	Gortyna, Phaestos, Ayia Triadha and Matala (80 km.) or Leben (111 km.) or Tombs of the Messara (89 km.) Rethymnon and Khania (150 km.) Ierapetra via Ayios Nikolaos (109 km.) or Ano Viannos (105 km.) Kamares for Cave (57 km.)	Phaestos, Ayia Triadha and Gortyna via Iraklion (143 km.) or Spili (105 km.) Anoyia for Mt Idha Summit and Cave (54 km.)

Khania	Ayios Nikolaos
Major Archaeological Museum (Church of St Francis) Janissaries' Mosque Church of St Nicholas Church of Ayii Anargyri Minaret, Harbour	*Major* Archaeological Museum *Minor* 'Bottomless Pool' Almyros
Minor Historical Museum, Inner and Outer Walls Other Venetian buildings and churches Cathedral of Our Lady, Arsenals Khalepa Quarter	
Half day The Akrotiri including Ayia Triadha Monastery (17 km.) *Full day* Rethymnon and Arkadhi Monastery (94 km.) Gorge of Samaria (44 km.)	*Half day* Mallia (33 km.) Kritsa and Lato (16 km.) Gournia and Ierapetra (38 km.) *Full day* Mallia, Knossos and Iraklion (76 km.) Sitia and Eastern Crete including Kato Zakros (122 km.)
Half day Aptera (15 km.) Ghonia Monastery (24 km.) Theriso (17 km.) Mournies (5 km.) *Full day* Khora Sfakion (74 km.) Kastelli-Kissamou for North-west Crete (42 km.) Palaiokhora for Selinos Province (77 km.)	*Half day* Elounda and Spinalonga (11 km.) *Full day* Psira and Mokhlos Islands (by boat) Lasithi Plain and Dhiktaion Cave (48 km.)
Rethymnon and Iraklion (150 km.) Gavdhos Island (by boat from Palaiokhora, 77 km.)	Arvi via Ierapetra (86 km.) Myrtos (53 km.)

the fact remains that one has only to leave the main streets, the major sites, the tourist routes, and then the old Crete can still be experienced – the Crete of rough overland trails, simple cafés, isolated archaeological sites, unspoilt beaches.

Statistics show that most tourists arrive in June, July, August and September, with another slight rise around April due to Easter activities. And it is true that Iraklion and Knossos, in particular, can occasionally give the impression that organized tourism has taken over, what with several cruise parties ashore for the day and planeloads of vacationers who fill the hotels and bungalows along the coast from Iraklion to Ayios Nikolaos. Those who simply can't abide crowds should pick off-season weeks or visit the main attractions at off-peak hours.

Apart from these situations, all real travellers can still feel as though they have the island to themselves. This guide is designed for such travellers, whether they come to spend one day or one year on Crete. It is organized into three sections: the travel data and practical information for planning a trip; essays on the background of the island; and the actual sights and itineraries, fanning out from the main centres. To help each visitor in planning a holiday, we have included the Chart of Excursions, (pp. 12–13) showing the various major and secondary sights that can be visited from each of the main centres. All the principal archaeological sites, incidentally, are accessible throughout the year, though some of the caves, mountain peaks or remote villages and chapels – and, of course, the Gorge of Samaria (p. 278) – are cut off by winter weather.

The natural centre for visiting the major archaeological sites – Knossos, Gortyna, Phaestos and Mallia – is Iraklion, commercial hub of the island and also home of the world's greatest collection of Minoan art. While Iraklion is a bustling city with varied facilities and popular diversions, it does not have the nostalgic appeal of the Venetian and Turkish remains of Khania. This town, which can be reached directly by ship or air from the mainland, provides a base for visiting some of the wilder and lesser-known parts of Crete – Sfakia Province and the Gorge of Samaria in the south, and the extreme western regions. At the other end of the island, lazing on the beaches of the attractive little towns of Ayios Nikolaos or Sitia can be combined with visiting such sites as Gournia or the palace at Kato Zakros. And Rethymnon – on the north coast, halfway between Iraklion and Khania – offers its attractions, from historical buildings to a sandy beach.

Apart from a trip across the island to Phaestos and the interesting sights of the Messara Plain, the whole interior provides endless inducements to explore: spectacular mountains to be climbed or just looked at, ancient myth-haunted caves, isolated monasteries and villages where the life has changed little over the centuries. Increasing numbers of foreigners are also finding their way to the under-developed villages and beaches along the south coast, and visitors with more time will have the opportunity of discovering lesser-known sites and fragmentary ruins, as well as remote villages and deserted beaches, in every corner of the island.

All of this is described in this guide. But apropos of the changes referred to earlier, it should be said that Crete, for all its agelessness and traditionalism, is changing. New archaeological finds, new tourist facilities, changes in the contemporary scene, reinterpretations of the past – these are occurring year in and year out. No book can keep up with all the details, but we can advise the visitor to be prepared to meet these developments.

A final word about discovering Crete. On the one hand, the island appears to yield easily to the curiosity of the foreigner; the people seem open and spontaneous, their hospitality encourages everyone to feel they have broken through the surface. But Crete has hidden depths. To a transient foreigner, it may appear to have become a tourist-centred island; but Cretans take little pleasure in this if true, and resent your perceiving this if false. Whatever foreigners or Cretans may feel about current developments on the island, it retains much of its unique, intense way of life. For the discerning, even the shortest visit to Crete can be a stimulating and rewarding adventure.

Note on Changes in Accommodation, Prices, Travel Costs, Visiting Hours, etc.

In recent years, a number of factors have created a situation of almost constant uncertainty in many of the details that people would like to find pinned down in a guidebook. But it is misleading – even potentially ruinous for some individuals' holiday plans – to pretend that all such details can be provided much in advance.

Consider the prices of everything from travel costs to hotels and other accommodation, meals, admission fees, etc.: about all that can be said for certain is that they will rise. So rather than give a lot of specific information for every class of boat ticket, every hotel category, every admission fee, this edition offers various comparisons, characterizations, or 'baselines' that should allow travellers to make reasonable calculations. Relationships, in particular, will remain the same: that is, if Class A was $2\frac{1}{2}$ times as much as Class C in 1990, it will probably be that way in 1993.

Or take the visiting hours to museums and archaeological sites. Not only do these change continually – daily schedules, closed days, half days, etc. – but many churches and chapels and minor archaeological sites that once remained open to all are now kept locked so that you must find the custodian or the key in some nearby village. Especially if you have a limited time or special goals for your holiday, it can be most important to know which places are open when. Our advice now is to enquire from a Tourist Information Office about all such matters immediately upon arriving in Iraklion, Khania, or any centre on Crete itself.

As for sleeping and eating facilities on Crete, this guide has never engaged in rating them but tried to list everything available. With the increase in the numbers of hotels, restaurants, and all such facilities, it seems meaningless to go on adding names, addresses, etc. Instead, we feel we provide something far more helpful: general conditions and essential characteristics (with occasional praise or warning when it seems called for).

With the increase in the numbers of people who come to Crete – especially during the summer months from May until September – aeroplanes, car ferries, hotels and the many package tours to Crete can be booked up. (August is probably the most crowded month – come some other time if at all possible.) Anyone who has a tight schedule and particular wants should make reservations well in advance. However, with a bit of flexibility, no traveller will ever be forced to spend the night in a Minoan tomb.

Final Warnings: Presumably users of this guide won't need to know this, but Greeks are ruthless when they apprehend foreign drug-users or smugglers.

Meanwhile, females report unpleasant encounters with Greek males: probably no more than elsewhere, but still, be wary.

Finally, and for the first time in over 25 years this guide has been in print, it seems necessary to say something about a change in the 'atmospherics' of tourism on Crete (and wherever in Greece tourism has blossomed). It can undoubtedly be explained if not justified by the sheer volume of tourists and the demands they place on the people as well as the resources, but whatever the cause, the issue must be faced: increasing numbers of visitors to Crete report unhappy encounters – not necessarily illegal, not threatening, but unhappy. Typical situations include: taxi drivers who overcharge or take passengers to hotels or restaurants other than those requested (presumably because the drivers get commissions); car rental agencies that produce vehicles other than the one reserved; facilities that simply do not live up to their advertisements (e.g. some still under construction); ticket agents that don't warn of special limitations or conditions on ships, etc.; restaurants or bars that charge inflated prices for items not on the menu; etc. So travellers beware: insist on getting what you are paying for.

GETTING TO CRETE

AIR

There is occasionally a service from London to Iraklion and, at least in the summer, to Khania as well. However most people taking scheduled commercial flights to Crete will be coming via Athens, which is itself served by most of the major international airlines. Internal air traffic in Greece is a monopoly of Olympic Airways – which has an excellent safety record – and all Olympic flights, international and domestic, operate from the West Air Terminal of the Hellenikon (Athens) Airport. Almost all other airlines use the (newer) East Air Terminal; there are frequent buses running between these two terminals, but you should consult the airline offices or travel agents about allowing for sufficient transfer time. Passengers who commence their flights within Greece may be limited to 15 kilos of luggage free of charge; those connecting with flights abroad are allowed two pieces of luggage and one carry-on. Olympic Airways provides a bus service between its airports and the cities for a nominal fee (although groups of 2–3 or more may find it almost as cheap to share a taxi to and from the airports of Iraklion and Khania).

There has long been a direct service between Iraklion and Rhodes with Olympic Airways – several weekly; flight time is about 45 minutes. And there is now an Olympic service between Rhodes and Sitia, in north-eastern Crete; three flights weekly, with stops at Karpathos and Kasos, the two islands between Rhodes and Crete. In 1980 Olympic introduced direct flights between Iraklion and Santorini (Thera) – several flights weekly only during the tourist season – and now there is direct service between Iraklion and Mykonos and between Iraklion and Paros during the tourist season; there is also direct service linking Iraklion and Saloniki, Greece's second largest city, up in the north. Meanwhile, Olympic Airlines has had some flights direct between Iraklion and Cyprus: enquire to see if this service is operating.

Over the years, Olympic and other airlines have occasionally offered direct flights between Crete and certain European cities such as London or Frankfurt-am-Main, Germany. Enquire at travel agents to learn if any are operating at present. Such flights should not be confused with the numerous charter flights that now connect Crete directly with several European cities; these charter flights are usually part of a package holiday (including accommodation, at least some meals, various extras, etc.), and have come to be very attractive economically as they can sometimes provide complete holidays for little more than a regular air fare. Most of these group charter flights place people in large hotels, but some may offer separate villas or village houses. (For a discussion of villas on Crete, and a list of some of the companies in Great Britain and the USA that can make arrangements, with or without air tickets, see pp. 42–3.)

The cost of air travel has been rising so in recent years that it can only be misleading to give precise fares in a book like this. But just to provide some general basis for planning, in 1990 a one-way fare between Athens and Iraklion or between Iraklion and Rhodes was about Drs 7,500, while that between Athens and Khania was about Drs 6,500. There are reductions for children and infants. Enquire at travel agents.

SEA

From Outside Greece

Most visitors travelling to or from Crete by ship will be using Piraeus, the port for Athens, but there are some possibilities for direct links to foreign ports. Several lines that ply the Mediterranean, especially during the spring-summer-autumn months, put in at Crete (usually Iraklion) on their way between French, Italian, or Yugoslavian ports and Turkey, Lebanon, Israel, Egypt, Rhodes, or Cyprus. The most recent service is one provided by Adriatic Lines; it moves back and forth between Venice, Italy; Dubrovnik, Yugoslavia; Piraeus, Greece; Iraklion; and Alexandria, Egypt. And Stability Line offers service between Piraeus, Iraklion, Limassol (Cyprus) and Haifa (Israel). The problem with all such services is that they tend to change from year to year. Still, anyone interested in travelling to Crete this way should enquire at a travel agent about (or attempt to contact directly) such shipping lines as: Extra Value Line, Karageorgis Line, Hellenic-Mediterranean Lines, Louis Cruise Lines, Ltd (and possibly others). Most of these lines, by the way, take vehicles as well as passengers. None are cheap.

Occasional freighters from foreign ports put in at Crete, but only if they have cargo to discharge or load, and the average traveller will be unable to arrange to get to and from Crete by such ships. Enquiries, however, could be made at a travel agent specializing in freighter travel. Lines that have traditionally serviced Crete include: Swedish S.O.L., Deutsche-Orient Linie, Argo Nah-Ost Linie, Atlas-Levante Linie, Hellenic Lines, P & O, and K.N.S.M. Co.

There remain the principal shipping links between Crete and foreign ports – the cruise ships that start from Italian and other Mediterranean cities. Many of these now include Crete in their itineraries, but such ships are restricted, in most instances, to taking only those people who remain with the ship for the complete cruise. These cruise ships usually put in at Iraklion for only one day. Travel agents should be able to provide up-to-date information on the constantly changing schedules and fares of such cruise ships. And in any case, it should be pointed out that most people start such cruises from Athens-Piraeus, where the Greek shipping lines offer a much wider selection of cruises that include Crete.

From Within Greece
There is a frequent and regular service direct between Piraeus and Iraklion or Khania – at least once daily (usually twice) to Iraklion, and about eight sailings a week to Khania (or actually its nearby port, Soudha). The voyage takes about twelve hours to either port; most sailings involve getting on the ship early in the evening and arriving at the destination early the next morning. Minoan Lines (owned by people of Iraklion and eastern Crete) and A.N.E.K. (owned by people of Khania and western Crete) operate the ships that service both cities. Tickets may be purchased at the offices of the lines in Piraeus, Iraklion, and Khania, as well as at various agents for the lines and some travel agencies.

The fares to both ports in Crete are almost the same (Khania's being a bit cheaper). Because of a different way that the harbours are organized, the fares from Crete *to* Piraeus are a few percentage points higher (but this would be included in the return ticket as you purchased it). There are reductions for young children.

There are four classes (five including the Luxury suite), and with the understanding that the fares will undoubtedly keep increasing, here are the approximate fares between Piraeus and Iraklion as of 1990: First class (2-bed cabin with private bath), Drs 6,500; second class (2 beds), Drs 4,000; Tourist class (2–5 beds), Drs 3,200, Deck class, Drs 2,400. Deck class means spending a night in a rather cramped bunk, stacked alongside a varied crowd, or in a chair; some prefer to spend the night camping out on the actual deck. No meals or service are included in the fares; drinks or simple snacks, a light breakfast, and one main meal may be bought (although deck class has no access to the dining room for the meal).

These ships take vehicles; usually you drive right into and out of the hold, but occasionally your car might have to ride on the deck (if the hold is filled – usually by trucks). The cost for the one-way trip (in 1990) was about Drs 7,500 for vehicles up to 750 kilos, and Drs 10,000 for up to 1,000 kilos.

Connections between Crete and the Peloponnese

Yet another possibility in recent years is to take a ship between Kastelli-Kissamou, some miles west of Khania (p. 287), and the Peloponnese or the islands between it and Crete (such as Kythera). There are 2–4 sailings each week each way, and the ships start and end their runs at Piraeus (putting in at Neapolis and Monemvassia). Just to give some point of comparison, in 1990, the first-class fare between Kastelli and Neapolis was about Drs 2,900, between Kastelli and Kythera Drs 2,500. This route might appeal to some people as an alternative way into or out of the island of Crete.

Connections between Crete and Rhodes

We have already indicated that it is possible to fly direct between Iraklion and Rhodes. It is also possible to get a once-weekly ship passage between the two islands – but usually not to Iraklion: the ships traditionally put in at Ayios Nikolaos (and Sitia). The ships (and their owner-lines) tend to change over time, as do exact schedules and fares. Anyone interested should wait until arriving in Greece or Crete to obtain the exact details. But because Ayios Nikolaos is only a way-station on the run between Rhodes and Piraeus, the departure times usually come at awkward hours, so you may have to make special plans to be in Ayios Nikolaos or Sitia. These ships also put in at the islands between Crete and Rhodes – Kassos, Karpathos, and Khalki. Again, for comparison, in 1990 the first class from Ayios Nikolaos to Rhodes was Drs 5,000, tourist class was about Drs 3,000. The trip lasts about fifteen hours.

Through some combination of air and ship journeys, it should be possible to include a side excursion to Rhodes in your visit to Crete, or at least to use Rhodes as a point of entry or departure.

Connections between Crete and other Greek islands
With the various exceptions described in this section, there are few
scheduled links between Crete and the other Greek islands: but note
that the ships linking Crete to Rhodes, Santorini (below) and the
Peloponnese do include quite a few other islands. Most people
wanting to 'island-hop' find that they often have to return to Piraeus
to get the regularly scheduled ships to the Greek islands. However,
adventurous travellers with time to spare might eventually find one of
the smaller freight or fishing boats in a Cretan port that would take
them to one of the other islands. (See p. 30 for a further discussion of
the boats known as *kaíkis*.) It is safe to assume the boat will sail only if
it is going to have a comparatively smooth crossing: no one has more
respect for the winds and seas than the native sailor. Fees would be
negotiable, but you must realize that the sailors of today are well
aware of the time and money you would be saving by not going via
Piraeus.

Connections between Crete and Santorini (Thera)
An even more stimulating excursion awaits visitors to Crete who
would like to go to Santorini (Thera), the island that lies about
100 km. due north of Crete and that, since the late 1960s, has been
rivalling Crete in the headlines of archaeological developments. Quite
aside from the fact that the new finds on Santorini show direct links
with the Minoan civilization, it seems worthwhile describing this
possibility in some detail, since increasing numbers of visitors to Crete
have the time for such side-trips.

Santorini had long had its own appeal, of course, and even some
minor archaeological remains. But in 1967, Professor Spyridon Marinatos (who also had several 'digs' on Crete to his credit) began to
unearth the site at Akrotiri. The years since have produced a most
impressive series of remains under Professor Marinatos's supervision
until his death in 1974 and excavations continue to this day. The
structures on the site – including remains of three-storeyed houses –
are protected by synthetic roofing so that visitors can continue to
enjoy them. Some of the most dramatic finds, however, have been
displayed in the National Archaeological Museum in Athens; these
include not only vases, sculptures and other artefacts, but some truly
lovely frescoes. The larger ones are the equal of those from Minoan
Crete in their colouring and style; in their portrayal of two youths
boxing and stylized antelopes, they have no equal. Another series of

frescoes is unique for another reason: a band of frieze (20–45 cm. wide, and running some 6 metres in its extant version) depicts what Marinatos has interpreted as a narrative of Aegeans attacking a Libyan city – full of realistic and dramatic details, and quite different from the usual Minoan frescoes. If Akrotiri turns out to have been in some sense an outpost of the Minoans, it certainly was not subordinate to the capital in the art of frescoes.

The Akrotiri frescoes were remarkably well preserved by the volcanic ash that fell out from the great eruption of Santorini itself about 1450 B.C.: considered by some geologists to have been the single most powerful natural disaster known to man, this is the same volcanic eruption that other authorities believe to have had a part in the destruction of some of the Minoan palaces. (So great was its impact on the world's atmosphere that it affected the growth rings of trees throughout the world; some experts wonder if the great Santorini explosion wasn't either in 1628 B.C. or 1191 B.C., based on tree rings – thus casting doubt on the whole Minoan chronology.) Meanwhile, some people have been quick to claim that it was this explosion, with the resultant 'end' of Minoan civilization, that was the progenitor of the tale of 'lost Atlantis'. Without taking sides in that age-old controversy, we may at least say that all this adds to the special thrill of sailing into the spectacular harbour of Santorini – the collapsed cone of the former volcano. What with the new Minoan-period excavations, the previously excavated Doric–Roman remains, the boat-rides to adjacent islets to see the volcanic fumes, the various Orthodox–Byzantine associations, the beaches and landscapes, Santorini definitely rewards those who make their way there. Santorini, by the way, has a couple of decent hotels as well as various pensions and rooms, and taxis can get you anywhere.

Aside from taking the Olympic Airways flight between Crete and Santorini (p. 18) or between Athens and Santorini, there are the regularly scheduled ships to and from Piraeus and Santorini and ships between Crete and Santorini (often referred to in schedules as Thera, or Thira). The Crete–Santorini service tends to change somewhat from year to year, but for some time now at least one of the ships that passes through Ayios Nikolaos (and usually Sitia) to and from Rhodes is also connecting with Santorini on its way to and from Piraeus. This ship usually services other islands, too, such as Anafi, Folegandros, and Milos. Then there is usually ship service between Iraklion and Santorini – in recent years, in fact, several such ships weekly during the tourist season; these ships also put in at such islands as Ios, Naxos, Paros, Syros, Sifnos, or Mykonos en route to and from Piraeus. Details about schedules and fares are best obtained when you arrive in Greece or Crete. Incidentally, no vehicles can be taken on to Santorini except by making complicated arrangements, and the average traveller is well advised to explore Santorini by other means.

As with the ships to and from Rhodes, there are often some inconvenient arrival and departure times for these ships connecting with Santorini. The best thing to do is to chalk them up to the fun of travelling. Meals are not included in any of the fares quoted; snacks, drinks, and other light refreshments are available, as are full meals in the dining room.

All the services mentioned allow for some flexibility in planning a vacation in Greece, not only in making side-excursions between Crete and Santorini but also to other points on these ships' routes. It is unlikely that many people will want to make a return trip from Crete to Mykonos, say, but it is not at all unlikely that some people, before or after a stay on Crete, might want to make their way along these Aegean islands. It requires some time and planning, but it can be done.

RAIL

There are no railways on Crete, of course, but some people still prefer to travel by train to Athens and there change to ship or plane for Crete. Another possibility is to take a train to either Ancona or Brindisi, Italy, and then take a ferry ship over to Patras, on the western corner of Greece; from there bus or train connects with Athens.

ROAD

In addition to the air and sea routes to Greece and Crete, and the rail connections with Athens or points along the way, there is the possibility of driving to Greece (or Italy) and then bringing the car over to Crete – a possibility that many foreigners now take advantage of. The drive down Yugoslavia's Adriatic coast is especially enjoyable; there is also a motorway through the centre of Yugoslavia to the Greek border, but although this can be a faster drive the road is not especially attractive. An alternative is to drive to Ancona or Brindisi, bring the car to Patras, and then drive on to Athens–Piraeus; there is also the above-mentioned service direct from Venice via Piraeus to Iraklion (p. 19). But the usual precautions prevail: since such services tend to vary from year to year, check at a travel agent for up-to-date details. A full discussion of motoring on Crete comes later (p. 34) but below we provide some basic data for anyone planning to drive a car to Greece and then on Crete. To be extra safe, you might check with your local automobile association or the National Tourist Organization of Greece to make sure there are no new regulations.

CAR DOCUMENTS

The following documents are required for driving a car in Greece:
(1) Although an International Driver's Licence is required (it is merely a multi-language translation of your licence), your valid licence, if you are British, Canadian, or American, may be accepted. If you wish to be extra safe, you can obtain the International Licence through your own automobile association; if you have come to Greece without it, you may obtain one upon presentation of your valid driving licence at offices of the Hellenic Automobile Club (E.L.P.A.) in Athens or in Iraklion or Khania. Two passport photos and a fee of a few hundred drachmas are required.
(2) The log book (or registration) of your car.
(3) The green international insurance card issued by your own insurance company. (Required in Yugoslavia and Greece.) AA or similar coverage will get the car out of Greece if you can't drive it out.

Car control

Upon arrival at the Greek border or port of entry in the absence of a *carnet de passage*, the Customs officials will place a stamp in your passport that allows your vehicle free entry for twelve months; this may be extended for another four months upon application at the Finance Ministry in Athens – or at the Customs Office in either Iraklion or Khania. The same regulations governing entry of vehicles into Greece extend to Crete, so that once you are in the country you may bring your car over to Crete without any further documents or formalities. (If you have come to Crete direct from some foreign port, of course, then you must go through all the formalities at the Cretan port of entry.) Incidentally, it is not that difficult for a foreigner to buy or sell a car in Greece – provided the vehicles changing hands have entered Greece with custom-free plates. This means that the vehicles are largely being bought and sold among foreigners, although there are dealers in Athens who handle custom-'sealed' vehicles. Warning: you must comply with the Greek Customs formalities, and get the car officially entered *and/or removed* from your passport.

PASSPORTS AND CUSTOMS

Since Crete is part of the Greek State, there are no special arrangements required for entering Crete. If you come over to Crete from the Greek mainland, there is not even any question of producing your passport; for travellers coming to Crete direct from a foreign country, there will be the usual passport control and Customs formalities.

While you may take in any sum of money in travellers' cheques and foreign currency, you are allowed to bring in only Drs 25,000 of Greek money (although in practice most foreigners are never questioned about this). Only 200 cigarettes (or 300 for citizens of EEC nations) and 1 litre of spirits (1.5 litres for EEC nationals) are admitted free; cameras, typewriters, radios, tape recorders, sport guns, etc., may be brought in so long as they are clearly for personal use. You cannot import narcotics, explosives, weapons (or parrots!).

As for export restrictions, if you wish to take foreign currency in excess of US$500, you will need the original customs declaration issued on entry. Technically only Drs 10,000 may be taken out of Greece and there is also a limit on how much olive-oil an individual is allowed to take out duty-free. Finally, taking out 'ancient works of art' (which are defined as anything dated before 1830) is prohibited unless you have been given a proper certificate with your purchase. Above all, do not try to take any 'souvenir' remains from archaeological sites.

Anyone planning to stay for an extended period or intending to bring in a lot of special equipment would do well to check first with the nearest Greek Consulate. And when it comes to getting unusual amounts of luggage to Crete, one of the large international freight agencies – such as American Express or Schenker & Co. – can save an individual a great deal of time and temper. Olympic Airways, of course, has air freight service.

If your stay in Greece and/or Crete is to be over three months, you must apply for a renewal or extension of your passport privilege at the

Department for Foreigners (head office in Athens at 173 Alexandros Avenue; there is an office in Iraklion (*Map* 4, pp. 140–1) and another in Khania, at 5 Solomon Street. Three passport photos and about Drs 100 are required; you must also produce solid evidence that you are self-supporting.

Foreigners whose stay in Greece has been one year or more must obtain a tax-clearance certificate from the Finance Ministry; for further information, consult the Tourist Organization or Tourist Police.

It should be said, after all this, that the average tourist will hardly be aware of any of these formalities.

As for regulations and changes that will take effect in the coming years with the European Economic Community, see pp. 28–9.

REDUCTIONS AND DISCOUNTS

Certain discounts and courtesy services may be available for certain tourists who visit Greece and Crete, but these are restricted to certified journalists, travel writers, academics, and such. Those who think they might qualify should enquire at the Greek Embassy or Consulate or at the Greek National Tourist Organization. In general, hotels, restaurants, shipping lines and such facilities offer no discounts to individual travellers.

Holders of valid International Student Identity Cards (which must be obtained through one's own institution) are allowed a reduced entry fee at many of the museums and archaeological sites. This card must have a photo.

Foreign students of classical subjects and relevant disciplines (e.g. Mediterranean archaeology) may apply for a pass that allows a 50 per cent reduction at all national archaeological sites and museums; but proof of status plus two passport photos must be produced; this pass is obtainable at the Directorate of Antiquities, 14 Aristidou Street, Athens; this office keeps limited hours for this service – enquire upon arriving in Athens.

Free entry to national museums and sites is granted to special professionals – archaeologists, museum curators, professors of art, architecture, and classical studies, certain UNESCO personnel, and such. Enquiries should be made at the Directorate of Antiquities (see above) but solid proof of status will be required. Children 12 years old and under are also admitted free to almost all museums and sites.

NOTE ON CHANGES AFFECTING TOURISTS FROM EUROPEAN ECONOMIC COMMUNITY MEMBER STATES WHEN VISITING GREECE

There is increasing talk, if not concern, over the changes that will take place among the member states of the European Community – which includes the UK, Ireland, and Greece among others – as the much-heralded threshold year of 1992 approaches. Specifically, what will be the effects on travellers to and from Greece?

The first thing to be said is that many of the changes are already in place and/or are being phased in over the coming months, so there will be no one day at the end of 1992 when everything suddenly or drastically becomes different. Beyond that, it appears that for *the average tourist or short-term traveller* there will actually be few major differences. The citizen of any member state of the European Community should be able to cross the borders of all member states, including Greece, without any 'passport control' or customs inspection (with some exceptions, as discussed below) – but this is the case today for most tourists. Many of the changes affect commercial operations, large scale financial transactions, permanent residents, etc.

That said, it should be emphasized that, despite all the relaxations that will occur, there will not be a total or absolute abolition of all restrictions, even on short-term tourists. For one, there will remain numerous restrictions on many commercial transactions – that is, the importing and exporting of products for other than personal use. For another, member states will still be allowed to impose some limits on the importing of tobacco products, alcoholic beverages, coffee and tea, even perfume and toilet water. Meanwhile, the duty-free allowances will still not apply to young people – under 17 years for tobacco and alcohol, under 15 years for coffee, etc. There will also remain in place restrictions on the movement of pets (and plants!) across national borders – and certainly there will be stringent efforts to restrict the movement of drugs (except legitimate medicines). Likewise, there will not be a totally unlimited movement of currencies if there is the suspicion that the money is for something other than an individual's expenses during a temporary visit in the other member states. And specific countries may for some time impose their own restrictions on certain types of goods: Greece, for instance, will probably try to restrict the import and sale of private vehicles by transient tourists.

Also to consider is the fact that although you may not need a passport or various other papers to enter Greece – if, that is, if you are a citizen of one of the European Communities – you may still need a passport and other papers to travel through or to non-member states (such as Turkey, Yugoslavia, or Switzerland, for that matter). And don't forget that although the European Community may work out special trade arrangements with such countries as the USA, Canada, Australia and New Zealand, the individual citizens of these countries will still be expected to comply with Greece's requirements regarding passports, customs, etc.

What, then, will be the difference for citizens of the EEC when they travel to and from Greece? For one, all matters having to do with the VAT taxes on gifts and goods should be more easily resolved. All matters having to do with banks and the postal service should also be easier (and cheaper). If you have a medical emergency, you should be able to receive treatment and have the cost refunded just as though you were in your home country – provided, that is, you have the proper forms. (For British citizens, this means obtaining Form E 111 from a DHSS office.) And although most tourists will not have the option, it should be easier to extend your stay and even take employment in a member state such as Greece.

All the details on these and related matters will be widely publicized as 1992 approaches. Meanwhile, the restrictions and policies described in this edition – on matters of passport, customs control, currencies, etc. – are as up-to-date and reliable as possible. If you have any special situations or conditions, contact the nearest Greek Consulate or Embassy.

TRAVEL ON CRETE

SEA

YACHTING

Yachting is probably the ideal way to get round Crete. There are small but safe harbours all round the island, and in certain places, such as Iraklion, Khania, Rethymnon, Ayios Nikolaos and Sitia, there are adequate facilities for emergencies and repairs. By putting into various harbours you would have access to every site on the island; no place would be much more than 30 km. from the sea. Sailors should remember, though, that the sea off the north coast can be quite rough, especially during July and August.

It is possible to charter motor cruisers and sailing yachts, with or without crews, in Piraeus, and arrangements can be made through the travel agencies. There is considerable range in accommodation, but when the cost has been divided among a party of six to twelve adults it is less heavy than one might expect. With a cook aboard, doing one's own food-buying and no hotel bills, it might even become a fairly cheap way for a group of friends to get about.

For further information, write to the Yachting Department of the National Tourist Organization, 2 Amerikis Street, Athens. On Crete, information may be had at the Yacht Club office by the harbour in Iraklion (see town map **2**, pp. 140–1).

KAÍKI (CAIQUE)

A *kaíki* is the type of boat used in the local coastal and island traffic. They vary in size from yacht-style boats to plain little fishing boats. All have motors. They may vary in comforts and conveniences, but all are perfectly reliable for what they set out to do.

There are two ways of hiring a *kaíki*. One is to make arrangements through the travel agents on the mainland or on Crete itself. Naturally, the boats they deal with tend to be more elegant than the ones you might pick up for yourself in some little fishing cove. Ayios Nikolaos offers the best possibilities for excursions to various sites in that area.

The second way arises when you find yourself on the coast and you want to get somewhere farther along. The old days, when there were often Cretans lounging about and ready to accommodate foreigners, are gone. But you might approach the men on a *kaíki* and ask if they are willing to take you. What you can expect to pay depends on whether the men were going to make the trip as part of their normal work or whether you are hiring them to make the trip especially for you. Assuming that you hire a *kaíki* for a special excursion to a point some one or two hours' sailing along the coast, with a short wait while you explore the site, you can expect to pay at least Drs 20,000. For a small group trying to visit an inaccessible site in a limited time, the cost may be fairly reasonable.

BUS

Many people still depend on buses to get around the island. And in spite of the run-down appearance of some of the public buses, they always get to their destinations. There are scheduled connections with practically every village and site on the island, usually departing from the capitals of the four nomes (administrative areas, or districts): Iraklion, Khania, Rethymnon, and Ayios Nikolaos. Only a very few out-of-the-way places involve any change or wait at a junction, although the independent traveller who is trying to see the most in a limited time might choose to make some connections at various points in order to link excursions.

The main towns and sites are served by quite a few buses each day, but the Sunday schedule usually differs considerably, and there is often only one bus a day between the main towns and the smaller villages and sites. Moreover, the timetables have been arranged for the convenience of the villagers who come into the city early in the morning and go home late in the afternoon – exactly the reverse of most tourists' excursions. By careful planning, combining excursions and some overnights and possibly a bit of walking, a traveller could take maximum advantage of these schedules.

The island's bus lines operate throughout the year, with the possible withdrawal of an occasional bus to some remote area in the winter. Summer and winter schedules differ slightly – the summer season is from April 15th to October 15th – but most travellers will not be inconvenienced by this. Check at the bus station for the latest schedules.

The bus stations in the major cities have been indicated on their respective plans, but just to be safe you might enquire at the Tourist Information offices about possible changes. Tickets are bought at the bus stations, and since many of the routes are heavily used, especially during the tourist season, you are advised to get yours well in advance. (The tickets are often assigned to numbered seats, but few Cretans seem to pay much attention to this.) Save all tickets until the end, even on short local runs, in case the inspector comes through the bus. And when flagging a bus down on the road, get right out there and wave; don't assume that the bus will stop because you are at a bus stop.

TOURIST COACHES AND GUIDES

There are now several tourist agencies on Crete that offer a selection of tours that use buses of one size or another. (The heavy, modern touring bus is called by Greeks a 'pullman'.) English-speaking guides are usually assigned, depending on the nature of the excursion. Such tours have obvious advantages for some people, and the better ones provide a quite attractive alternative when, say, a return trip by public transportation in one day is inconvenient. Ask the National Tourist Organization offices in the main cities to recommend you one. In addition to tours to the well-known points of interest, some of the Cretan travel agencies arrange trips to villages for local music, dancing, wine, and meals. Some people would find this a bit forced, but others find it the closest thing to 'authentic' Cretan life they can experience.

Another variation is for small groups or an individual to engage a private guide who speaks the language desired and keeps to the itinerary and schedule contracted for. (An obvious example of when such a guide might be needed is for a small group of inexperienced walkers who want to go through the Samaria Gorge, p. 278.) These guides have been to special schools and are licensed; the National Tourist Organization and private travel agencies can contact such guides. Their fees are regulated and depend on the time involved and the number in the touring party.

TAXIS

In certain situations, hiring a taxi is the best way to get to some place. It is not as extravagant as it might sound. Nor will it mark you as a 'rich tourist': Greeks use taxis at the drop of a hat and think nothing of it when three or four people decide to share one and avoid the crowded or inconvenient buses. In the cities and large towns, it is easy enough to find a taxi, and even comparatively small villages support at least one cab. Foreigners, indeed, are sometimes surprised to see remote and otherwise backward villages supporting a modern vehicle, but in places where no private individual owns a car it is a necessity to have some means of fast transport.

As some of the excursions described later can take longer than one would wish – owing to the fact that bus schedules are not arranged for the tourists – an excursion that might take two days to make by depending on buses could be done in one day if you had a taxi at your disposal. When three or four people share expenses, the cost can be quite reasonable. In addition, there are valuable fringe benefits – such as the taxi-driver's knowing many people, cafés and obscure sights en route.

Taxi rates are officially regulated, but like everything connected with petroleum these days, they are constantly increasing. When the meter starts, a flat rate hiring charge goes into effect, and then you pay so many Drs per km.; if you go outside city limits and dismiss the taxi at your destination, you naturally pay more Drs per km.; if you ask the driver to wait, you pay a rate-per-hour. The rates should not change with the number of individuals sharing a taxi. There may be extra charges for luggage, for nights (midnight to 6 a.m.), at Christmas and Easter, and for boarding a taxi at an airport or ship port. To avoid misunderstanding, any major trip should be negotiated with the driver before setting out. If there are any problems, either the Tourist Police or the National Tourist Organization could help.

CAR, MOTOR-BIKE, AND BICYCLE HIRE

It is now easy to hire a car to drive yourself, whether at the airports of Iraklion and Khania or in the major cities. The National Tourist Organization or private travel agencies can help you in this matter when you are on Crete; but during the high season it might be advisable to make arrangements before arriving – especially if you have particular requirements (as to size, model, etc. of vehicle). The well-known international agencies such as Hertz are well represented on Crete, but many other agencies also operate; indeed, the impression around Iraklion is that everyone who owns a car is prepared to rent it. The rates are officially regulated, so that one agency's ends up much like another's – at least in its class; if the larger agencies charge more, consider that they are better organized to service or substitute your car should there be any problems.

Most of the cars are recent European and Japanese models. Rates vary tremendously with the size of the car and with the particular arrangements (e.g. daily with minimum kms. required; weekly with minimum kms. required; weekly with unlimited mileage; etc.); about the only thing certain is that they are high and will go higher. Look into the various contracts offered and try to calculate the best for your plans; some agencies will let you change to the most favourable terms after you return. Rates are naturally higher during the main season – which tends to be from July 1st to September 30th. Petrol is never included in the rates. Third-party liability and property damage insurance are included, but full protection is a bit extra and is recommended. Be sure to offer the names of all individuals who might be driving the vehicle – all of whom, by the way, must be at least 23 years old. A largish deposit is usually required (but waived for most credit-card holders). Anyone knowing their exact plans well in advance should consult a travel agent or one of the international car-hire firms (Avis, Hertz, etc.) about any special rates available (e.g. for making arrangements from abroad and in advance).

Still other possibilities are to hire a motor-bike, motor-scooter, or a bicycle. There are now several firms handling the first two types of vehicles, located in Iraklion, Khania, and Ayios Nikolaos. Rates vary considerably, and you might like to consult the National Tourist Information office or a private travel agency for a recommended firm. Anyone renting a motor-bike or motor-scooter must be eighteen years old and licensed to operate such a vehicle. You should always wear a helmet (as should your passengers). And you are advised to be fully insured.

MOTORING

Every year many visitors from abroad discover the pleasures of touring Crete by car. It is fairly expensive, of course, to bring a car over to Crete, or to hire one, but in the end it may repay you. If you have only three to five days, it probably will not be worth bringing a car over; hiring one should be considered (as discussed above). But anyone planning to spend over five days – particularly with a family or a party of friends – may discover that it is the most reasonable proposition, especially if – as can be expected from many users of this book – you have already brought your car as far as Athens. And certainly a private car will allow you to see places and things that could not be managed in a limited time with public transport.

We have elsewhere (pp. 25–6) described the means of getting a car to Greece and then to Crete. Once ashore, you will find that petrol and oil are available all over the island, including 'super' (high octane) and diesel – although only about six stations in or near the main cities along the north coast sell unleaded petrol, so plan ahead! Many of the well-known international brands are available. But although there are many filling stations around the cities, it is well to keep as full a tank as possible, especially in the more remote districts. (In an emergency, small quantities of diesel can be bought in grocery stores.) Petrol is sold by the litre and its cost has risen so that in recent years it is among the most expensive in Europe (by 1990, it was at least Drs 85 per litre).

For rough calculations, 4·5 litres equal one Imperial gallon and 3·8 litres equal one U.S. gallon.

In the smaller towns and villages, filling stations offer little except petrol and oil, but there are plenty of repair shops in the larger towns and cities. Perhaps you will not get the *most* expert service and repair work in the world, but the men are certainly experienced with foreign cars – since that's all Greeks have. And more and more of the world's major firms now have authorized dealers and garages in at least Iraklion and Khania.

Most of the roads that a majority of travellers will be using are fine to adequate. Indeed, the new national highway is a first-class asphalt highway whose main fault is that it takes some of the peculiar fun out of driving on Crete's curving roads and makes the island into another speedway. (Still, great caution is advised on this as on all roads in Crete: curves are never far ahead – shoulders are seldom on your side – rockfalls are often in your way, and there are increasing numbers of potholes.) For many stretches it merely replaces or uses the older road, but for much of its length between Khania and Ayios Nikolaos it is a brand new road. Since it by-passes many of the villages and sights of interest to the traveller, this guide's itineraries will continue to refer to the old route (and indicate the new stretches as alternatives for fast trips between two distant points). One of the great pleasures of the new highway, by the way, are the miles and miles of flowering bushes.

After the many asphalt roads come some hard-packed dirt roads: they can get dusty during the long dry summer and slippery in the rainy winter, but by and large they are good solid roads. Here again, however, you must always be prepared for pits and rocks and washboard patches. And finally there are still a few roads to remote sites described in this book that are, frankly, very rough going. Yet with a little patience and care you can get over them. Heavy low-slung cars are at a disadvantage on these stretches, but it is largely a matter of being willing to crawl. Considering Crete's situation – geographically, historically, economically – the island has better roads than one might expect. If you do have car problems, membership of the RAC or the AA will bring you free aid from ELPA, Greece's automobile club.

The use of seat belts is obligatory for all persons in the front seat. Driving is on the right. Roads, it cannot be said too often, are not as well marked as one might like them to be: curves, soft shoulders, steep gradients, hazardous conditions – you cannot count on signs for all of these. Nor will crucial turnings always be marked. You may have been directed to go straight ahead to the site you seek, and two minutes later there will be a fork – one road as good as the other, and with no sign to indicate which leads to your destination. If you do get lost or go exploring on your own, care is needed when asking directions, for the average villager is not that precise about distances or times. Your destination, furthermore, tends always to be 'straight ahead' (*kat' efthian*): for local people, those forks and turns are accepted as part of the route. Best advice is to get a good *big* road map.

By the way, parking regulations are strictly enforced in the cities and towns and even foreign plates don't necessarily exempt you from compliance. (Police may impound plates of illegally parked cars and it costs many drachmas to get them back.)

Finally, it must be said that Greek drivers have their own ways of driving. They can be careless about giving turning signals. They may ignore through traffic and turn on to the main road from some little by-road just when you are convinced you must have the right of way. The right of way in Greece, in fact, seems to go to the fastest and foolhardiest. Greeks rely on their horns, and especially on curves you should be prepared to use yours. Pedestrians technically have the right of way in cities and villages, and the fact that the new breed of Greek drivers shows little patience with them should not give you licence to do the same. Some years ago, when there were far fewer vehicles on the roads of Greece and Crete, earlier editions of this guide could claim with amusement that driving on Crete 'is like finding yourself in an old Keystone comedy'. Now that Greece has one of the highest mortality rates for vehicular accidents, it all seems less amusing.

MAPS

Any serious traveller will want a detailed map of Crete; there are several available – with more or less accuracy. The best are large-scale maps produced by the Efstathiadis Group and by Christoforakis. They are in English, among other languages, and employ the Roman alphabet. They can be found in shops in Athens and Crete. There is also a very clear and readable map of Crete published by Clyde Surveys Ltd, Reform Road, Maidenhead, Berks, and available from them or from Edward Stanford Ltd, 12 Long Acre, London WC2, who also stock the useful Toubi's Road Map of Crete. The map in the endpapers of this book, of course, plus the verbal descriptions of routes, would suffice for the places that most tourists will be visiting.

ACCOMMODATION AND RESTAURANTS

Taking the island as a whole, travellers on Crete have a wide choice of accommodation when it comes to sleeping and eating. The greatest concentration of amenities, of course, is in the Iraklion area, but the whole north coast from Khania to Ayios Nikolaos offers considerable variety. Many hotels and other accommodation can now be found in quite remote parts of the island; from luxury villas to spare rooms in private homes, from 'continental cuisine' to simple snacks, most people will find what they seek. All accommodation is regulated and inspected by the National Tourist Organization and the Tourist Police (as throughout Greece); although the officials inevitably find it hard to keep up with all facilities every year, standards are relatively well maintained in respect to fair prices and required amenities.

A word of warning: if you write ahead to a Greek hotel to make a reservation, do not necessarily expect any written acknowledgement or confirmation. If this bothers you, use a travel agent.

HOTELS

There are six classes of hotels (and the same classes are applied to other accommodation like pensions, guest houses, apartments, etc.). These categories are assigned on the basis of such things as whether there are telephones in rooms, elevators, the size of the public rooms, etc. – not all of which concern all travellers. Clean linen and safe water are provided by all, but other conveniences may vary. For many years the Greek government enforced a quite rigid schedule of prices on the basis of a hotel's classification but since 1982 more flexibility has been allowed within classes. Most travellers, of course, don't want to spend their valuable hours walking around town 'comparison shopping', so the best thing to do is to go into the National Tourist Organization Office or a travel agency and get some advice. The variations within a class presumably reflect various advantages and disadvantages – more modern plumbing, a quieter street, etc. In any case, the variations are not that wide within a class. Then, to further unsettle matters, it is rumoured that the Greek government is going to convert to the European system of rating hotels by stars: what effect this will have on actual accommodation or service is unclear, but it should result in Greek hotels' compliance with international standards. Meanwhile, the price of each room is posted in that room so that you can at least know the amount you are supposed to pay.

The names of some hotels and their telephone numbers are listed according to geographical location. These are Class C or higher, and are chosen because they can be expected to be reliable sources of accommodation if you need to book in advance. The National Tourist Organization and travel agencies tend to discourage foreigners from patronizing Class D and E hotels; some, indeed, can be unappealing, but certain people might be prepared to put up in them to save money – and, after all, not too many years ago these were the principal accommodation Crete had to offer! The main lack as far as many people are concerned will be that of private toilets. Class C hotels are really quite fine, especially since most of them are relatively new. Class B and Class A are increasingly elaborate in their ambience and services, while Luxury can be just that. In the main cities, many people might be more interested in a quiet street than in a marble bathroom, so that the location of a hotel can be important. Likewise, if the décor or style of some of the new hotels seems a bit anonymous, or even in need of some touching up, ask yourself how much of your time on Crete is going to be spent in your hotel. (The Greek word for hotel, by the way, is *xenodhokhíon*.) If one hotel is full, the receptionist or proprietor traditionally will help you to find a room in the vicinity, but do not expect to haggle down to lower rates (except in the off season).

Prices

Hotel prices have been increasing annually and it is impossible for a book like this to keep up with them. But as a base for comparison, here are some rounded-off rates (see the table opposite) as posted by the National Tourist Organization for 1990.

To repeat: these are rounded-off prices and subject to change. Furthermore, they do not tell the full story of variations of hotel rates (the minimum–maximum listed here reflects the low and high seasons).

Prices in Drachmas

Class	Single Min. – Max.	Double Min. – Max.
Luxury	15,000–18,000	23,000–35,000
Class A	10,000–14,000	12,000–16,000
Class B	6,000– 9,000	7,000–11,000
Class C	4,000– 6,000	4,000– 6,500
Class D	1,400– 1,800	2,000– 2,700
Class E	1,200– 1,500	1,800– 2,100

Since there can be misunderstandings about differences in hotel bills, you should be aware of some of the other variables:

(a) Prices are quoted per room (rather than per person). If you are alone and the hotel lacks single rooms but you want to stay there, the hotel can offer you a double room at 80 per cent of the full cost. If you want to add an extra bed to a room, the hotel can charge an extra 20 per cent.

(b) Prices quoted for Greek hotels include the service charges; any extra tipping is at the discretion of the Individual (see p. 63).

(c) The prices given above do not include the three taxes that will usually be part of the total price quoted (but you will want to ask about this to make sure you know what you're agreeing to): the 8 per cent 'business turnover', or VAT tax; a 4.5 per cent municipal tax; and a 1.2 per cent stamp tax on the total bill. If you are in doubt about any of this, ask for clarification before taking a room and/or paying the bill.

(d) There are two basic seasons for Greek hotels – the 'on season', or tourist season, which runs from approximately March 15th to October 31st; and the 'off season', which covers the other months. But in addition, hotels in Crete have the option of charging an additional 20 per cent for the 'high' period, July 1st to September 30th. Likewise, hotels are allowed to offer reductions (from 10 to 40 per cent) during the off season. Any price quoted for that period should include the central heating (assuming there is any). The prices shown here are for the on season.

(e) Air conditioning, when offered, may be charged as an extra, with rates for double rooms running about one quarter more than those for a single room.

(f) Since most rooms in hotels from Class C and above now have private baths, the prices shown here – and those usually quoted – are for this type of accommodation. However, some hotels still offer rooms without private baths – usually, though, with a basin in the room. You can make arrangements to take a bath or shower in the bathroom on the corridor, and an extra fee may be charged. (Incidentally, even in the best of hotels, hot water may not be running at all hours of the day.) Moreover, bathrooms now usually have showers, not tubs: if this is of prime concern, enquire ahead of time to see if the hotel offers at least one room with a bathtub.

(g) Hotels are also allowed to charge an extra 10 per cent any time during the year if your stay is for only one or two nights.

(h) Luxury, Class A, and Class B hotels usually require their clients to take half board (breakfast plus one other meal); these meals can be quite expensive – and are not included in the rates shown here. During the tourist season, all hotels are allowed to require clients to take breakfast along with the rooms; these hotels will have at least breakfast lounges if not full restaurants, but you could ask for breakfast to be served in your room. The cost of the breakfast (not included in the prices shown here) was up to Drs 250–600 by 1990 and will obviously get no cheaper over the years. As for what you get for breakfast, see pp. 48–9.

BEACH HOTELS AND BUNGALOWS

For some years now the popular attractions of Crete have included the various hotels and bungalows located on the beaches away from the cities, thus offering the relaxation and quiet of a resort in a natural atmosphere along with the traditional possibilities of the island's unique cultural heritage. Some of these are essentially hotels situated on the coast, while others combine central hotel-like buildings with free-standing bungalows or clustered suites. The appeal of such facilities is obvious. They often have fine private beaches with facilities for water-skiing, boating, etc.; they offer amenities from conference facilities to tennis; and they provide trips to towns and sites while at the same time allowing people to stay in one place. Many of the clients now come with charter or package tours, so that the combination of air fare and first-class accommodation ends up being remarkably cheap. Some of these beach hotels close during the winter, but many remain open at reduced rates. Most are in the Luxury or A or B classes, and they generally require everyone to take half board. But there are a few Class C hotels located on beaches, and at today's prices for hotels, even the Luxury accommodation of Crete is something of a bargain.

There are now so many of these beach developments to choose from, and the prices are so variable, that it does not make much sense just to list them all. What is more important is to know that they tend to fall into five 'clusters': several on the immediate outskirts of Iraklion; many in the area some 20–35 kms. east of Iraklion, mainly from Limin Khersonisou to Mallia; another group at Ayios Nikolaos; and smaller selections near Rethymnon and Khania. Consider your preferences and then enquire at the National Tourist Organization or a travel agency as to which of these Cretan beach facilities best fits your plans.

PENSIONS, GUEST HOUSES, AND ROOMS

Throughout Crete, in scores of small towns and villages, there are available several thousands of rooms and beds in what are classed as pensions, guest houses, or simply 'rooms to let'. In the larger tourist centres, some of these are fairly ambitious operations – they may even offer private showers with the rooms. At the other extreme, in remote villages they are merely a room in a private home, 'bed and break-fast', essentially. All, however, must comply with certain officially regulated standards. Their rates are considerably cheaper than hotels. There is not space to list all these places here, but in the Routes section it is indicated when something is available in any town or village. In the main cities, the National Tourist Organization will be able to advise you; the local Tourist Police will help in smaller communities. In really small villages, almost anyone should be able to direct you.

One special type of guest house is the tourist pavilion, located at several tourist attractions and maintained either by the National Tourist Organization or by the local community. Most travellers use them only for welcome refreshments during a day's excursion, but some people appreciate the convenience of staying overnight close to a particular destination. The rooms are limited, meals can be basic, and the facilities are not always the cleanest, but the location compensates for these. They will be indicated at their appropriate places in the Routes section.

FURNISHED HOUSES AND VILLAS

There is now a large selection of completely furnished private homes around Crete – several hundred of them available during the main season. Some have been erected deliberately to take advantage of the demand; others are Cretans' homes made available for the season. The term 'villas' suggests something rather grand or luxurious, while in fact many of them are quite modest; what tends to distinguish a 'villa' from a 'house' is more apt to be that the former has a bit of land and gardens while the latter is just the house. But even this distinction doesn't always hold good, and both villas and houses can vary in style, grounds, amenities, and price. Many of the villas are now rented in advance through large travel agencies, especially by those based in European countries. Here are several agencies in Great Britain and the USA that specialize in arranging for villas or furnished apartments, with or without the other travel arrangements (air fares, etc.):

Beach Villas Ltd, 8 Market Passage, Cambridge CB2 3QR (tel. 0223-311113)

Cretasun, 12 Roland Close, Horndean, Hants (tel. 0705-596441)

Hellenic Resorts Corp., 566 7th Ave., New York City 10018 (tel. 212-391-0200)

Homeric Tours, Inc., 595 5th Ave., New York City (tel. 212-753-1100)

Inter-Island Holidays, 152 Shirland Road, London W9 (tel. 01-286 9185)

Kosmar Villa Holidays, 85/86 Tottenham Court Road, London W1 (tel. 01-323 4705)

Niki Tours, Inc. 373 N. Western Ave., Los Angeles, CA 90004 (tel. 213-464-8427)

Rent a Home Int'L, 3429 Fremont Place North, Seattle, WA 98103 (tel. 206-545 6963)

Simply Crete, 480 Chiswick High Road, London W4 5TT (tel. 01-994 4462)

Small World Travel Ltd, 850 Brighton Road, Purley, Surrey CR2 2BH (tel. 01-660 3999)

Sunmed (Go Greek), 4–6 Manor Mount, London SE23 (tel. 01-699 8833)

Timeway Holidays, Penn Place, Rickmansworth, Herts (tel. 0923-771 266)

Vacation Home Rentals Worldwide, 253 Kensington Ave., Norwood, NJ 07648 (tel. 201-767-9393)

Villas International, 71 West 23rd St., New York City 10010 (tel. 212-929-7585)

Almost any good travel agent, of course, should be able to help make arrangements. And on Crete itself, if you have let things go or only then decide you prefer something other than a hotel, you could contact:

Creta Travel Bureau, 20–22 Epimenidou St., Iraklion (tel. 081-222.761)

Cretan Holidays, 34 Daedalou St., Iraklion (tel. 081-222.339)

Polytravel, 60 25th of August St., Iraklion (tel. 081-282.476)

Zeus of Crete, 1 Kalergon St., Iraklion (tel. 081-221.103)

The National Tourist Organization office in Crete is another place to start making enquiries (although it cannot be expected to be responsible for the actual arrangements or details). Villas and houses rent directly for many thousands of drachmas, especially in the high season, but once more – divided among several people, and assuming many meals are prepared at home, they are not all that expensive.

TOURIST VILLAGE

One distinctive variation on Crete is the hotel-village of Koutsounari on the south coast, about 6 kms east of Ierapetra, on a hillside overlooking the Libyan Sea. Several old houses in an abandoned settlement were acquired by a developer, totally restored and renovated, then new houses in the same style were erected; all were furnished in a traditional and tasteful style; all offer fully equipped kitchens, bathrooms, and rooms with sleeping accommodation for two to six people. A taverna on the site sells meals and basic food supplies. The village is actually a couple of kilometres from the beach, and guests find they need a car to get around. Prices may sound steep at first (in 1990, a cottage sleeping six cost some Drs 62,000 a week during high season – but only some Drs 38,000 during the months of November to mid-March), but divided among several people, and considering you can make your own meals, you might find it a reasonable alternative to a hotel.

LONG-TERM RENTALS

It is interesting, if not ironic, that during the very era when the traditional and indigenous monasteries are dying out, a very modern phenomenon has been growing on Crete: the many foreigners who come to live on the island for extended periods, from a month to a year or more. Some of these people make arrangements in pensions or private homes, but most prefer to settle in their own quarters, with some kitchen-cooking facilities and at least the basics of running water and a toilet. Until relatively recent years, there were not many apartments or houses to accommodate such people, but now this has all changed. At the same time, there are so many variables in individual requirements – the type of location, the location, the price, the season – that this guide cannot elaborate on all the details. But some general points can be made about the main types.

FURNISHED APARTMENTS

These are modern buildings that provide apartments with an equipped kitchen, a bathroom, a living room, and at least one bedroom. They are usually on or near beaches; indeed, most of the apartments are located on a stretch of the north coast between Iraklion and Mallia, with another selection around Ayios Nikolaos and around Khania. They all tend to be in the A or B class. Typical rates in 1990 would be some Drs 8,000 per week for one double room, some Drs 9,500 for one single and one double room, and some Drs 12,000 for two double rooms (all in a Class A apartment; Class B accommodation runs about 70 per cent of these rates). These apartments may seem a bit impersonal and isolated, but some people find them convenient to use as a base to make their own contacts with Crete.

UNFURNISHED APARTMENTS OR HOUSES

This is another alternative, and although most of those advertised for rent are really looking for minimum one-year rentals from Cretans, you might well come to terms. (The sign to watch for in cities and towns is the word ENOIKIAZETAI – 'for rent' – usually printed in red on a white band of paper. 'Rooms to rent' usually refers to furnished rooms.) You should be able to calculate whether what you save on rent may be spent on furnishings that – with any luck or skill – can be sold at the end of your stay for perhaps as much as you paid for them. On the other hand, there is not that much trading of second-hand or used items among Cretans – refrigerators, beds, and such; and there is no denying that a considerable capital outlay is required at the outset. There is usually a circle of transient foreigners, however, and you could certainly sell back most of the items.

Check list for rentals

Here is a rundown of items you will want to consider, whether you are renting a furnished or unfurnished dwelling:

Electricity: now in virtually all areas, but if you want to go off and live in a field or on a mountain, forget it.

Running cold water: should be available everywhere; check the source to make sure it is potable.

Running hot water: cannot be assumed except in newer quarters; most likely a small electric tank that must be budgeted. (Incidentally, you always pay the electric and water bills; usually you will have to leave a deposit for these services beforehand – just as you may have to leave a security deposit on the house or apartment.)

Toilet: adequate except in the oldest dwellings; always needs care.

Central heating: this cannot be expected except in a few of the newer or more expensive apartments; nearly everyone heats individual rooms with some combination of electric heaters, bottled gas, or oil stoves – all of which can be bought or rented and all of which can be expensive. But there are about four months when you'll want some heat in at least a room or two.

Cooking stove: should be included in any furnished quarters; most use bottled gas; ovens not always very adequate.

Refrigerator: now provided by furnished villas and houses, but a small model; you get around this by shopping almost daily.

Utensils: basic cooking, eating, and household utensils should be included with all furnished quarters.

Blankets and linen: should be included with all furnished quarters, although you may want to add a few items.

Lights: you will probably want to replace the dim light bulbs and maybe even add a lamp or two.

But to conclude: many foreigners now live on Crete for long periods, and if you really want to, all the obstacles can be overcome.

YOUTH HOSTELS

The youth hostel situation on Crete tends to change constantly, with one or another changing hands or temporarily closed. But the hostel in Iraklion always seems to be functioning, and there is usually one at Khania, Rethymnon, Ierapetra, Myrthios, Sitia, Mallia, and Ayios Nikolaos. Enquire at the National Tourist Organization or the Tourist Police. By 1990 the charge was about Drs 300 for a bed, and use of the kitchen and showers. Normally you must produce a membership card from the Youth Hostels Association if you want to stay in one of these hostels, or you can purchase an International Guest card from the Greek Youth Hostels Association for several hundred drachmas from their headquarters at 4 Dragatsaniou Street, Klafthmonos Square, Athens (tel. 32.34.107).

CAMPING

At the time of publication, there were only 14 official camping sites on Crete. These provide electricity, toilets, showers, drinking water, washing facilities, and some sort of eating possibilities. All are on or close to beaches, and all tend to open about April to October. Fees are based on the number of individuals, and the tent or vehicle space. These official camping facilities are: near Iraklion, Amoudra (west) and Gouves (east); at Khania, one on east edge, one farther east at Ayia Marina; near Rethymnon (east), at Messina; one at Limin Khersonisou; one at Drapana, east of Kastelli-Kissamos; one at Sissi, east of Mallia; one at Pakhia Ammos; and then along the south coast, one each at Palaiokhora, Ayia Galini, and Matala; and two near Ierapetra (both to east). There may be others opening, so enquire at the National Tourist Organization or at the Tourist Police.

In order to protect the environment, camping is now allowed only in these authorized camping grounds. In practice, however, many people camp at various 'unofficial' places – beaches, mountains, parking lots, harbour quays. In general, the authorities tolerate such unofficial campers as long as they don't overdo things. Certainly no one will be allowed to camp anywhere on an archaeological site; and if you want to camp near a village or in what is obviously someone's olive grove or a beach café's parking lot, you should ask permission. Water and toilet facilities can become a problem – and are among the reasons the official places have been set aside – and fires and litter are obvious issues. An overnight here and there in a self-contained camper vehicle is one thing; setting out a tent for an extended stay is another. Enquire at the National Tourist Organization or the Tourist Police and see what the latest policy is.

MONASTERIES

Until recent years, several of the monasteries and convents of Crete were pointed out as yet another alternative for overnight lodging and even simple meals. Several monasteries actually encouraged guests. But this possibility has essentially been closed off on Crete. There are so few monks and nuns left, they tend to be old, and the monasteries' resources are so limited, that foreigners are no longer made to feel welcome. Part of the change, too, is due to the sheer numbers of foreigners now roaming Crete: it was a different thing when the occasional individual came tramping into the cloister. Even today, it is not impossible that an individual with the right mixture of language, manner, and time might be allowed to stay overnight. (One thing is certain: even if you are just visiting a monastery to admire its architecture and frescoes, you must respect the dress code. This means a minimum of bare flesh – no shorts, and covered tops.) As to payment, much depends on the circumstances. If you simply use a bed, then offer to pay a reasonable sum or at least leave a generous offering in the chapel. If you have been fed or received some special attentions from the abbot in charge or from one of the monks, then offer some gratuity directly to the individual; if he refuses, you can then leave it in the chapel. But money is not really the issue. The monasteries are dying out and your presence may simply not be appreciated.

RESTAURANTS AND NIGHT-LIFE

If there is one thing that Greece and Crete have an abundance of, it is eating and refreshment places. The quality and atmosphere may vary, but no one need ever go hungry or thirsty. Even the meanest village will have a café or two where some sort of meal can be scraped together – hard-boiled eggs, cheese, olives, bread, vegetables and fruits in season. Even when drinking just a glass of wine or beer, it is customary to munch something – a bit of cheese, fresh artichoke leaves, shrimp: these are known as *mezés*, or *mezedákis*. (Similar hors d'oeuvres served before full meals are called *oretiká*.) Incidentally, 'café' is *kaphenéion*, but in the villages it may be called *magazí* – 'the shop.'

In the larger cities and towns restaurants are classed 'A', 'B', 'C', etc., depending on the extent of the menu, the facilities, and such matters. In addition, there is a class of eating-place known as a *tavérna*, and to most foreigners these will look like restaurants. The point is that, although there can be a wide gap between the best and the worst, the majority conform to a general pattern. Some may have white table-cloths, some will have plastic table-tops; some offer a large choice of foods, some can offer only what they have on the stove at the moment. Indeed, there is an inevitable sameness to the Greek restaurant menu: in each season, relatively few items are offered.

Meanwhile, in recent years a new phenomenon has shown up on Crete, or at least in some of the locales more frequented by tourists: restaurants and cafés that are really more international than indigenous – in the menu they offer, in the style of service, often in the personnel, and certainly in the prices. There is no denying that many of these places offer a more varied choice of food and refreshment, and some of it is quite good. But you have to ask yourself if this is why you have come to Crete. Of course, if you must have your cappuccino or your Scotch, go ahead – but be prepared to pay international prices. Or take the latest fad – croissant shops, serving croissants and similar baked goods with a variety of fillings: all very tasty – but Cretan? If you stick to the more indigenous cafés, restaurants and eating places, you will leave Crete with a more memorable experience – and more drachmas in your wallet.

A more detailed discussion of the Greek menu and Cretan specialities follows. But when in doubt, or when you are just seeking a change, step into the kitchen or over to the cooking area and see for yourself what is available – it is an old Greek custom. (Besides ensuring that you get what you want, it saves a struggle with the menu.) Point to what interests you, find out what it is, and indicate whether you want it. Don't hesitate to specify exact cooking instructions – and good luck if you get exactly what you want! If what is brought to your place is definitely not what you ordered, don't hesitate to express your disapproval: Greeks send food back for all sorts of reasons. In one matter, though, Greeks differ in attitude from most foreigners: they don't care for their food to be that hot. If you do, stress – with good spirit – that you want your food *zestí*.

Most restaurants do not serve breakfast – indeed, they're not even open at breakfast time, although they're very good about producing some kind of food at almost any other time of day. For a breakfast you must go to a hotel dining room or certain cafés. (Likewise, Greek restaurants in general do not serve coffee or desserts: for these you go to separate cafés). As for Greek breakfasts, even in the better places they have in recent years become routine, to put it mildly: instant coffee, sweet fruit juice, bland bread, plastic jellies. Consider going out and assembling your own breakfast – fresh fruit, perhaps a cheese pie (*tirópita*) or some sort of sweet cake, and then a coffee at a café.

Prices vary – and increase yearly – but not that greatly. You can get a simple meal (e.g., omelette, bread, basic salad) in a plain little place for Drs 500; you can get a full meal in a decent restaurant for Drs 900. Beer or wine would add Drs 110–170 to these prices. Service is almost always included in the bill. The standard menu is set up with double columns, one with the price of the item itself, the other with the item after the service percentage is included. Any further tipping is up to you. As with so much else in Greece, the attitude of waiters, the quality of service, and the general atmosphere in restaurants have changed in recent years. With so many foreigners passing through, it is hard for every waiter to extend the full 'Zorba' treatment to every client. Service at times is best described as casual. But by and large, you should be pleased, and even impressed, by the efforts of Greek waiters.

NIGHT-LIFE

Particular facilities for night-life will be indicated under each centre, but a few general remarks might be made here. Essentially, outside the main cities and the major tourist resorts – where, to be sure, most visitors will be at night – tourists will have to make their own night-life, and it will be of the informal, impromptu variety: late meals, lingering drinks, moonlight strolls. There are cinemas in the larger towns, where mostly foreign films are shown. These are usually in the original language, with Greek subtitles; they are usually not first-run films. If you are lucky, you may just run into the odd folk-dance performance or folk-music concert at some formal or festive gathering. For those who insist on doing something, it comes around to dancing – in a stylish night-spot in Iraklion, a roadside tavern or one of the new discos, from a fox-trot to a folk-dance. For those who want to be entertained, the best thing is to park oneself in a café and watch the world go by.

FOOD AND DRINK

In Greece, as with most national cuisines, many foods that might not appeal to you if taken separately turn out to be most satisfying when blended with a full meal. The notorious resinated wine – *retsina* – is a case in point: by itself, it leaves many foreigners aghast, but when drunk with Greek foods it combines with the other textures and flavours to make a real Greek 'bouquet'.

Crete has several specialities: a few are even confined to limited areas of Crete (a list of these follows). Menus also reflect the season: when something is in season you will see it everywhere; then quite suddenly it will disappear and you switch to another food.

BREAD
Even in the villages, people have generally given up baking their own bread. But in some bakeries and restaurants of the cities there is a choice. The word for bread is *psomi*, but there are special words for varieties. On saints' days and special occasions when a priest blesses bread that is passed around, it is usually a slightly sweet bread that is used, and this is known as *ártos*, or *áyios ártos*. In some villages they make an almost stone-hard bread – *paximádhia*: this must be soaked in water before you can get your teeth into it, but then it goes surprisingly well with other foods.

OLIVE OIL
Greeks like a lot of olive oil, but with a little persistence you can persuade them to reduce the quantities for you. The fact remains, though, that many foods are cooked in olive oil, and if you don't care for this you must order selectively.

FISH AND FOWL
Fish are far more of a rarity than one might expect on an island, but they should be fresh when you do have an opportunity to try some – especially grilled and especially in harbour-side eating places. The *barboúnia*, red mullet, and the red snapper are especially good. Try squid (*kalamares*) or octopus, for a change; or shrimps or shellfish if you can find them. A new item that has begun to appear in more stylish restaurants is 'fish kebab', chunks of fish on a spit with onions, peppers, etc. – quite tasty!

Chickens and eggs are plentiful. You might chance on partridge or quail.

MEAT

The staple meat of Crete for centuries has been some form of lamb or mutton, but in recent years – due to rise in demand – it has become expensive (and indeed Crete now imports some lamb). In the villages, though, it is still the most available meat. In towns and cities, beef, veal and pork are available – and occasionally rabbit. Charcoal-grilled chops are known as *brizóles*. Beef (sometimes pork) grilled in small chunks on a spit is *souvlákia* (now often 'anglicized' as kebabs). Scraps of meat packed on to a vertical spit and then sliced off when cooked is known as *yíros*. What we would call 'offal' is wrapped around a large horizontal spit to make what is known as *kokorétsi* – and, despite the sound of it, it is delicious.

PREPARED DISHES

The well-known favourite is *moussaká*, made in a casserole of layers of aubergine (eggplant), chopped meat, potato (sometimes macaroni) and egg.

There are *dolmádhes*: vine leaves stuffed with minced meat or rice – especially delicious when served with an egg-lemon sauce. Then there is *pastitsio*, a sort of macaroni pie that, at best, is a cheap meal.

VEGETABLES AND SALADS

There are plenty of tomatoes, cucumbers and courgettes (small marrows); aubergines (eggplants) are widely eaten, as are a variety of green beans. Onions are used freely as a garnish. 'Greek salad' can be a real treat: tomatoes, cucumbers, olives and *féta* cheese (possibly bits of green pepper and onions and occasionally with cabbage). Ask for pepper, vinegar or lemon juice if you want to enliven the basic oil and salt dressing. Lettuce or salad greens are not easily come by but try a plate of plain fresh tomatoes for a change. In the spring, Cretans enjoy eating raw artichoke leaves.

FRUIT

Oranges, tangerines, peaches, water-melons, grapes and bananas are perhaps the most common; there are also quinces, pears, apples, mulberries, apricots, cherries and strawberries. The prices fall rapidly from day to day as the various fruits come in season. And try the less familiar ones – fresh figs, or pomegranates.

CHEESE AND DAIRY PRODUCTS

There are a variety of local goats' cheeses, but the best-known and best-liked are *anthótiro*, *mizíthra*, *manoúri*, *graviéra*, *kefalotíri* and *féta*. Fresh cow's milk is now easy to find, at least in tourist centres and large towns. The fresh yoghurt makes up for anything lacking in the cheeses – Cretan yoghurts are one of the treats of the island. Also popular is the *tirópita* – cheese enclosed in pastry.

DESSERT

Most of the typical Greek sweets are some variety of *baklavá* – a flaky layered pastry with finely chopped nuts, soaked in honey; most foreigners find it excessively sweet. There is also *halvá* – a mildly sweet, crisp paste made of honey and sesame seeds; *loukoumádhes* – doughnut-like lumps covered with honey; and *bougátsa* – flaky pastry with a cream or cheese filling. In the villages one can sometimes get *tighanítes*, a typical Cretan delicacy – a plain flour pancake covered with honey and sesame seeds. Until recently, most restaurants didn't serve desserts other than the odd baklava; now many offer ice-cream, fancy cakes, etc. – even with coffee.

DRINKS

Water

Oddly enough, water is the 'national drink' of Crete. Cretans like it cold, and they like to savour its taste; they also like compliments about it. There is good, safe drinking-water over the entire island throughout the year; all the towns and larger villages have chemically treated supplies, while fresh springs are abundant elsewhere. In the towns, bottled mineral water (*metallikó neró*) is available; and even the most obscure villages always seem to have some sort of bottled lemonade.

Indeed, it has now come to pass that many cafés and restaurants no longer provide the famous, free, cold fresh water; when you order water you will be brought bottled (in plastic) spring water. But before becoming indignant at another tourist trap, consider that there is a serious shortage of water in many parts of Greece, particularly where tourists are now making extraordinary demands on the water supply: it does not seem unreasonable to ask foreigners to pay for at least some of this precious commodity.

WINE

Cretan wines have not the quality of good Continental wines, but they go with the local food. *Retsina* is not so popular on Crete as it is in Athens; ask for *aretsinoto*, just to be sure – 'unresinated wine'. Two of the better Cretan red wines are *Broúsko* and *Kissamos*; a good white wine called *Mínos* is generally available; others are *Górtinos* and *Phaestós*. Try a glass of the taverna's own wine – certainly cheaper. The sweet dessert wine, *Malevízi*, is a speciality. Local vermouths and Greek brandy should be tried.

BEER

Beer is popular, and actually is drunk more with meals – at least in restaurants – than wine. Several Greek brands of beer stand up well to better-known brands. The German beer Henninger now has a brewery outside Iraklion, so this beer is widely available. Two sizes are usually offered – specify if you want the smaller. Draught beer is appearing.

OUZO

Ouzo is the well-known Greek spirit; it is made by distilling the crushed mash after the wine juice has been pressed from the grapes, with anisette added to provide a slight flavour. On Crete the men are distinguished from the boys by drinking *rakí*, a stronger, unflavoured version (and known in Crete as *tsípouro* or *tzikoudhiá*). An even stronger spirit is *mournóraki*, made from mulberries and a speciality of Rethymnon.

COFFEE

In spite of the claim just made for water, coffee-drinking will strike the visitor as the national pastime, and most foreigners come to enjoy the ritual, the locales – and sometimes the coffee. For Greek coffee is served Turkish style (but definitely ordered now as *ellenikós kafés*): a small cup with the muddy lees in the bottom, and usually very sweet. You soon learn how to make the little cup last an hour. As for the dregs, plan to stop about two thirds of the way down! As a rule, the sugar is boiled together with the coffee. If you don't want any sugar, insist on *skétos*; if you require just a little, say *me olíghi*; medium, *métrios*; sweet and well-boiled, *glyko vrastós*; and very sweet, *polí glykós*. These are only some of the gradations. The waiter will bring you sweet coffee unless you indicate otherwise. In the better restaurants or cafés you may be able to order a cup of 'American' or 'French' coffee, but in many cases this will turn out to be Nescafé, although espresso coffee is now being served at some of the smartest restaurants and cafés. If you send out for breakfast, be prepared to get Greek coffee unless you have made yourself very clear on the point.

HERB TEA

One speciality of Crete is its herb teas, made from dittany and other herbs. They have various names – *karteráchi*, *diktamo tsái* or *tsái vounoú*.

Regional specialities

IRAKLION NOME

Stiffádo (beef with onions and spices).

Dolmádhes or *dolmadhákia* (vine leaves stuffed with meat and rice).

Giouvarlákia (meatballs with egg-lemon sauce).

Bougátsa (soft cheese or cream filling between flaky pastry).

Fresh grapes: *rosakí* and *sultaniá*.

Oranges from Fodhele.

Mageirítsa (soup of lamb's liver, vegetables, rice and eggs – traditional on Easter Eve).

KHANIA NOME

Honey from Akrotiri and from Sfakia.

Wines and chestnuts from Kissamos.

Olive oil of Apokorona.

Chochlioí (snails with potatoes).

Boiled *radhikia* (chicory) as salad.

Oranges and tangerines.

Kallitsoúnia (mint cream-cheese pastries – traditional Easter food).

RETHYMNON NOME

Pork with *máratho* (fennel).

Mizíthra (white soft cheese) with honey.

Graviéra (cheese) from Mount Idha.

LASITHI NOME

Grilled fish.

Local cheeses.

Wine from Mouliana.

Soumádha (a drink made from almonds and either hot or cold water).

Yoghurt-and-honey in Kritsa.

PRACTICAL INFORMATION

CLIMATE AND WEATHER

It once seemed adequate to say that Crete enjoys one of the more favourable climates of the Mediterranean, to point out the attractions of the hot summers and mild winters or the differences between the coastal plains and the mountains, and then retire. But as increasing numbers of people come to Crete with more sophisticated goals, it seems necessary to provide a more detailed account. The chart shows the temperature and rainfall for Iraklion, not only because it is the city most people pass through, but because these averages hold for at least most of the northern coastal region where far and away the majority of foreigners spend most of their time. The south coast tends to be somewhat warmer, while the hills and mountains, obviously, are cooler and wetter.

AVERAGE TEMPERATURES AND RAINFALL IN IRAKLION

Month	Average Temperature		Average Rainfall		Average Rainy Days
	°F	°C	inches	mm	
January	54	12	3·7	94	14
February	54	12	3·0	76	12
March	57	14	1·6	41	7
April	62	17	0·9	23	4
May	68	20	0·7	18	3
June	74	23	0·1	3	0·7
July	78	26	0·0	0	0·1
August	78	26	0·1	3	0·4
September	75	24	0·7	18	2
October	69	21	1·7	43	5
November	63	17	2·7	69	8
December	58	14	4·0	102	13

In general you can count on about 300 days of sunny, clear skies each year, with moderate to hot temperatures. For those who have the whole year to choose from, May or September are the ideal months to travel on Crete.

Spring moves over Crete during March and April and is distinguished by a virtual 'explosion' of flowers. May brings a further warming and a drop in the rainfall. By the end of the month, there will be hardly a drop of rain, or for the next three to four months. Summer is undeniably hot, although breezes play along the north coast (the *meltemi*, or etesian wind from the north) and through the mountains, somewhat relieving the dead heat. But foreigners must be careful not to overexpose themselves to the sun, and they are advised to avoid ambitious expeditions during the middle of the day. That still leaves many hours for sightseeing, and late afternoon–early evening is an especially pleasant time to visit certain sites. Summer evenings, too, are surprisingly mild, cooling to 60°–70° F even during the hottest spell.

Autumn moves in during October, a lovely month, and November, often a rainy month, is marked not so much by a change in foliage as by a re-greening. Winter – December, January, February – can be raw and chilly, especially if you lack proper heat, which is generally the case: Cretans, like all Mediterraneans, pretend that each winter's cold is 'unusual'. But many foreigners now winter on Crete and find it quite manageable. Beware, though, of travel posters that suggest water sports in Cretan waters during the winter: the water temperature drops to about 60° F (16° C) from December to March. Freezing air temperatures, though, are rare in most places where travellers are apt to be and snow is all but unknown along the coastal plains. Mountain winters, of course, are quite different, and snowfalls on certain slopes or roads makes travel all but impossible. One plus for the winter on Crete, however, is that the haze that enshrouds the island vanishes, and the whole atmosphere takes on clarity and detail. It should also be said that the rainy and raw weather seldom lasts for more than two to three days, and then the clear, sunny days return.

There are two minor exceptions to this moderate climate, but neither need deter the prospective visitor. One is the hot, dry sirocco that occasionally sweeps up from North Africa in the summer – at most a temporary nuisance. The other consists of earthquakes, but these occur so infrequently and are so slight as to count for nothing in a traveller's plans.

HEALTH AND WATER

The main cities have a selection of doctors, dentists, specialized clinics, and hospitals. Iraklion, naturally, has the fullest range of medical facilities. The National Tourist Information offices or major hotels should be able to aid you in an emergency.

In the villages or remote areas, you would probably have to get a ride to a doctor – unless, of course, it were an extreme emergency. The Tourist Police and other authorities would assist. By the way, since so many of the doctors have studied in England, America, Germany, or France, even in the provinces language will probably not be a problem.

Cities, towns, and even larger villages have chemists (pharmacies) selling more or less all the familiar medicines: such shops are marked by a distinctive red cross. And if prices seem high, they are that way for everyone. People intending to go off on their own and into the hills might consider taking a small first-aid kit. Anyone with special needs or worries should obviously consult their own doctor before leaving for abroad.

Not too many years ago, travellers to places like Crete were concerned about finding safe drinking water. That should no longer be anyone's concern (although a sudden shift to any new water supply may temporarily upset some people's internal processes). Any water you will be drinking will be perfectly safe especially now that so many cafés and restaurants have taken to selling bottled water (in place of providing free water). However, a new water problem has arisen recently. Because of the tremendous demand created by the concentrations of people in large hotels and cities, there may be occasional times of low supply or pressure. A much more likely situation is to find that your hotel rations its hot water: ask as you are signing in when hot water is available, and plan accordingly.

Finally, and unfortunately, it still must be said that many public toilets – including some in restaurants and other facilities frequented by foreigners – leave much to be desired. Although not a threat to anyone's health, these places are certainly unappealing. You might consider travelling with spare toilet paper and hand wipers.

TOURIST INFORMATION

Before setting out for Greece and Crete, you can obtain certain kinds of information from the National Tourist Organization of Greece. Besides its offices in Athens and Crete, it maintains offices in some of the world's major cities. The main office is in Athens, at 2 Amerikis Street. It also maintains information offices convenient for the public in the centre of Athens: one at 2 Karageorgi Servias (in the bank at the corner of Syntagma–Constitution Square), the other at the General Bank of Greece, 1 Ermou Street. In all fairness to the staffs at these offices, there is a limit to the details they can provide about every aspect of Greece or Crete: many questions must simply wait until you are on the scene. But you might get a general sense of things if you were to contact one of these offices:

London: 4 Conduit Street, London, W1R 0DJ.
New York: 645 Fifth Avenue, New York City 10022.
Los Angeles: 611 West 6th Street, Los Angeles, Calif. 90017.
Chicago: 168 No. Michigan Avenue, Chicago, Ill. 60601.
Montreal: 1233 rue de la Montagne.
Munich: Pacellistrasse 2.
Paris: 3 Avenue de l'Opéra.
Rome: Via Bissolati 78–80.
Frankfurt-am-Main: Neue Mainzerstrasse 22.
Brussels: Avenue Louise 173.
Stockholm: Birger Jarlsgate 8 IV
Zurich: Loewenstrasse 25.

Greek Embassies and Consulates in all cities will assist where possible. There are also, of course, the many private travel and tourist agencies.

Once on Crete it is possible to get help and advice from several sources. The following cities have offices of the National Tourist Organization:

Iraklion: Xanthoudhidhou Street (opposite Archaeological Museum).
Khania: Janissaries' Mosque (on the old harbour).
Rethymnon: E. Venizelos Ave. (at Beach Centre).

If you want to know where there is to be a village festival, find out about ships connecting to Santorini, or just book a room in a hotel, you can start at one of these offices. But do not expect the clerks on duty to be very conversant with subtle points about Cretan art or archaeology.

Another official institution which you may find yourself relying on during your stay on the island is the Tourist Police. This is simply one of the main branches of the Greek National Police and is to be found all over Greece. Its members wear a greenish uniform. Tourist Police are to be met all over the island, and will do anything possible to help the traveller. The main offices of the Tourist Police are:

Iraklion: Dikeösinis Avenue.
Khania: 44 Karaiskaki Street (in Nea Dimotiki Agora).
Rethymnon: Arkadhiou Street (beside Loggia Museum).
Ayios Nikolaos: Voulismeni Pool ('bottomless pool').

Incidentally, any complaints you may have – about prices or anything else – should be directed to the Tourist Police, but it might be more discreet to start at the National Tourist Organization's office.

MUSEUMS AND SITES

Specific information about museums and sites will be given where they occur in the Routes section. Details about hours of opening, free days, etc. now seem to be in a constant state of flux, especially since the Greek government claims it is going to impose more conventional work hours on shops and businesses. So rather than mislead travellers, we advise everyone who is determined to visit a particular site or museum – especially anyone who has limited time to do so – to enquire at the National Tourist Information Office immediately upon arriving in one of the major Cretan cities. If your travel plans depend on a tight schedule, insist on getting the latest details. Better still, go straight to the museum or site and check out the hours.

Here, though, we might point out what seem to be a few reliable constants. Almost all museums and sites have a reduced schedule during the winter – officially from November 1st to April 31st – and are open mornings only on Sundays, so-called half-holidays, and regular holidays. These include: January 2nd, January 6th, the first Saturday of Carnival, the last Monday before Lent, Maundy Thursday, Easter Saturday, Easter Monday, Easter Tuesday, Whitsuntide, August 15th, October 28th, and December 24th, 26th and 31st. Everything in Greece, including sites and museums, closes completely on January 1st, March 25th, Good Friday afternoon, Easter Day, and Christmas Day. (Note that from Maundy Thursday to the Wednesday of Easter week, there are very restricted hours.) These schedules, by the way, refer to those museums and sites administered by the national departments; local sites and museums may follow their own hours – and also need not recognize the various passes, etc. for reduced rates.

Admission charges will vary greatly, but all the nationally-administered sites and museums are open free to visitors on Sundays and half-holidays. (For details about reductions available to certain classes of visitors, such as students, teachers, artists, or journalists, see p. 27.)

To conclude: be prepared for variations on the above – and enquire as soon as you arrive close to your destination.

BANKS AND CURRENCY

You should check exchange rates with your bank as they are apt to fluctuate. And it is not always true that you get a better rate abroad than you will in Greece.

The maximum amount of drachmas that a foreigner is allowed to bring in is 25,000, while the maximum to be taken out is 10,000 (although in practice the average traveller is never questioned about this). If you should overstock, it is possible to buy back your own currency, but only at the Bank of Greece. You must produce the receipts of your original purchase of drachmas, and you will lose at least 1 per cent on the transaction. If for any reason you have to send money out of Greece to some other country, this may also be done through the Bank of Greece; here again you will also need to take all receipts and official documents.

Travellers should work out their own personal system for making easy conversions and relating to known values. For example: if the English £ were around Drs 260, it should be possible to remember certain basic equivalents: Drs 20 equals 8p; Drs 100 about 40p. If the US dollar is pegged at around Drs 150, then Drs 10 is about 7 cents; Drs 50 about 33 cents; Drs 100 just over 65 cents.

Banks on Crete are open from Monday to Friday, usually from 8.00 to 14.00, except for the public holidays listed on p. 67. In Iraklion you can usually change money in one bank during the afternoon, at least during the high season; there have even been banks that opened at limited hours on Saturday and Sunday for foreign exchange, but you cannot count on that. Travellers cheques can also be cashed in hotels, restaurants, souvenir shops, at the airport, etc. Major credit cards, including Access, American Express and Visa, are a useful standby (especially when hiring a car).

And now there is a new alternative – at least in a few major cities (including Iraklion and Khania): the Greek Post Office maintains a few (bright yellow) trailer-like offices in central locales where you can buy Drachmas (with your passport) and postage stamps. Hours are fairly steady, certainly an improvement over traditional services.

SHOPPING AND SOUVENIRS

Smaller towns and villages can provide little beyond the basic amenities, but several of the larger towns and the main cities offer a full range of shops and services – including laundry and dry-cleaning, films and photographic supplies, chemists (pharmacies) and jewellers, clothing and hardware, English-language newspapers and magazines, etc. Many of the manufactured items will bear familiar names, since Greece is forced to import a great deal. Dry-cleaners are surprisingly cheap, laundries surprisingly expensive. In general, prices are marked and usually fixed (but see Bargaining, on p. 62). Many of the better shops now have some English-speaking personnel, and people around will always help you with any difficulties.

With regard to souvenirs and handicrafts, Crete's specialities include basketry, hand-woven materials, bags, carpets, lace, knitware, embroideries, shawls, hand-made gold and silver jewellery, leather-work, wood-carving and ceramics. The larger towns have a wide selection in the shops; if you are lucky you may be able to pick up some things in the villages. The Cretan knives are of particular interest. Some of the reproductions of Minoan artwork are fairly attractive. Among the best buys are textiles – wool, linen, silk, cotton, embroideries, knitwear, lace – made into handbags, rugs and various articles of clothing. Some of it has been produced in the villages on the old looms and with the old patterns but most of it is now mass produced. As for the claims of proprietors of souvenir and gift shops that this or that item is 'old', the best thing is to forget all about such matters, and buy an object because you like it and because it costs what you feel it's worth to you. Many items do seem to be overpriced, but you are free to walk away from them. And if many items seem unappealing, that is a matter of taste.

Hours for Greek stores have been in flux for some years as Greeks vacillate over adopting the conventional European work day. In general, though, all stores are open every morning, Monday to Saturday (major holidays excluded: see p. 67). Exactly when the morning ends and which shops – such as food or clothing – are open on which afternoons not even Greeks are sure. You must ask each day and plan accordingly. Pavement kiosks in the larger cities are open at almost any time of the day or night; here you can get cigarettes, toilet articles and cosmetics, pencils and postcards, sweets, etc.; those in the centre of cities often sell postage stamps (with a slight surcharge).

BARGAINING

Many tourists believe that haggling is a required constituent of all transactions in Mediterranean lands, and are more or less nervous of it according to their individual aptitude for this pastime. It may not be entirely avoided on Crete, but it need not be so unnerving. And there is haggling – and haggling: if you are going to engage in it, at least do so in the proper spirit, not with hostility, which will change the relationship and get you nowhere. We give here a list of some goods and services, and show how the custom applies.

Hotel rooms: These charges are fixed by law and are posted in the room as a matter of course. Extra fees are usually for extra services. Reductions are usually only for off-season rates.

Restaurants: Prices are clearly marked on menus. Where there are no menus, you may find yourself paying a few drachmas more than a native 'regular' – but only a few more, and this is standard throughout the world.

Bus and taxi fares: These are officially fixed, although for a long trip by taxi it is a good idea to make sure you and the driver understand all that is involved.

Groceries, fruit, etc.: Prices in shops and markets are usually clearly marked. It is as well to memorize standard prices of a few basic commodities and allow for small differences according to locality. And don't get too excited if the merchant rounds off a few lepta in his favour; the next time it will be someone rounding it off in your favour.

Souvenirs: Prices are usually marked, but this is a competitive business and shop-owners must be allowed a few 'ploys' to survive in this trade. If a shop-owner knocks 30 – or even 50 – drachmas off an article he has been asking Drs 550 for, it may be that he has seen you waver. Haggle if you feel like it, and see what happens. There comes a moment, though, when you must be prepared to walk out the door – and the proprietor may just let you go.

Other goods: You need a lantern or a stove for camping, and so you go to a shop. You are quoted a price that is 300 drachmas more than a Greek acquaintance told you it would be. It may be that your Greek friend doesn't know the real price of the moment. But if he did, and if the dealer is in fact trying to get Drs 300 more from you than he would from a native Cretan, you must decide just how much it is worth to you and play the game on that basis. You can walk out and try elsewhere. Nor should you feel cheated when the price is reduced; that is why you are haggling. And for all you know the shopman may need your money so badly that he is prepared to cut down on his fair profit.

As for outright cheating, undoubtedly there are incidents; the sheer numbers of transient tourists has led to a certain 'carelessness' in many transactions. Again, each person must decide how much of himself he wants to expend to right a wrong when a few drachmas are involved. At least go into each situation with the presumption of good faith – and with good spirits. Many incidents involve true misunderstandings (often as not due to language difficulties). If you should really feel that you have been cheated, you should quietly ask for a receipt – completely itemized – before handing over your money. Then take the receipt to the Tourist Police at the first opportunity, and you will have their assistance. And in recounting it later, why not remember all those acts of impulsive generosity by other Cretans?

TIPPING

Tipping often presents a problem to tourists. On Crete many people will be helpful to you and there will be occasions when you just do not know whether to tip or not. Cigarettes – especially foreign brands – can be used with men as a discreet gratuity, sweets with children.

Hotels: There is a 10 per cent, and in some cases a 15 per cent service charge on the bill, but it is customary to give a personal tip to anyone who has been particularly helpful – the man who carries your bags, and the chambermaid, for instance.

Restaurants: After a meal it is customary to tip over and above the service charge included in the bill. Give your waiter, personally, a few drachmas extra when he returns your change, or leave the tip on the plate with the bill. You should know that drachmas left on the table are for the boy who sets the table, brings the water, etc.: it is customary to leave several drachmas for him if the party consists of two or three people. In little tavernas or village cafés where it is obviously the proprietor himself who is serving you, tipping is not customary.

Taxi-drivers: You are not required to give taxi-drivers any fixed percentage of the fare, but it is customary to give them 10–15 per cent.

Ladies' hairdressers: For a shampoo and set, the tip is usually 10 per cent to the hairdresser in charge and perhaps half that to the assistant.

Shoeshine boys: They get about Drs 10 tip for a shine that will cost you Drs 50.

SPORT

SWIMMING

Crete is ringed by beaches – some like Pacific lagoons, others of a harsher grandeur. They will be indicated on the routes, but here we point out a few general features. Only a few of the main cities have public beaches with full facilities (changing rooms, etc.) and none really provide lifeguards. At less frequented beaches, precautions are advised: there can be dangerous and unexpected undertows and currents!

There is no denying that Crete's shores have been under heavy attack in recent years. Large tourist resorts are monopolizing many of the most accessible sandy beaches, leaving rocky or more remote beaches to the general public. The water in many places close to cities is not especially clean or refreshing. And the oil that fouls so many Mediterranean shores is inevitably present on many Cretan beaches: even when they appear clean on the surface, your feet pick up tar from walking around. Most people now bring roll-up mats to beaches to avoid spoiling good towels. Yet there is still good swimming to be enjoyed around Crete – especially at the more remote beaches.

Topless bathing by women of all nationalities is now pretty much the norm on most of the beaches of Crete – perhaps less so on those that really serve as 'town beaches'. As for nude bathing, attitudes vary and do change. Some Cretans – both communities and individuals – are strongly opposed to it and seem able to get the authorities to arrest people found nude on certain beaches. Yet some resorts invite it, and individuals are able to get away with it in remote places. Discretion is advised.

WATER-SKIING, WINDSURFING, PEDALBOATS

Water-skiing facilities are available at most of the Class A and B beach hotels and resorts. Many of the public beaches now have sailboards and pedalboats for hire, and some now have water-skiing operators. Private resorts at Elounda (p. 313) offer instruction for a fee.

SKIN-DIVING

Scuba-diving (that is, with tanks) is now forbidden in all Greek waters (unless done with special permit). But snorkelling – with tube, mask and flippers – can be practised, and Crete offers some special attractions. In addition to the chance delights of underwater flora and fauna, there are several places where submerged archaeological remains may be examined: Olous at Elounda, Limin Khersonisou, Loutro, and Mokhlos. Incidentally, anyone with some knowledge of geological matters will often be able to see evidence of the rising of sections of Crete by examining coastal strata. The basic gear can be purchased in Iraklion, Khania, and in a few other places such as Rethymnon and Ayios Nikolaos.

TENNIS

Both Iraklion and Khania have tennis courts where the public can play for a reasonable fee. Enquire at the National Tourist offices in those cities. Several of the larger, more expensive resort hotels have tennis courts for their guests, and may hire them to non-residents: enquire in advance.

HORSEBACK RIDING

In recent years there have been two private stables that offer horses for hire or for lessons. Both are near Iraklion: enquire at the National Tourist office there if you want to pursue this.

WALKING AND CLIMBING

For those who would like to see something of Crete on foot, there are touring and climbing clubs in Iraklion, Rethymnon and Khania (pp. 131, 246 and 259), which arrange frequent excursions – some involving only a few hours of walking, others quite ambitious climbs. (Protection for the lower legs and feet is advised.) Foreigners would always be most welcome, and contacts can be made through the Tourist Office. For those who prefer to go alone and would like some hints from men who have actually walked over much of Crete, the following books in English are best: Pendlebury's *The Archaeology of*

Crete, Grantham's *Minotaur and Crete* (Alexiou, 1960), Trevor-Battye's *Camping in Crete* and Fielding's *The Stronghold*. There are several quite rewarding climbs to be made on Cretan peaks, but most people go to the mountains to enjoy their beauties rather than for spectacular ascents. Snow stays on some slopes through many months, and the Cretan mountains can be cold and windy. Proper preparations should be made before setting out. The single most attractive climb – the ascent of Mount Idha – is described in some detail on pp. 194–9, while the passage through the Gorge of Samaria is described on pp. 278–85. Experienced walkers' advice: wear proper shoes.

SKIING

Some skiing is now done in the White Mountains in western Crete, centred at Kallergi. There is no lift but there are some simple facilities – beds and basic amenities. All arrangements should be made through the Hellenic Mountain Club in Khania.

HUNTING

There is some small game on Crete, including rabbits and hares as well as birds like partridges, woodcocks, ducks, thrushes, etc. Seasons are strictly observed and there are various requirements and restrictions for foreigners. Start your enquiries at the National Tourist Organization's offices in the nearest large city.

It has been stressed for some years now that it is forbidden to shoot the Cretan wild goat (see p. 81). However, in 1977 the Greek government announced it was going to allow some hunting of the goat, but only on the largest of the three island preserves, Dia, off Iraklion. The preserved population had become so large that hunters were to be allowed to shoot some older male goats. The fees involved, however, make this prohibitive to all except the wealthy: Drs 30,000 for a special licence, Drs 1,000 for a special fee, Drs 3,000 per animal taken (limit of six), plus the expenses (Drs 10,000–20,000) of hiring a boat for a day's visit. There are also restrictions on the type of weapon and ammunition allowed – so anyone interested must make exact enquiries before setting off for Greece. And when it's all over, the hunt is hardly a true challenge: on the relatively small and restricted range, the wild goats are more like sitting ducks.

FISHING
Although the coastal waters in this part of the Mediterranean are no longer as productive as might be expected, there is still some fishing for the amateur. No licence is required, but anyone intending to use fishing guns or spears should consult the Tourist Police or harbour-master about restrictions.

PUBLIC HOLIDAYS

We list here the Greek holidays when banks, museums and most shops (including many restaurants) are closed:
January 1st – New Year's Day.
January 6th – Epiphany.
Last Monday before Lent.*
Good Friday.*
Easter Monday.*
March 25th – Greek Independence Day.
May 1st – Spring Festival, or Labour Day.
August 15th – Assumption of the Virgin Mary.
October 28th – Okhi (No!) Day (Second World War episode).
December 25th – Christmas Day.
December 26th – Boxing Day.

HOLIDAYS AND FESTIVALS

Hardly a day passes on Crete without a celebration in honour of somebody or something – a saint, a village festival, a harvest, a patriotic event. Each nome (p. 120) has one place – either a chapel, a monastery or a village – where on major saints' days the people bearing the name of that saint tend to gather. These 'name-days' are more important to Greeks than their birthdays. Often dancing and general celebration takes place on the night preceding the actual church observances, and extra services are run on the regular bus routes. Sometimes festivities are extended over two or three days, and the lavish Cretan hospitality sets itself no limits.

The data of the official holidays are listed above. What follows is a list of the major events of the Cretan year. As celebration of certain events may vary from year to year, enquire at the Tourist Office for details.

*See note on Greek Easter, p. 68.

Date	Occasion	Where and how observed (Nome given in parentheses)
Dec. 30th– Jan. 1st	New Year	In homes, cafés, hotels and public assemblies; observed by feasting, card-playing and gambling, and rituals such as opening the windows at midnight to let evil spirits out, or sharing cake with lucky coin baked in it.
Jan. 6th	Epiphany	At harbours and seashores: a cross is thrown into the sea to bring luck and blessings.
2 weeks before Lent*	Carnival	Cities such as Iraklion and Rethymnon make the biggest display, but eating, drinking and good spirits are general throughout the island.
Last Monday before Lent*	Clean Monday	This marks the end of Carnival and the beginning of Lent; no meat is eaten, but a feast is contrived all the same. Kites are flown – by all ages.
*(See note on Greek Easter)	Lent	Observed by everyone to a certain extent, but a Holy Week of almost total fasting is the culminating feature of Lent.
*(See note on Greek Easter)	Good Friday to Easter Monday	On Friday evening there is a funeral procession through the streets. On Saturday evening a long church service ends with rejoicing at midnight, the lighting of candles, and fireworks. Easter Sunday is celebrated with eating, drinking, dancing. Many flock to military installations where the soldiers entertain the local population.

* *Note on Greek Easter:* The Greek Orthodox Easter is calculated in a way which baffles all but the initiated. As with the Western Christian Churches, it must fall after the first full moon following the first day of spring, but it must also fall *after* the Jewish Passover. Holidays dependent on Easter (printed with an asterisk), of course, must also fluctuate in relation to this date.

Date	Occasion	Where and how observed (Nome given in parentheses)
Mar. 25th	Greek Independence Day	Observed mainly by parades in large towns.
	Annunciation of Our Lady	Church of Prassa (Iraklion) and Apokorona (Khania).
1st Sunday after Easter*	St Thomas	Monastery of Vrondisi, Ayios Thomas (Iraklion) and Neo Khorio of Apokorona (Khania).
April	Orange Festival	Skines Kydonias (Khania): Cretan music and dances, folk-craft exhibition.
April 23rd †(See note below)	St George	Monastery of Epanosifi (Iraklion); religious feast with Archbishop celebrating Mass. Selinaris Monastery (Lasithi): religious feast.
*(See note on Greek Easter, p. 68)	Ascension	Almyros Church near Ayios Nikolaos (Lasithi): service and feast. Local dances and fireworks.
May 1st	Spring Festival	Throughout the countryside people picnic, dance and weave flower-wreaths.
May 5th	St Irene	Village of Kroussonas (Iraklion): religious feast.
May 20th–27th	Anniversary of Battle of Crete (Second World War)	City of Khania celebrates with athletic events.
May 21st	St Constantine and St Helena	At various chapels named after these saints.

† *Note on St George's Day:* If this festival happens to fall in Holy Week, it is postponed until after Easter. This is because there are so many Cretans with the name Georgios, who would not be able to celebrate their name-day with proper enthusiasm during the austerities of Holy Week.

Date	Occasion	Where and how observed (Nome given in parentheses)
May 26th–27th	Anniversary of Declaration of 1821 Revolution	Khora Sfakion.
June 1st–7th	Amateur fishermen's week	Arranged by local Hellenic Club in Ayios Nikolaos.
June 24th	Birthday of St John the Baptist	With bonfires (which are actually observing the summer solstice) on which are burned wreaths of flowers which have been hanging over people's front doors since May 1st. If you are lucky, you may see people jumping the fires.
	Klidona Festival	Kroustas (Lasithi): music and dancing.
June 29th	St Peter and St Paul	At various chapels named after these saints.
1st week in July	Marine Week	Various naval observances and sea sports along the coast.
July 17th	St Marina	Village of Voni (Iraklion): major religious feast.
	Watermelon Festival	Khersonissos.
July 26th and 27th	St Paraskevi and St Panteleimon	Observed at villages of Kounavi (Iraklion) and Fournes (Khania).
End of July	Wine Festival	The city of Rethymnon has instituted a modern festival, with several days of wine-sampling. Dances in Cretan costumes.
August	Sultana Festival	Sitia: celebrations for five days
Aug. 6th	Feast of the Transfiguration	At a small church on Mt Iouktas (Iraklion). Also observed at Skine (Khania).
Aug. 8th	St Myron	At the village of Ayios Myron (Iraklion): there is a cave where the saint lived, with sacred water.

Date	Occasion	Where and how observed (Nome given in parentheses)
Aug. 15th	Assumption of Our Lady	At the town of Neapolis (Lasithi): feast starts on 14th with local dances, athletic sports; ends on 16th. At the village of Mokhos (Iraklion): festival organized by Greek Touring Club, with Cretan food, local dances in Cretan costumes, exhibitions of local hand-weavings and embroidery, fireworks. Religious feasts at villages, convents and monasteries throughout Crete.
Aug. 25th	St Titus	Iraklion: religious procession from Church of St Titus.
Aug. 27th	St Fanourios	Monastery of Vrondisi (Iraklion): religious feast.
Aug. 29th	Beheading of St John the Baptist	At Giona, beyond village of Rodhopou (Khania). Also at various churches named after John.
Aug. 31st	Holy Sash of the Virgin Mary	Village of Psykhro (Lasithi): religious feast and local dances, hundreds of people descending to the plain on mules.
Sept. 14th	Raising of Holy Cross	Observed in city of Iraklion and villages around Mount Idha. Also at Alikianos (Khania).
October	Chestnut Festival	Villages in Khania Nome.
Oct. 7th	St John the Hermit	At the monastery of Gouverneto and the near-by cave where the saint died (Khania).
Oct. 26th	St Demetrios	Observed at many chapels, as this is a popular name.
Oct. 28th	Okhi Day	Observed all over Greece to commemorate the occasion when the Greek Premier replied 'Okhi!' ('No!') to the Italian ultimatum of 1940.

Date	Occasion	Where and how observed (Nome given in parentheses)
Nov. 7th–9th	Anniversary of Explosion of 1866	Monastery of Arkadhi and at Rethymnon: Crete's own 'national' holiday, with people from all over the island gathering at the monastery (p. 251).
Nov. 11th	St Menas	Town of Iraklion: religious procession for patron saint of town.
Dec. 4th	St Barbara	Village of Ayia Varvara (Iraklion).
Dec. 6th	St Nicholas	Town of Ayios Nikolaos (Lasithi).
Dec. 25th	Christmas	This is less important to the Orthodox Church than Easter, but the whole season of Twelve Days is marked here and there, with singing on Christmas Eve. Popular diversions are gambling and fortune-telling. Fear of evil spirits – the *Kalikántzari* – prevails.

SPECIAL EVENTS

Several activities which have appeared on Crete include:

The Heraklion Festival: Throughout July and August, concerts, dances, recitals, major symphony orchestras, ballet companies, dance troupes, jazz groups, individual performing artists (some Cretan and some Greek). Some of these events take place at the Venetian Fort in Iraklion's harbour (p. 146) and this setting adds greatly to the performance. For details about the schedule, prices, etc., enquire at the National Tourist Organization office.

Kandra Kitchen: A cooking school emphasizing Greek cuisine-cum-culture, now based on Oia on Santorini but including a visit to Crete. Contact: 23b Orinda Way, Orinda, CA 94563, USA.

Hiking and climbing trips around Crete sponsored by the Appalachian Mountain Club. Contact: S. Graham, 1195 Burts Pit Road, Northampton, MA 01060, USA.

POSTAL INFORMATION, TELEPHONES AND TELEGRAMS

Every village on Crete has some place where it is possible to buy stamps, and send and receive mail. In the main towns you can sometimes buy stamps at kiosks as well as at the post offices (the word for stamp is *grammatóssimo*). Postal rates on Crete are the same as on mainland Greece and, as everywhere in the world, increase so often that it would be misleading to give specific figures. But it should be kept in mind that there is a basic fee for airmail letters (the first 20 grammes for Europe, including the United Kingdom, the U.S.A. and Canada); then a fee for the next weight (20–50 grammes for Europe: 20–110 grammes for the U.S.A. and Canada); and then extra fees for successive increments. Postcards, of course, have their own rates.

MOBILE POST OFFICES AND EXCHANGE BOOTHS
One of the most convenient additions to the Greek cityscape in recent years are the yellow trailer-like offices that have been set down at a few centres most frequented by foreigners and tourists (in Iraklion (2), Khania, Rethymnon, Sitia, Matala, and Stalis): usually open most of the day from 08.00 to 20.00, they sell postage stamps and exchange reasonable sums of foreign currency and travellers' cheques.

REGISTERED MAIL
If you intend to send a registered letter or package, this should not be sealed until the post office has approved its contents.

PARCEL POST
If you are sending a package out of Greece, you must be prepared to show the entire contents to the postal authorities; this means undoing even gift wrappings – often for each individual item. There is also a considerable amount of form-filling, stamping, etc. The Greeks themselves take their various gifts and items to the post office, get them inspected, and do all the wrapping-up there, and this seems to be the easiest way. Supposedly some of the procedures will become easier for those sending small packages and gifts to other member nations of the European Community after 1992.

AIR FREIGHT
Olympic Airways has a relatively cheap service for both light freight and for oversize packages (because the post office has strict limits).

TELEPHONES AND TELEGRAMS
There is at least one telephone to be found in every village on Crete; both local and long-distance calls may be placed, but long-distance calls are usually made from offices of the Telephone Service (open

Monday to Friday 07.30 to 15.00 most places, 22.00 in towns, and shorter hours at weekends). Local calls cost Drs 5. In the main cities, telegrams may be sent from the telegraph offices; in other places this may be done by telephone.

International Direct Dialling is prefixed by the code 00 followed by the country code (1 in the case of the U.S.A., 44 in the case of the U.K.). An English-speaking operator can help on 162.

Note: Hotels charge different rates depending on their class. Enquire before placing a call to avoid unpleasant surprises.

WEIGHTS AND MEASURES

The international metric system is used, officially and generally. The few exceptions that linger among the older village folk are noted below.

WEIGHT
Kilo (1,000 grammes) = approx. 2·2 lb.
Half kilo (*missó kiló*) = approx. 1·1 lb.
Quarter kilo (*tétarto*) = approx. $\frac{1}{2}$ lb.
(The *oká* – 1,282 grammes or 2·8 lb. – has been officially abolished, but it is still sometimes used by older people.)

VOLUME
1 litre = approx. $1\frac{3}{4}$ pints Imperial (British) = approx. $2\frac{1}{10}$ pints American measure.
Petrol is sold by the litre. Other liquids are often sold by the kilo. In restaurants wine is sold by large or small bottles or by the glass; but in the wine taverns by the kilo.

LENGTH
1 metre = 39·37 inches.
1 kilometre = 0·62 mile (roughly, 5/8ths mile).

AREA
1 hectare = 2·47 acres.
1 square kilometre = 0·39 square miles.

TEMPERATURE
The Centigrade scale is used. To convert Centigrade to Fahrenheit, multiply by 9/5ths and add 32. To convert Fahrenheit to Centigrade, subtract 32 and multiply by 5/9ths.

ELECTRICITY

All the cities and towns, and almost all the villages, now have electricity. The voltage is 220 and the current AC (unless you have reason to believe that it is provided by a private generator). Americans planning a long stay on Crete with elaborate electrical equipment would need to bring transformers to convert the voltage. Plugs are usually Continental three-pin or two-pin size (which also means that one must have converter plugs).

TIME

Crete, like the mainland, lies in the Eastern European Zone, two hours ahead of Greenwich Mean Time. (Crete, like the rest of Greece, observes Summer Time from March to September.) Officially, Greece uses the Continental 24-hour system, where 1 p.m. is 13.00 hours), 2 p.m. is 14.00 hours, etc. In practice, people say 'one this noon' or 'eight this evening'.

All Greece – except Mount Athos – uses the Western Gregorian calendar. With the exception of Easter and its dependent holy days (pp. 68–9), most Greek holidays and festivals coincide with those of the rest of Europe.

THE LAND AND ITS RESOURCES

General situation and features

Crete lies in the Mediterranean, almost equidistant from central Greece, Asia Minor and Africa – a fact to be kept in mind whenever the point is being made that Crete is the first recognizably *European* civilization. After Sicily, Sardinia, Cyprus and Corsica, Crete is the fifth largest island in the Mediterranean. It is nearly 260 km. long, and varies in width from about 12 to 60 km.; its area is about 8,300 square km. Altogether Crete has some 1,050 km. of coast-line. The north coast is irregular, with several bays, the chief of which is Soudha Bay, considered to be one of the finest harbours in the Mediterranean. The south coast is less irregular, but possesses no natural harbours of any great extent. Crete is distinguished by several physical features: its many fissures and ravines (*pharángi*); its upland plains – some quite large, flat and fertile; numerous caves; one freshwater lake and three brackish water-holes (*almyrós*); and many unique species and endemic varieties of flora. The predominant aspect of the island is its rocky, scrubby, mountainous terrain.

Geological background

Crete's underlying formation is the limestone deposited during the Cretaceous period. In this dim geological past, Crete was part of a great arc of mountains connecting it to the mainland masses of Europe and Asia Minor. For the layman, perhaps the most dramatic evidence for this is the fossil remains of such animals as the dwarf hippopotamus that have been found on Crete – proof, also, that the island was still connected to the mainland up to the beginning of the Pleistocene Epoch. But this was at least one million years before the first humans appeared on Crete. In the relatively few thousand years that human beings have inhabited the island, Crete has been racked by innumerable earthquakes, but a more lasting impact has resulted from the steady and progressive vertical movement of the island that has occurred. Most of western Crete (from a line running from Rethymnon south-east to Matala) has been uplifted, with the island of Elaphonisi, off the south-west corner, raised some 8·5 metres, the maximum; the north-western region has been uplifted slightly less, but the site of Phalasarna (p. 292) has ancient port facilities that are now many yards inland. The central and east-central parts of Crete have not moved in any consistent direction, but there has been some submergence from Limin Khersonisou to Erimoupolis (in the very north-east corner). Olous (p. 314) has some sunken harbour installations still visible; and it is known that the islet of Mokhlos (p. 315) was joined to the mainland in Minoan times. The south-eastern corner has been uplifted.

Mountains

If one feature of Crete's geography had to be singled out as the most influential, it would be the mountains. They are not that spectacular in height, but they do express the Cretan character, and they are certainly impressive in their changing effects and views. As on the mainland, they have probably influenced the island's history by isolating various settlements and shaping the independent character of the people. There are four principal mountain ranges, and one is never very far away from them: they are the back-bone of Crete.

(1) In the west are the White Mountains (*Lefka Ori*); the highest point is Pachnes, 2,452 metres (8,045 feet) above sea level.

(2) In the centre is the Idha Range, now generally known as the Psiloritis. Its peak, the highest point on Crete, is Timios Stavros – 2,456 metres (8,058 feet).

(3) East of the Idha Range are the Dhikti, or Lasithi, Mountains; the highest point is Mount Dhikti, at 2,148 metres (7,047 feet), although another peak, Aphendis Christos, is almost the same height.

(4) At the extreme east are the Sitia Mountains, whose highest point, Aphendis Stavromenos, is 1,476 metres (4,843 feet).

In addition to these principal ranges there are the Asterousia Mountains, which separate the Messara Plain from the south coast in central Crete; the highest peak is Kofinas, some 1,231 metres (4,039 feet). The Kouloukonas Mountains extend along the north coast from Fodhele to Perama; and various other mountains form the peninsulas – and much of the rest of the island.

Flat land and plateaux

The largest flat area is the Messara Plain, which is about 30 km. long and averages 5 km. in width. It runs roughly on the east–west axis in the south-central region of Crete. Rich in history, it is also one of the richest agricultural areas of the island. The other intensively culti-vated flat lands are found chiefly on the narrow coastal plains bordering segments of the north and south coasts.

Crete also has several upland plains – basin-like plateaux formed of irregular mountain masses with flat bottoms that furnish excellent pasture and farmland. The one of greatest interest to most visitors is the Lasithi Plain below Mount Dhikti, at an elevation of about 900 metres (3,000 feet). The three other major plateaux are: the Omalos Plain (about 1,138 metres or 3,780 feet) to the west, in the White Mountains; the Askifou (about 750 metres, or 2,500 feet), above Khora Sfakion; and the Nidha (about 1,315 metres, or 4,560 feet), on the east slope of Mt Idha. All these tend to draw the precipitation from the adjacent slopes so that they are especially fertile, but the water drains through the limestone and potholes rather than forming rivers.

Water sources

There are only a few rivers of any consequence on Crete – the Keritis, west of Khania; the Mylopotamos, between Iraklion and Rethymnon; the Yeropotamos, running through the Messara; the Anapodharis, running down to the south-central shore; the Platis, draining the Idha mountains down to the south coast – but none of these are navigable. Their watershed basins cover one-fifth of the island and account for the major grain and fruit areas. Although travellers even throughout the nineteenth century spoke of an abundance of water on Crete, there has been a drastic decline, and most rivers and streams today are narrow, shallow, short, and seasonal. The one freshwater lake, Kournas (p. 254), about 40 km. west of Rethymnon, has an area of only some 65 hectares (160 acres). There are numerous springs – much appreciated for their refreshing water – and conditions are generally good for sinking wells. But the highly seasonal nature of the rains and the scarcity of permanent rivers, together with the porous limestone that forms so much of the island, make storage dams impractical – at least on any grand scale. Water shortages remain a serious challenge to Crete's development, especially with increasing concentrations of people in a few cities and tourist centres and the heavy demands of modern life.

Climate

Crete's climate is what the geographers call 'Mediterranean', characterized by the dry, generally hot summers and the relatively mild but wet winters. Almost all precipitation falls from October to April, but the rainfall varies considerably over the island as a whole, with the mountain and upland regions getting more than their share. This variation in locale and season plays a major role in the type of vegetation, as well as irrigation needs for cultivation. The prevailing winds blow across the Aegean from the north, often with such force as to keep down tree-growth in many exposed places along the coast. Despite the narrowness of the island, the winter months along the south coast are milder than those on the north coast, but the island enjoys sunshine for about 300 days of each year. (For a discussion of the weather as it affects the visitor, see pp. 55–6).

Trees and forests

Now we come to one of the main reasons for the water shortage: there are no really extensive forests left on Crete. Yet the island is reputed to have been covered with dense cypress forests in ancient times, the export of timber being one of the chief sources of Minoan prosperity. Cedars grew, too, and the island was famed for its trees well into classical times. Centuries of subsequent neglect, deforestation, grazing and charcoal-burning left Crete denuded. Today small forests of pine, cypress and oak scatter the island and the western half certainly seems lush and green, even if the trees are not that large. The ilex tree is plentiful in the eastern half, the cypress in the western half and upland regions, there are chestnut trees in Selinou Province; particularly noteworthy are the fine old plane trees that flourish near springs and water sources and grow to an astounding size. Olive trees and carob trees are discussed in some detail on pp. 83 and 84.

Flora

Crete provides unusually interesting territory for the botanist, for it has a great variety of flowers, plants, trees, herbs, etc. There are said to be some 1,500 species or varieties, at least 100 of which seem to be endemic or indigenous, or at least varieties and subspecies peculiar to Crete. Quince, for instance, is said to be an indigenous Cretan fruit (reflected in its scientific name, *Cydonia*). Some are more familiar Mediterranean species, modified by the environment; the mountain heights, with their sharp climatic changes, have been the chief influence here. Flowers will be with you wherever you go on Crete. And there are many thorny bushes and spiky plants – hence the high boots worn by the mountain men. Spurge is the most common plant in such situations – especially *Euphorbia acanthothamnos* (thorn-bush spurge) which produces compact, golden-yellow bushes on the bare mountain-sides early in the year.

Spring is undoubtedly the best time to appreciate the wealth of wild flowers on Crete, and it is interesting to notice at this time how extraordinarily localized plants are. One valley may produce wild lupins (*Lupinus hirsutus*), another the huge, sinister-looking dragon arum (*Dracunculus vulgaris*), the only specimens in the area. Many of the plants are the wild forms from which garden and house plants have been bred. Beside the path to the Dhiktaion Cave there is wild cyclamen (*Cyclamen persicum*); the lower-lying areas near the Messara Plain have an abundance of small pink gladioli (*Gladiolus communis*); towards the Omalos Plain the mountains are covered in tree heather (*Erica arborea*); the scrubby hillsides at the east round Ano Zakros are bright with rock roses (*Cistus*) of many different types, a shrub which is probably the source of myrrh. There is an attractive wild iris with a distinctive orange stripe on its blue flower which takes its name from the island – *Iris cretica*; another iris, larger and white in colour (*Iris florentina*), is the model for the fleur-de-lys motif. Orchids may be found in abundance, including some rare yellow varieties. Anemones of many colours brighten waste ground and olive groves. The Samaria Gorge (p. 278) is noted for several endemic species: *Ebenus creticus*, *Petromarula pinnata*, *Paeonia clusii*, etc.

Beside roads, particularly in fairly damp situations, the traveller cannot fail to notice *Agave americana* with its huge rosette of tough, sharp-pointed leaves and flower stalks often twenty or more feet high, bearing numerous heads of greenish flowers. The plant flowers once only when it is ten to fifteen years old, and then dies, though side-shoots often continue to grow, so that colonies become established. In shady places may be found the mandrake (*Mandragora officinarum*), famous in literature for shrieking when pulled up and for its aphrodisiac properties. It is an unimpressive, low plant with wrinkled oval leaves, and bell-shaped, pale-blue flowers and yellowish berries.

Herbs are among Crete's most distinctive vegetation, and if one species of all Crete's flora had to be singled out it should be the endemic herb, Cretan dittany (*Origanum dictamnus*, perhaps from Mount Dhikti, where it flourished). A plant of the mint family, it is of the same genus as wild marjoram. It is given several names by the natives – *Erondas*, *Stamatóhorto*, or – as it is most widely known – *Dictamo*. Cretan dittany is mentioned in many classical texts, where it was said to expel arrows, and it is still prized for its pharmaceutical qualities. It is supposed to act as a relaxant and is believed to be of special comfort to women in childbirth. (It is also claimed that a bath in an infusion will increase sexual desire.) It may be found growing throughout the island, particularly in the mountainous reaches, and even in the gorges and caves. You may find yourself eating it as a flavouring with some Cretan foods; it is especially popular as a herb-tea.

Fauna

Crete also offers a variety of wild-life. The following mammals have been reported by reputable observers in recent decades: shrew, hedgehog, bat, badger, marten, weasel, wild-cat, rabbit, hare, mouse and rat. There are no poisonous snakes; tradition credits St Titus with expelling them from Crete (as St Patrick did from Ireland). Scorpions may be encountered, but they are not the dangerous kind. There is also reported to be a poisonous spider, known as the *rogalida*, but no one ever encounters it. The fish population is scanty, but there are many butterflies. There are some surprises among the native and migrant birds, including many species of warblers, Cetti's, Savi's, Rüppell's, etc., though the most common small birds are brightly coloured goldfinches, crested larks and shrikes of different types. The mountainous areas, particularly the White Mountains and the Omalos Plain, support several rare birds of prey – lammergeyer, griffon vulture and booted eagle, while rough-legged buzzards are quite common. The coast, especially where there are brackish marches, is also rewarding; near Gournia, for example, little egrets, pratincoles and glossy ibis may be seen. There is reported to be a breeding colony of the rare Eleonora's falcon on Ayii Theodhori island off Khania. Archaeological sites too are rich in ornithological interest; at Knossos there are ortolan buntings and the lesser kestrel; at Kato Zakros night-herons and black-tailed godwits may be seen. More exotic birds include hoopoes, rollers and bee-eaters. In 1974 ornithologists from the University of Aberdeen (Scotland) began studying the migrant birds that set down on Crete as they fly from Europe, Turkey, and the Aegean to Libya and Egypt – southward in autumn, northward in spring. They found far more species (over 250) and individual birds (literally millions) put down on Crete than had been suspected.

The one really notable and unique animal on Crete is the wild goat – *Capra aegagrus creticus*. Zoologists deny it the rank of a species, but it is not to be confused with the ibex and bouquetin of the European Alps; it is related to the wild goat found in the Caucasus and Mount Taurus and down into Iran and Pakistan. Cretans refer to it as *kri-kri* or *agrími* – a generic word for wild animal – and have admired it since Minoan times, as various works of art in the Iraklion museum prove. It has been known to weigh up to 45 kilos and have horns up to 78 cm. in spread, but it is chiefly noted for its nimbleness at racing and leaping around the White Mountains – its last natural habitat. It is so adept that it would seem almost impossible to catch or kill, but over the years so many *agrímia* were taken for their flesh or hides that they almost became extinct. Some years ago, however, the government and local organizations instructed the inhabitants of the region about the need to protect these goats. Hunting was prohibited, strict penalties for poaching were imposed, and sanctuaries established on several off-shore islands: Ayii Theodhori, near Khania; Dia, near Iraklion; and Ayii Pantes, near Ayios Nikolaos. The future of the species on

Crete, therefore, now seems secure; indeed, the population on Dia is so dense that hunting is now allowed there (see p. 66). And there is usually at least one Cretan wild goat kept at the little zoos of Khania, Iraklion and Athens National Gardens.

Land use

Two thirds of the land area of Crete is taken up by largely barren mountains, leaving only one third for crop production, although nomadic grazing, wood for fuel, oils, honey and some other produce are also provided by the mountain areas. More crucial is the fact that the best soils for cultivation comprise less than 7 per cent of the total area of the island – and more than two thirds of these better soils are located in the Messara Plain, where lack of water poses a serious problem. A large percentage of the soil lacks nitrogen and phosphorus, and only in recent years has full advantage been taken of modern fertilizers and soil conservation techniques. The land problem has been further complicated by the custom of dividing land among children upon the death of the owner or as dowries for the girls. This has reduced the size of the farms and scattered the land in each holding, until many farms have become impossibly small and inefficient.

Animal husbandry

In the sheep and the goat we see the paradox confronting Crete: they have been the mainstays of a way of life, yet they devastated the land. Their meat, of course, provides a staple flesh diet (although in recent years Cretans have begun to consume so much meat that a great deal is now imported – including lamb from New Zealand!); the wool has a multitude of uses; they provide cheese and milk – you will see very few cows on Crete. For that matter, you will not see many sheep and goats, considering how many there must be, unless you chance across flocks as they are passing to or from spring and winter pastures. Chickens and pigs are fairly plentiful; rabbits less so.

Agriculture

Throughout most of its history – and despite this history – Crete managed to feed its population. In the sixteenth and seventeenth centuries A.D. under the Venetians, Crete was virtually a garden, famed for its fruit, olives, wines, grain and cheese, which were exported – together with products such as silk and leather – all over

Europe. Today the most remarkable aspect of Cretan agriculture is the extent to which the primitive methods survive. Many of the implements used are classic – although tractors and some other farm machinery are increasingly on the scene. If you are fortunate enough to observe a grain harvest you may see grain being cut by hand, gathered and carried to the threshing-floor, where cattle tread it – or perhaps a sleigh is dragged over it. The winnowing may still be done by tossing it to the wind until the chaff is blown away. At any time of year you may observe the extremes farmers must resort to for water: many of them now have small petrol pumps for their wells; but some make do with windmills; others use donkeys to turn the crank; and a few are forced to haul water by hand, hour after hour, in the heat of the summer, pouring bucket after bucket into little irrigation ditches. Much of the cultivation, moreover, is on far from desirable terrain – burnt-out soil or mountain sides. And now that synthetic fertilizers and petrol-powered machinery are available, their costs are putting a tremendous pressure on Cretan farmers' resources.

The wonder of it all, then, is that yields are as high as they are. Crete cannot grow enough grain for self-support, but its own fresh fruit and vegetables make up a large part of the island's diet. Nuts – almonds, chestnuts, peanuts – provide a supplement. Almost any edible plant is made use of somehow. In the end, Crete is able to export considerable quantities of its vegetables and fruit, largely to Athens but increasingly to various European countries. In particular, grapes, oranges, tomatoes, cucumbers and table-flowers provide Crete with an export income, and there has been considerable planting of these in recent years. More adventurous new farmers are also experimenting with such exotics as avocadoes and kiwi fruit.

Olives

The number of olive trees on Crete is said to be thirteen million. If you keep to the main routes you may find this hard to believe; it is only when you wander in the hinterland and among the foothills that you begin to realize how many olive trees there are. They thrive in the most unlikely places – not, as is commonly supposed, because they don't require water, but because their roots strike deep to underground sources. The olives are picked during the late autumn and early winter, and although the oil is widely used on the island there is still plenty left for export. (A threat lurks in the difficulty of getting Cretans to harvest the olives, but this has been at least temporarily avoided by spreading plastic dropcloths around the trees and just letting the olives fall – then fewer people are needed to gather them.)

In addition, after the oil has been extracted, the crushed seeds and pulp are dried and pressed and subsequently burned as a cheap, if foul-smelling fuel. And last but not least, the aged gnarled trees have traditionally provided hiding-places from the oppressors and occupiers of the island.

Grapes

The delicious table grape known as *rosakí* is a favourite for domestic and export consumption, but, in terms of economic value, it is the *sultani*, the pale dried grape – alias the raisin – that has the greatest importance. Thanks to its mild climate and fertile soil, Crete's wines have also been noted from earliest times. Dionysus and the grape are motifs of early Cretan coinage, and classical authors often extolled the fine quality of Cretan wines. By the fourteenth century wine was a principal export; vine cuttings from Crete were so highly regarded that Prince Henry of Portugal is said to have sent for plants to stock the island of Madeira. By the sixteenth century the English were foremost among the Europeans who sang the praises of Crete's malmsey. The first English consul on Crete, indeed, was a merchant appointed by Henry VIII in 1522 to supervise the wine exports. But by the eighteenth century Cretan wines had lost their international popularity and were forced out of the market. Today their quality varies considerably; some claim that only the monasteries have first-rate wines – thanks to the care that they lavish. Nevertheless it is still possible to be served with an attractive wine in some isolated *tavérna* or home.

Carob tree

The carob is a small evergreen tree found throughout the Mediterranean; on Crete it grows most extensively in the eastern part of the island. It has long pods looking like overgrown green beans which are rich in sugar and proteins and have been used since ancient times for animal fodder, human food and fermented beverages. They are still much in demand as fodder. In addition, a gum made from the pods is used in paper-making and tobacco-curing, as a stabilizer in food products and as a celluloid in photographic supplies. Sometimes the actual pods are exported for these purposes, but usually it is only the gum that has been extracted. The bean has many names, including

'Saint John's bread', for it was the carob that St John the Baptist ate when he wandered in the wilderness. This is an interesting example of a crop, all but unknown to most of us, providing an income for a whole people. But, in fact, we have all come in contact with the carob; the carat, standard unit for precious stones and gold alloys, is derived from the Greek *kératon* – 'little horn' – the carob bean that once served as standard measure. And in recent years, 'health food' fanciers have turned to the carob as a substitute for chocolate in certain mixtures.

Mineral resources

Both copper and iron have been mined on Crete, even in modern times, but it seems probable that the Minoans imported the bulk of their raw ores. Stone quarries, talc, lignite and gypsum mines, in any case, are all that operate today. Surveys have also turned up some lead, manganese, copper, iron, sulphur, zinc, gold, silver, tungsten, platinum, emery, graphite, tin and magnetite. But these latter deposits are unlikely to be worth mining.

Occupations

About one-third of Crete's income still comes from agriculture, and one-half of its labour force is still engaged in agricultural occupations; most are self-employed, eking a living out of scattered plots of land. Outside the few large towns the visitor will hardly be aware of any other occupations. There are some, though. In addition to the many olive-crushers and grape pressers and distilleries that require operators at harvest time, there are a number of small factories and plants (such as those that must bottle all the drinks to quench visitors' thirsts – and including a brewery that makes a 'German' beer). Most employ only a few people and utilize little power or equipment, but they process and pack foods, produce soap and make building materials. Then there are harbour installations to be manned, as well as numerous garages and repair shops in the towns. And a stroll through the side-streets of cities such as Khania and Iraklion will reveal many other crafts and trades being practised. Crete has always been famous for its metalwork – especially its knives. (Once, too, the black mulberry tree and the silkworm were cultivated on Crete, and the island could boast of a domestic silk industry.) What the foreigner seldom gets a chance to see are the many people working at small home 'industries': spinning, weaving, knitting, embroidering, basket-making and turning out various other handicrafts and tourist articles. But as Crete advances through the twentieth century, more and more Cretans find employment in construction, transport, trade, government and office work, as well as in the many new tourist facilities.

Human resources

As with any organic society, the real potential finally lies in the people. Crete's population today numbers about 450,000 – compared to the up to one million inhabitants that some scholars estimate there were during the peak of Minoan civilization. Because of the climate, soil, harbours, and general orientation of Aegean life, the majority live in clusters along the north coast; less than a quarter – including some 50,000 inhabitants of the rich Messara Plain – live in the southern half of the island, where Ierapetra is the only large town. The capital resources of Crete have become increasingly concentrated in Iraklion and Khania, and this has also been accompanied by a concentration of the educated and skilled in these two cities. Athens, too, has come to represent an irresistible magnet for the young and ambitious, but although many young people have left the countryside and villages, the island's population seems to have stabilized in recent years. One benefit of tourism – at least in the short-term sense – has been that Crete has avoided the high unemployment rates that afflict other societies. Indeed, Crete conveys a sense of hustle and bustle that makes it almost unrecognizable to those who remember the island as a place of sleepy villages and lounging Cretans. Everyone seems to be working. At the same time, new problems have arisen. The cities are experiencing many of the pressures of modern urban life. Meanwhile, much of Crete's economy has become dependent on the prosperity of foreigners and many Cretans are beginning to express a certain uneasiness about the direction in which their island is going. The prospects for Crete's people, then, if challenging, are unsettled.

CAVES AND MYTHS

The 3,000 or more caves of Crete are among its most remarkable attractions. They are of every conceivable size and location. Some are simple grottoes – mere holes in the ground or on the sides of mountains. Others are many-chambered, with complicated passages, stalactites and stalagmites, or pools of water. Some have been thoroughly explored and have yielded rich archaeological treasures; others have barely been looked into. As recently as 1961, for instance, a large cave was discovered on the Omalos Plain and the first investigators estimated its length at 2 kilometres and its depth at 1,000 metres; they also reported an internal river or lake. Another large cave was discovered in 1969 just west of Rethymnon (p. 253) during the construction of the new highway.

The first settlers on Crete probably used the caves as dwellings. Gradually they came to use them increasingly as religious shrines and burial sites. Finds from some of the caves have been most valuable in piecing together Crete's history – from fossil remains of prehistoric animal life to human skulls and bones, and later to votive offerings of pottery and bronze. The caves attracted pilgrims and petitioners long after the Minoan era, and even now many of them are still approached with veneration, for they were long ago recognized by Christians as special locales and used by hermit-monks, or for chapel sites. In addition they have provided a refuge for the islanders in times of trouble – as for instance the Cave of Melidhoni (p. 244) and the Cave of Milatos (p. 304).

But, exploring aside, it is the mythical associations of the caves that generate the most controversy. Take the matter of Zeus' birthplace. There are many caves throughout the ancient world that claim to be the site. Obviously, in such a matter, everything depends on the classical sources that you accept. Hesiod in his *Theogony* seems to link Zeus with a cave near Lyttos (p. 191), and somewhere along the way the honour was attached to the Dhiktaion Cave at Psykhro (p. 187). But many students in this field (Robert Graves, for one) dispute this cave's right to the honour. And technically – i.e. on the basis of geographical allusions – the Cave of Zeus should be farther east. Another strong candidate is a cave near Arkalokhorion (p. 191), which was frequented and famous during the first millenia of Crete's history; some scholars have begun to advance this cave as the site of a Zeus cult.

And even after reaching agreement as to where Zeus was born, a second question arises as to whether he was brought up in the same cave. In the end neither 'true believers' nor classical scholars can decide, and the Tourist Organization has the last word. For them Zeus was born in the Dhiktaion Cave (p. 187) and was brought up, under the protection of the *Curétes*, in the Cave of Idha (p. 198).

There are many other myths involving the caves of Crete. Minos was said to have returned every nine years to the birth-cave of Zeus, where he was re-consecrated by Zeus and given a 'refresher course' in law. Elsewhere it is mentioned that the sixth-century B.C. Cretan mystic, Epimenides, slept fifty-seven years in the Cave of Idha. Several myths and legends are also attached to the Cave of Eileithyia (p. 296), a cave which is easily accessible from Iraklion. And finally, a cave on Mount Iouktas (p. 179) is claimed as the burial site of Zeus – although not by the mainland Greeks of classical times, for whom Olympian Zeus could never have died.

Those who have had no experience of cave-exploring are advised not to go unattended. Some of the caves are soon explored, but others are true labyrinths. Candles and strong flash-light are minimum requirements; rolled newspapers, ignited, provide a clear view for a short time. A good length of string is a necessity for ambitious expeditions; rubber-soled shoes and a light stock of food and water are also advised. Old clothes should be worn, as the floors of the caves are generally filthy, wet and slippery.

HISTORY

With every year that passes, our knowledge of the Minoan era is having to be reassessed, for modern archaeology and scholarship do more than reveal the history of a place such as Crete; they force a continual reappraisal of this history. The earlier concept of a unique and indigenous Minoan civilization has been revised. Crete has now been placed in the Mediterranean and Near East complex, and this whole world, in turn, is viewed as a dynamic process, not as a set of building-blocks. Just on the island itself, excavations continue to reveal that the roots of Cretan culture run far deeper and farther afield than had been imagined, both in the pre-Minoan and in the post-Minoan contexts. And one of the major developments in recent years has been the discovery of more and more pre-Minoan and Minoan remains in the western half of Crete; nothing as spectacular as the great sites in the central and eastern regions, but enough to force an expansion of previous concepts of Minoan civilization.

It is not surprising, therefore, that some of the theories and conclusions of Sir Arthur Evans have had to be modified. The problem of chronology, however, always seems to remain. 'Minoan' was the name given by Evans to the specifically Cretan culture that would otherwise be classified as Chalcolithic and Bronze Age. Evans decided – using chiefly the evidence of changing pottery – that there had been three definite periods: Early, Middle and Late Minoan, each of these being subdivided into three phases. The findings of archaeologists since Evans's pioneering days have necessitated many adjustments in his dating, but one of the most recent and authoritative chronologies assigns the following dates:

Began B.C.		Began B.C.		Began B.C.	
EM I	2500	MM I	1950	LM I	1550
EM II	2400	MM II	1850	LM II	1450
EM III	2100	MM III	1750	LM III	1400

Not all scholars or published accounts agree on this, and in any case there will probably have to be further adjustments. Therefore, since the average layman cannot always be sure which chronology has been used in assigning dates to artefacts and sites, a different scheme has been adopted for this book. It is one accepted by some scholars in the field and, based upon internal evidence from the principal palace sites, it uses the terms Pre-, Proto-, Neo- and Post-palatial, covering the following periods:

	B.C.
Pre-palatial	2600–2000
Proto-palatial	2000–1700
Neo-palatial	1700–1400
Post-palatial	1400–1100

Not all of Crete, of course, participated in the 'high' Minoan culture from the outset. In the early centuries it seems to have been confined mainly to eastern and central settlements, although the new discoveries in western Crete are forcing a revision of even this view. Moreover, even where several sites are contemporary, they are not necessarily at the same stage of development.

STONE AGE (?–2600 B.C.)

I. PRE-NEOLITHIC
On some of the other Greek islands there have been finds indicating Paleolithic inhabitants. But although fossil remains of animals indi-

cate that Crete was once attached to the mainland of Europe and Asia, there is no evidence that man arrived on Crete before Neolithic times.

II. NEOLITHIC (6500–2600 B.C.)

In general, archaeologists postulate that the first people to settle in Crete were seafarers or semi-nomadic groups from Asia Minor and/or North Africa. A reasonable date for their arrival would be about 6500 B.C. Their way of life must have been quite primitive for many centuries: hunting and fishing, using stone and bone tools, making simple clay pottery, dwelling in or near caves. Later migrants introduced elementary agriculture, domesticated animals, decorated pottery and simple dwellings of clay bricks on stone foundations. They soon turned to making a variety of vases and clay figurines of familiar animals. From the finds of small steatopygous idols, known from many primitive cultures, it is suggested that they worshipped some aspect of the maternal fertility goddess. Most important for what was to come, some of the earliest settlements were at Knossos, Mallia, Phaestos and Ayia Triadha, as well as at such sites as Katsamba, the caves of Eileithyia and Trapeza, and on the Akrotiri peninsula near Khania.

CHALCOLITHIC AND BRONZE AGE: THE MINOAN ERA (2600–1100 B.C.)

I. PRE-PALATIAL (2600–2000 B.C.)

Cretan culture was developing naturally through late Neolithic stages when, about 2600 B.C., a new wave of settlers evidently arrived. This was not an invasion, and the Neolithic population was gradually absorbed by the newcomers who were, in any case, most probably close relatives. Where these new people – or peoples – came from cannot be said for certain. But certainly in the next few centuries Crete was to show many influences from Anatolia, Syria, the Cyclades, Egypt and Libya. Whatever cultures they brought with them, however, the people intermingled, and the new environment stimulated an individual culture that we know as 'Minoan'. (The Minoans, by the way, were short, the men averaging just a little over five feet.)

Copper was worked (there was a mine on Crete) and later bronze. How much trade there was is not certain, but obsidian knives from the earliest times have been found – and obsidian had to be imported, probably from the islands of Melos and Yali (south of Kos) or Anatolia. A new artistry appeared in the treatment of pottery – the incised Pyrgos style, the painted Ayios Onoufrios style, the spiny-shelled Barbotine style and the Vasiliki 'flameware'. The handling of metals and stone revealed an advance in craftsmanship, and the carving of ivory, rock-crystal, precious and semi-precious stones in the sealstones indicates a remarkable sensitivity. The circular and vaulted *tholos* tombs that appear in the south-western fringes of the Asterousia Mountains (e.g., Leben, Kaloi Limines, etc.), on the Messara Plain and at the Phourni necropolis at Arkhanes, have not only yielded many of the treasured possessions buried with the dead – jewels, tools, sealstones, vases – but their construction suggests relationships with the later 'beehive' tombs of Mycenae. The commu-nal nature of the tombs suggests that society was organized around some group such as a clan.

The major sites such as Knossos and Phaestos remained settled, but the principal centres of life and culture through most of this period were on the Messara Plain and at the eastern end of the island (sites such as the islands of Mokhlos and Psira, Vasiliki, Kato Zakros and Palaikastro).

II. PROTO-PALATIAL (2000–1700 B.C.)

The construction of the first palaces at Knossos, Phaestos and Mallia shortly after 2000 B.C. accompanied what would appear to have been a rather sudden concentration of power in the ruling families at these settlements along with a general shift of vitality to central Crete. And it is no coincidence that these palaces were in the most productive regions of Crete. A more systematic and hierarchic society came into being. Increased trade with Egypt, Asia Minor, Africa, the Aegean islands and the Mediterranean world in general laid the foundations for the Minoan maritime economy ('thalassocracy') as well as provid-ing immediate cultural and commercial gains. (There was a Minoan colony on Kythera by about 2300 B.C.) Situated in the centre of major sea routes, Crete was something of a 'middleman', importing tin and copper, processing them to make bronze, and then exporting the products as far as Troy and Italy in ships made of native cypress and cedarwood. Incidentally, the Keftiu who appear later in Egyptian tomb-paintings are generally accepted to be Minoans; most likely, too, they are the same people as those from the island of Kaftor mentioned in the Bible.

A native pictographic script – perhaps suggested by the Egyptians' hieroglyphics, but more likely an independent development – was in use by at least the year 2000 B.C. There were many achievements in arts and crafts – seal-engraving, goldwork, jewellery, clay-modelling, pottery (most notably the Kamares polychrome style and 'eggshell' ware).

In about 1700 B.C. the main palaces seem to have been struck by an earthquake, but there is no break in the continuity of Minoan culture. What appeared about this time, though, is Linear A, a script probably used to record commercial and administrative affairs. Linear A script developed out of the pictographic script in use on Crete, but scholars have not agreed on what language is recorded by Linear A; various Indo-European and Semitic languages have been put forward as candidates.

III. NEO-PALATIAL (1700–1400 B.C.)

At Knossos, Phaestos, Mallia and Zakros, new palaces were constructed, and additions brought about the grand structure we know as a Minoan palace: several storeys, majestic stairways, great courts, murals, corridors, columns, workshops, ritual chambers, together with all the technical achievements that would mark them as advanced in many parts of the world even today. There seems to have been a concentration of power at Knossos, but numerous towns and villas, as well as paved roads, irrigation works and other structures throughout the island indicate the extent of wealth and energies during this period.

It should be remembered, however, that most of the refinements were confined to the palaces and upper classes; there are no grounds for thinking that the mass of Cretans enjoyed any of this style or comfort. Their life was probably at least as good as that of most people of their day, but most Minoans were farmers and workers who supported the society that culminated in the Priest-King of Knossos, the legendary Minos. ('Minos', by the way, was possibly a generic title, like 'Pharaoh', and applied to several rulers; moreover, it is now believed that the Minos who passed into Greek myth and legend was a Mycenaean – not a Minoan!)

The epitome of aristocratic refinement is to be seen in the role that women seem to have enjoyed in the life at court. This is the sophisticated Minoan social life that can be deduced from frescoes and other remains. Crete was not a matriarchal society, however, even if some women at the palaces may have had a fair amount of independence and influence.

The Mother Goddess was worshipped, with symbols such as the double axe, the pillar, horns, the dove, snakes and flowers. The familiar Snake Goddess was only one of various manifestations of this Mother Goddess, the object of devotion throughout much of the ancient world at this time. The Minoans adopted most of their symbols, but probably developed some rituals on their own; their bull-leaping, for instance, may have been based on some imported religious ceremony, but the Cretans seem to have developed it beyond any known people.

By now Crete was one of the chief maritime powers in the Mediterranean. Its influence can be detected in the finds of artefacts in many distant corners of the ancient world. There is one theory, too, based on resemblances of burial structures and some few artefacts, that Cretan merchant ships went through the Straits of Gibraltar and up the coast of Europe as far as Scandinavia. But even if the Minoans were not physically present in these lands, they took part in the widespread trading operations of the time. For example, Crete imported amber that came down across Europe on the amber routes from the Baltic.

Crete's far-ranging ships not only enriched the island's economy but protected the island to the extent that the great palaces needed virtually no special fortifications, though undoubtedly they had a defensive warning system along the coasts. The so-called Minoan thalassocracy, or 'sea empire', is best characterized more as a vast commercial complex than as a militaristic power. All the arts and crafts were practised. Vase-making particularly flourished, with decoration becoming more naturalistic in its use of marine and floral motifs.

Around 1500 B.C. the Linear A script was adapted to record a new language, at least at Knossos. Until 1953 the revised script was known only as Linear B, but, primarily owing to the efforts of Michael Ventris, it is now accepted to be recording an early form of Greek. The extant records are largely inventories and other such mundane accounts, but the implications cannot be dismissed. If Greek was being written, there must have been mainland Greeks on Crete – and in positions of some influence. If so, they were most likely the Achaeans of Mycenae. It has long been accepted that the Minoans were involved with the Mycenaeans. What is now coming to be recognized is that the Mycenaeans played a more active role in Minoan life (at least at Knossos) and from an earlier time than had been supposed.

About 1600 B.C. the new palace centres were disrupted by a major earthquake. They were quickly restored and then about 1450 B.C. Knossos and many of the other centres of Minoan society seem to have been simultaneously overwhelmed. The most widely publicized theory has been that there was a catastrophic explosion of Santorini (Thera), the volcanic island due north of Crete, accompanied by a rain of volcanic matter, a tidal wave and an earthquake on Crete itself. But this theory is not generally accepted and some scholars think that invaders or rebel forces attacked and burnt the palaces; still others have suggested that a natural disaster merely exposed the island to new influences.

And the most recent scientific findings still further confuse the issue: dendrochronologists – that is, experts in tree-ring dating – have established that there were major volcanic eruptions about 1628 B.C. and 1153 B.C. and they are inclined to attribute at least one of these to the great explosion of Santorini; the trouble is that neither comes close enough to the circa 1500 date that most archaeologists have been relying on for the events and finds of Santorini and Crete. It remains to be seen now how this apparent discrepancy is reconciled.

Whatever the cause, Knossos alone of the major palaces seems to have recovered from this catastrophe and enjoyed a brief period known today by its pottery as the Palace Style and attributed to Mycenaeans. Then about 1370, the palace of Knossos was destroyed by yet another catastrophe. Sir Arthur Evans and his supporters believe that, whatever the calamity, it marked the effective end of Minoan society and culture. According to this view, 'squatters' took over the abandoned palaces, merely biding their time until the coming of the Dorians some centuries later. But this version has generally been rejected and, in general, students of history are sceptical of such catastrophic 'ends': the palaces and other structures may have been destroyed suddenly, but Crete's people and their culture probably reacted less drastically.

IV. POST-PALATIAL (1400–1100 B.C.)

Whatever or whoever was responsible for the collapse of a distinctive Minoan culture, the Achaeans were certainly on the scene during the years that followed. Although some of the peculiarly Minoan social, religious and artistic patterns seem to have been broken up, the arts and crafts did not completely disappear. At least parts of some of the sites – including Knossos, Tylissos, Ayia Triadha, Palaikastro – were restored and reoccupied. Some of the Minoans seem to have founded new villages elsewhere on the island, especially in eastern Crete. And as more and more excavations and finds of recent years fill in the missing links, the strengthening impression is one of the continuity of Cretan culture.

With the balance of power shifted to the mainland, the commercial importance of Crete disappeared, although the island still exported and imported. And when the Mycenaean Greeks undertook the expedition against Troy, Crete joined in the struggle, led by King Idomeneus, according to Homer.

The real significance of the struggle at Troy, however, was that it signalled the disintegration of the Bronze Age world, already weakened by wars, economic strains and general social stresses. New peoples were on the move, and power was shifting throughout much of the ancient world during the thirteenth and twelfth centuries B.C. Among the people on the rise were the Dorians, one of several Greek tribes from the north-western Balkans who had been encroaching on the Aegean world for some time. By the end of the twelfth century B.C., the Achaean strongholds had been totally overrun by the Dorians, and the Mycenaean domain, including Crete, lay exposed. The Bronze Age was ending.

IRON AGE: THE GREEK WORLD (1100–67 B.C.)

I. Sub-Minoan – Geometric – Orientalizing – Archaic periods (1100–500 B.C.)

Although it has been claimed that Knossos was destroyed in the twelfth century B.C. along with other Achaean strongholds, this is not generally accepted. In any case, the coming of the Dorians to Crete was not marked by widespread destruction, nor was it sudden. Crete went, rather, into a state of gradual decline, during which some of the major sites were deserted. As the Dorians moved on to the island, there was probably little organized resistance and so little need for violence. The native population, however, was reduced to a serf class, so that some of the Minoans took refuge in hill sites. Others withdrew to sites in the far east of the island, where for hundreds of years they kept alive some of their Minoan heritage, thus becoming known as Eteocretans, or the indigenous Cretans. (See the remarks on Eteocretans under Sitia, p. 328, and Praisos, p. 340, or see Homer, *Odyssey*, Book XIX).

For a while Crete was lost in the Dark Ages that settled over much of the Greek world. The island was isolated and inactive, although such arts and crafts as vase-making were kept up and, if anything, stimulated by the new Dorian forms. Iron, meanwhile, was gradually replacing bronze. Then some of the old sites were reoccupied and there were new signs of life in western Crete. As Crete renewed contact with the outside world, influences from the Near East – in particular, Syria, Phoenicia, Assyria and Egypt – appear. And out of the mixture of the various elements – from Minoan to Dorian to Near Eastern – a new culture emerged; it can be thought of as starting about 900 B.C. It was no longer a specifically Cretan culture, for Crete was now part of the broader currents known as the Geometric, Orientalizing and Archaic periods. In the case of its pottery and sculpture, however, Crete made distinctive contributions. Sites such as Lato, Dreros and Prinias witnessed notable architectural achievements.

Perhaps most surprising is to find on Crete the full-fledged Dorian social system similar to Sparta's, with the Dorian aristocrats ruling over the native serfs and the young male citizens raised in communal houses to be warriors. The Dorians on Crete were especially advanced in their constitution and laws, too, judging from their reputation and such evidence as the Code of Gortyna (p. 205).

II. CLASSIC – HELLENISTIC PERIODS (500–67 B.C.)

In the end, though, the Dorians were unable to consolidate their governments or resources, and each city-state went its own way. During the great days of the Attic-Athenian civilization, Crete remained a provincial outpost, sharing in neither the struggles nor the glory. It is tempting to speculate as to why Crete failed to develop into another Athens – but then who else did? Crete had had its day. Yet the Greeks of the classic age paid their respects to Crete, for they saw it as the source of much of their culture, especially in the matter of myths and the law (p. 110). During this period Crete produced nothing notable of its own, but trade brought a certain prosperity and there was also some building. Cities issued their own coinage. Knossos, Gortyna and Kydonia exercised some rule over lesser settlements. Around the year 300 B.C. certain cities in the west – Elyros, Lissos, Hyrtakina, Tarrha, Syia, Poikilassos – formed the Confederation of

Oreioi, with Gortyna, and Cyrenaica under King Magus, joining later.

During the next 250 years Cretan cities and settlements made and broke alliances with various Mediterranean powers – Sparta, Macedonia, Egypt, Rhodes. There were continual feuds, skirmishes and wars, and the island came to be known as the haunt of lawless pirates, mercenaries – and liars! In actual fact, there was a fair amount of building during the twilight years of the Hellenistic period, but Crete as a whole declined. By the first century B.C. the Romans were interfering more and more in the island's quarrels. Rome was perturbed, moreover, by its alliances with such foreign powers as Mithridates the Great from Pontus.

ROMAN AND BYZANTINE ERA (67 B.C.–A.D. 1204)

I. ROMAN OCCUPATION (67 B.C.–A.D. 395)

The Romans came to settle the island's feuds; they stayed to conquer. After sporadic campaigning for three years – with Quintus Caecilius Metellus gaining the final triumphs – they acquired another province. Gortyna became the capital of Crete and Cyrenaica (part of North Africa). The Romans had ambitious plans for Crete, and after initial repressions prosperity of a sort was established. There was extensive building at Gortyna and elsewhere on the island, including an impressive settlement near Knossos. The Romans left their familiar landmarks all over the island – villas, mosaics, temples, sculptures, aqueducts, roads and brick-work. The Apostle Paul is supposed to have made his first landing on European soil in about A.D. 60 at Kaloi Limines ('Fair Havens') while on his way to Rome as a prisoner. Tradition has it that he appointed Titus as Bishop of Gortyna, and it was Titus who spread the Christian faith on Crete.

II. FIRST BYZANTINE PERIOD (A.D. 395–824)

With the division of the Roman Empire into the western and eastern sections, Crete fell under the sway of Byzantium. Christianity prospered, with considerable building of basilicas; the most notable was Ayios Titos at Gortyna, around the sixth century A.D. In the political-economic sphere Crete was virtually an abandoned outpost. By the end of the third century, Goth pirates were making attacks on Crete. Then as power and trade shifted in the eastern Mediterranean, the Arabs began to menace Crete as well as other European territories.

III. ARABIC OCCUPATION (A.D. 824–961)

Abou Hafs Omar, having been driven out of both Spain and Alexandria, came to Crete with his band of brigands, attacked and destroyed Gortyna and overran the island, establishing a fort at Rabdh-al-Khandak – the nucleus of what was to become Iraklion. During the next century or so Crete was used by the Arabs as a pirates' base; all attempts to regain the island for Byzantium failed. There was no colonizing on any scale, but there were probably inter-marriages and conversions.

IV. SECOND BYZANTINE PERIOD (A.D. 961–1204)

Eventually the Byzantine general, Nikiphoros Phokas, liberated Crete. It is said that he catapulted the chopped-off heads of his Muslim prisoners against the garrison. Aristocratic families from the Greek mainland, Christians from eastern territories and European merchants were 'imported' to effect a revival of Crete. A variety of feudalism developed, the former Muslims being retained as slaves. Phokas, meanwhile, had moved on to become (in A.D. 963) one of the great Byzantine emperors – and patron of the Great Lavra, first of the major monasteries on Mount Athos. Crete once more had a place on the perimeter of affairs.

VENETIAN OCCUPATION (A.D. 1204–1669)

Byzantium fell during the Fourth Crusade, and in 1204 Crete was 'given' to Boniface of Monferrato, who in turn sold it to the Venetians for a thousand silver marks. In the meantime the Genoese had set themselves up there, and together with the native Cretans they resisted the Venetians. But in 1210 Jacopo Tiepolo was appointed first Governor, and the Venetians began their long occupation. They named the island and its capital city 'Candia' and set to work to organize, fortify and adorn their new territory. Many of the fortifications and castles remain to this day. The island was divided up on feudal principles: six sections, corresponding to the six quarters of Venice, were thrown open to Venetian colonizers and entrepreneurs. But the native Cretans were never quiet for very long and there were several bloody revolts. The Venetians had hoped to impose their own way of life, but actually many of the Italian colonists joined the Cretans in revolting against the unjust taxes and privileges of the mother city, Venice. In fact, it became clear that the Venetians were there to convert only one thing: produce into gold.

With the decline of the Byzantine Empire and the fall of Constantinople in 1453, Crete had become a refuge for artists and scholars from the mainland. Orthodox monasteries, schools, literature and painting flourished, borrowing details from the Venetians but essentially preserving Greek traditions (see p. 112). Now and again the Cretans pressed their attacks on the Venetian overlords. In certain parts they practically had self-rule; but also many Cretans had accepted positions and privileges from the Venetians – the barriers were falling down.

In the meantime, during the sixteenth century, pirates under the Turkish 'Barbarossa', Khair Eddin, were ravaging the Cretan coastal towns. The Venetians set about restoring and enlarging the various walls and forts. The Turks had come to see Crete as one of the last barriers to the west and in 1645 they mounted a fleet and took Khania; Rethymnon fell the next year, and in 1648 there began the epic siege of Candia (Iraklion).

For the next twenty-two years all Europe waited and watched what was probably the longest siege of its kind in history. Candia was the last outpost of Christianity against the Ottoman Empire in that part of the world, and when its downfall seemed imminent Pope Clement IX appealed for aid. Louis XIV sent a French force under the Duc de Beaufort, but it was wiped out. In the final two years Candia's defence was undertaken by Francesco Morosini, but he was finally forced to surrender. The Turks let the defenders leave with honour, and most of the Cretans deserted the city. Some Cretans went to settle in Mani, the southern tip of the Peloponnese, and also in the Ionian Islands: from Mani, some moved on to Corsica, where a variation of the Cretan dialect has been reported as surviving until quite recently.

TURKISH OCCUPATION (A.D. 1669–1898)

I. YEARS OF SUPPRESSION (A.D. 1669–1821)

The island was once again divided among foreign conquerors and administrators – this time the Pashas. There were, however, no great numbers of Turkish colonists.

At first the Cretans willingly traded Turks for Venetians. But relations soon deteriorated. The Turks took over the cities, the Cretans clung to their mountains, and the Janissaries roamed at will. Under the non-administration of the Turks, agriculture and commerce declined, roads fell into disrepair, walls and forts crumbled, and building largely ceased – even the mosques were converted churches. Taxes and tariffs took so much that the Cretans lost all incentive; the population declined, and earthquakes and insurrection defeated construction.

In spite of this sad history, however, it is estimated that by the mid-eighteenth century there were 60,000 Christians and 200,000 Muslims on Crete – and almost all of the latter were converted Cretans! This may not be one of the proudest statistics of Crete's history, but for most people it was a simple question of survival. Moreover, many of them were Muslim in name only; the Orthodox faith was practised and sustained. Nor were the Cretans entirely passive during these years. There were several uprisings, the best-known being the one led by Daskaloyiannis in 1770. Unfortunately, though, mountaineers like the Sfakians, who raided and then retired, brought persecution and bloodshed to the exposed villages.

II. YEARS OF REVOLUTION (A.D. 1821–98)

With the uprising against the Turks on the mainland in 1821, Greece set off on the road to independence. Crete joined in, but was unable to keep up the pace. When the new Greek state was proclaimed in 1832, the Allied Powers ceded Crete to the Egyptians – who had actually been called in by the Turks to put down the revolution in 1822. But by 1841 the Turks were back in possession.

The nineteenth century on Crete is one of the most shameful episodes in Great Power politics. Decisive action by England, France, Italy and Russia – acting in consort or in any combination – could have resulted in the final handing over of Crete to Greece. Instead there were compromises, intrigues, rivalry – and inaction. But on Crete there was insurrection and bloodshed. Every decade has its uprising, but these fail to tell the full story of suffering and slaughter. The rallying cry during these years was 'Freedom or Death'; for most Cretans there was only the latter.

Finally, in 1898, after a relatively minor incident – which happened to involve loss of life among some of the British soldiers stationed on Crete – the Allied Powers forced the Turks to leave, and granted the island autonomous status under a High Commissioner, Prince George, younger son of the Greek King.

TWENTIETH-CENTURY CRETE (A.D. 1898–present)

I. TOWARDS UNION (A.D. 1898–1913)

Prince George was warmly welcomed in December 1898; in the next year a Cretan assembly met to draw up a constitution, and a new spirit of order and co-operation prevailed. Many Cretans refused to settle for half, however; they wanted union with Greece or no outside interference. Turmoil set in once more and in 1905 Eleftherios Venizelos led an abortive revolution. Venizelos, a Cretan, was destined to become the only modern Greek statesman who can be classed in the grand European tradition. His ancestors, it is true, had come from the mainland, but Venizelos, born in 1864 at Mournies (p. 272), was forged in the Cretan struggles. A staunch republican and politician, he first raised his banner by forming a party pledged to seek union with Greece. In 1905 he convened a revolutionary assembly at Theriso (p. 272), in violation of the government of Prince George and the Allied Powers. When he resorted to arms he was beaten down, but he forced the retirement of Prince George and gave notice that Venizelos and Crete would be heard of some day soon in the parliament of Greece. Eventually he had his way; he was Premier of Greece during several tempestuous administrations; he was listened to at the Treaty of Versailles; he lost a great deal, for himself and for Greece, but the net gain was the modern Greek nation.

After the 1905 revolt, the next few years were merely a biding of time until Crete could openly be taken into the Greek nation. Finally in 1913 – and not until the whole Balkan region had been embroiled in a war – the union of the island of Crete with Greece was officially recognized.

II. SETTLEMENT – AND OCCUPATION (A.D. 1913–45)

Crete quietened down and went unscathed during the First World War. But in 1923 it was exposed to another severe strain by the exchanges of population between Greece and Turkey. The Turkish population – about 30,000 – left, and about 13,000 Greek refugees from Asia Minor came in their place. Once more Crete settled down, to build and prosper. Agriculture and commerce were increasing; archaeology and tourism gave promise of a new future. Then in 1941 the Second World War descended on Crete in the person of British and Commonwealth troops driven from the Greek mainland by the invading Germans. The British decided to make a stand, and on May 20th the German paratroops and gliders began to land. The British forces were assisted by the Cretan citizenry, using any weapons they could get their hands on, and for several days the Germans got the worst of it. (After the war, in fact, it was revealed that the German

High Command regarded the Cretan airborne operation as something of a disaster, owing to the high mortality rate, and Hitler had called a halt to further campaigns in Cyprus and the Near East that might have strengthened the German cause.) But once the Germans held the airport at Maleme, west of Khania, reinforcements poured in. By May 30th the battle of Crete was over. Thousands of British troops managed to get across the mountains to the south coast and were taken off to Egypt. But many failed to get away.

For the next four years Crete was an occupied land. At times it was a bitter one, with forced labour, insufficient food, deprivations of all kinds and punitive retaliations against many villages. The Cretans continued the struggle as guerrillas and partisans, assisted by special British agents, against the German and Italian troops. The latter occupied the eastern end of Crete. The most famous incident of this period was the kidnapping of the German Commandant Kreipe, who was then taken off to Egypt by an English motor launch. With the end of the occupation in May 1945 – and after the Germans had made a last-ditch stand at Khania – Crete surveyed the damage. Iraklion had been particularly hard hit, and so had several other coastal towns; many villages lay in ruins; transport, roads and commerce were idle; food was a pressing problem.

III. POST-WAR YEARS (A.D. 1945–present)

The United Nations moved in to help Crete during the first months of peace, and in the next few years, although there were some lingering conflicts between the several resistance groups, Crete even had an advantage over mainland Greece in avoiding the divisive civil war. Gradually its agriculture and commerce were restored, but it was about 1960 before the island was ready to move ahead. The 'explosion' of tourism in the 1960s, that decade's general mood of expansionism, the specific attractions of Greece's sites and sunshine – all these combined to launch Crete on to the twentieth-century highway. There was a tremendous amount of new construction – roads, commercial structures, hotels and touristic facilities – but there were also more significant changes in traditional Cretan ways. In April 1967 the Colonels' coup (and Cretans were among the few Greeks who offered overt resistance) put a damper on the Cretan spirit, but during the seven years of that regime – although individual Greeks paid a high price – the expansion of the economy, tourism, and construction proceeded.

With the restoration of democracy in 1974, Crete became committed – for better or worse – to its participation in the contemporary-international way of life. Roads into the most remote villages, electricity into every home, the telephone and television into increasing numbers of homes, hotels and bungalows on many beaches, souvenir shops on every corner, women in the offices, motor vehicles on every kerb and lot, foreigners on every site and peak – there would seem to be no turning back. Many individual Cretans profess to worry about the impact of all this on their island's traditional ways, but as often as not these worriers are themselves participating in the process and prosperity of change. With the entry of Greece into the European Economic Community, Crete has become even more exposed to foreigners and their ways. Crete has survived some 8,500 years of invaders; it remains to be seen how well it survives its new friends.

HISTORY OF EXCAVATIONS

One of the most frustrating sensations while exploring some ancient site is to know nothing about the circumstances of the excavations themselves. When were the remains discovered? Who excavated them? For how many years have visitors been able to view them as we know them today? Such questions often rush to mind, and usually must remain unanswered. Here we offer a brief survey of the exploration and excavation of Crete in order to put the whole field into some perspective. For it is one of the most common fallacies in the entire realm of archaeology to say that until Sir Arthur Evans excavated the great palace at Knossos no one had ever suspected that Crete had a past. According to this version, Evans was the first to stumble on to Crete, the first to dig, the first to reveal the existence of a Cretan culture; before Evans there was nothing but vague mythology and a few classical allusions.

It is true that Evans was the first to advance the evidence and concept of a peculiar Minoan civilization. But the plain fact is that Crete had never been completely lost to men's eyes or minds. Indeed, the list of those who had come to Crete before Evans is a long and honourable one, which includes the Homeric heroes as well as Schliemann. In the *Iliad* and the *Odyssey*, Crete appears only indirectly, but it is cited as the home of populous cities – respectively 100 or 90, only a few of which are named – and as a land of great wealth. (In Hesiod, on the other hand, Crete is a land of the gods; it is he who sets the tone of mythology that is later associated with Crete.) The disguised Odysseus pretends to have come from there – he even mentions the Cave of Eileithyia; and part of Menelaus' fleet is blown ashore south of Phaestos – but in general Crete is a distant prospect.

By the time of the classical mainland civilization the Cretan cities and their glories were all but legendary, although one, Gortyna, was still to enjoy a revival. Numerous classical sources refer to Crete: historians, commentators, geographers, travellers. To men such as Thucydides, Aristotle, Apollodorus, Diodorus Siculus, Pliny, Strabo, Appian, Ptolemy, as well as many others, Crete was a very real place, even if all their facts were not quite correct. But Strabo, in the first century A.D., gives quite accurate distances between Cretan sites.

After the Roman occupation of the island, Crete passed into obscurity. The *Stadiasmus*, an anonymous 'Admiralty Chart' of the sixth to eleventh centuries A.D., mentions many places and routes on Crete, but like much of the Mediterranean world Crete fell into disrepair. For hundreds of years its cities and sites, temples and tombs were abandoned to the ravages of time and climate, earthquakes, marauders and – perhaps most destructive of all – Cretans themselves, seeking materials for new structures.

The arrival of the Venetians in the thirteenth century provided both losses and gains, but at least Crete re-entered the awareness of the western world. The Venetians' name for the island, 'Candia', began to appear in dispatches, and men passing through the eastern Mediterranean on the way to the Levant or Asia often made a point of calling at Crete. The Italian Buondelmonti, in the fifteenth century, was among the first to record his visit; he was able to say of Gortyna that he 'counted two thousand columns and statues upturned by time. For grandeur it is the equal of our Florence.' Belon and Belli in the sixteenth century; Boschini and Lithgow in the seventeenth; Tournefort, Savary and Pococke in the eighteenth; Tancoigne, Olivier, Sieber and Hartley in the early decades of the nineteenth – these are only a few of the men who set down their impressions of Crete. In addition, scholarly works such as those of Meursius (1675), Dapper (1688), Cornelius (1755) and Hoeck (1825–9) kept the academic light burning for later archaeologists.

With the publication of Robert Pashley's *Travels in Crete* in 1837 a new era began. Pashley was one of England's indefatigable scholar-travellers; after finishing his book the reader is left feeling that there was nothing for anyone else to discover. He had in fact a remarkably high score in his identification of sites. However, when he reaches what he feels is 'undoubtedly the site of Knossos', he says, 'All the now existing vestiges of the ancient "metropolis" of Crete are some rude masses of Roman brickwork . . .' The fact is that Pashley, like his predecessors, had no idea of how much he was missing; despite all they did see and despite all they knew of Crete's past, they neglected one simple tool – the spade.

Pashley was followed by men such as Raulin and Spratt, just as knowledgeable in their own ways, so that by 1870 most of Crete had been brought into the area of the *known*. But what these men had settled for were fragments protruding above ground, or random surface finds of artefacts. Some were scholars, of course, and cited a classical allusion for every one of the remains they saw; at most they might dig up a column or a sarcophagus. Yet if none excavated, as we understand the term today, some of them certainly looked very hard, and turned up things that provided material links to Crete's past. From the time of Pashley on, there could be no doubting the existence of prehistorical Crete; it was only a question of digging it up.

Two events in the year 1878 gave the impetus to Cretan archaeology. One was when a Cretan merchant and amateur archaeologist (most fittingly named Minos Kalokairinos) was digging in an olive grove a short distance south of Iraklion, not far from the known Roman ruins. His spade struck a buried structure, and before long he was uncovering extensive walls, stones with masons' marks on them and huge storage urns. W. J. Stillman, an American archaeologist-journalist, who had once served as consul on Crete, went off to explore with Minos. Before they could proceed much farther, the Turkish authorities put a stop to the excavations, but not before Stillman had sent out various dispatches. Heinrich Schliemann read the accounts and in 1886 he arrived in Crete, determined to buy the land concerned. He was unable to come to terms with its owner, however, and abandoned his 'hope of discovering the original home of Mycenaean civilization'. What Minos Kalokairinos had excavated, by the way, were storerooms of the palace of Knossos.

In that same year of 1878 a group of prominent Cretans formed an association to advance the education and culture of the islanders. Within a few years they were concentrating on preserving the historical and archaeological remains, collecting antiquities and generally encouraging excavation. (From this enterprise, incidentally, developed the Archaeological Museum in Iraklion.) The guiding spirit behind all this was Joseph Hadzidakis of Iraklion. Scholar, active archaeologist, first curator of Cretan antiquities, not the least of his achievements is the aid he lent to the various foreign archaeologists during the early years of 'digging up' Crete.

In the meantime – starting in 1884 – an Italian mission was travelling about the island making significant discoveries of both epigraphical materials and ancient sites. To the Italians, in fact – headed by Professor Federigo Halbherr – should go the credit for the first really sustained and professional excavations on Crete. By 1900 parts of Gortyna, the Caves of Idha, Eileithyia and Kamares, many tombs and other sites had been revealed by the combined efforts of Greek, Italian and other foreign archaeologists.

Then came the spectacular excavations at Knossos. Sir Arthur Evans had originally come to Crete in 1894 in search of linguistic materials. He was looking for sealstones with pictographs, and in the course of his searches he uncovered several sites, explored caves and tombs and made finds that were later to occupy many other archaeologists. After several attempts he was finally able to buy the entire plot of land at Knossos. There, armed with his personal fortune, his knowledge and his insight, and aided by a staff of technicians, archaeologists and artists, he supervised the literal unearthing of Minoan civilization. It was to take many decades, and the whole world looked over his shoulder. It is little wonder that Evans has come to stand as the Columbus of Crete, but it does not belittle his achievement to recognize all those who had gone before.

From 1900 onwards, the excavation of Crete proceeded by leaps and bounds, stimulated by the finds of Knossos. Some were the results of individual quests; others came about through patient searching by teams of archaeologists. The Greeks were active throughout the island, finding the tombs of the Messara, the palace at Mallia, and the *megarons* of Tylissos, Nirou Khani and Amnisos. The Italians were uncovering many sites; concentrating on the Messara, they excavated Phaestos, Ayia Triadha and Gortyna. English archaeologists spread over the island and were particularly active in eastern Crete, as well as exploring caves generally. The French undertook such sites as Mallia, Lato and Dreros. Americans excavated Gournia, Vasiliki, Mokhlos and Psira. By 1940 the major patterns of Cretan archaeology had been established.

Excavating by no means ceased. Even during the German occupation it went on to some extent. The Greek government and various archaeological missions from foreign lands bear the burden of the expenses now, and some of the glamour may seem to have passed. But to dedicated archaeologists the day-to-day finds at even some of the more modest sites can be exciting. And since the war there have been some quite dramatic finds, at both old sites – along the 'royal road' at Knossos, on the slopes of Phaestos, in the fields adjacent to the palace at Mallia – and new 'digs'. Among the more spectacular of the new discoveries are: the manor-house at Vathypetro, the tholos tombs at Phourni, the temple at Anemospilia, and the palatial site at Turko-geitonia (all in or near Arkhanes), the vast necropolises at Armenoi (near Rethymnon) and Ayia Fotia (near Sitia), the villa at Pyrgos (near Myrtos), the sanctuaries at Kato Sime (near Ano Viannos) and on Mt Iouktas, emerging remains at Kommos and Khania and, of course, the fourth great palace and town at Kato Zakros. (And, although not strictly speaking Minoan, there have been the obviously related finds on Santorini, p. 22). And these are only the ones that most appeal to the layman. To report all the finds of archaeologists on Crete in the last decade or so would require pages of listing. Many of these sites go unmentioned in a book like this, too, because as important as they are for reconstructing Crete's past, the actual remains are often meaningless to most travellers. These places have often yielded handsome artefacts, though – many of which are to be seen in Iraklion's Archaeological Museum or in the expanding local museums.

With the refinement of techniques, e.g. stratigraphic excavation (the precise recording of levels), and new dating methods, some of the previous conclusions about the history of Crete have had to be modified. Crete now stands like some great jigsaw puzzle: most of the pieces are there, but the problem of arrangement still remains. And although it is unlikely that anything as spectacular as Knossos or Kato Zakros lies buried, there is a good chance of major finds yet to come.

ART, LEGENDS AND LITERATURE

Considering its size, its isolation, its unsettled history, Crete has made some truly remarkable contributions to both Greek and Western European culture. The art and artefacts of the Minoan civilization are widely known: vases and ceramics in a dazzling variety of forms, techniques and motifs; seal-stones and jewellery with an unusual delicacy of style and observation; statuettes and carvings created with a perception and freedom transcending their times; frescoes almost bewildering in the range and reality of their subjects. These have all been pictured and publicized, although one should still make the pilgrimage to the Iraklion Archaeological Museum to see them in their glory. (The Ashmolean Museum at Oxford has the second-finest collection of Cretan art and antiquities, thanks to Sir Arthur Evans's bequests.) Even when adapting or transmitting the art of others, Crete gave its inimitable imprint.

In one medium above all Minoan Crete attained unique dimensions. That was architecture. Its palaces were Crete's distinctive achievement. Nor is there any possibility of confusing Minoan architecture with that of classical Greece; to put it briefly, in place of symmetry there is accumulation. Small rooms and various structures cluster around a central court; additions seem to be accidental; the sites themselves are irregular; the total complex seems to 'erupt' at random levels. Yet the more one examines the different palaces, the more one appreciates the design of the whole. In fact, recent studies have revealed that the Minoan palaces were probably far more carefully planned than was hitherto thought: some report finding standard linear measurements (a 'cubit' and a 'foot') used in both Minoan and Mycenaean structures, and claim that a Minoan palace can be described in terms of a gridwork of large squares, with rooms being simple subdivisions within these squares. But even accepting this, Minoan architecture strikes us as dynamic, organic – an architecture that anticipates the style of a Frank Lloyd Wright.

As regards literature, the Minoans left none that we are aware of. But when all the evidence is collected who knows how influential – even crucial – Crete was in transmitting the alphabet to the western world? One thing seems certain: the Minoans must have had a rich stock of folk-lore if they were anything like their descendants. Songs, tales, ballads, proverbs, popular lore of every kind, were surely passed on orally from generation to generation. And, of far more importance than a barren legacy of fragments and minor texts, Crete left a vital corpus to the classical world – and to our own – in mythology.

The traveller to Crete who wishes to recognize its oldest traditions should prepare himself by reviewing these myths. 'Review', because it is surprising how many of the familiar personages and episodes of classical mythology concern Crete. In a book such as *The Greek Myths* by Robert Graves, almost every page contains at least a passing allusion to Crete. It must, however, be admitted that many of these myths were transplanted to Crete long after the decline of the indigenous culture. On the other hand Crete must have offered a fertile soil for the proliferation of such myths.

There is the birth of Zeus himself, involving Cronus and Rhea, as well as several episodes in his youth; these are associated with specific Cretan caves, although scholars have not agreed as to which is which (p. 87). Later, Zeus returns to Crete, this time in the guise of a bull, carrying Europa on his back; the associations here run through three thousand years of European art. Europa bears Zeus three sons – Sarpedon, Rhadamanthys and Minos. It is the last-named who became the dominating force in Crete's myth-history; the repercussions have never really stopped.

There is a certain ambiguity in the figure of Minos. On the one hand, he is the harsh tyrant whose ships scour the seas while he sacrifices to the Minotaur; on the other hand, he is the just and benevolent lawgiver who attains immortality as a judge in the afterlife. But that is only part of Minos' drama. He had a wife, Pasiphaë, who had a god-willed lust for a bull; their union produced the Minotaur. This was the occasion for the Labyrinth, constructed by the legendary craftsman Daedalus to hide the Minotaur. Then comes Theseus – who would seem to embody some semi-historical figure or event – the slaying of the Minotaur, the flight with Ariadne. Later, Theseus marries Phaedra, another of Crete's ill-starred daughters, and there follows the classic tale of her passion for Hippolytus. It is an endless thread, indeed. Meanwhile, Heracles had accomplished the seventh of his Twelve Labours on Crete. There is also Daedalus, back in the Labyrinth; his escape with his son Icarus has never ceased to engage man's wonder. (Perhaps the most striking and recent example of this was the flight in April 1988 of a human-powered (pedalled) aircraft from Iraklion to Santorini – widely publicized as the Daedalus Project.) In addition there are all the secondary figures – Britomartis, Miletus, Talos the Bronze Monster. Crete may not have given birth to all these gods and heroes, but they have all wanted to claim Cretan ancestry.

At the time of the Homeric Age the balance of power had shifted, but in some versions of the Trojan War the Cretan Idomeneus was accepted as an equal of Agamemnon. Judging from the behaviour of

Idomeneus in the *Iliad*, the Cretans had a reputation as rather rugged fighters. This same Idomeneus appears some three thousand years later in a considerably less boisterous setting – Mozart's *Idomeneo*, which deals with his return to Crete after the Trojan War.

With the coming of the Dorians, Crete entered into the mainstream of the cultural world as it was developing in that part of the Mediterranean. There was a minor resurgence of the Cretan genius in ceramics, and, although it cannot be claimed that Crete originated the forms, it certainly contributed its share to the emerging art of the Geometric and Oriental styles. By the seventh century B.C. still another force was at work, this time in the Archaic sculpture of the Greek world. Crete has generally been credited with playing a major role in the development of the 'Daedalic' style, which was named after the mythical craftsman. In addition to the Daedalic sculptures on view in Iraklion, there are the 'Lady of Auxerre' in the Louvre, a bronze statuette at Delphi and figures in New York and other museums.

With the ascendance of the Attic-Athenian culture, Crete was completely overshadowed. It can, however, be fairly claimed that Crete was the cradle of many of the manifestations of the classical civilization. Various students have claimed to see a Cretan influence in much of its art and architecture; certainly it can be said that Crete played a dominant role in its mythology and religion – there was, for instance, a legend that the first priests at Delphi were Cretans from Knossos. Then, too, there is a fragment of a lost tragedy by Euripides, *The Cretans*, that appears to deal with a religious cult. Beneath the classical veneer a Cretan influence often seems to be lurking. Cresilas, the sculptor of the well-known bust of Pericles, was from Kydonia in Crete. There is even a theory that Plato's 'Atlantis' is really Crete. Or take, for instance, one of the most famous Cretans of this period – Epimenides. Said to have flourished around the turn of the sixth century B.C., he came to Sparta and Athens and is credited with shaping the legislation of the times. Numerous works are attributed to him, including the constitution of Crete and mythical-mystical texts. In due time many myths accrued to him, such as that he was a son of Zeus, slept in a Cretan cave for fifty-seven years, had prophetic revelations and was reincarnated. Obviously something of an apocryphal figure, his most famous line, alas, is his claim: 'All Cretans are liars!'

It was in the domain of law, however, that Cretans were particularly honoured. Both Minos and Rhadamanthys were installed as judges in the underworld. Lycurgos, the lawgiver of Sparta, was said to have studied on Crete. Solon was also inspired and influenced by Cretan law; indeed, it was Solon who counselled Athens to bring Epimenides from Crete to help purify the city. Plato and Aristotle paid frequent tribute to Crete. And if more tangible evidence is required, we have only to consider the Code of Gortyna (p. 205), still standing as irrefutable testimony to Crete's pre-eminence.

Gortyna also stands as a symbol of the Romans' ambitions on Crete. They came, conquered and built, but the Empire declined before Crete could contribute to the greater glory of Rome. And Rome did little for Crete. Instead, the winds blew from the East. Paul of Tarsus passed through. Paul's immediate heir on Crete was Titus; his testament is in Acts xxvii and the Epistle to Titus. With the absorption of Crete by the Eastern Empire at the end of the fourth century A.D., the island was left pretty much to its own devices. Church buildings and mosaics seem to have been the sole expressions of any aspirations. The Arabs came and went, from A.D. 824 to 961; then mainland Greeks asserted themselves on Crete under the banner of Nikiphoros Phokas. In the thirteenth century all Greece became prey to the plundering Crusaders and warring commercial states of Europe; Crete fell to the Venetians.

For the next four and a half centuries Crete was a Venetian colony. During the first half of this occupation there were frequent and bloody uprisings, but the Venetians imposed their *castelli* and order, and a cosmopolitanism gradually took over in the main city-ports. Yet, somehow, Cretans survived as such, in their language, their religion, their folk-lore, their dances, their art and their traditions; the people kept their identity. As described in the History section, after the fall of Constantinople in 1453 Crete was one of the last outposts of Orthodox Greek culture; scholars and artists, fleeing from the mainland, often landed there. A fascinating footnote to history, by the way, is the fact that many Cretans, both natives and transients, went on to western Europe, where they played a crucial role in transmitting the actual texts of the Classics and promoting Greek studies, thus helping to advance the Renaissance. Venice, in particular, had a large colony of Greeks, among whom Cretans were prominent as printers, copyists and editors. To single out but one, the native Cretan Markos Musuros was influential in bringing out the famous Aldine Press editions of the Greek Classics.

Thus, the three traditions met: the indigenous vigour, the links with the West via Venice, and the cultivated forms of Byzantium. The result was Crete's version of the Renaissance during the sixteenth and seventeenth centuries. The literary products of this period are not generally known outside Greece, which is a pity. There is the poetry of Sakhlikis, who recounts his escapades in a Rabelaisian manner. There is a pastoral poem – *The Fair Shepherdess* – perhaps somewhat incongruous on an island of such real shepherds. The most notable work is the long epic poem *Erotokritos* by Vincenzo Cornaros; it strikes those who read it today as a mausoleum of conventions, but it exercised considerable influence on modern Greek literature, and even now can still be heard in the villages of Crete. (Georgios Seferis, the 1963 Nobel prize-winner in Literature, in his poem, 'On a Foreign Verse', speaks of his boyhood in Smyrna and says: '... like certain mariners who ... recited to me in my childhood the song of *Erotokritos* with tears in their eyes ...')

It was the drama, however, that experienced the finest flowering. Eight plays and various interludes (not all intact) have been preserved from the period 1550 to 1670, and if none is a masterpiece – and all are highly derivative – they represent a significant achievement. The finest is *The Sacrifice of Abraham*, attributed to Cornaros. It is the familiar vein of the medieval mysteries, but individual touches and its insight make it truly Cretan. Two other Cretan plays of distinction are *Gyparis*, a pastoral comedy, and *Erophile*, a tragedy. Some of these plays have been revived by Greek theatre groups in recent years, and it is occasionally possible to see them at some summer festival. There have also been occasional productions of translated versions by foreign theatre companies.

But it is in another medium that medieval-Renaissance Crete has held the attention of the world: in painting, both of frescoes and icons. Scholars have not yet separated all the strands in the tapestry of Cretan-Byzantine painting; besides indigenous art there is an imported influence. The Byzantine schools of Macedonia and Mistra evidently made some impact; later there was the influence of Italy. Yet it is agreed that there is a recognizable 'Cretan school' of Byzantine art, even though this may be more a style and technique than the work of a circle of friends. In either case, the Cretan spirit speaks with an intense masculine energy. Figures are often exaggerated in length, realistic detail is emphasized, a chiaroscuro effect is achieved by the use of bold colours over dark backgrounds.

When used in a restrictive sense, the term 'Cretan school' refers to the fresco painting that flourished during the fifteenth and sixteenth centuries, although frescoes of other periods – as well as icons of that era – reveal some of the same spirit. Among the thousand or more chapels and churches on Crete, there are many that still have their wall-paintings intact – albeit restored. The most notable examples are at Kritsa (p. 311), Ayios Fanourios (p. 196), Potamies (p. 183), in the chapels around Kastelli-Pedhiadhos (p. 190), and in the provinces of Amari (p. 236) and Selinos (p. 286). In more accessible places many of these would attract thousands of viewers. In the sixteenth century several Cretan painters worked on the mainland: Theophanes, Anthony and Tzortzis are the best-known, and their works – perhaps the master-works of the 'Cretan school' – are to be seen in the monasteries of Mount Athos and Meteora.

By the end of the sixteenth century the Cretan spirit tended to express itself in icons rather than in large-scale frescoes. The tradition, of course, had been long established: recognizably *Cretan* icons can be found from the fourteenth century. Here again mainland influences came into play; by the later sixteenth century Italy – particularly Venice – exercised her spell; and eventually, in the seventeenth century, a Creto-Venetian school flourished in the Ionian Islands. Michael Damaskinos, one of the true Cretan masters, absorbed much from his years in Italy. When he returned to Crete to paint his major works – largely from 1582 to 1591 – he blended the Italian-Renaissance style with his own Byzantine manner. Finally there came the man who made a bridge between the Byzantine and Western forms, the medieval and modern worlds, the Orthodox and the Catholic – the man from 'Candia' who moved on to other lands but who could never quite forget his homeland – its landscape, its patterns, its eyes: Domenico Theotokopoulos, 'El Greco'. He was born in 1541 and died in 1614. None of his work is to be seen on Crete, but Crete is to be seen in much of his painting. Not all Westerners find the Byzantine iconography congenial, but even for such El Greco vindicates the tradition.

To round out the picture of Crete's peculiar vitality during this period, three other Cretans who left their mark on the world must be mentioned. In 1340 a certain Peter Philargos was born outside Neapolis; he went to study in European universities, advanced in the Roman Catholic hierarchy, and crowned his career by being elected Pope in 1409. As Alexander V he served for only ten months; it is suspected that he was poisoned – a typical end for a Cretan and a pope of that day. Then there was Kyrillos Loukaris (1572–1638), another

Cretan who wandered forth to get a European education some two centuries later. A man of true culture and learning, he became Patriarch of Constantinople and took the lead in educating Greeks in their traditions, even to the extent of introducing the printing-press into Constantinople and sponsoring a translation of the Bible into a less archaic, more colloquial Greek. But such activities were too advanced for the times; he only succeeded in offending Orthodox, Muslim and Catholic, and he paid with his life. Finally, there was yet another Cretan scholar, whose achievements would seem to have gained him the blessings – or curses – of all faiths. Nathaniel Kanopios was at Balliol College, Oxford, for ten years, until Cromwell expelled him in 1648. In the course of his time there, he is credited with having introduced coffee-drinking into England.

By the end of the seventeenth century and with the final conquests of the Turks, Crete once more passed out of the mainstream of European history. Again, though, popular traditions – songs, poetry, music, dancing, folk-lore of all varieties – kept the Cretan character alive, renewing the life and language of the land. Every event provided its hero, and subsequent songs and epics. The most admired of these poems is *The Song of Daskaloyiannis*, based on the uprising of the Sfakians in 1770. But in the nineteenth century, when the rest of Greece had gained independence and was sharing the artistic harvest of the new spirit. Crete was still occupied territory. Its energies went into the continual struggles and uprisings against the Turks.

Yet when Crete re-entered the Western community in the twentieth century, it produced two great men who achieved international reputations in very different ways. One was Eleftherios Venizelos, whose career is described under the History section (p. 101). The other was Nikos Kazantzakis. He left Crete as a young man, but he could never get it out of his mind. *Zorba the Greek* and *Freedom and Death* are literally set there; *Christ Recrucified* is animated by a Cretan energy; and even his Odysseus becomes deeply involved with Crete. Philosopher, poet, dramatist, novelist – a genuine man of letters – the translations and the publicity of his last years gave Kazantzakis a somewhat exaggerated status in relation to the total Greek literature of this century. But no one can deny his power, his intensity and the provocative nature of his work.

Nor was he the only Cretan artist of this century. Several others have made significant contributions to Greek literature: Kondylakis, Prevelakis, Dimakis, Hadzidakis. (The 1979 Nobel prizewinner in literature, Odysseus Elytis, was born in Crete, but his family and upbringing were actually not Cretan.) The musician, Mikis Theodorakis is of Cretan descent. And the leading Greek actor of our time, Alexis Minotis, is from Crete. What is the secret? Why should this small isolated island have produced so many strong art-forms across the centuries – and what do they have in common? It could be that if there is one theme peculiar to the Cretan spirit, one thread that links Minoan pottery, Cretan frescoes and the novels of Kazantzakis, it is an affirmation of life in all its diversity, a spontaneous – yet intense – celebration of nature's joys and mysteries.

RELIGION

Commentators on modern Crete all remark on the continuity of Cretan culture. Despite a history of violent disruptive forces, Crete seems to have maintained intact many fundamentals from even the earliest eras. In nothing is this more apparent than in its religious beliefs and practices. The Orthodox Church of Crete is not under the Greek mainland Church but is an autonomous institution which owes its allegiance directly to the Patriarchate of Constantinople. It stresses its own continuity, taking pride in its own faithfulness to the roots and sources of earliest Christianity. For the visitor, Crete provides a fascinating glimpse of age-old sources of the religious impulse and of religious behaviour. To Cretans, who are almost all Orthodox, there is nothing contradictory or curious about worshipping in the ways of their ancestors, but it is one of the most interesting and attractive features of a stay on Crete.

The priest, or *papás*, in his stovepipe hat and flowing gown, soon becomes a familiar figure as he strides across the fields or sits in the café. In the Orthodox Church, if a priest wants to rise in the hierarchy or to enter a monastery, he remains celibate, but the village priests are allowed to marry and are encouraged to take part in the life of the community. It is therefore no cause for surprise to see a bearded old *papás* showing off his grandchildren. The village priests will often be obliged to do some other work to support their families, despite the fact that they receive part of their salary from the government, since Orthodoxy is recognized as the official State religion. The Church's hierarchy, in fact, has a status analogous to the civil service or the military: the Metropolitan of Iraklion, who is head of the Church on Crete, has the 'rank' of a general – and should even be saluted by members of the military when he passes in his official capacity.

The Greek clergy, by the way, have always been associated with the political and national life of their people. During the centuries of Turkish occupation, for instance, it was the Orthodox clergy who helped to keep the Greeks' identity and aspirations alive, both by word and deed. The Greek Independence Day celebrates the occasion on March 25th, 1821, when Bishop Germanos of Patras raised the flag of revolution at the Monastery of Ayia Lavra on the Peloponnese. On Crete, the monks at such monasteries as Arkhadi and Preveli may be said to have taken a truly active role in the islanders' struggles against foreigners. And many monasteries conducted 'secret schools' in which they taught the Greek language and heritage to young people.

Of the chapels and churches on Crete (there are reputedly over a thousand) many are tiny, and are used only on one day of the year to commemorate a particular saint, or the name-day of the donor. Some are new and have no significance for the visitor. But some are very old indeed, and many of these have frescoes and other works of art that are worth going out of one's way to see. They are to be found everywhere – on the barren coast, perhaps, or high on a peak. They are worth looking into, frescoed or not, for they have a special atmosphere. Until fairly recently most chapels were open or the key was left above the door. Now, because of the threat of thieves, all chapels with any valuable contents are locked; the key is usually kept by the priest or by someone that others in the nearby village will know about. Frequently candles will be burning in the most isolated chapels. The simple icons are often interesting, and sometimes, flanking the picture of a saint, many little silver or base-metal tags are to be seen. These are *támata* or *taxímata* – simulacra moulded in the image of the afflicted part of the body, or an animal, or someone the petitioner wants cured or protected.

LANGUAGE

The history of the Greek language will here be described briefly in so far as it impinges on modern spoken Greek. One thing should be said at once: there *is* a definite relationship between classical Greek and modern Greek. Having been given the impression that there is little or none, most students of the classical language are amazed at how far it can take them.

After the decline of the classical Attic civilization, a common Greek tongue came into use throughout the Hellenistic-Mediterranean world; this was the *koiné*, the Greek of the New Testament. It is the basis of modern Greek. Over the centuries, through the rise and fall of the Byzantine Empire, a gap developed between the language of the masses and the more refined language of the lettered. The higher clergy especially tried to maintain the archaic Greek, but the vulgar tongue was evolving on its own. Foreign words were absorbed, idioms crept in, and each region developed its own dialect. When the independence of the modern Greek nation was established in the nineteenth century, the movement to impose a unified and purified language gained the support of many educated men; this was the *katharévusa* – the pure, correct, formal language. But for all their sincere intentions, the proponents of this somewhat artificial language were doomed from the start, because the colloquial tongue, the *dhimotikí*, or 'popular' language – despite its inconsistencies – was an organic living language. At the end of the nineteenth century the struggle between the adherents of the two languages was still in full swing, affecting every aspect of national life and capable of causing academic quarrels and popular riots. To a certain degree the struggle is still going on, but the *katharévusa* is now largely confined to the law, science, advanced textbooks, academic circles, government administration and formal use in general. The demotic, among other victories, has won over most modern creative writers in Greek and has proved itself an expressive instrument. When a classical Greek drama is performed today, for instance, it is usually in a modified demotic version; most newspapers employ the *kathomiloúmeni*, which is a modified version of the demotic. The 1967–74 government tried to restore the *katharévusa* in schools and elsewhere, but as with all such efforts it made little headway. One of the first acts of the government that restored democracy was to disavow the *katharévusa*.

To understand what it means to have two languages in competition with each other, the English speaker need only imagine all those situations where he employs only the most formal and literary language (legal documents, scholarly papers, formal announcements, conversations with foreign dignitaries) and oppose them to situations where he uses more colloquial and familiar language. In other words, English – as well as every other language – is subject to the same forces. The significant difference, though, is that strict boundaries were never set up between these other pairs of languages, so that there has always been some intermingling. Britain could support a Dr Johnson *and* a Robert Burns; America could produce a Henry James *and* a Mark Twain. But the Greek language found them incompatible. Contemporary educated Greeks, all the same, are finding it easier to bridge the two languages in speech, literature, radio and the theatre. The differences – in sounds, grammar and vocabulary – still exist; everything depends on how much modern Greeks want to make of them.

Few visitors to Greece ever come to grips with the language and fewer still master it. The alphabet defeats most people in the first place. Until one is in control of that there is no gratuitous gain in vocabulary, as is the case when the English-speaking traveller tries other European languages. The result is that most foreigners give up, or at best struggle along with about three words.

This is to be regretted, because the Greeks are among those people who truly enjoy having a foreigner use their language – even when it is not used well. So few do try to use it that the Greeks are pleased when anyone does make the effort. The foreigner need never feel embarrassed while he is learning, and he will never lack encouragement and praise, even though accompanied by good-natured laughter.

Anyone who wants to try to use Greek needs at least a phrase-book. The really ambitious may try to teach themselves Greek before setting out, and there are several courses available. Useful books include Constantinos' *How to Say It in Modern Greek* and Pring's *Modern Greek* in the 'Teach Yourself' series. Record courses include the Linguaphone Institute's, another by the Institute for Language Study, Conversaphone's Modern Greek, Dover's *Listen and Learn Modern Greek*, Doubleday's *Learn Modern Greek in Record Time*, and Cortina's *Modern Greek*. There is also Dun-Donnelley's *Take-Along Cassettes*, a Greek course you can take with a cassette player. Between phrase-book and complete course lies the dictionary, a necessity for anyone planning to strike out on his own. There are many available; but be sure you are getting a dictionary of *modern* Greek.

When travelling with a dictionary, it is of little use to hand it to unschooled people and expect them to pick out words for you. They are not accustomed to treating their language as an alphabetical list and are apt to be as baffled as you are by the mass of words. Moreover, just as important as learning the proper sounds of Greek pronunciation is learning the correct syllable to be accented. The accent is a crucial element in the Greek language – a mark is always written over the syllable which must receive the major stress – and when the accent is misplaced it leads either to confusion or to a complete blank (see stress accents in the Index). The average Greek finds it hard to dissociate the sounds from the accent. It can be most frustrating when you have taken the trouble to learn some long, difficult word and you know you have the sounds correct – and still no contact is being made. When you finally do shift to the proper syllable, your word will be greeted with immediate recognition and a 'Why didn't you say so?' look.

There is a slight dialect spoken on Crete, and as might be expected the farther one goes into the hills the more pronounced it becomes. In the matter of vocabulary, too, there is a rich fund of local words and expressions. The main pronunciation variations are as follows: the Greek *gamma* – γ – thickens into a sound as in 'rou*g*e' before ι, ε, η and ν; the *kappa* – κ – behaves like the Italian 'c', being hard before α, ο and ω and soft (like English 'ch') before ι, ε, η and ν; and the *kh* – χ – ordinarily a guttural 'kh', on Crete behaves like the Italian 'sc', becoming a soft 'sh' before ι, ε, η and ν.

Cretans, like all Greeks, use many nicknames, diminutives and terms of affection. Even the commonest words will frequently have affectionate diminutives, such as '-aki': thus, *neró* is 'water', while *neráki* is more like 'lovely bit of water'. Incidentally, if you meet a Greek whose name ends in '-akis' – 'son of' – the probability is that the ancestry is Cretan.

English language

Many of the younger people speak a little English. Some are learning it in state schools, while others study at one of the many 'institutes', or private evening schools. People of all ages and all walks of life give up a considerable proportion of their time and money to acquire this new 'passport' to success. You will be doing a real service by exchanging a few words with such students when opportunity presents itself. French, by the way, was traditionally the second language of the older, educated generation, but many younger Greeks now speak German that they learned while working abroad.

Almost every town and village, no matter how isolated, has its resident 'Greek-American', an ex-emigrant who has returned to live out his retirement in his home town. He will make your acquaintance very quickly, and although his English may not be highly polished, it will probably be better than your Greek. He can be of great help, saving you a lot of time and trouble in some situations, but you may not gain in the eyes of the other inhabitants of the town or village if you let yourself be monopolized by him. Preserve your independence with goodwill, and try to make your own contacts.

GOVERNMENT

As one of the eleven major regions of the highly centralized Greek administrative system, Crete's nomarchs, or prefects, who head each of the four traditional nomes are appointed by Athens, not elected by Cretans. There has never been a common legislative body for Crete itself; its elected representatives, whatever their title and number, and however chosen, go off to Athens. Each town has traditionally elected a mayor and each village its 'community president', but they have never had many actual powers. Taxes are collected and disbursed by Athens. Education and teachers are essentially controlled from Athens. The police belong to the national force, although the rank and file are usually Cretans who have been more or less permanently assigned to the island. Individual Cretans are often prominent in Greek political life, and Cretans share the traditional Greek interest in partisan politics, but the mass of Cretans find little to identify with in either the elected government or the appointed bureaucracy. Finally, though, if the initiative comes largely from Athens, and local officialdom is powerless, it can still be said that Crete's true 'parliament' is to be found in its cafés.

PEOPLE AND CUSTOMS

Contemporary Cretans probably represent a mixture of many ancestries and traits, which makes it somewhat questionable whether there is a people that can still be called 'Cretan'. Physical appearances among Cretans, too, vary considerably – from the short, wiry 'Mediterranean' to the tall, fair 'Dorian'. This second type is only found among certain isolated communities, usually in the mountains, but you can still run into men in the villages who look and bear themselves like gods – whether it be Zeus or Pan. The traditional costume – black knee-length boots, baggy, wrap-around pantaloons (*vráka*), sash, embroidered jacket, black head-wrapping (*kefalomándilo*) – is generally disappearing, although some of the older men still wear it. Among the younger village men, however, boots and riding-breeches are stylish.

Women are increasingly in evidence in the Cretan villages but you still see them lurking in doorways or behind windows, bundled up in rather graceless, timeless dresses. They often go about their work in the fields with their heads wrapped up Arab-fashion. The wearing of black is also common in the villages – signifying that a close family member has died. Only if you happen to arrive at some special festival will you see women in gay traditional costume and they are most likely to be members of some organized folk dance group. In the larger towns, of course, Western clothes have taken over and people dress very stylishly at promenade-time on Saturday night.

The old ways, it is true, are gradually dying out, but not without a good deal of delaying action and rearguard tactics. Family ties are still strong and they serve as brakes. Young men's careers are often settled by their parents; marriages are usually arranged, to some degree. (Even the Code of Gortyna (p. 205) dealt, among other things, with the need to marry heiresses within the 'tribe' – to prevent the breakup of families.) The village people, too, are surrounded by rituals and formulas, traditions, superstitions, proverbial ways. And as is to be expected, the younger generation and the urban types comprise the 'modernist' element. Yet the dominant tone of the island is set by the conservative, orthodox groups, and the more intelligent and balanced young people do not find it necessary to turn their backs on all the old ways. They are the first to appreciate the traditional social and personal relationships; they still love to dance the old dances, sing the old songs.

Folk-music and dancing

Dances provide the most authentic evidence of the continuity of Crete's popular traditions and rhythms. Homer in the *Iliad* describes how 'Daedalus in Knossos once contrived/A dancing-floor for fair-haired Ariadne', and the Cretans have always been known for their dances: the *pendozális* – a lively, swinging dance, with the arms interlocked; the *khaniótikos* – a circle dance; the *syrtós* – a sedate circle dance; and many others, such as the *soústa, órtzes, kastrinós, malevysiótikos, sitiakós*. Today there are groups who revive and perform the traditional dances. But perhaps the really true Cretan dance is that to be seen in any village café or festival – or, for that matter, in some Iraklion *tavérna* – when a man or several men spontaneously move into the centre of the floor and start to dance. And the young people of Iraklion can be just as proud and graceful when they circle in the old dances. It makes no difference that the old melodies are played on electric guitars, or even on a gramophone; the dancing is still performed to the old rhythms and with the old enthusiasm. But undoubtedly the most picturesque occasions for the traditional music and dances are at village ceremonies – weddings, baptisms, saints' days.

As for the music of Crete, it strikes the ear as one would expect: an amalgamation of all the styles and cultures that have entered Crete. Into Near Eastern music the familiar strains of European folk-music intrude. If you are lucky, you will see one of the old instruments played – the *lýra*, a small, three-stringed lute-like instrument that is bowed as it is held on the knee. Or you may hear some really old ballads. Most exciting of all are the *mantinádhes*, improvised rhyming couplets that follow the inspiration of some occasion, joyful or mournful. Although traditionally improvised there is actually a repertoire of *mantinádhes* on which to draw. In Iraklion – and possibly Khania – you may also hear *bouzoúki* music. Taking its name from the instrument (something like a mandolin), it has now come to stand more for the mood of the songs and the atmosphere of the places where it is played – a mood akin to jazz 'blues'. Greek music, then, traditional or otherwise, is very much alive, and it will be a long time before international hit songs– which, to be sure, often blare out from some radio – obliterate the native melodies.

The koumbáros

In Greek life, family loyalties take precedence over all others. This is not so hard to comprehend, but there is one relationship which the foreigner may not have encountered elsewhere but which is essential to an understanding of Greek social-family life. This is the role of the *koumbáros* – technically the best man at the wedding and/or the godfather, but the obligations and significance of his office go beyond anything that most of us know. As best man at the wedding, the *koumbáros* participates by holding the little wreath over the heads of the couple. But that is only the beginning of his bonds with the couple, because, as Greeks tend to stay close to their circle of intimates, the *koumbáros* will probably be the couple's closest friend throughout their lives. Thus, when the first child is born, the *koumbáros* is traditionally asked to serve as godfather. There is also a *koumbára*, the bridesmaid and/or godmother, but like so many female roles in Greek life hers is overshadowed by the man's. She will usually be the wife of the *koumbáros*, if he is married. (On Crete the godparents are also known as the *sýnteknos* and *syntéknissa*.) As a godfather, the *koumbáros* takes on truly serious responsibilities, which he has sworn to uphold in the course of the christening service. As the child grows, the parents will consult the *koumbáros* on all vital matters; and when the child comes of age, he may still turn to his *koumbáros* for counsel. The *koumbáros*, on his side, will have provided aid and favours of all kinds throughout the years. He may be of the same social and economic status as his godchild's family, or he may be of considerably higher standing, but the links are just as strong, whatever the distinctions to be observed. The *koumbáros* will be an honoured guest at family gatherings, but while sharing in the family's lighter moments he does not take his relationship of *koumbáros* lightly.

Hospitality

Greek hospitality is a byword among foreigners; by now everyone except the native has marvelled that the Greek word for 'stranger' – *xénos* – is also the word for 'guest'. But this hospitality is quite complex: on the one hand it reaches out to embrace the stranger-guest, on the other it is restrained by procedure and ritual. For example, when a stranger walks into a village its inhabitants normally will not speak until spoken to. But once the newcomer speaks he will be overwhelmed with friendly greetings.

Perhaps nowhere is Greek hospitality seen in such intensity as on Crete. There it becomes almost aggressive at times, and the traveller who really wants to understand and take part in local life must be prepared to go all the way. It is no good going into the villages and mixing with the people and then – when the going becomes a bit strenuous – discreetly retiring. If you are welcomed into a home you will be plied with drinks and sweets that must not be refused; you will be given meals that cannot be paid for except with thanks. The less they have the more they will produce for you. Food, drink, flowers, souvenirs – these are their welcome to a guest and should be gracefully accepted. You will find yourself stared at or asked quite personal questions; if you get the impression that everyone for miles around has been called in to 'inspect' you, that is probably exactly what has happened. The greater the number of people who are packed into a small space, whether it is the front parlour or the back seat of a car, the more successful is the hospitality. And everything said here about hospitality becomes still more intense at holidays, especially Easter, when the stranger will find himself truly an honoured guest.

Drinking and eating traditions

In view of this great tradition of hospitality it is useful to know about some of the customs and rituals that often accompany a meal. When you enter a private home, for instance, no matter how humble, you will, as a guest, be offered a little glass of liquor; men take it in one gulp, women usually just wet their lips with it. This is followed by a sweet, a little dish of preserves or candied fruit (very sweet!), or a spoonful of vanilla paste. A glass of refreshing water is then brought. Don't feel embarrassed when you alone are treated to this round of good things, while your host and other natives sit by; traditions of hospitality demand this ritual.

If you stay to eat a meal, you may notice other unfamiliar ways. In the towns, among more sophisticated people, and in restaurants, manners are much the same as everywhere. But if you should become involved with village life or with rural families or festivals, it is as well to be forewarned about several things. There is, for example, considerable eating from common dishes. Plates and bowls are set on the table, you are handed a fork and knife – and it's every man for himself. At a high festive occasion, such eating can become quite intense. Then, a sort of duel with forks may ensue: a man will thrust his fork into a piece of meat and plunge forward, offering it to some table-companion – perhaps you! You are expected to eat it straight off the fork, then swallow a chaser of wine. As a guest, indeed, you will find yourself getting far more than your share of such attentions. You are not expected to return the service at once, but if you are with the spirit of things you will eventually pass your fork round. A banquet like this can become almost aggressive, to put it mildly.

Drinking, as in every land, is surrounded with a great deal of ritual. One is the snack – *mezés* – taken with drinks. Then, too, almost every gulp is accompanied by a toast: glasses are knocked against each other or on the table, a toast is shouted, another is returned, and the drink is swallowed. These are a few toasts that might prove useful:

'*Stin iyássas!*': 'Your health!'
'*Iss iyía!*': 'Your health!'
'*Pánta yiá!*': 'May you always be happy!'
'*Epíssis!*': 'Same to you!' (used in reply to any toast).
And as do most Europeans, Greeks wish each other 'bon appétit', which is '*kalí órexi!*'

Café life

On Crete the café is the man's world. Men sit there and nurse a single drink for hours, talking, reading newspapers, watching the world go by. Two active café occupations may puzzle visitors. One is a board game, *távli*, which many will recognize as backgammon; it is played at a furious rate, with much slamming and argument. The other occupation involves the little strings of amber beads which so many men finger while they are sitting or standing about. At first glance they look like rosaries. They are the *kombolóia* – the 'worry beads' – and their function seems to be simply to relieve tension. Men can get quite attached to their 'worry beads', and it is said to be a sign of a well-spent life if a man can show a string of highly polished beads in his later years.

The vólta

Walking is another feature of Cretan social life. Not tramping overland to get somewhere, but the very special walking known as the *vólta* – the promenade which takes place at given hours along a defined route in towns and villages all over Crete. The basic pattern is for a considerable section of the local population to put on its finery and stroll up and down a certain stretch of the town's main street. The usual time is in the early evening. It is quite a complex social ritual for those involved – who wears what, and who is seen with whom, and who looked at whom, are matters of interest.

Time and punctuality

If you get to know individual Cretans well enough to make appointments with them, it is as well to remember that on Crete 'morning' extends until 12 noon. 'Noon' is from 12 to 3 p.m.; 'afternoon' is from 3 to 7 p.m. If a Cretan says he will meet you 'at noon', he may mean 2 p.m.; 'this afternoon' for him may be 6 p.m.

Roadside sights

Cretan life takes place largely out of doors. It is particularly fascinating to be present during the summer grain harvest, when some farmers may still be seen using tools and techniques that have remained unchanged for thousands of years. Or if you are lucky you may see flocks being moved to or from the summer pastures by shepherds straight out of Kazantzakis. In the fields women often stand guard spinning wool on the distaff – a scene off an ancient vase-painting.

If you should want to photograph such scenes, you must observe a few proprieties. Not everyone wants to be treated as a 'subject', and so you should somehow make sure you have the person's permission. On the other hand, once some people realize you are going to take their picture, they will become stiff and formal. The basic rule is to remember that you are the stranger-guest in Crete.

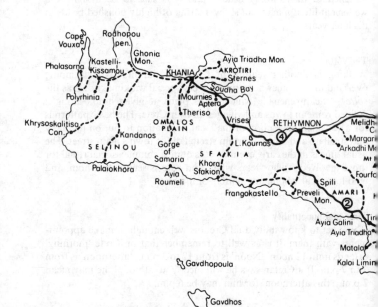

INTRODUCTION TO ROUTES

The centres and routes described in the following section are shown in the Diagram of Routes below. The plan has been to start with Iraklion and the various excursions that use this city as a base. Then, after this, Route 1 is to Phaestos, followed by excursions from Phaestos to sites around the Messara Plain. Route 2 describes the trip from Phaestos up through the mountainous centre of Crete to Rethymnon. Starting again from Iraklion. Route 3 moves westwards along the coast to Rethymnon. Route 4 continues on to Khania, which then becomes the base for excursions to Khora Sfakion, the Gorge of Samaria and western Crete. From Iraklion again, Route 5 goes eastwards to Mallia and Ayios Nikolaos; and Route 6 continues east to Sitia, which is the base for various excursions into eastern Crete, including Kato Zakros. In the text, links between the main routes and cross-references between the excursions are indicated; numerous detours and alter-

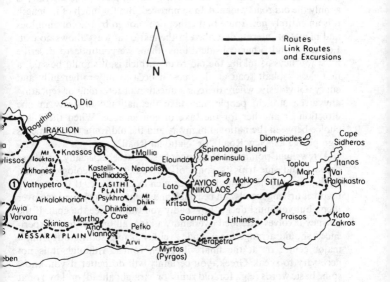

native routes are also described. In general, the excursions cover places that are either not conveniently placed along the main routes or would take too much time to visit when travelling from one centre to the next.

Distances given along the margins of the routes refer to the distance along the direct route up to that point and do not include detours, the distances for which are given in the account of the detour. In some instances, particularly in remote or mountainous regions, distances can be only approximate.

On the Chart of Excursions, pp. 12–13, distances are one-way from the centre indicated. The times allocated for excursions assume that private transport is available (i.e. your own car, hired car or taxi) and are minimum times for visitors, rather than the time recommended for maximum enjoyment. The number of days allotted to each centre refers to the minimum time for seeing the sights within the city and does not include excursions.

It should also be understood that the routes or excursions as described do not assume the use of the national highway that runs almost the entire length of the north coast. In places this highway is simply the old road widened and improved. But for much of its length it is an entirely new route that either does not go by the communities and places of interest described in the text or at least allows no exit. For these and other considerations, then, we continue to describe most journeys as taking the old road – which is, it should be said, a first-class asphalt road at all times, if occasionally rather hilly and curvy. Obviously, where there is a question of returning or repeating any given stretch, people may take the national highway in one direction or another for the sake of convenience. When there is a choice between the national highway and the old route, the former is sign-posted as 'New Road', or 'National Road'.

A few final pointers before people set out – especially on those detours and side-trips to some of the remote archaeological sites, Byzantine chapels, natural features such as caves, etc. If the journey involves driving, roads can be rough and rocky: others have gone over them, but you must decide how badly you want to see the goal. If the journey involves extended overland walking, all but the most experienced should arrange for a guide – either before setting out from a major centre or at the final village en route. Although it is not necessary to speak Greek, you certainly will do better if you know some basic words (e.g., for 'old ruins' or 'straight ahead' or 'key') or at least are able to 'mime' your wants. Finally, if it is not always clear in the text, many of these remote places are not spectacular in the 'four-star' touristic sense; what is involved is the fun of tracking down a place, the satisfaction of arriving and – often – a rewarding setting.

IRAKLION

The largest and best-known city of Crete (and the fifth-largest of all Greece), Iraklion is the governmental-administrative capital and commercial centre of the island as well as the focal point for most visitors. Although the city itself lacks ancient remains, it has far more historical attractions than many people realize – particularly from its Venetian era. Above all, it houses the world's supreme collection of Minoan art and is the gateway to Knossos, the foremost Minoan site, and to many other points of interest for the traveller.

Population About 84,000.

Air and sea connections For schedules, etc., see pp. 18–24. Iraklion Airport is about a 15-minute ride along the coast east of the city. Olympic Airways' town office – where passengers are picked up or left off by the bus – is in Liberty Square (*Map* **15**). The A.N.E.K. Line, which operates some of the ships to Piraeus, has its office in 25th August Street; the Minoan Line has its office in Platia Kallergon.

Information *National Tourist Organization of Greece*: Zanthoudhidhou Street (opposite Archaeological Museum, *Map* **13**) (tel. 222.487).
Tourist Police: Dikeosinis Avenue, *Map* **12**) (tel. 283.190).

Hotels Listing all the hotels of Iraklion by name no longer seems worthwhile: there are now so many, and the variables that individuals seek to satisfy are too many to be detailed. It is more important to know that the National Tourist Organization in Iraklion will send its annual listing of all hotels of Crete and this provides certain details. The Class A hotels all have their own swimming pools and restaurants. Some Class B hotels have their own restaurants. (Not all A or B class hotels can provide air conditioning – while a few Class C can.) Many of the Class C hotels are quite new and more than adequate for most tourists. In making enquiries or reservations, specify such wishes as location (some of Iraklion's hotels are now some distance from the centre of town), bathtub (*vs* shower), quiet room, etc. The Class D and E hotels are not all that bad: enquire at the Tourist Information office when you arrive.

Bungalows and beach hotels Along the coast (especially to the east) not far from Iraklion are several modern hotel establishments that have free-standing bungalows and a central building with restaurant and other facilities. They are normally open only during the summer season from April to October, and they usually require you to take half board.

Pensions and guest houses Iraklion has many of these; they are usually classed – and priced – as Class B or C. There are also plain rooms to rent. The National Tourist Information office can provide details.

Youth hostel 24 Khandakos Street (tel. 222.947) (*Map* **20**).

Restaurants There are countless restaurants, tavernas, and other eating places in

Iraklion, not all first-class but offering a wide choice in menu and atmosphere. (There are even several places specializing in pizza.) At the places listed below, full meals can be obtained from about noon to late evening (with a break from about 3–6 p.m.):

Caprice, Venizelou (Fountain) Square.

Glass House, Sophocles Venizelou Street.

Ionia, Evans Street.

Klimataria, Daedalou Street.

Knossos, Venizelou (Fountain) Square.

Kostas, Daedalou Street.

Maxim, Koronaiou Street (on El Greco Park).

Minos, Daedalou Street.

Portofino, Minotauros Street.

There are still others – and, of course, the Class A hotels also have their own restaurants that are open to the public. Then there are the many smaller restaurants and *tavérnas* scattered throughout the city that serve limited menus and tasty snacks. And no one should leave Iraklion without visiting one of the little eating-places lining the street familiarly known as 'Dirty Alley'. This connects Evans Street with Market Street, one block up from the traffic lights. It provides a fascinating glimpse of a perhaps vanishing world. Each little restaurant jostles the next, spilling out into a narrow street filled with tantalizing smells, noises and people. The food is appetizing too – especially the charcoaled meats. To sit over a meal here is to realize that you are indeed on a unique island.

There are also several outdoor *tavérnas* on the outskirts of Iraklion on the road to Knossos, in the suburb known as Ayios Ioannis: *Kolobotsis*, *Tzobanakis* and *Verikokes*.

There are also the numerous cafés and sweet-shops where cold drinks, coffee, ice-cream, cakes, yoghurt and light snacks can be bought, especially round Liberty Square, Dikeosinis Avenue and Venizelou (Fountain) Square, where people sit till late on summer evenings.

Dining and dancing There are various types of eating places or nightclubs that offer some combination of food and dancing. For the young crowd there are discothèques that open and close each season. Or there is the *Ariadne* nightclub on the road just before Knossos (5 km. from Iraklion) that has a large outdoor dining and dancing area, but the music is not especially Greek. Other *tavérnas* might even produce some spontaneous music and dancing. But the most recent attractions are the several eating places in and around Iraklion that feature traditional Cretan music – usually the lyra – along with some dancers. Although catering especially to foreigners, the music is at least relatively authentic and you can join in the dances. If you do not take a meal, expect to pay heavily for your drinks and consider the amount a cover charge.

Entertainment There is a special organization of young people, the Lyceon Ellinidhon, who study and perform the authentic Cretan dances; if you are lucky, they will be giving a public performance during your stay. Shows with costumes, music and dancing could be arranged through the Tourist Organization, but they are too expensive except for largish parties. Also, in recent years there have been performances of plays (including those from the Cretan Renaissance; see p. 112) at the Venetian Fort in the harbour, as well as events of the Heraklion Festival (p. 72). Enquire about all such possibilities as soon as you arrive in Iraklion. Another possibility that can be combined with a walk around the old Venetian walls is to stop and see the little zoo (*Map 27*) – nothing very grand, but perhaps of interest to those with children in tow.

Cinemas In the summer season, films are shown out of doors (beginning about 20.00); in the winter, film shows are in regular cinemas – many of them around Liberty Square – beginning about 16.00 on weekdays and 14.00 on Sundays. Tickets average about Drs 100.

Consulates The following countries have consulates or consular agents in Iraklion: Belgium, Denmark, Finland, France, Great Britain, Netherlands, Norway, Sweden, West Germany. Americans might try the British Consulate in an emergency (16 Papalexandrou Street, tel. 224.012). (The U.S. Embassy is in Athens.)

Churches In addition to the many Greek Orthodox churches, there is a Roman Catholic Church on Patros Antoniou Street (*Map 5*), a Protestant congregation sometimes holds private gatherings (enquire at Tourist Office).

Shops and souvenirs Everything said about shops, services and souvenirs on p. 61 applies especially to Iraklion, as the biggest city on the island. It has the largest selection of souvenirs on Crete – ranging from cheap touristic items to authentic native handicrafts (and a few genuine antiquities). Of special interest to foreigners will be Astrakianakis and Ekthesis bookshops on Venizelou (Fountain) Square, which have good selections of books, periodicals and daily papers in English and other foreign languages; newspapers and magazines from abroad are also available at several news-stands in the city.

Public toilets There are public toilets in El Greco Park, at the harbour and in the Public Gardens, just behind the memorial to Phokas.

Laundromat There has been one on Mirabello Street, below the street at the back of the Archaeological Museum. It has both coin-operated washing machines and dryers; it seems to be open virtually all day but bring your own supply of 25-Drachma coins.

Left luggage One of the more recent convenient services that have begun to appear in those parts of Greece where so many young people travel with backpacks, these offices (usually part of travel or car rental agencies) will hold your luggage for agreed-upon periods at set fees. In Iraklion, they tend to be along 25th of August Street.

Sport and swimming There is a tennis club on Beaufort Avenue, behind the Archaeological Museum; if you want to play the odd game, you may do so for a modest fee; for a longer stay, you might want to become a member.

The Hellenic Touring Club arranges excursions around the island; so, too, does the Hellenic Alpine Club, but its emphasis is more on walks and climbs. The National Tourist Information office can provide information about both clubs.

The closest swimming is to be found at Poros, on the eastern edge of the city, but it is not an especially attractive beach. Farther along the road, 8 km. east of Iraklion, is Karteros – better known as Florida Beach – and just beyond that is a more ambitious beach facility, run by the National Tourist Organization, with cabins and refreshments. Frequent buses run here from the centre of the city. There is also a beach at Stomion, about 5 km. to the west of Iraklion, which has facilities. And then all along the north coast to the east – especially over as far as Stalis and Mallia – are beautiful beaches. There are two other attractive beaches west of Iraklion – Ayia Pelaya (21 km.) and Fodhele (25 km.), both easily reached by the new road.

For further information about sport facilities on Crete, see pp. 64–5.

Buses Buses for the various cities, towns, villages and sites leave from different points in Iraklion; these have been indicated on the town map (pp. 140–1) and are roughly as follows:

On the harbour (also at other places in town, e.g. Kallergon Square, near Ayios Titos Square): Knossos, Arkhanes.

In square near Historical Museum and behind Xenia Hotel (Map 23): Rethymnon and Khania and points en route.

Khania Gate (Map 24): Phaestos, Timbaki, Matala, Platanos, Lendas, Ayia Galini, Tylissos, Anoyia, Rogdhia, Fodhele, Zaros, Kamares, and all points south-west of Iraklion.

Megaron Phitakis (on the harbour, reached by steps leading seaward from end of Beaufort Ave.) (Map 29): Kokhini Kanni, Khersonissos, Mallia, Ayios Nikolaos, Sitia, Ierapetra, Lassithi Plain, Psykhro.

Oasis (outside Kainouryia Gate) (Map 26): Viannos, Arvi, Myrtos, Kastelli-Pedhiadhos, and points south-east of Iraklion Nome.

Taxis and car hire The main taxi ranks are at Liberty Square, Kornarou Square, Daskaloyiannis Square, Khania Gate and El Greco Park (for rates, etc., see p. 32). The car-hire agencies are clearly advertised all over the city (for rates, etc., see p. 33).

Car parking This has become such a problem in the central city during busy times of the tourist season that you might do better to park at the waterfront lot near the Historical Museum (*Map 21*) or in the moat outside Kainouryia Gate.

HISTORY

Iraklion's history is best glimpsed through the changes in its name. If the place had a name in Minoan times, it is unknown: no Minoan remains have been found in the centre of the city – only tombs on the fringes. The same holds true for the first millennium B.C. Not until the first century A.D. did Strabo the geographer refer to a port of Knossos as Herakleium; this was derived from Herakles' Seventh Labour, but we cannot be sure of the exact site. Some time during the early centuries of the Christian-Byzantine era, the place became known as Kastro, a reference to a castle-fort. And when the Arabs took over the island in 824, they either enlarged this fort or made another and called it Rabdh-al-Khandak (Castle of the Moat). Phokas drove the Arabs out in 961 but their name remained, becoming corrupted by the local Greeks into something like Khandax. When the Venetians took over in the thirteenth century, this became further transformed into Candia; moreover, the name was applied both to the city and the whole island, and thanks to mariners, merchants and mapmakers, Candia was widely known (Shakespeare called it Candy). The Venetians maintained the city's associations with notable fortifications (p. 147), but even though they were among the strongest in the world, the city fell to the Turks in 1669 after a 22-year siege. Europeans continued to call the city Candia, while Cretans called it Megalo Kastro (Big Fort). In the nineteenth century some prominent citizens

– wanting to affirm their island's Greek links – began to advance the name of Iraklion, and in 1922 this was officially adopted. But elderly Cretans often call it Kastro, as if to defy the increasingly modern appearance and pace of the city since the Second World War.

In the last few decades, Iraklion has become the island's centre of transport and communications, the market for exports and imports of central and eastern Crete and the administrative 'capital' of the island. Although it still retains remnants of the almost Near Eastern bazaar atmosphere that was for long its peculiar charm, Iraklion has now irrevocably tilted towards the modern international style. The streets in the centre have become dominated by the new façades and new shops – jewellers, touristic items, appliances, banks, and chemists (make of that mixture what you will!). There has been considerable renovation of the public areas and structures – walls, boulevards, squares, and such – and although it is all certainly more grand it is also somewhat more pretentious. During a few months of high season, moreover, Iraklion takes on the feel of yet another touristic mecca: elbow-to-elbow foreigners looking at gift shops and each other (and bumper-to-bumper vehicles emitting fumes and noise).

But if a superficial chic has all but banished the indigenous from the centre of Iraklion, if you wander off to the edge or down through back streets you can still discover some of the old Iraklion: people living in old, overhanging houses, with fine trees and gardens, shops selling unexpected goods, smiths plying their craft by an open forge, artists painting icons by the age-old method. Although most travellers tend to treat Iraklion as merely the gateway to Minoan culture, we hope to show in the account that follows that the city has historical landmarks of its own to interest the curious visitor.

MUSEUMS
Archaeological Museum
Map 14.

Hours The hours have been changing so often in recent years that it would be misleading to provide specific information here. Go and check at the Tourist Information office as soon as you arrive in Iraklion. However, the museum will almost certainly be closed on the major holidays (see p. 67), and the winter hours tend to be shorter than the summer hours. Also, various rooms are often closed.

Entrance charge Drs 200. Free days seem to have been abolished. Student passes accepted for discounts.

Fee for taking photographs Drs 100 (flash allowed, but not tripod, and some displays cannot be photographed).

Director Dr Ioannis Sakellarakis.

By far the most important sight in Iraklion itself is the world-famous collection of Minoan art and artefacts in the Archaeological Museum. As the world's unrivalled collection of Minoan art and culture, this museum would require several visits to be explored in detail. But the finds are well displayed in rooms arranged chronologically and geographically, and there are many labels in English, so that the visitor with a limited schedule can move through in a fairly short time and still obtain a good impression of the highlights. Ideally, you should visit the museum both early in your stay on Crete and then again after you have seen the sites themselves.

For a thorough study of the collection and its background, the visitor should buy the official guide by the museum's former director, Stylianos Alexiou; there is an English-language edition available in the museum's entrance hall. In the tour that follows, we single out only the principal displays and the most striking individual pieces.

ROOM I: NEOLITHIC AND PRE-PALATIAL PERIODS (6500–2000 B.C.)

Case 1: Neolithic vessels, ritual objects and tools from Knossos and the Cave of Eileithyia.

Case 2: Neolithic and sub-Neolithic pottery from Knossos, Phaestos and Phourni, and a stone figurine of a male worshipper.

Case 3: Sub-Neolithic pottery from burial caves, including some in the Pyrgos and Ayios Onoufrios styles (these being among the oldest painted vases in Europe).

Case 4: Pre-palatial pottery from the tombs at Leben.

Case 5: Jewellery, vases and other finds from the Leben tombs.

Case 6: Pottery in the Vasiliki style – a mottled flameware produced by uneven firing.

Case 7: Stone vases from the cemetery on the island of Mokhlos: note especially the handle carved in shape of a recumbent dog (with an identical one found during the Zakros excavations); included in this case are some of the earliest examples of carved stone vases.

Cases 9, 11–17: Finds from the tholos tombs of the Messara, including vases, sealstones, jewellery, weapons and tools; and note especially the Cycladic-style idols.

Case 10: Pottery from Palaikastro: note the model of a four-wheeled cart; also the clay bowl with a shepherd and his sheep.

Case 12: Note the bull with three men on the horns.

Case 18: Sealstones from central and eastern Crete.
Case 18a: Jewellery, ivory, Cycladic heads from Phourni-Arkhanes.

ROOM II: PROTO-PALATIAL PERIOD (2000–1700 B.C.): KNOSSOS, MALLIA, PEAK SANCTUARIES
Case 19: Vases, pottery and moulds from Mallia: note vase in form of Mother Goddess.
Case 20: Small jugs and bell-shaped figurines from Gournes and Tylissos.
Case 21: Votive figurines of men, women and bulls; vessels from the peak sanctuary of Mount Kofinos in the Asterousia Mountains.
Case 21a–21b: Stone offering tables and objects from the peak sanctuary on Mount Iouktas.
Cases 22–23: Polychrome vases in Kamares style and 'eggshell ware' from Knossos.
Case 25: The *Town Mosaic*, made up of several small earthenware plaques depicting Minoan structures; the modern reconstructions at Knossos have drawn heavily on these plaques. Also here are examples of early pictographic writing on Crete.
Case 27: Vases in the Kamares style from Knossos.
Case 28: Sealstones of the Proto-palatial period from Knossos, Mallia and elsewhere.
Case 29: Large Kamares-style vases from Knossos.

ROOM III: PROTO-PALATIAL PERIOD (2000–1700 B.C.): PHAESTOS
Case 30: Vases of the Kamares style; a utensil, probably a charcoal pan.
Cases 31–36: Kamares and other styles of pottery: note the clay idols and rhytons (libation vases).
Case 33a: Column with dolphins from Phaestos.
Case 34: Note especially the Kamares-style pitchers (next-to-bottom shelf) with the spiral designs – a masterpiece for any age.
Case 39: Vases in barbotine style – decorative relief produced by pinching wet clay or adding thin strips.
Case 40: Clay scalings and 'eggshell' sherds from Phaestos and Knossos.
Case 41: The *Phaestos Disc*: found in 1908, it is a terracotta disc almost 7 inches in diameter, with pictographic signs imprinted on both sides and spiralling from the edge into the centre. It was made by punching a set of metal signs – 45 different ones – into the clay, which

qualifies this as one of the earliest, if 'freak', examples of 'printing' with movable type. It is dated to about 1650–1600 B.C. Signs may be ideograms and/or syllables. It is believed that the text has some religious significance – perhaps a hymn – and there seems to be some rhythm to the order of the signs. Many decipherments and translations have been proposed, but none has been generally accepted.

Case 42: Altars and offering tables from Phaestos.

Case 43: Vessels of remarkable shapes and decoration: note a vase from Phaestos with added clay flowers, perhaps imitating metal or stonework.

ROOM IV: NEO-PALATIAL PERIOD (1700–1450 B.C.): KNOSSOS, PHAESTOS, MALLIA

Case 44: Pottery, including inscribed vessels from Knossos.

Case 45: Vases, wool-holder and lantern case from Knossos.

Case 46: Pottery from Knossos; vases used for libations in the worship of snakes.

Case 47: Sceptre, bronze saw and bowls from Mallia.

Case 49: Pottery and inscribed objects from Phaestos.

Case 50: Sacral relics from temple repositories at Knossos: note especially the famed snake-goddess.

Case 51: A remarkable bull's-head rhyton from the Little Palace, Knossos.

Case 52: Swords from Mallia: note the acrobatic figure in gold foil on one pommel; also the highly decorated miniature objects.

Case 53: Tools and domestic implements from Knossos.

Case 55: Sacral relics from temple repositories at Knossos: note especially the faience plaques representing the deity as a cow suckling a calf, and a wild goat caressing kids. See, too, the stone cross and the balance weights.

Case 56: The *bull-jumper*: unique ivory acrobat from Knossos.

Case 57: The *royal gameboard*, about the size of a chessboard, made of inlaid ivory, found at Knossos.

Case 59: Alabaster rhyton in the form of a lioness's head.

ROOM V: LATE NEO-PALATIAL PERIOD (1450–1400 B.C.): KNOSSOS

Case 60: Pottery of the 'floral style'.

Case 61: Stone friezes from Knossos.

Case 62: Stone lamps from Knossos; Egyptian objects crucial to dating Minoan civilization. Note on top shelf: carved hair-piece; and in corner, a porphyry weight (29 kilos).

Case 65: Sealstones from several sites (note 2096: a wild boar).
Case 69: Clay tablets inscribed with Linear A and B.
Case 70: Fragments from Knossos, including carved stone representing the netting of a bull.
Case 70a: Minoan model of a two-storey house, from Arkhanes.

ROOM VI: NEO-PALATIAL AND POST-PALATIAL PERIODS
(1450–1350 B.C.): CEMETERIES
Case 71: Idols representing a ritual dance, a cult scene and pottery from the vaulted tomb of Kamilari near Phaestos.
Case 73: Vases from cemeteries at Knossos: note idol of goddess carrying infant.
Case 75: Bronze vases and utensils from cemeteries at Phourni, near Arkhanes, and from Knossos.
Case 75a: Skull and skeleton of horse from Tholos A at Phourni (Arkhanes).
Case 77: Bronze weapons and golden cup from Knossos cemeteries.
Case 78: The helmet made out of boar's tusks from near Knossos: unique on Crete and probably imported from the mainland by Mycenaeans.
Case 79: Libation vases from Phaestos: note glass vessel.
Case 79a: Ivory cosmetic box from Katsamba, with relief depicting the capture of a wild bull.
Case 81: Lids of jewel boxes, bronze mirrors and ivory boat from the tombs near Knossos.
Case 84: Spear-heads, swords and daggers from tombs near Knossos.
Case 85: Bronze helmet from tomb near Knossos.
Cases 86, 87: Jewellery from tombs at Knossos, Phaestos and elsewhere: note the fine granulated work and the gold rings.
Case 88: Jewellery, ivories and mirror from the tholos tombs of Arkhanes.

ROOM VII: NEO-PALATIAL PERIOD (1700–1450 B.C.): CENTRAL CRETE
Case 89: Vases, stone lamps, ritual vessel of obsidian from Tylissos and Nirou Khani. Note the three worshippers giving sacred 'salute'.
Case 92: Bronze votive offerings from various caves.
Case 93: Note carbonized wheat and figs on bottom shelf.
Cases 94–96: Three of the masterpieces of this museum, black steatite vases with relief carvings from the Royal Villa at Ayia Triadha: the *Harvesters' Vase* (Case 94); the *Chieftain's Cup* (Case 95); the *Rhyton of the Athletes* (Case 96).

Cases 97, 98: Swords and double axes from Arkalokhorion cave.
Case 99: Bronze talents (i.e. currency ingots) from Ayia Triadha.
Case 100: Bronze tools and weapons from Ayia Triadha; potter's wheels from Vathypetro.
Case 101: Gold jewellery from central and eastern Crete: among so many prizes, we can only single out the incomparable 'honeybee pendant' from Khrysolakkos, near Mallia.
Case 102: Votive idols from Ayia Triadha: note especially the triton shell carved from liparite.

Round the room, note the large bronze double axes from Nirou Khani and the three large bronze cauldrons from Tylissos (the largest weighing about 49 kilos).

ROOM VIII: NEO-PALATIAL PERIOD (1700–1450 B.C.): KATO ZAKROS
These are the most spectacular of the finds at the recently excavated palace site of Kato Zakros (pp. 329–36). All the various ceramic and stone vessels on display are worthy of attention and appreciation, but we single out the following displays:
Case 105: Stone vases and a bronze incense-burner with ivy-leaf decoration.
Case 108: Pottery, a little stone column, stone vases.
Case 109: Libation vase of rock crystal.
Case 111: Libation vase with relief representation of a Minoan peak sanctuary: note the incredible liveliness of the goats. Also note traces of gold-leaf.
Case 112: Bronze swords and double axes.
Case 113: Copper ingots and elephant tusks; the pitcher (upper corner) decorated with nautili, by the way, is like one (from Crete) in a Marseilles museum.
Case 115: Bronze saws.
Case 116: Libation vase in form of a bull's head.
Case 117: A head of a cat, a little silver vase, ivory fragments, a shell vase in faience, a butterfly, double axes and shells.
Case 118: Libation vessels of stone and faience from the palace treasury.

Note, too, on the wall a spiral-decorated frieze in relief from the palace 'banquet hall'.

ROOM IX: NEO-PALATIAL PERIOD (1700–1450 B.C.): EASTERN CRETE
Cases 119–22, 125–6: Stone lamps, bronze figures, libation vases and offering tables from Palaikastro, Gournia and island of Psira.

Case 123: Figurines and sacred insects, models of shrines from Piskephalo.
Case 124: Ivory idols of children, miniature works, seal impressions.
Case 127: Tools and weapons from eastern Crete.
Case 128: A fine collection of sealstones.

ROOM X: POST-PALATIAL PERIOD (1400–1100 B.C.)
Cases 130–31: Clay rhytons, goblets and pottery showing Mycenaean characteristics.
Case 132: Women in sacred dance, incense-burners.
Case 133: Clay figures of goddesses carrying sacred symbols on their heads.
Case 135: Votive figurines of goddesses with unusual head-dresses.
Case 137: Sacred horns with socket for double axe, jewel box with contents.
Case 138: Double vases from Knossos, clay *larnakes* and figurines.
Case 139: Necklaces and moulds.
Case 140: Offering table from Phaestos: goddesses and models of shrines, libation vases in form of human head, and stone altar decorated with double axes and horns in relief from Knossos.
Case 142: Figurines of goddesses and ritual vessels.
Case 143: Votive figurines, sacred swing, sacred ship from Ayia Triadha.
Case 144: Bronze weapons.

ROOM XI: SUB-MINOAN AND EARLY GEOMETRIC PERIOD
(1100–800 B.C.)
Case 146: Vases, figures of horses, bronze tripod.
Case 147: Votive figures in bronze.
Case 148: Model representing a chariot drawn by oxen; clay statuettes of goddesses in benediction: note three with movable feet.
Case 149: Interesting clay figurines and ship models from Inatos cave.
Case 151: Finds from tombs near Prinias: bronze brooches, gold-leaf work, ceramics.
Case 153: Iron weapons and tools; brooches.
Case 154: Cult objects, including clay model of house or sanctuary.
Case 158: Head of goddess, jewellery, statuettes and offerings from Inatos cave.

Iraklion

1 Venetian Fort (p. 146)
2 Yacht Club
3 Venetian Arsenals (p. 147)
4 Customs and Aliens Offices
5 Roman Catholic Church
6 Telephone/Telegraph Office
7 Church of Ayios Titos (p. 148)
8 Loggia (p. 148) and City Hall
   (Armoury)
9 Basilica of St Mark (p. 149)
10 Morosini Lion Fountain (p. 149)
11 Nikiphoros Phokas Square (Traffic
   lights crossroads)
12 Tourist Police
13 National Tourist Information Office
14 Archaeological Museum (p. 133)
15 Olympic Airways Office
16 Post Office
17 Cathedral of Ayios Menas (p. 151)
18 Church of Ayios Menas (p. 151)
19 Church of St Katherine (p. 151)
20 Youth Hostel
21 Historical and Ethnographic
   Museum (p. 144)
22 Fountain of Priuli (p. 152)
23 Bus Terminal
24 Bus Terminal
25 Santa Maria dei Crociferi (p. 152)
26 Bus Terminal
27 Zoo
28 Martinengo Bastion: Kazantzakis
   Tomb (p. 147)
29 To Bus Terminal

A route to
   Fodhele
   Tylissos
   Gortyna, Phaestos and Ayia
      Triadha
   Mt Idha and Kamares Cave
   Rethymnon
   Khania
   Matala and Ayia Galini
B route to
   Knossos
   Arkhanes, Vathypetro and
      Mt Iouktas
   Ano Viannos and Arvi
C route to
   Poros
   Airport
   Lasithi Plain and Dhiktaion Cave
   Mallia
   Ayios Nikolaos
   Sitia
   Ierapetra
   Kato Zakros

N

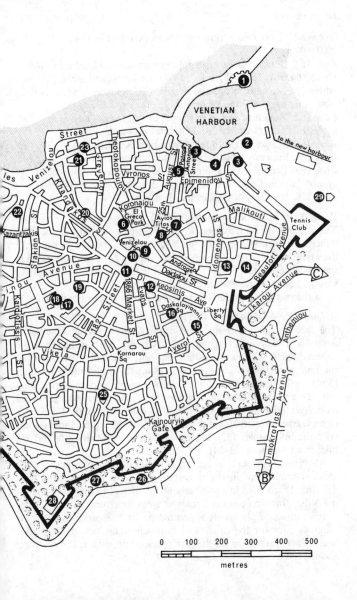

VENETIAN HARBOUR

to the new harbour

Street

Neotokopoulou

Kydonias

Venizelou

les

Kazantzakis

Stakion St.

Inou

Kardoulisis St.

Avenue

1821 Street

Vikela

Vyronos St.

August St.

Epimenidou St.

Koronaiou

El Greco Park

Ayios Titos

Venizelou Sq.

Androgeo

Daidalou St.

1866 (Market) St.

Ikeosinis Ave

Evans St.

Daskaloyannis St.

Averof St.

Kornarou Sq.

Kainouryia Gate

Pausaniou

Antoniou Street

Malikouti

Idomeneos

Tennis Club

Beaufort Avenue

Ikarou Avenue

Liberty Sq.

Anthemiou

Dimokratias Avenue

C

B

0 100 200 300 400 500

metres

ROOM XII: LATE GEOMETRIC AND ORIENTALIZING PERIODS
(800–600 B.C.)

Case 159: Unusual Geometric pottery with blue and red on white.
Cases 160, 161, 161a, 161b, 161c: Votive animals and archer, Hermes with a lyre, centaur, bronze votive plaques, figurines, and other finds from sanctuary of Syme Viannos.
Case 162: Models of sacred trees with doves, from Knossos.
Cases 163, 168: Geometric and Orientalizing tomb vases.
Case 164: Bronze belt with relief from near Knossos.
Case 166: Funerary urns from Knossos cemeteries.
Case 169: Bronze decorations from Idhaean cave: note 'master of animals' in relief on arrow quiver (see drawing on wall opposite).
Case 170: Jewellery of the Geometric period.

ROOM XIII: MINOAN SARCOPHAGI (1400–1100 B.C.)

The sarcophagi here belong to the Post-palatial Period; they are either of the 'chest' or of the 'bath-tub' shape. The body's legs were drawn up tightly – hence the small size. The later ones are decorated in the so-called decadent style. Note, too, in the corner, the impressive wooden model of the Palace of Knossos.

At the end of Room XIII a staircase leads to the upper floor.

ROOM XIV: MINOAN FRESCOES (1600–1400 B.C.)

The frescoes in this room come from Knossos, Ayia Triadha or Amnisos. The original fragments may be easily distinguished from the restored parts. All are interesting, but note especially: sections from the long processional corridor of Knossos (2–4) and the cup-bearer (5); the wild-cat and birds (9), the scenes from a religious procession (10–12), and the painted stucco floor with marine subjects (13) – all from Ayia Triadha; the figure-of-eight war shields (14), the Lily Prince (with feather crown) (15), the bull's head in relief (16), the dolphins (18), the bull-leapers (22), all from Knossos; and the white and red lilies from Amnisos (23–24).

Also here (*Case 171*, in centre) is what is considered perhaps the most valuable item in the museum – the sarcophagus from Ayia Triadha. Discovered in a tomb about 100 metres to the north-east of the Villa, the sarcophagus is carved from limestone with a surface coating of white plaster. It is painted on its four sides to show the religious rites for the dead, and thus represents one of the major sources for speculation on Minoan religion and rituals. It dates from about 1400 B.C.

ROOM XV: MINOAN FRESCOES (1600–1400 B.C.)
Among the many fine smaller frescoes here, note: the ritual dance in a sacred olive grove (1) and the so-called 'La Parisienne' (3).

ROOM XVI: MINOAN FRESCOES (1600–1400 B.C.)

ROOM XVI: MINOAN FRESCOES (1600–1400 B.C.)
Among these fine frescoes, note: the two restorations of the saffron-gatherer (1–2: it is now agreed that it was a monkey); the leader of the Blacks (3); the dancing girl (4); and the blue monkey (10).

Owing to lack of funds, the remaining four rooms (XVII–XX) are often closed to the public. If you have some special requirement or qualification, ask at the Museum or the National Tourist office what arrangements might be made.

ROOM XVII: THE GIAMALAKIS COLLECTION
Dr Giamalakis, an Iraklion physician, was one of the few individuals allowed to purchase Minoan art, and over the years he amassed an important collection. It was acquired by the government for the museum in 1962, and is here displayed in its entirety. (Note that it includes many post-Minoan materials.
Case 178: Bronze statuette of man carrying ram on his shoulder; exact provenance is unknown, but it probably dates from about 750 B.C.
Case 181: Proto-Geometric shrine, with goddess inside, two votaries and a dog on the roof.
Case 191: A finely worked gold diadem (Minoan) with goddess as queen of the animals; other jewellery of various periods.

ROOM XVIII: MINOR ARTS OF ARCHAIC, HELLENISTIC AND ROMAN PERIODS
As the title of this room indicates, it contains a diverse collection of pottery, glass vases, bronze and clay figurines, armour, jewellery and coins, covering the periods from the seventh century B.C. to the fourth century A.D. Note the especially handsome bronze funerary statue from Ierapetra.

Down again to the ground floor, where there are two rooms of sculpture.

ROOMS XIX AND XX: SCULPTURE FROM ARCHAIC, CLASSICAL, HELLENISTIC AND GRAECO-ROMAN PERIODS
These friezes, sculptures, bronzes and other works are mainly from such sites as Prinias, Gortyna, Eleftherna, Dreros, Palaikastro,

Praisos and Roman Knossos. Although they may not be great works in the pure aesthetic sense, they are of great importance in tracing the development of Greek sculpture, and several pieces are most enjoyable. Do not miss the original work from the Archaic temple of Prinias, over the doorway between the two rooms.

Historical and Ethnographic Museum
Map **21.**
Hours Has usually been open 09.00–13.00 and 15.00–17.30; closed on Sundays and major holidays. Enquire.
Entrance charge Drs 100.
There is a *Guide to the Historical Museum* by Stylianos Alexiou in an English translation, but it was out of print. Enquire if it is available.

Taking up where the Archaeological Museum leaves off, this is a collection of art, historical mementoes and handicrafts dating from the first years of the Christian era. It thus reveals the continuity of Cretan culture from that period on into medieval, Renaissance and modern times throughout the island's lulls and storms. It is housed in the former home of Andreas Kalokairinos, a student and benefactor of Crete's heritage.

BASEMENT
Here are remains of the early Christian and Byzantine periods as well as sculpture from the Venetian period and some Turkish remains from Iraklion.

MAIN FLOOR
This houses a collection of early Christian objects found at the Basilica of Ayios Titos at Gortyna (p. 205); also icons and frescoes from various churches and monasteries of Crete. These latter are of particular interest to students of Byzantine painting from the fourteenth to the sixteenth centuries. There is also a collection of Byzantine coins and a reconstruction of a Byzantine chapel.

UPPER FLOORS
Here are some interesting manuscripts, books and maps associated with Crete's past; a collection of photos of the Battle of Crete, 1941; examples of popular wood carvings and textiles; and a reconstruction of a Cretan rural home, furnished as it would have been about 1900. Of particular interest to many will be the reconstruction of the study of Nikos Kazantzakis, Crete's gift to modern letters (p. 114), with his furniture, belongings and books; there is also a reconstruction of the

study of Emanuel Tsouderos, a prominent Greek statesman – he was Prime Minister of Greece at the time of the Battle of Crete in 1941 – who was a native of Rethymnon.

Basilica of St Mark
Map **9**.

Hours Very flexible. Officially, they are 10.00–12.00 and 17.00–19.00, except on Sundays and public holidays, but the building is often closed for lectures or meetings, and occasionally open on Sundays. It is often closed for the entire period from September to February.

Entrance charge Variable. Drs 50 when there is no exhibition being held in the building, but free when there is an exhibition!

Since this old Venetian church was restored in 1961 (p. 149), it has housed a collection of reproductions of early Byzantine frescoes from the churches and chapels of Crete, an exhibition sponsored by the Society of Cretan Historical Studies.

The thirty-odd copies of frescoes from Cretan churches – some of which are quite remotely situated – show the artistic flourishing of Cretan painting in the thirteenth, fourteenth and fifteenth centuries. (Among the more distinctive characteristics are those cited on p. 112). It is hoped that this exhibition will encourage some people to seek out the churches themselves around the island.

Church of St Katherine
Map **19**.

Hours Variable, but usually open every morning and several late afternoons. Closed Sundays.

Entrance charge Drs 60.

Photographs forbidden.

This church, so rich in its own historical associations (see p. 151) has been restored in recent years and now serves as a museum for religious art of the Middle Ages on Crete – icons, frescoes, wood carvings, manuscripts and other works from the churches and chapels of Crete. Perhaps the most valued works are the six paintings by Michael Damaskinos, the contemporary of El Greco (see p. 113): these paintings, considered to be his masterworks, date from 1582 to 1591 and long reposed in the church of Vrondisi (p. 195); then they were brought to the Cathedral of Ayios Menas (across the square from St Katherine) where they were lost in the shadows. The six icons are recognizable as: *The Adoration of the Magi, The Burning Bush, The*

Last Supper, Noli me tangere, The First Ecumenical Synod (Nicaea) and *The Sacred Mass*.

PRINCIPAL SIGHTS

The major sights of Iraklion are described below, following a route from the harbour up to the cross-roads at Nikiphoros Phokas Square (where the traffic lights are), and then radiating from that point (*Map* **11**).

Harbour

Since Iraklion has traditionally been approached by sea, we begin with the view as you enter the bay. Just off to the east is the barren island of Dia, named after the nymph – one of Zeus's extra-marital amours – cast there by Hera. (The English-speaking community call it Dragon Island because of its shape.) It is now a refuge for the wild goat (p. 81). To the west of the city the land rises steeply, with the remains of a Venetian fort, the Palaiokastro, to be seen; above this is the village of Rogdhia (p. 181). Inland and to the west is the prominent cone of Mt Stroumboulas; more central are the peaks of the Idha Mountains and the Zeus-profile of Mt Iouktas (p. 179). The city itself is most dense around the harbour but now overflows on to the inclined plain that is backed by the mountain spine of Crete.

Ships tie up in the New Harbour, which has been dredged and enlarged over the years and is still developing its facilities. The entrance to the inner and older harbour – now used by yachts and small fishing boats – is guarded by the impressive Venetian Castle.

Venetian Castle
Map **1**.
Hours Variable, but usually weekdays 09.00–13.00: 16.00–19.00.
Entrance charge Drs 100.

The Arabs (back in the ninth–tenth centuries A.D.) may have been the first to build on an islet here – now joined by a mole to the mainland; then came the Genoese with a simple fort; they were soon ousted by the Venetians, who worked on the ambitious fort we see today, constructing the major part between 1523 and 1540. Its battlements and exterior texture are essentially intact, and the Lion of St Mark, in several relief carvings, is a resonant echo of the old glory. The interior with its many chambers has been restored in recent years and is now one of the most impressive such forts most of us will ever get to see outside of a movie set. It is well worth a visit. The upper level is now used in the high season for performances of Greek dramas. (Incidentally, the fort is still known by many Iraklion residents as the *Koúles*, the name the Turks gave to it.)

Venetian harbour installations
Map 3.

The Venetians expended a great deal to develop the harbour of Candia, a vital link in their commercial route to the East. Little remains except a section of their sixteenth-century *arsenali* – great vaulted and arcaded chambers where ships were built and serviced. The surviving portions have been cleared and restored in recent years. At the west end, rear, of the larger group is a doorway (restored) leading to the former salt warehouse, from the days when salt was controlled and taxed as a government monopoly.

Venetian Wall and Gates

The dominating structure of Iraklion is the Venetian Wall. First erected in the fifteenth century, these ramparts were greatly enlarged and improved in the sixteenth and seventeenth centuries; Michele Sammicheli of Verona, one of the leading sixteenth-century military engineers, came in 1538 to supervise. These walls were considered the strongest of their day in the Mediterranean world; in spite of their long siege by the Turks (p. 99), they were well preserved and still impose a distinctive character on the city. Perhaps the most impressive reminder of the reality of these walls are two of the gates:

(1) The Pantocrator or Panigra Gate – best known as the *Khania Gate* – a gateway to the west and south. Carvings date it *c.* 1570.

(2) The Gate of Gesu (Jesus), or *Kainouryia Gate*, with ornate stonework and decorations. Dated to 1587.

A novel – and sometimes surprising – perspective on Iraklion may be had from walking around the entire perimeter of the walls, a distance of about 4 km. They are now particularly dramatic since the recent clearing away of the old dwellings and vegetation that had spread on to the ramparts. On the very southern side you will see the city's gardens and a small *zoo* (*Map 27*). And alongside and above these sits the *Martinengo Bastion* (*Map 28*), which holds the grave of Nikos Kazantzakis (1883–1957), the celebrated Cretan-Greek author.

Because of his somewhat unorthodox beliefs and writings, the Greek Church refused to bury him with its full rites. Now he lies under a massive but simple, rough native stone. On it an inscription from his own works reads: 'I hope for nothing. I fear nothing. I am free.' It is also possible to visit the 'birthplace' of Kazantzakis in the street now named after him, but the actual house has now been replaced by a new building (No. 18). More stimulating for those who want to pay their respects is the reconstruction of his last study in the Historical Museum (p. 144).

True devotees of Kazantzakis will also want to know of the so-called Kazantzakis Museum opened at Varvari-Myrti (some 20 km. south of Iraklion), the home village of Kazantzakis's father. It has various mementoes, manuscripts, books, photographs, and archives (TV, radio, film) associated with Kazantzakis. It has been open only from November to February; you are strongly advised to telephone ahead (tel. 741689) to find out about hours, route, etc.

Church of Ayios Titos
Map 7.

Proceeding from the harbour, you climb 25th August Street up to the centre of the town; the street is lined with shipping offices, tourist agencies, souvenir shops and banks. About halfway up, on the left, is the Square of Ayios Titos, named after the patron saint of the island (p. 111), whose church dominates the square. An early Greek Byzantine church on the spot was evidently greatly modified by the Venetians in the sixteenth century; earthquakes, fires and restorations followed, until the Turks made a major reconstruction as a mosque in 1872; in 1923 it reverted to the Orthodox. This 'ecumenical' history accounts for its unusual mixture of architectural elements. Its two most famous treasures – the icon of The Virgin Messopanditissa and the head of St Titus – were taken to Venice when Iraklion fell to the Turks. In 1966, however, a reliquary containing the skull of St Titus was returned by Venice, so that it once again reposes in its rightful home. (The icon remains in Santa Maria della Salute in Venice.)

Venetian Armoury and Loggia
Map 8.

Off the corner of Ayios Titos Square is the Venetian Armoury, now the City Hall, fronted by the once renowned Loggia. Constructed early in the seventeenth century in a mixed 'Palladian-Renaissance' style, the Loggia disintegrated, owing largely to earthquakes. Now it has been given a total and authentic reconstruction, and it may be seen as a handsome structure. There are plans to use it for some kind of civic or public functions. In the north wall of the armoury, by the way, may be seen the somewhat damaged fountain of Sagredo, erected in 1602–4; the woman is thought to represent Crete.

Fountain Square
Map **10**.

Higher up along 25th August Street, on the right, is Venizelou Square – but more commonly known as 'Fountain Square' after the delightful fountain erected in 1628 under the Venetians. Along with being the centre of many bookstores and souvenir shops, the square has long been a favourite place for people to sit and enjoy a *bougátsa*, the delicious filled pastry, while watching the world pass by.

Francesco Morosini, the Venetian governor-general in the early seventeenth century, is credited with supervising its construction – as well as that of the Loggia, the armoury, several other fountains and an aqueduct from Mt Iouktas to Iraklion. (This Morosini should not be confused with his nephew, the famous Proveditore Generale who surrendered Iraklion to the Turks in 1669 and later led the attack on Athens during which the Parthenon was so badly damaged.)

The four lions on the fountain date from the fourteenth century and were probably brought from another Venetian fountain. There was once a statue of Neptune on the top. The eight lobes or basins have bas-reliefs, not especially fine workmanship but worth a close look: nymphs, tritons, dolphins, bulls and mythical marine animals, some playing musical instruments.

Across from the fountain is the *Basilica of St Mark* (*Map* **9**), which contains the exhibition of copies of frescoes in the churches of Crete (p. 145). Built in 1239 under the Venetians, it was reconstructed after an earthquake in 1303 as the Church of the Duke, with a campanile (since destroyed); under the Turks it was transformed into a mosque. It has now been restored to the original Venetian style, and is used as an auditorium for lectures and concerts.

To the north-west of Fountain Square – that is, a few steps back down 25th August Street – is *El Greco Park*, a modern public park, with a bust of El Greco beyond the entrance. There is a children's playground here, and public lavatories beneath the park.

Dikeosinis Avenue and Liberty Square

Continuing along 25th August Street, you arrive at the cross-roads with the traffic lights – officially Nikiphoros Phokas Square (*Map* 11). If you turn left, you proceed along Dikeosinis Avenue, where many of the better shops are found along the left, while administrative buildings line the right. (Just a few storefronts in from the corner, on the left, there have been visible (at the rear of a small open lot) some remains of the old Venetian walls.) Proceeding on, to the right, at the entrance to the Court House is clearly distinguished the Venetian Portal from the destroyed monastery church of St Francis (once on the site of the Archaeological Museum). Old Turkish barracks once stood along the right-hand side of the avenue, until they were converted into these governmental buildings. Near the end, on the right, there is an opening up to Daskaloyiannis Square: the bust of this revolutionary hero (p. 276) is situated here.

Continuing to the end of Dikeosinis Avenue, you come out on to Liberty Square, with its cinemas, cafés and swirling traffic. On Sunday and holiday evenings in particular, pedestrians take over the streets from the traffic, and here is where you sit to watch the *vólta*, or promenade. Off at the far left, where the road swings down through the St George Gate, is the office of the National Tourist Organization (*Map* 13) and the Archaeological Museum (p. 133). In the garden of the museum is a small *monument*, erected by the French, to the Duc de Beaufort and the French troops who lost their lives in 1668–9 while trying to raise the siege of Candia (p. 99). Looking across to the St George Gate from this garden, you see the *epigraphic collection* of the museum built into the gateway (and kept locked for specialists).

Around the square are various other points of interest. At the far edge of the centre terraces is one with a *portrait bust of Kazantzakis*; across from this, on a terrace on the wall, is a larger-than-life-size *statue of Eleftherios Venizelos*. Leaving the square by Dimokratias Avenue, you pass on the right the *public gardens*, which contain quite a number of unusual flowers, bushes and trees. (There are also public lavatories just inside.) Alongside the gardens is the commemorative *column* to Nikiphoros Phokas (p. 98); farther on is the rather grandiose *monument to national resistance*.

Market and Kornarou Square

Back at the traffic lights (with 25th August Street and the harbour to your back), the street that leads straight ahead is officially 1866 Street, but no one can fail to recognize it as the market. Everyone should stroll down it at least once. At the far end is Kornarou Square, where a lovely Turkish fountain stands (now housing a souvenir shop). Behind this is the *Bembo Fountain* (1588): the headless statue built into it is Roman, brought from Ierapetra. And now standing in the middle of the square is a handsome statue by the modern Cretan sculptor, Ioannis Parmekellis. Titled 'Erotokritos and Arethusa', it commemorates the hero and heroine of the Cretan epic poem by Cornaro (p. 112).

Cathedral of Ayios Menas
Map 17.
Back once more at the traffic-lights cross-roads, keeping your back to the harbour you turn right and start down Kalokairinou Avenue, a street lined with shops of all kinds. After about four streets (depending on where you start to count), you turn left into Ayii Dheka Street, which emerges into the Square of Ayia Ekaterini, where stands the Cathedral of Iraklion, Ayios Menas. Erected between 1862 and 1895, it is quite imposing in its size and situation, but otherwise not especially notable. At the west (lower) corner of the cathedral is the little *Church of Ayios Menas* (*Map* 18); it contains some notable wood-carving, as well as icons dating back to the eighteenth century. (If closed, the key may be obtained from the cathedral staff.) It is not known exactly how old this structure is, but presumably it dates well back to the Middle Ages; it served for a period from the eighteenth century as the metropolitan church of Iraklion, until replaced by the large Cathedral.

Church of St Katherine
Map 19.
Off this same square, in a lower court, is the Church of St Katherine. It dates from the fifteenth century, and is of a plain style except for the elegant seventeenth-century doorway. During the sixteenth and seventeenth centuries, this was the site of the Mount Sinai Monastery School, a centre of the Cretan 'Renaissance', where painting, theology and humanistic studies were taught. It has been claimed that El Greco studied here as Domenico Theotokopoulos before he left for Italy and Spain, but this is largely speculative. Much more certain as pupils here were the other major figures of Crete's Renaissance: Cornaros and Khortatzis, the dramatists; Damaskinos, the painter;

and Meletios Pigas and Kyrillos Loukaris, famous Orthodox theologians, the former Patriarch of Alexandria and the latter Patriarch of Constantinople. Today the church serves as a museum of Cretan icons (see p. 145).

Other sights

These are the principal landmarks of Iraklion, but there are still other surprising, if minor, attractions to be seen in strolling through its back streets. There are several other fine churches – including the *Santa Maria dei Crociferi* (*Map* 25) in the southern area of the city (on the corner of Dhiktaion Antrou and Markos Mousourou streets): this is an Italian structure of the fourteenth century in the basilica style, with a nave and two aisles; its exterior has been repaired, and its interior changed to accommodate the Greek Orthodox (and its name changed to Panayia Stavrophorou). Restoration has also begun on another of the Venetian churches, *St Peter's*; this is down behind the Xenia Hotel. There are also several charming little fountains – for instance, the *Fountain of Priuli* (*Map* 22), dating from 1666. And everywhere, in addition, are the pleasures and surprises of contemporary Iraklion.

EXCURSIONS FROM IRAKLION

By consulting the Chart of Excursions, pages 12–13, you can get an over-all impression of the many excursions possible from Iraklion. And since such a large proportion of visitors to Crete do use Iraklion as a base, we repeat here what was said in the Introduction to this section (p. 128); all routes and excursions described that make use of the roads along the north coast assume that the old road – where there is a choice, instead of the new highway – is being used. Again, too, where you are returning or repeating stretches, you might decide to make use of the new highway. The main exit–entrance for Iraklion and this new highway is on the southern edge of the city, out on the road to Phaestos. For trips to the east, there is also an access road on the outskirts of Katsamba, on the old coast road (p. 296), and one on the road to Knossos in the suburb of Ayios Ioannis also leads east or west.

Knossos

Knossos is, of course, the goal of all visitors to Crete, and it lives up to its reputation. There will always be some who feel that Sir Arthur Evans carried his reconstruction rather too far, but no one ever leaves without being impressed by the majesty of the whole. While its breadth and complexity are apparent even to those who merely stroll through, we have provided a description that allows visitors to move through with some awareness of their surroundings. Still more details may be had by using more detailed guides such as Pendlebury's *Handbook to the Palace of Minos, Knossos and its Dependencies*, Alexiou's *Guide to the Minoan Palaces*, or Cadogan's *Palaces of Minoan Crete*. And private guides may be hired through the National Tourist Organization.

A bit of advice: during high season, the organized tours and cruise ships tend to go out to Knossos early in the day; if you have a choice, put off your visit till later in the day – say, after 16.00.

Route Leaving Iraklion by Dimokratias Avenue off Liberty Square (Route Exit B), you continue through several suburbs until you reach the site of Knossos. As Knossos is only 5 km. from Iraklion, some people may consider making the 'pilgrimage' by foot. (Apropos of pilgrimage, Kazantzakis describes his own journey to Knossos in his autobiography, *Report to Greco*.)
Bus Buses leave for Knossos from the harbour of Iraklion about every fifteen minutes, joining Dimokratias Avenue at the edge of town. A convenient pickup point is on 1821 Street, just above the El Greco Hotel. Several tourist agencies arrange guided tours to Knossos with their own buses.
Hours These have been the hours, but enquire:
  April 1st–Sept 30th. Mon–Sat. 7.30–19.00
  Sundays and holidays: 10.00–18.00
  Oct. 1st–March 31st. Daily 08.00 to sundown.
Closed at Christmas, New Year, Greek Easter, March 25th and October 28th.
Entrance charge Drs 200. Students get discount with proper pass.

[1 km.] To the left, a paved road descends into a ravine and leads eastward to the plateau of Ayios Ioannis, from which there is a fine view of the city and the bay. Not far from here were the remains of the Tomb of Isopata, a remarkable domed tomb of the middle Minoan period, but what survived when Evans excavated it was destroyed, accidentally or otherwise, under the German occupation. Now you can see it only through the restoration-drawing drawn by Piet de Jong, one of Evans's assistants, in the Iraklion museum.

There was a day when you could walk from this area across the field to Knossos, but now it is becoming built up. There are other tombs in the region, but it would take a knowledgeable guide to locate them – and all their valuable finds are in the museum.

Continuing along the main road to the south, you wind up and down through various suburbs.

[4 km.] On a curve, you pass, to the left, a large *hospital* (originally a sanatorium, built after the Second World War with donations from Greek-Americans); this commands a fine view of the valley of Kairatos, where Knossos lies. Many Minoan tombs were discovered when the sanatorium was being built; more recently (while the area was being prepared for the new medical and science schools of the University of Crete), near by has been found an extensive cemetery with tombs from the Dark Age (post-Minoan) to Roman periods and an early Christian basilica, dating from about A.D. 500.

[4¾ km.] Continuing on several hundred metres, you should begin to look up to the field to the right for the red-roofed structure that covers the well-preserved mosaic floor of the Roman *Villa of Dionysus*. To visit this, you may park just off the road before the 5-km. stone and scramble up the slope – taking care to avoid the barbed-wire fence – and walk the several metres across a field. The mosaics of the villa, some marble slabs of the main living-room, some columns and fragments of the peristyle and a few other odds-and-ends in the area are all that survive of the *Colonia Julia Nobilis*, the Roman colony that began when a group of Roman veterans settled here after the conquest (p. 97); although they hardly rivalled the glory of Knossos, it must have been a fairly ambitious town. The villa itself was evidently a religious centre in which the Dionysus ritual was prominent.

Proceeding on along the main road a few more metres, you pass a side-road that leads off to the right past the gatehouse and up to the *Villa Ariadne*, built by Sir Arthur Evans for his private residence. During the war it became the headquarters of the German commandant; it now belongs to the Greek Archaeological Service. Since 1965 there has also been established near by a Stratigraphical Museum for specialists in Minoan archaeology. And just a little farther down the main road, again on the right, is the entrance to the *Little Palace* and *Unexplored Mansion* (p. 170).

(5¼ km.] A stretch of little cafés along the main road proclaims your arrival at Knossos. Just across from the first of these cafés, to the left of the main road and below it, you can see the end of the excavations of the 'royal road' (p. 169) from the Palace, but there is no access to the site at this point. For that, you proceed to the white pavilion at the car park; there is a souvenir shop here with some choice of handicrafts.

HISTORY OF EXCAVATIONS AT KNOSSOS

It had long been known that there must be ancient remains at the site of Knossos; by the last half of the nineteenth century there were frequent reports of finds in the area, but they were usually remains of the later, Roman structures. After the revelations of an amateur Cretan archaeologist, Minos Kalokairinos (p. 105), Schliemann tried to acquire the site, but it remained for Evans to begin the real excavations in 1900. Week after week produced some amazing find; year after year continued to reveal the immensity of the site. Evans soon realized that if the various levels and the general complexity of the structures were to be presented – not to mention protected from the elements – there would have to be a certain amount of reconstruction. Working carefully with all the fragments and evidence available – cf. the Town mosaic in the Archaeological Museum – Evans supervised the restoration of considerable parts of the palace: columns, window casements, stairways, walls. All these were rendered in reinforced concrete, and whenever possible actual remains were incorporated in the restoration. Over the decades, Evans was assisted by a staff of archaeologists, architects and artists, and the palace and the dependencies assumed their present appearance.

In 1960 there began a scholars' dispute that might appear to cast doubt on the whole site of Knossos; in point of fact it concerned such matters as chronology, the script and the relationships among Minoan Cretans, Mycenaean Greeks and other Mediterranean and Near Eastern peoples. (The principal points in contention are: What was behind Evans's assigning certain Linear B tablets to a particular level? And can these tablets be used to move the date of the end of the palace from about 1370 B.C. to about 1250 B.C.?) Whatever the final adjustments, the achievement of Evans can in no way be diminished. Excavations have continued, under the British School of Archaeology, and still turn up valuable finds both at the palace and in the surrounding areas. In addition to amplifying the extent of the Minoan community, the discoveries have revealed the Neolithic remains going as far back as 6300 B.C. and also show the extent to which this area was populated in the post-Minoan period. The whole area around Knossos seems to be honeycombed with post-Minoan tombs, for instance – many of them turned up by the emergency excavations required by the advancing modern construction projects.

One other point. The more recent excavations at Knossos are typical of a much more modern archaeology in being problem-oriented; that is, they reflect the specialists' desires to resolve specific questions on matters of dating, fortifications, and such. Many of the finds are crucial to understanding Minoan civilizations but do not necessarily yield remains of artefacts that interest the average visitor.

PALACE OF KNOSSOS

Before plunging into the labyrinth, it seems best to have some general concept of what you will be seeing. First, it must be emphasized that what the visitor tours at Knossos today is largely the remains of the great palace that arose during the Neo-palatial Period – approximately 1700 to 1400 B.C. At the same time, remains from both earlier and later periods are everywhere, the Cretans themselves having continually built upon and absorbed previous structures. (Scholars' estimates of the population of Knossos, as both palace and dependent city, range from 30,000 to 100,000; the complete city must have spread over a very large surrounding area.) What we see, then, is a great sprawling palace complex, amazingly modern in its treatment of space and terrain. This is not the Greece of classical proportions, but Knossos never was that; the amalgam of periods and structures we view is a legitimate effect. At the same time, as mentioned elsewhere (p. 108), careful measurement of this and other Minoan palaces suggests that more thought was given to the design than was previously realized.

As the archetype of the Minoan palaces, Knossos has at its heart the great central court, used for everything from religious rituals to moonlight strolling. (The great courts at Mallia and Phaestos, incidentally, are each as impressive in their own ways.) And like the other Minoan palaces, Knossos has no particular walls or defences. Its location, on a relatively modest mound in a valley, hardly made it impregnable; but as signs and remains of fortifications are slight, it evidently relied for defence on sea power, coastal installations – and reputation.

In addition to being the residence of the royal family and their circle of attendant nobles and functionaries, the palace served as the Sacred Precincts, and many rooms and remains are associated with the Minoan religion. There were little chapels and shrines everywhere, as well as lustral baths used for purification during sacred rites. Other indications of the religious atmosphere that must have pervaded the palace are the sacred pillars, the carved signs and symbols, the double axes, as well as all the artefacts, such as Snake Goddesses, now in museums. This great complex also housed the commercial and industrial quarters, with their administrative adjuncts. There were sizeable storerooms for basic foods, and workshops for many of the common crafts. There are also indications that a close check was kept on such affairs: included here are the inscribed clay tablets that are just beginning to yield information about the Cretans of those days.

Most of the works of art and craftsmanship have had to be removed to the Iraklion museum. But the original drainage pipes function, and bathtubs are in place, as well as the gigantic urns and jars (*píthoi*) – some 2 metres high and 4·5 metres in girth. The original frescoes are in the museum; what you see at Knossos are copies of reconstructions, although the parts that had been found are distinguished from what is conjecture. (Two Swiss painters, the Gilliérons, father and son, are responsible for most of the imaginative restorations, based on surviving fragments and archaeologists' hints.) Perhaps the most dramatic original still *in situ* is the throne – generally conceded to be the oldest throne in Europe; it is made of gypsum and is well preserved.

The drainage and sanitation systems were probably superior to any known in Europe until the nineteenth century. Particularly notable is the system around the Queen's quarters. Remains in her toilet room suggest that there might have been running water from cisterns on a higher level, and the toilet itself has the means for flushing, as well as drains and a sewer. And the hydraulic technology displayed on the East Bastion is quite amazing: the channel bordering the stairs is constructed so that it breaks and governs the flow of water.

Still another distinguishing feature of these palaces is the method of lighting. Building on several storeys as they did, the Minoans solved their interior lighting problems by leaving open courts and shafts so that the daylight could illuminate the lower quarters. The stairways, too, are remarkable. Some were narrow, some on a grand scale, but all suggest a kind of modern sensibility at work. The amazing thing about all these technical accomplishments is that the Minoans combined them with artistic refinements. There are drain-pipes – and the frescoes; a network of roads – and the Snake Goddess.

Is it any wonder, then, that such a complex structure gained the reputation of being a labyrinth? Think of the effect such a place must have had on visiting merchants or passing travellers (and possibly the odd captured enemy). And perhaps more to the point, there is a pre-Hellenic word *labyrs*, meaning 'double axe', and a pre-Hellenic ending -*nthos* (a survival familiar from such sites as Corinth): Knossos was literally the labyrinth, 'the house of the double axe'.

DESCRIPTION OF SITE

In the 'guided tour' that follows, the main rooms and features of the palace are keyed to the plans on pp. 160–2. These show the basic lay-out of the restored levels and the restored upper storey known as the Piano Nobile. Owing to the several overlapping levels of the palace, the visitor will be constantly moving from one level to another: our directions should provide the thread that makes this as little confusing as possible. This reminds us, by the way, of another distinctive feature of Knossos: a Minoan viewing the palace from the valley of the Kairatos, just below to the east, would have looked up at a four- or five-storey structure (including those storeys built into the hill's slope).

Entrance and South Wing
(*see plan on pp.* 160–1)
You approach the palace from the official entry by a path that leads to a bronze bust of Sir Arthur Evans (1) on the edge of the West Court (2). Off to the left are three large walled pits (3): whatever their original function – as granaries or for storage – they were used by later Minoans for waste disposal. A paved causeway runs diagonally, to the left, across the court, but you proceed straight ahead on the causeway that leads to the west façade; there, just to the left, is an altar and behind that are charred traces of the fire that presumably destroyed the palace by the West Porch (4): the base of its single column is to be seen (and it was originally decorated with frescoes). Proceeding past its guard-room (to the right), you go along the Corridor of the Procession (5), once lined with frescoes. At the far end you come to a small flight of stairs down, but you turn left (through a break in the wall), then right through a restored doorway, and then left through a

restored double doorway, and continue on to a southern wing of the palace, just alongside the Great (or South) Propyleum (**6**). Before turning left into the Great Propyleum, you might proceed on to the sacred horns on the edge and look down and to the left on what was the South Entrance (**7**): this once connected to the road that led across a bridge and viaduct, past the Caravanserai and Spring Chamber (p. 170), and on across the island to the south coast – the main route to Phaestos and points south of Crete. And if you look left across some low-lying walls on your present level, you will see the Corridor of the Priest King (or Lily Prince) (**8**), which leads into the Central Court (**9**). However, we shall be examining these sections later, so you now turn back to the Great Propyleum (**6**) and proceed through it (noting the reconstructions of the frescoes found there) and ascend the broad open staircase (**10**) leading to the Piano Nobile, the level with the state chambers.

Knossos: Principal Remains

1 Bust of Sir Arthur Evans
2 West Court
3 Walled Pits
4 West Porch
5 Corridor of the Procession
6 Great (South) Propyleum
7 South Entrance
8 Corridor of the Priest King (Lily Prince)
9 Central Court
10 Staircase to Piano Nobile
10–18 See Knossos: Piano Nobile (p. 162)
18 Stairs from Piano Nobile
19 Corridor of the Magazines
20 Stirrup Jars Room
21 North-West Portico
22 Lustral Area
23 Theatral Area
24 Royal Road
25 Propyleum
26 Pillar Hall
27 Northern Entrance
28 Ramp
29 Antechamber
30 Throne Room
31 Staircase
32 Columnar, or Tripartite, Shrine
33 Lobby of the Stone Seat
34 Room of the Tall Pithos
35 Temple Repositories
36 Pillar Crypts
37 Site of the Greek Temple
38 Grand Staircase
39 Hall of the Colonnades
40 King's Room (Hall of the Double Axes)
41 Queen's Megaron
42 Bathroom
43 Queen's Toilet Room
44 Treasury (closed)
45 Eastern Portico
46 Potter's Workshop
47 Court of the Stone Spout
48 Giant Pithoi
49 East Bastion
50 Corridor of the Draughtsboard
51 North-East Hall
52 Workshops
53 Royal Pottery Stores
54 Magazine of Medallion Pithoi
55 Corridor of the Bays
56 Bathroom
57 Room with jars
58 Shrine of Double Axes
59 Lustral Basin

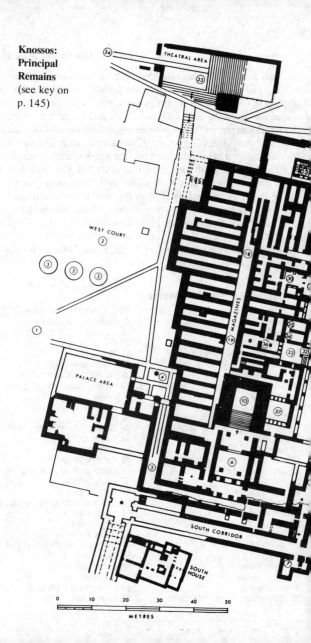

**Knossos:
Principal
Remains**
(see key on
p. 145)

THEATRAL AREA

WEST COURT

PALACE AREA

MAGAZINES

SOUTH CORRIDOR

SOUTH
HOUSE

0   10   20   30   40   50
METRES

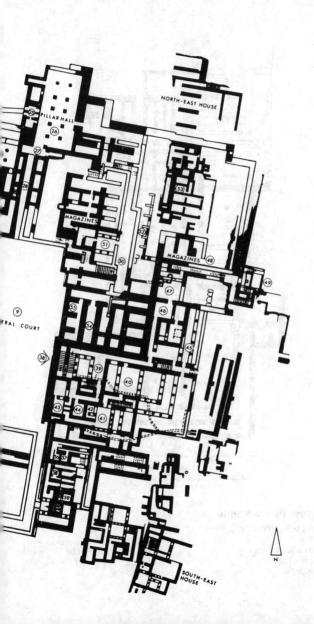

NORTH-EAST HOUSE

PILLAR HALL

㉕

㉖

㉗

㉘

MAGAZINES

㊾

㊸

㊼

㊻

㊺

MAGAZINES

㊳

㊴

㊵

㊶

㊷

㊹

㊼

㉝

㉞

㊽

⑨
CENTRAL COURT

㊳

㊴

㊵

㊸

㊹

㊶

㊷

㊺

㊻

㊾

㊿

SOUTH-EAST
HOUSE

N

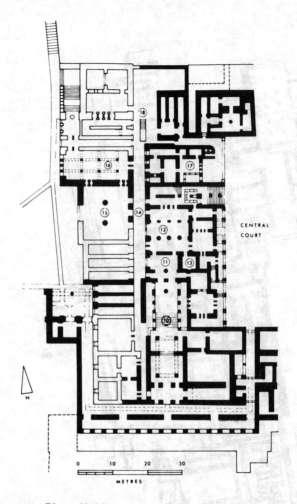

CENTRAL
COURT

N

| 0 | 10 | 20 | 30 |

METRES

Knossos: Piano Nobile

10 Stairs from Grand Propyleum
11 Lobby
12 Tricolumnar Shrine
13 Temple Treasury
14 Corridor

15 Great Hall
16 Sanctuary Hall
17 Reconstructed terrace and rooms
18 Stairs to Corridor of the
   Magazines

Piano Nobile
(see p. 162)
At the top of the stairs, you pass through a lobby, or anteroom (11) into the Tricolumnar Shrine (12), to the right of which was the Temple Treasury (13). A long corridor (14) originally ran down through the centre of the Piano Nobile, but only part of it has been restored; you enter that from the north, or far left, corner of the Tricolumnar Shrine. Off to the left of the corridor was the Great Hall (15), with the bases of its two columns to be seen.

At this point you are advised to stand along the edge of this restored cement floor and look down over the Corridor of the Magazines (19) and the adjacent storerooms on the main floor. That area was once accessible to visitors, but the surge of numbers in recent years has put it offbounds. From above, however, you get a good sense of the extent of these storerooms. But you must remember that they were actually roofed over and did not have much natural light; thus there were undoubtedly torches or oil lamps about, and whatever the original cause of the destruction of the palace, the oil stored here must have turned the storerooms into an inferno. If you look closely you can even see some of the charred gypsum slabs where the boiling oil ran. You can also see some of the sunken chests in the narrow storeroom floors, cists that presumably held especially valuable goods; the larger jars, or *píthoi*, several of which are still in place, held wine or oil.

Moving back along the corridor (14) you come, on the left, to the Sanctuary Hall (16), with traces of its six columns. Opposite, you make your way across a low-walled area and pass into the completely enclosed room (17) that Evans reconstructed over the Throne Room complex (29, 30 on main plan): in this upper room are reproductions of some of the noted frescoes found at Knossos. You should proceed straight through this room and out on to an open porch that provides a fine overview of the Central Court and palace. Then go back out of the room as you entered it, but immediately turn right and step across the low-walled area to its far corner; there proceed (carefully) down the narrow flight of concrete stairs (18) that bring you down on to the north end of the Corridor of the Magazines (19 on the main plan, pp. 160–1).

Ground Floor, West Wing
(see plan on pp. 160–1)
You proceed north along the corridor; the narrow, rather un-

distinguished room immediately on your right is where tablets inscribed in the early pictographic script were found. Upon reaching an open dirt area, you turn right, take a few steps, then turn right again on to a paved walk; you proceed south along that, then turn left along the paved corridor. When you have come to a door covered by a metal grille on your right, you turn left and go north along a downward sloping path. On the right are several rooms that in the New Palace may have formed some kind of shrine; in one of them (**20**), were found some stirrup jars and Linear B tablets that have since become the focus of the controversy over the dating of the end of the palace (p. 155). Beneath these shrine rooms are visible (under metal grilles) six small, deep rooms from the Old Palace: Evans called this a keep, or dungeon, but it has since been decided they were granaries. Proceeding down the sloping path, you turn right on to cement steps. Descend them and then turn left and pass through the double doorway of the North-West Portico (**21**). Outside this, and off to the left, is the reconstructed Lustral Area (**22**), used for ceremonial and purificatory bathing. At this point, you leave the palace proper and step over some metres to the left, or west, to arrive at the edge of the so-called Theatral Area (**23**).

Theatral Area and Royal Road

Originally this was a flat paved area, but eventually the Minoans added stairs on the southern side and then on the eastern side. It has been suggested that this was a 'theatre' used for dances or ceremonies, but of course there is no tangible evidence for this. Leading straight away to the west is the 'royal road' (**24**), often called 'the oldest road in Europe' which once joined the major Minoan road to the Little Palace (p. 170) and to the north coast. This road has been quite thoroughly excavated by the British only since the 1960s, and now it lies there, still well paved and drained; it is a unique experience to walk some 130 metres down this road, seeing the remains of houses, workshops and other structures along the side (most of the walls, of course, are modern, added to hold back the earth). Among the more suggestive of the recent finds are Minoan structures that appear to be grandstands for viewing events on the Royal Road.

North Quarter

You now return to the palace, walking below its north side; you descend a dirt path with the North-West Portico above to the right, and enter the Palace through the remains of the Propyleum (**25**) and pass into the Pillar Hall (**26**) (also known as the 'customs house'), with its large square pillars. Proceeding into the palace by the Northern Entrance (**27**), you go on up a ramp (**28**): originally this was walled, but later the Minoans added the present bastions and the colonnaded porticoes above – of which the one to the right has been restored. Proceeding up the ramp a bit, you come to a staircase (on your right) that leads up to the second storey of this portico, where you can examine the reproduction of the bull relief-fresco that was found here. Back on the ramp, you proceed up the small stairway that takes you on to the Central Court (**9**).

Central Court

Built on almost an exact north–south axis, this great court is 55 by 28 metres. The original Neolithic site of Knossos lies under this court; trial soundings and limited digs have revealed many Neolithic remains (including a 'cemetery' of seven children); the earlier buildings were simply levelled and covered over by the palace builders. In general, as you face south down the court, the official and ceremonial rooms are to the west, or right, while the private and domestic quarters lie to the east, or left.

West Wing

You now cut across to the right (noting the drainage system exposed under the metal grilles) to approach the Throne Room (**30**). First you descend a few steps into an antechamber (**29**), with stone wall benches, and a great stone basin on the floor (and a wooden reproduction of the throne). Until the late 1960s you could enter the Throne Room itself and actually sit on the original gypsum throne, perhaps the oldest such object in the world that the average tourist could so enjoy: now, though, the great numbers of visitors have required that this room be closed, so that you must be content with looking at the room. Its wall paintings reproduce some frescoes found in the room (although not on that wall); across from the throne is a sunken lustral area – again, for purificatory, not functional, bathing. (At the far left corner of the Throne Room are two small rooms; one is a small shrine, and the other is known as the 'kitchen'.) Leaving the antechamber, you step back out on to the Central Court and turn right, passing a broad flight of stairs (**31**) that lead up to the Piano Nobile (and still another flight up to obtain a good view of the palace). You proceed along the edge of the Court past the foundations of the columnar or tripartite shrine (**32**) and then descend a few steps into a small open court, the Lobby of the Stone Seat (**33**). (This whole area is now protected by a plastic roof.) Off to the right of this is a small room with a tall *píthos* (**34**); beyond that are the Temple Repositories (**35**), in which were stored the treasuries and offerings for the shrine: in one of the crypts here were found the Snake Goddess and attendant statuettes in the Iraklion Museum (*case* 50). Back on the Lobby of the Stone Seat, on the right, or west side, are two rooms (**36**): each has a pillar in the centre, and if they weren't now closed to the public, you could make out the signs of the double axes scratched on these, indicating that these pillar crypts had some sacred character. Coming back out on to the Lobby of the Stone Seat again, you leave to the right by the double doors and proceed south, ascending a few stairs on to an open space (**37**) where was found remains of what is now believed to have been a Greek temple – the only such late structure found directly in the palace site itself. You leave this area at the far left and step out on to the extreme south-west corner of the Central Court. Proceeding along the southern edge, you pass the other end of the Corridor of the Procession (**5**): you may step down and examine, on the left, the reproduction of the relief-fresco of the Priest King (or Lily Prince) (**8**) that was on the original wall of the corridor here. You then cut across the Court to about the middle of its east side, to meet the Grand Staircase (**38**), leading down to your right (and now protected by a plastic roof).

East Wing: Domestic Quarters

This Grand Staircase is considered one of the major architectural achievements of antiquity, with its several flights, and a superb setting for ceremonial processions. You descend to the first landing, the Hall of the Royal Guard (also known as the Upper Hall of the Colonnades) with its reproductions of the great Minoan shields. As you reach this landing, you proceed directly around to your left and descend down an enclosed flight of stairs to come out on to the Hall of the Colonnades (**39**), with its typical light-shaft to the right. You leave this hall by proceeding along the side you entered it and through the passageway; you proceed about 4·5 metres along the east-west corridor, then turn right into the King's Room (**40**), also known as the Hall of the Double Axes (from the many masons' marks on the wall blocks, to your right). Against the wall, beneath the glass case, are the remains of the plaster that fell on to a wooden throne that stood there – suggesting that the King held court here. Off to the left is a second large room, which once had partitions that could be closed separately and now contains a reproduction of the throne in the adjacent room. Outside this is a columned arcade; this whole area is now closed to the public. You leave the King's Room by the door opposite the one you entered, and walk along an enclosed dog's-leg corridor into the Queen's Megaron (**41**), with its reproduction of the Dolphin Fresco. To the right, as you enter, is a small room with a tub, the bathroom (**42**). You leave the Queen's Megaron by the door to the right and pass along an enclosed corridor that leads into the Queen's Toilet Room (**43**); around to the right are the remains of the famous 'flush' toilet, and you can see other signs of the drainage system on the floor. Following the only exit passage of this room, you pass a closed room, to the right (**44**), where many inscribed tablets were found; you then wind back into the Hall of the Colonnades (**39**). You leave this by the door in the north-east corner, as you did earlier, but proceed straight along the east-west corridor to its end and then turn left to go outdoors and enter the north-east wing.

North-East Wing: Palace Workshops

Heading north along this short passageway, you at once pass, on your right, some small workshops; the second one, with a metal gate, is known as the Lapidary's Workshop. (And off to the right, or east, are the remains of the Eastern Portico (**45**).) You proceed straight out into the Potter's Workshop (**46**), once known as the Schoolroom, with its benches and receptacles. Proceeding straight on through this, you enter the Court of the Stone Spout (**47**), so named from the spout (upper left wall) that drained water from the upper storey. You proceed straight ahead and on to the stairs; here you find yourself facing the enclosed magazines with the giant *píthoi* (**48**). You descend the stairs to the East Bastion (**49**): you are advised to go as far as possible to examine the ingenious system of checking the water's flow, built into the side of the reconstructed stairs. (Evans suggested that the palace laundry was down here; he also suggested that the flat ground between the palace here and the Kairatos River below was the site of the arena where the famous bull-leaping ceremony was performed.) You now go back up the stairs from the East Bastion, on up past the magazine with the giant *píthoi* (**48**), to your right, and up to the very top, where you turn left up on to the flat paved area, the

Corridor of the Draughtsboard (**50**), so named for the gameboard found here (and now in *Case 57* in Iraklion's Museum). You will note the drain-pipes exposed beneath the metal grille: these survive from the first palace. If you stand at the top of the stairs where you entered the Corridor of the Draughtsboard and face north, you will see, to the left, the North-East Hall (**51**) and, on the right, below, a series of openings (**52**), which may have been workshops; beyond these, to the north-east, were the Royal Pottery Stores (**53**). You now turn around and walk straight ahead, or south, and face three sections. The one straight ahead is an open court, in which is a rain-water conduit that leads down to the Court of the Stone Spout (**47**). To the right of this, enclosed, is the narrow Magazine of the Medallion Pithoi (**54**), so named from the decorations on the giant jars – still in place. The section to the far right of this is the Corridor of the Bays (**55**) (not always sign-posted), and you enter this; note the massive piers that probably supported the Great East Hall above (and in which, it has been suggested, may have stood a giant statue of the Minoan goddess). You proceed southwards along the Corridor of the Bays and enter the Hall of the Royal Guard again. (This is the landing of the Grand Staircase with the Minoan shields.)

South-East Wing

After entering the Hall of the Royal Guard, you immediately turn left, and then turn right and proceed out past the reproductions of the shields into an exposed area. As soon as you are outside, turn right and proceed ahead (with the Upper Queen's Room to your left) and meet the Room with Stone Seat in the royal apartments. (These rooms may no longer be sign-posted.) You turn left here – noting the remains of the toilet in the south-western corner – and keeping this room on your right, you step down on to a roofed-over area. As you turn right on to this area, the first small room to the left (**56**) is a bathroom, with a fine bathtub preserved there; behind it, around the corner, is a small room (**57**) with three jars. Back at the corner of the bathroom, you turn right and proceed south under the roof, crossing over some remains of a stairway; you then turn right and step over a threshold to pass, on your right, the small enclosed Shrine of the Double Axes (**58**), built after the destruction of the great Palace. So many sacred objects were found in this small room (now protected by a concrete roof and a locked gate) – sacral horns, double-edged axes, a tripod altar, male and female figurines, etc. – that it has been suggested that priests had taken over this whole wing of the palace. You turn left on to the corridor, and passing the Lustral Basin at your left (59), you arrive at the south-east corner of the palace.

South Slopes and Exit

On adjacent slopes are various houses that might be investigated by those with some time to spare. They have been assigned names derived from special finds in each – House of the Fallen Blocks or House of the Sacrificed Oxen. The totally enclosed one, down to the left, is the House of the Chancel Screen, so named for the dais with balustrade that was found here. Down below this house, also enclosed, is the South-East House, with its Pillar Crypt and libation table. Adjacent to it is a furnace, perhaps used for metal-working. In any case, you now have two choices for leaving the palace. One is to turn right at the south-east corner of the palace and proceed up the earthen ramp to the edge of the Central Court, turn left there, and make your way over to the south-west corner and the Corridor of the Procession (5) where you entered the Palace. The other possibility is to proceed straight along and below the southern edge of the palace, passing the South Entrance (7) on your left, and making your way to the narrow flight of stairs, at the far corner (the impressive South House and Stepped Portico are accessible down the slope) that leads up to the Corridor of the Procession (5) and the way out; or you might make your way up the dirt path just past the flight of stairs and walk along the edge of some of the outlying remains of pre-palatial structures, to come up on to the edge of the West Court (2). At that point, those with still more time and interest may want to explore some of the structures that are located in the environs of the palace.

Palace Dependencies

(*see plan on p.* 171)

The remains of several subsidiary structures lie around the palace – to remind us that Knossos was more than just a palace. Another hour or two might well be spent in climbing about the gentle slopes; we shall attempt to call attention only to the more obvious ones, referring more serious students to the detailed guides mentioned on p. 153. However, the Little Palace, the Royal Villa and the Temple Tomb are behind locked gates and may be visited only with special permission; if you are serious, start your enquiry at the Archaeological Museum in Iraklion the day before (and plan to visit them at off-peak hours).

The Little Palace, Unexplored Mansion, and Roman House (**1**). This is off the main road from Iraklion to Knossos (p. 154), on the right, about 250 metres north-west from the palace; you leave the main road by a flight of steps over the bank and across a small bridge. The Little Palace is the second-largest building excavated at Knossos and is quite impressive in its own right. It dates from the time of the second palace, but its exact function is unknown. Behind (and south) of the Little Palace lie the remains of what Evans called 'the unexplored mansion'; the British archaeologists finally got around to excavating it in the late 1960s and 1970s. The mansion was begun about 1550 B.C., but rough interior additions suggest that 100 or so years later other people (Mycenaeans?) had small regard for the fine Minoan architecture. To get down to this Minoan mansion, the archaeologists had to remove material as late as the third century A.D.; they also revealed remains of a Roman house (about first century A.D.), with two unusual features – frescoes with geometric patterns and artificial marble effects, and a group of sculptured plaster heads of exceptional realism.

Royal Villa (**2**). This is situated below the main palace, about 100 metres away to the north-east; it is best approached from the East Bastion (**49** on plan on pp. 160–1).

The South House (**4**), *The Stepped Portico* (**5**), *the Piers of the Minoan Viaduct* (**7**), *the Caravanserai and Spring Chamber* (**8**). These lie below the southern side of the palace. Their names identify their functions, a caravanserai being a sort of reception house for travellers and caravans. The South House and Stepped Portico are only accessible from within the main palace grounds. The Caravanserai and Spring Chamber and piers are reached by leaving the palace and walking about 500 metres south on the modern road to a sign.

A few hundred metres farther along this road, below on the left (and sign-posted) are the scant remains of the *House of the High Priest*. In addition, about 1 km. farther south along the main road (towards Arkhanes) set into the hillside on the right of the road is the *Temple Tomb*, a two-storey structure, still quite impressive.

Many other houses, tombs and sacred structures have also been excavated in the immediate neighbourhood of the palace, and digging continues to turn up still more remains attesting to the extent of the Knossos complex – not only in Minoan times but in later periods.

There is still one more point of interest in the area. If you stay on the main road, past Knossos, and follow its curves for about 2 km.,

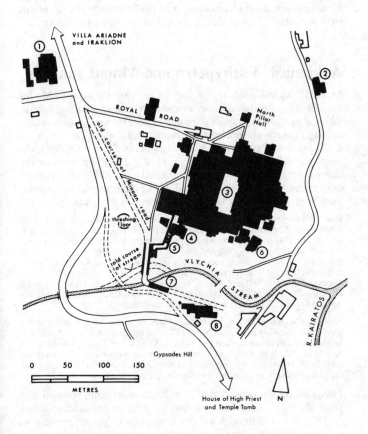

VILLA ARIADNE
and IRAKLION

ROYAL ROAD

old course of Minoan road

North
Pillar
Hall

threshing
floor

old course
of stream

VLYCHIA
STREAM

R. KAIRATOS

Gypsades Hill

| 0 | 50 | 100 | 150 |

METRES

N

House of High Priest
and Temple Tomb

Knossos: Environs

1 Little Palace, Unexplored Mansion,
  and Roman House
2 Royal Villa
3 Palace of Knossos
4 South House

5 Stepped Portico
6 South-East House
7 Piers of Minoan Viaduct
8 Caravanserai and Spring Chamber

you come to the head of the valley of Spilia. Arching across the gorge is an *aqueduct*, dating from about A.D. 1838; although the Egyptians were in control of Crete then, it is credited to a Cretan architect.

Arkhanes, Vathypetro and Mount Iouktas

Most visitors will probably be content to enjoy the peak of Mount Iouktas from a distance; from almost anywhere around Iraklion, in fact, the monstrous recumbent profile of Zeus is visible, and it is easy to imagine that a god lies buried beneath those slopes. (This god-who-died should not be confused with the immortal Zeus of Olympia; the name was taken over, but the concept of a dying god predates the classical version.) For those willing to make the trip, however, there are various 'fringe benefits', including the important newer excavations in and around Arkhanes – not to mention the landscape.

Route Mount Iouktas is best approached from Arkhanes, which is reached by following the Knossos road (Route Exit B) out of Iraklion (p. 141); continuing past Knossos (p. 154) to a point at 9 km., you turn right for Patsides and Arkhanes [13 km.]; all the excursions described below start from Arkhanes.

Bus There is a regular hourly bus service from the harbour and Kallergon Square, just across from the Venetian Loggia in Iraklion.

Accommodation Apart from rooms to let in the town, there has been one Class B hotel, the *Dias* (tel. 751.810), 1 km. south of the town centre and open at least from April to October. (Enquire if this hotel is still operating.)

Note Since several of the sites and goals of this excursion are now enclosed and locked, you should enquire at the National Tourist Information office in Iraklion as to where you can obtain the keys and/or guide. Usually both keys and guides are to be had in Arkhanes itself, but there is always the possibility of a change in procedures. Meanwhile, if you are not that interested in the details but simply enjoy the general settings, you can visit these locales and get some sense of them.

Following the Knossos road southwards from Iraklion, you pass that great site (p. 154) and move on into the hills, past the old aqueduct (p. 172), and wind through a region famous for its grapes: growing on the fields and slopes here is the fine table-grape, the *rosakí*.

[9 km.] Turn right for Arkhanes (via Patsides: sign-posted). It was at this junction, by the way, that the British and Cretans flagged down the car carrying the German commandant in 1944 and then abducted him (p. 102).

[12 km.] **Kato Arkhanes.**

[13 km.] **Arkhanes.**

A relatively large and prosperous town, Arkhanes until the late 1960s had been known mainly as the centre of a rich agricultural and grape-growing region. The modern town could boast few attractions for the tourist. There is, to be sure, the handsome white *Church of the Panayia* (with its fine collection of icons) and an unusual clock tower as you drive into town; following the signs down the one-way street, you could visit the little *Church of Ayia Triadha* on the edge of town, in which a few fragmentary Byzantine frescoes have survived. And the citizens of Arkhanes could boast of a long history of resistance to the Turks. But undeniably it is the Minoan remains that now promise to put Arkhanes on the list of travellers' goals on Crete.

Evans and other archaeologists had long ago indicated that there were Minoan remains in and around the town, but it was not until 1964 that systematic excavations began. These immediately produced some remarkable and valuable finds, and this has continued to be the case since. Archaeology is not supposed to measure its value by headlines, but the finds of Ioannis and Efi Sakellarakis, the husband and wife archaeologists, have generated considerable excitement – and controversy. As of publication there are three main sites in and near Arkhanes (see map, p. 177) that will reward those whose interest in Minoan archaeology goes beyond the more obvious finds.

'The Palace'

To visit this structure, you drive into town to where the road splits into two one-way streets; it is easiest to park as close to this point as possible and then walk the last 100 metres or so to the site. Take the street to the left (i.e., against the one-way traffic), then turn up the first street to the left; where the road splits, take the turn to the left and proceed right around the corner; turn immediately right into the street (there has been a sign, 'To the Palace'), at the end of which is the excavation. The site is locked, but the walls are clearly visible through the gates.

Evans, as mentioned, had discovered traces of Minoan remains at this locale, but it was the Sakellarakises who in 1964 confirmed that a major archaeological site was awaiting excavation. Serious excavations began in 1979 and seem to have many more years to go, as each year's dig reveals more extensive and ambitious remains stretching from the Minoan through Byzantine and the Turkish-occupation years. (Because this area was built up in that latter period, the site is sometimes referred to in the literature as 'Turkogeitonia' – to distinguish it from the Phourni site in Arkhanes.) Already a palatial building (dating from at least as far back as 1600 B.C.) has begun to emerge; it had painted walls, frescoes, and polychrome reliefs suggesting a certain prosperity. Much pottery, fragments of stone lamps, bronze objects, ivories, tripod altars and such finds confirm the sense of a typical Minoan palace. More unusual, however, is the large rectangular altar found in the open space before the palatial building; clearly designed for liquid offerings, it is the first such altar found intact at a Minoan site. There are plans to reconstruct parts of the two-storey complex (as at Knossos) because of the state of preservation of some of the elements. The portable artefacts and wall paintings will eventually be displayed in Iraklion's Archaeological Museum. The excavators look ahead eventually to revealing a site that will reward both specialists and travellers.

Phourni

Phourni is the name of a hill about 1 km. north-west of Arkhanes and overlooking the fields and food-processing structures at the edge of town. Excavating here since 1965, the Sakellarakis team has revealed over a score of structures and many lesser tombs dating from at least 2500 to 1250 B.C. and establishing this site as the richest and most extensive cemetery in the entire prehistoric Aegean.

You reach Phourni by turning right (there should be a sign-post) as you reach the first built-up part of Arkhanes. You drive down a (rough) road about 500 metres and cross a small bridge; you can park your vehicle here and proceed up the rest of the road on foot, as it is unlikely that you will want to subject your vehicle to the rocks; in either case, you continue up another 500 metres until the road gives out. There you see what is little more than a steep, stony gully leading up the edge of the hill; you make your way up this until you come along the fenced site; the locked entrance is on the east side (facing the main road).

As you enter, to your left will be a circular tomb, *Tholos E*, from the Pre-palatial Period (about 2500–2000 B.C.); in it and the attached rooms were found 31 sarcophagi and 2 *pithoi* burials, and among the other valuable finds, 6 early Minoan sealstones. Down the slope slightly south from this is a small circular tomb, *Tholos D*, from the Mycenaean period (about 1300 B.C.); women were buried here, and the finds included some fine jewellery. In other smaller graves in this area, dating from the Old Palace period (about 2000–1700 B.C.), were found ceramics in the lovely Kamares style.

Now, proceeding back up and along the crest (north) – a right turn as you enter – you come to Tholos Tombs C and B, which, along with their many attached rooms, form the most ambitious complex yet found at Phourni. *Tholos C*, the tomb projecting to the south, is thought to have been the burial place of a group of people of the Pre-palatial Period who identified with the Cycladic culture: Cycladic female idols and obsidian objects were found buried below the sarcophagi and *píthoi* that contained some 47 bodies. *Tholos B*, to the north, is part of a two-storeyed mortuary temple: you can enter by the doorway and note, around to the left, the *dromos*, or road, that had been the original entrance. On the ground behind was the ossuary, with three narrow rooms: it was filled with nearly two hundred human skulls, along with vases, bronze objects, sea-shells, and some carved sealstones. If any further testimony were needed, the sheer quantity of such finds in one relatively small locale attests to the populous and flourishing settlement here at Arkhanes.

Proceeding still farther north along the edge of the slope, and passing various remains, you come to *Tholos A*, a domed tomb dated to about 1400 B.C. Its 20-metre-long *dromos* and its 'beehive' interior inevitably evoke the great tombs at Mycenae. Although the main chamber was plundered in antiquity, the small side-chamber was left untouched, and in 1965 it yielded the first intact 'royal burial' of Minoan Crete. There was a sarcophagus containing a woman who, judging from the richness of the ornaments and other articles around her, was not only wealthy and royal but possibly of some status as a priestess. There were more than 140 pieces of gold jewellery, pottery, fine bronze vessels, ivory pieces, and necklaces of glass paste (now to be seen in Iraklion's museum). Among those many finds, some stand out as especially significant: gold signet-rings that confirm previous reconstructions of Minoan-Mycenaean religion; two iron beads that were probably rarer than gold at that time; the skull of a bull and a horse's skeleton, evidently sacrificed in honour of this highly regarded woman.

North of Tholos A is a grave complex with seven rectangular shafts and elsewhere along this hillside are other tombs and structures – some probably yet to be discovered after this is written. The Sakellarakis team continues to excavate here each year and turn up revealing finds almost every year. Altogether this site forms a virtual museum of the history of tombs during more than 1,000 years of Aegean pre-history.

The Temple (of Human Sacrifice)
(*near Anemospilia*)
This is the site that created considerable controversy among the Greek archaeological establishment when the Sakellarakis team discovered it in 1979. The remains themselves are nothing spectacular – a relatively small, low-walled structure. Furthermore, they are locked inside an enclosure so that without the key and a guide you cannot get within 50 metres. But the site enjoys such a dramatic panoramic view to the north and provides such a sense of exhilaration that the sensitive traveller will gain some insights into the very nature of the Minoan spirit.

You reach the site by following the map (p. 177) down the one-way street and winding on to the open area. Here you turn a sharp right and proceed to the point where the asphalt road bears left (and a dirt road goes straight on): you will have travelled about 1 km. from the one-way division and you have another 3 km. to go to the temple. Following the asphalt road you climb and wind until after about 1 km. you pass the town dump, on the slopes to the right; after this, the road becomes adequately hardpacked dirt. You continue winding, and off to your right you will see a low hill with an outcrop of rock filled with hollows and caves believed to have been carved by the wind: thus the name for this area, Anemospilia, 'caves of the wind'. You climb up a small pass and continue around a bend on what is actually the northernmost slope of Mt Iouktas. At the very 'prow' of this spur, and to the left of the road, lie the remains of the temple.

The temple was discovered when a field trip tracing the ancient Minoan road produced an unusual collection of surface finds at this site. Excavation quickly revealed the outlines and walls of a structure: a central *portico* on the north that led into an east-west corridor extending across the front and giving entry by three separate door-ways into three equal-sized rooms. Soon came a number of finds that suggested this was a very special and sacred structure – many vases (eventually almost 400), a sacred pillar in a pit, a tray with the bones of an animal, etc. In the *corridor* was found the skeleton of a human evidently crushed by falling stones during an earthquake – and

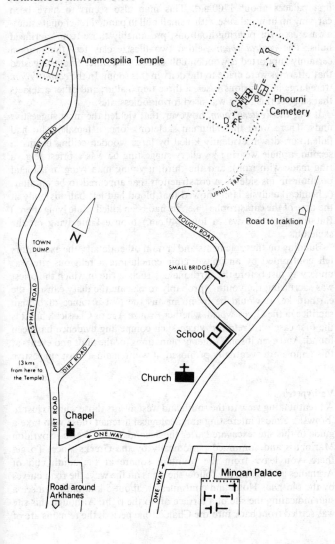

Arkhanes: Minoan Sites

Anemospilia Temple

Phourni Cemetery

A

B
C
D
E

DIRT ROAD

TOWN
DUMP

N

UPHILL TRAIL

ROUGH ROAD

Road to Iraklion

SMALL BRIDGE

ASPHALT ROAD

(3 kms
from here to
the Temple)

DIRT ROAD

DIRT ROAD

School

Church

Chapel

← ONE WAY

Minoan Palace

ONE WAY

Road around
Arkhanes

various finds linked this with the one that may have so damaged the first palaces about 1700 B.C. This man also seems to have been carrying an unusual vase with a small bull in painted relief on its side – a vase used for pouring libations, presumably those from sacrificed bulls. The *central room* yielded two lifesize clay feet that almost certainly supported a wooden cult statue, and other finds suggested that offerings were made to the deity in this room. In the *eastern room* were large jars, various vases, a three-tiered altar, and other artefacts that suggest this room was used for bloodless rites.

It was the *western room*, however, that yielded the most suggestive finds. There were three human skeletons: one, a female, who had fallen face down, evidently killed by large wooden ceiling beams; a second, a male wearing jewellery suggesting he was a priest (e.g., a ring made with iron); and the third, a young man lying in a foetal position on his side on a construction that appeared to be an altar. (Chemical analysis later showed that blood had left half his body at the time of the catastrophe – i.e., he had been killed while lying there.) But the final clue was a long (40 cm.) bronze knife lying on the skeleton.

Building on these elements and certain other details, the excavators felt confronted by an unavoidable conclusion: a religious rite was underway just before the earthquake struck, a rite in which the priest was sacrificing the youth – probably to placate the deity causing the earthquake. It would be by no means the first instance of human sacrifice in the Greek world, whether Bronze Age or Classical, but it is the first case on Crete for which such compelling evidence has been found. And even if some other explanations for the finds and events at this temple are eventually proposed, it will remain a most suggestive site.

Vathypetro

A breathtaking view to the south and west awaits those who go just to 'browse', a most interesting archaeological artefact those who take a guide to this site, excavated after the Second World War by Spyridon Marinatos and continued periodically by the Greeks since. To get there, you leave from the fountain square at the south end of Arkhanes and essentially follow the signs all the way: the road curves by the old Dias Hotel and continues on about 5 km. until you see a sign indicating the site of a terrace off to the right. Although this site was settled from back into the Chalcolithic period, the remains are of a manor-house built and then abandoned within the first half of the sixteenth century B.C.: a central court, a three-part sacred chamber, a main hall with columned façades, terraces, etc. But it was the basement workrooms that contained the most interesting objects, and to get in to see these, under their modern protective structure, you must be accompanied by a guide: along with the usual large *píthoi* were found a large oil-press, parts of a weaving apparatus and an almost completely preserved wine-press (of the kind later found at Kato Zakros), all of which remain in the (locked) rooms at the site.

Mount Iouktas

If you intend to make the ascent on foot – it requires a not too strenuous hour – you may want to engage a guide in Arkhanes. But there is a road along which a car can drive up to the peak: it follows the Vathypetro route (described above) – south from Fountain Square for about 3 km., where a sign indicates a turn to the right; from there it is another 3 km. up a relatively good dirt track. If you have any intention of locating the caves – for there are two candidates – said to be the burial-place of Zeus, you will need a guide; otherwise you may be content to enjoy the view – Arkhanes directly below, Iraklion in the distance, the vine-covered countryside between. Quite aside from Zeus, the caves yielded remains that indicate they were used as early as Neolithic times and well into the Neo-palatial Period. There was also a sanctuary on the summit in Minoan times. (Evans was the first to explore this site, but the Greeks returned in the 1970s and continue to make numerous finds including large offering tables – now in the Archaeological Museum, Room II, *Case* 21a, an onyx vase inscribed with eighteen Linear A signs, hundreds of votive offerings, and quite extensive remains.) The Orthodox, not to be outdone, have built a chapel to The Lord of the Transfiguration here, and the modern world has constructed *its* shrine on another peak – a radio transmitter. On August 6th, the whole town of Arkhanes turns out on foot and by car to celebrate the Feast of the Transfiguration on Iouktas.

Church of Archangel Michael at Asomatos

One last sight for those who have come this far is the early fourteenth-century frescoes commissioned by one Michael Patsidiotis in the tiny chapel of his patron saint; to get in to see them, you must obtain the key in Arkhanes (in recent years, from the Café Miriofito, in the square with the fountain at the south end of town). You leave from the fountain square by the same route described above, but about $\frac{1}{2}$ km. beyond the Hotel Dias, a sign (ASOMATOS) indicates the turn-off to the left; after about 50 metres, you bear sharp right and climb up and along a rough road for about 1 km., when a sign indicates that you bear left; continuing about another 1 km., you arrive at the chapel, below the road to your left, all but overgrown with the vines and trees. The frescoes are fine examples of the Cretan school and include a striking *Crucifixion*.

Fodhele

People who come to Crete mainly to see the home of the Minoans are sometimes surprised to be offered this excursion – to the birthplace of Domenico Theotokopoulos, known as El Greco. Beyond that, Fodhele is a village in an attractive setting, and the trip there has several other modest pleasures.

Route The best way now is to take the new road west of Iraklion, after leaving by Route Exit A, and follow it for 17 km. to a turn-off for Ayia Pelayia, where a detour may be made [4 km.] to this beach (see below); continuing on the new road for a further 5 km. you reach a turn-off for Fodhele.

Bus There is a regular twice daily bus service from Iraklion to Fodhele, from the Khania Gate.

Leaving Iraklion by the new Rethymnon–Khania road, drive along the coastal plain, with the cone of Mt Stroumboulas in the distance, then follow the coast north-westwards with splendid views back over the Gulf of Iraklion on your right.

[17 km.] A left turn-off leads around and under the new road, and after 4 km., to **Ayia Pelayia**, a locale down on the water that takes its name from the church near here. The beach is especially fine, and it may be possible to get a boat to take you here direct from Iraklion. A most ambitious tourist village (*Capsis Beach*, Class A) now dominates the promontory and has certainly changed what was a sleepy fishing settlement. Meanwhile, excavations in the early 1970s have produced both Minoan deposits and Hellenistic remains: Alexiou, the Cretan archaeologist, has identified the Hellenistic site as the Panormos cited by ancients.

Hotels Class A: *Capsis Beach* (tel. 233.395).
          Peninsula (tel. 289.404).
    Class B: *Panorama* (tel. 285.632).

[22 km.] Turn off the new road to Fodhele. A fine sandy beach lies to the right of the road here, while to the left the road leads in 3 km. to the village of Fodhele (see below).

The other possibility, though almost entirely on rough and very mountainous tracks, is to take the old road to Rethymnon from Iraklion, turning right at 7 km. for Rogdhia, then continuing through Akhlada to Fodhele [35 km.]. You can then continue through Fodhele and climb to rejoin the old road back to Iraklion just before the village of Marathos.

At 10 km., as you climb, you find yourself looking down a fairly sheer drop to the right where lies a dark pond about 20 hectares in area. This is the *Almyros of Malevizi*, the 'salt pond', one of the three such brackish pools along Crete's north coast; as usual, the natives claim that it is bottomless. At 17 km. is **Rogdhia**, the village that is seen from Iraklion as a glimmer of white in the day and a sparkle of light at night. It is worth stopping a few minutes at least to look at the façade of a Venetian *palazzo* near the church. A more ambitious excursion would be across the hills [5 kms.] to the *Convent of Savathiana*, where some 20 nuns still live and work. The nuns are known for their fine handwork (for sale). The convent has two churches, and one – Ayios Antonius – has icons worth viewing.

At 25 km. is **Akhlada**, a lovely village with its white *church* and *bell tower*. From here the road descends in bends to the sea, until it meets up with the new national highway and passes inland through orange and lemon groves, reaching Fodhele in another 10 kms.

[25 km.] Fodhele.

Today's residents of Fodhele probably prize it most for its orange groves and mild climate. There is a modest monument to El Greco, placed there in 1934 by the University of Valladolid in Spain, and a bust of the man in a small village park. For the non-sceptics there is a Venetian-style house that may be shown as his family's home; in the village chapel is a much-treasured album with photographs of his paintings and, on the walls, two or three not very professional reproductions of his work. Those who insist on seeing his *real* birthplace will be taken a bit out of the village to the ruins of an old house lying in a little gully; a plaque identifies it as the Theotokopou-los home, and imagination must do the rest. In the nearby orange groves is a lovely little domed cruciform Byzantine *Church of the Panayia*.

That El Greco (1541–1614) came from Crete is not disputed, for he often declared that he was a native of Candia, as the island and its capital was then known. But the actual place of his birth was not known until this century, when research established that references to a Theotokopoulos family living in Fodhele occurred in documents of the time; indeed, a family with a similar name still lives in the district. (The region near Gortyna later laid claim to being his birthplace but on such slender evidence that it has been discarded.) In any case, Fodhele has been designated as El Greco's native village.

Little is known of El Greco until he arrived in Rome in 1570. But he was referred to by a contemporary as 'a student of Titian', and it is accepted that he spent some years working in Venice, possibly under Titian. It has also been claimed that he studied at the School of Mt Sinai in Iraklion, that he learned wood-carving at Vrondisi Monastery and that he painted some of the frescoes at Valsamonero, but none of this is authenticated. He left Italy in the 1570s and settled in Toledo, Spain, and never returned to Crete. But El Greco carried the Byzantine style in his eye and the island landscape in his mind; he was never to free himself entirely from their influence on his technique and imagination.

In continuing on through Fodhele, you go south, passing (right) the abandoned *Monastery of Ayios Panteleimon* (where it has been claimed that El Greco studied). After 6 kms, mostly uphill, you rejoin the old Iraklion–Rethymnon road.

Lasithi Plain and Dhiktaion Cave

This excursion – which includes the birth-cave of Zeus and a plateau known as 'The Valley of the Windmills' as its destination – requires a full day, especially if some of the sites en route are taken in. The destination lies in Lasithi Nome and can also be reached from either Neapolis (p. 305) or Ayios Nikolaos (p. 306). Most people, however, will make it as a round trip from Iraklion, so that we describe the approach from there; those who are going on to the eastern sites might consider taking the alternative route off the Lasithi Plain towards Ayios Nikolaos.

Route Follow the road out of Iraklion (Route Exit C) described at the beginning of the route to Ayios Nikolaos (pp. 295–8); then turn right at 22 km.; proceed up into the hills via Potamies, Avdou, Gonies, Kera, Tzermiadhes, Ayios Constantinos and Avrakontes to arrive at Psykhro [67 km.], the jumping-off point for the Dhiktaion

Cave. From Psykhro you can either return to Iraklion by retracing the same route; or you can go on to Neapolis or Ayios Nikolaos: these latter possibilities involve going back only some 7 km. to the road at the Monastery of Panayia Kroustallenia (see below) and there turning right, winding up out of the plain and then down the long ascent, until at Drasi you have the choice of the left fork to Neapolis or the right fork to Ayios Nikolaos.

Bus There is a regular, thrice daily bus service from Iraklion to Psykhro and points en route; buses depart from the Megaron Phitakis station by the harbour. There is also a bus service from Ayios Nikolaos to Psykhro.

Accommodation Psykhro has one Class D hotel, the *Zeus*, and two Class E hotels, as well as various rooms to rent; the Monastery of Panayia Kroustallenia might provide a bed or two; Tzermiadhes has a Class E hotel and a Class B guest house, the *Kourites*; and Ayios Georgios has three hotels and several rooms to rent.

[22 km.] Having taken the road eastwards out of Iraklion, as for Ayios Nikolaos (pp. 295–8), you turn off to the right down a road sign-posted to Lasithi. It is a good asphalt road leading through olive groves as it slowly climbs into the mountains.

[30 km.] A right turn would take you in 10 km. to **Kastelli–Pedhiadhos** (p. 190), but you keep straight on for Lasithi.

[3 km.] Just before the village of **Potamies** itself, across a field to the left, stands the little Byzantine *Church of Christos*, with recently restored frescoes. (This – like the monastery church described next – is locked: enquire in Potamies village for the keys.) About 100 metres farther, a turn-off to the left leads up a hill to the *Monastery of Panayia Gouverniotisa*. Founded in the tenth century, this monastery had a distinguished history but is now deserted; its church has some fourteenth-century frescoes of some importance, especially a Christ Pantocrator on the dome.

[38 km.] The road goes through the village of **Avdou**. Those with an interest in these things might enquire about the *Church of Ayios Antonios*, with attractive fourteenth-century frescoes, including one of the Last Supper.

[40 km.] You pass through the village of **Gonies**, following the sign to Lasithi, and proceed to ascend more steep curves.

[43 km.] A turn-off to the left would take you to **Mokhos**, a village that has a road down to the coast near Mallia (p. 299) and is a favourite spot for excursionists seeking a typical Cretan mountain village. But you bear right (to Kera) and continue a still more dramatic ascent up the Lasithi Range.

[46 km.] The road passes around the edge of the village of **Krasi** (or **Krassion**). Those who have the time should take the turn-off to the left and go on up through the village 1 km. to see one of the most remarkable trees in the world: a gigantic plane tree that has been nourished by the endlessly gushing spring near by. You can sit under the tree and enjoy a glass of water while watching the people come and go at the fountains fed by the spring. Then move on past the fountains to rejoin the road to the Lasithi plateau.

[49 km.] Down to the right, just before you enter the built-up section of the village of **Kera**, sits the *Monastery of Panayia Kera* (also known as *Panayia Kardiotisis*). The frescoes in the church (many of which were only discovered under paint in the 1960s) and in the common room are quite notable and would be required viewing for anyone interested in Cretan-Byzantine frescoes. There are also several fine architectural details that make this well-preserved church worth stopping to see.

The monastery once possessed a famous twelfth-century icon of the Madonna of Perpetual Succour, and a small column in the churchyard is said to be connected with a story involving this painting. It was taken away three times to Constantinople, and each time it miraculously returned; after the third time, the Madonna brought with her a chain and the column to which she could be bound to prevent her being removed. However, something must have gone wrong because the icon was taken in 1498 to Italy and there it remains in the Church of St Alphonse in Rome. The present icon of the Virgin is a copy. The church celebrates the birthday of the Virgin on September 8th.

Back on the road, just opposite Kera, if you look up to the left you will see a distinctive peak, one that is called **Karfi** in Greek (meaning 'nail'). Rising some 1,100 metres above sea level, it is associated with an important post-Minoan settlement. Evans discovered it in his field-trips, but it remained for Pendlebury to excavate it just before the Second World War. The remains go back to Middle Minoan times, but it is the settlement dated to about 1200–1000 B.C. that has proved more suggestive. This post-Minoan settlement, located to the east on a saddle of the peak, is considered to be one of several isolated and secure refuges that grew in the aftermath of the Minoans' decline and the Dorians' rise. There is nothing much for the amateur to see (the important finds are displayed in Iraklion's Archaeological Museum) but there is a superb view to reward those who make the climb. You can start the ascent from a point about 1 km. after the village of Kera or from the windmill-pass (see below) or from Lagou, a village on the Lasithi Plain (p. 186), but it is a solid one-hour climb and not the kind of excursion one should undertake without some experience or preparations.

[52 km.] Proceeding on the road from Kera, and just when you think the road cannot go any higher or farther, you find yourself going through a pass, with old stone windmill towers banked along the steep ridges. Two have recently been put back in working order, and there has been a café-restaurant here. These mills ground grain and are worth pausing to examine. There is also a spectacular view to be enjoyed here – the Lasithi Plain spread out below like some enormous Olympic stadium, with the highest peak of the Lasithi Range, Dhikti (2,148 metres), ahead to the right. And if you look back to where you've come from, you see the Nome of Iraklion (and possibly Mt Idha).

Lasithi Plain

From 8 to 10 km. long and 4 to 6 km. wide, the plain appears almost symmetrical. After heavy spring rains or the thaw, the water may collect up to one metre in depth; this drains at the north-west entrance, forming a sizeable river as the water comes down on to the north coast. Thus the plateau is virtually an alluvial plain in that the run-off from the slopes has deposited a thick soil, making for some of the most productive land on Crete. Potatoes, apples and other fruit, and some grain are among the chief products. (The area is also noted for its wild orchids.) There are about twenty-one villages, tucked away in the foothills both to avoid the floods and to free the land for cultivation. Because of its peculiar situation, this whole area has always been somewhat independent, yet it has never completely cut itself off from the culture of the rest of the island. Ancient sites and remains have been found all over the plain and its slopes: caves, buildings, forts, temples, tombs, with shards and artefacts of all sorts – with the British taking the lead in exploring and excavating these places. The history runs from Neolithic times to the Roman period, and to describe all these sites would require a book in itself. The Venetians, determined to do away with such an enclave, removed the inhabitants and prohibited farming and pasturing on the plain from 1362 to the end of the fifteenth century; but eventually its fertility could not be denied. Some of the residents of the Lasithi today still claim descent from the northern Italians said to have been brought here by the Venetians.

What makes it a spectacle today is not just the lush, flat farmland. Wherever you look there are windmills. Yes, windmills – some very slight but others quite ambitious, and when they all have their white sails unfurled it is a unique sight. You cannot count on the sails being on display at all times: enquire at the Iraklion National Tourist office if you are intending to make a special excursion just to view them. A count taken some years ago is said to have revealed about 10,000 windmills here, but many of them no longer function; they have been used to pump water for irrigation, and petrol pumps are now preferred. It used to be said that a family's wealth here is measured by the number and size of their windmills – just like the Lapps with their reindeer.

[55 km.] The village of **Lagou**, from which the ascent to Karfi (p. 184) may be made.

[57 km.] Keeping to the left and the northern edge of the plain, you come to **Tzermiadhes** (also Tzermiadhon), the largest village on the plain. (It has a Class E hotel, the *Kri-Kri*, and a Class B guest house, the *Kourites*, tel. 22.194.) Travellers report a most pleasant reception in this village. A little to the north-east is the low plateau of Trapeza, where lies a famous cave. The *Cave of Trapeza* was discovered by Evans in 1896, but it was not until 1936 that the British got around to making thorough excavations. Many finds, including pottery, seal-stones, and figurines, were taken out of the cave, but they were so mixed up that it was hard to assign exact dates. It was claimed by the first excavators that the cave started out in Neolithic times as a habitation, then became a burial site, and finally a cult shrine in Minoan times; now the opinion seems to be that the cave was always and only a burial site. Over one hundred bodies were found in the two chambers, some in the ground and some in urns and sarcophagi.

[60 km.] As you leave Tzermiadhes, note the new, well-maintained church on the left. Following the sign to Dhiktaion Andron, you come at a point about 2 km. from the village to a junction. (The left fork would lead in about 1 km. to the village of **Messa Lasithi**; after that, climbing out of the plain, you would then descend a long, winding road to the east; after some 20 km., you come to the village of **Drasi**, where a left fork would take you into Neapolis (p. 305) and the right fork down to the old main road to Ayios Nikolaos (p. 306).) You take the right fork at the Lasithi junction, and pass immediately, on the right, the *Monastery of Panayia Kroustallenia*, perched on its rocky hillock and surrounded by trees. The monastery played an important role in Crete's revolutionary history, being twice destroyed by the Turks, so that the buildings are no longer noteworthy.

[63 km.] Having passed through the village of **Ayios Constantinos**, you proceed on by the next village, **Ayios Georgios**; this now has three hotels, rooms to rent, and restaurants, and can be used as a base for climbing the three main peaks of the Lasithi range – *Dhikti* (2,148 metres), *Aphendis Christos*, or *Lazaros*. But you would need an experienced guide and many hours; and for most people it would be better to approach these Lasithi peaks from the south, via villages to the north-west of Ierapetra (p. 318).

[64 km.] **Avrakontes.**

[67 km.] **Psykhro**, the starting-point for the visit to the Dhiktaion Cave, 'the birthplace of Zeus'. The village is a popular spot for excursionists from all over Crete as well as for foreigners, so that it can be quite over-run during many days of the year. There is a Class D hotel, the *Zeus*, and two Class E hotels, and of course meals and refreshments are available. You drive another 1 km. out of the village to the Tourist Pavilion and parking lot, and from there it is a steep climb (20 minutes) up to the cave entrance. Until fairly recent years, visitors were advised to hire a local guide who would provide light, support, and some information while visiting the cave. Now it is all more organized than that. There is a ticket table near the entrance (the charge has been Drs 50, but will undoubtedly go up); small candles are sold; then you get in line (especially during the high season) and make your way down rather steep and narrow, but reliable, stairs and ramps. The cave can be damp and chilly but you won't be in it that long. You must stay on the wooden 'track', but you can let others pass you by if you want to examine anything. The crowds take away from some of the mystery, but it is still a moving experience.

Dhiktaion Cave

The cave, a gaping split in the mountain-side, was brought to light back in 1881 by local men. Hadzidakis and Halbherr explored the exposed parts shortly afterwards, and Evans came there in 1894; but it was 1900 before the British, with the help of local people, undertook a thorough excavation, which was later continued by the French.

Blasting was resorted to, and the unsuspected inner depths revealed, with local youths bringing up hundreds of votive offerings from the muddy depths. There are large stalagmites and stalactites; a huge stalactite, hidden in the chamber usually isolated by water, is known as 'the mantle of Zeus' (i.e. his swaddling-clothes). And in one tiny chamber – where there were particularly rich finds of votive offerings such as double-axes and bronze statuettes – it is claimed that the birth occurred.

The myth, briefly, is that Cronus, once the master-god of the earth, feared that he would be overthrown by his children, and so ate all those that his wife Rhea bore him. After she bore Zeus she gave Cronus a stone to eat instead, and then left the baby to be reared by the goat Amaltheia and the bee Melissa. It must be recalled, too, that Zeus was no god for the Minoans; he was introduced into Crete by the later Greeks, and this story of his birth was evidently an attempt to relate the new god to the old mother, and to convert some Minoan deity into an acceptable Olympian figure. Hesiod is responsible for setting this down, and as noted elsewhere (p. 87) it is all further complicated by the question as to just where the Dhiktaion Cave should be located. In any case, this cave had a long history as a cult shrine from the middle Minoan period on. It would seem that the upper cave was used first; then the water receded and the lower cave was attended by votaries of the Mother Goddess. By 800 B.C. the cave's appeal was at its peak, but then it began to be superseded by the one on Mount Idha (which also replaced the female deity with a Zeus-cult).

After visiting the cave, you have several alternatives: overnight on Lasithi Plain (at Psykhro or Tzermiadhes); turn off to the east, as mentioned on p. 186, and go via Messa Lasithi either to Neapolis or Ayios Nikolaos; retrace the complete route back to Iraklion, or turn off to Mokhos, p. 183, and go down to the north coast near Mallia. And of course there are various mountains to climb from villages in this area.

Ano Viannos and Arvi

A trip to the village of Arvi on the south coast can be made an excursion in itself; combined with at least a few of the sights en route – and especially visits to the Byzantine chapels around Kastelli-

Pedhiadhos – it can be a full day that will require overnighting somewhere down along the south coast. There is no one place that makes this especially significant, but all the sights together add up to a true Cretan expedition. During the high season, it can be an escape from the mass of tourists; during the winter months, the south coast can be appreciably warmer.

Route Take the Knossos road (Route Exit B) out of Iraklion (p. 141) and continue past Knossos and on via Kounavi, Peza, Arkalokhori, Ano Viannos, and then on via Amiras to Arvi [85 km.]. Another, more strenuous route, leads from Ano Viannos more or less south to the coast via Keratokambos and then along the shore to Arvi [77 km.]. There are several possibilities after leaving Arvi, and these will be indicated at the end (p. 193), but a drive on to Ierapetra is recommended.

Bus There is a regular bus service from outside the Kainouryia Gate in Iraklion through Ano Viannos to Arvi and Myrtos. There is also a service from the same station to Kastelli–Pedhiadhos.

Accommodation Accommodation may be had at a Class C hotel, *Ariadne*, in Arvi. Along the coast to the east, at Myrtos, there is a Class E hotel; and of course Ierapetra has several fine hotels (p. 317).

[9 km.] Having left Iraklion by the road to Knossos (p. 153), you pass the right fork to Arkhanes (p. 172).

[15 km.] **Kounavi.**

[18 km.] **Peza**, the centre of one of the more prosperous and progress-ive agricultural districts of Crete, especially for the *rosakí* table grapes. The large buildings you pass are the processing plants and storehouses for olives, grapes, and other produce.

[19·5 km.] A junction, where you take the left fork and then, after 1 km., take the right route to Viannos via Arkalokhori. But two other major possibilities lie before the traveller with extra time, curiosity, and a bit of persistence.

The first would require a turn to the right at this first junction, toward **Kaloni** and **Ayios Vassilios**: the goal would be to cut due south across the mountains to come down on to the eastern edge of the Messara Plain. There are a few attractions along the way: the Byzantine *Church of John the Baptist*, with its thirteenth-century frescoes, is at the edge of Ayios Vassilios; and there is a right turn-off (of 3 km.) farther along to the *Monastery of Epanosiffi*, with its St George church dating from 1600, precious relics, and octagonal fountain. But mostly it is the drive – via **Tefeli** and **Ligortynos**, to join the Messara road at Pretoria: a turn to **Pyrgos** could lead east to Ano Viannos (by a route described elsewhere: p. 320), while a turn to **Asimi** could lead over to Ayii Dheka, Gortyna, and Phaestos (by this same route).

The other possibility is perhaps more of a day's excursion in itself: visiting the Byzantine chapels of Kastelli-Pedhiadhos and its region. This means taking the left at the first junction, but then bearing off again to the left 1 km. later and going via **Ayies Paraskies** toward Kastelli-Pedhiadhos. (As this lies some 16 km. away you might prefer to drive directly south from Kastelli and join the main route to Ano Viannos.) Assuming you take this detour-excursion, about 3 km. after Ayies Paraskies, a turn-off to the right (sign-posted) to Thrapsano brings you via **Voni** in another 8 km. to **Thrapsano**, a village famous on Crete for keeping alive the tradition and trade of hand-made earthenware pottery: don't expect anything very elegant, but it is worth a stop for those interested in ceramics. Proceeding on to the east and north, you pass by **Evangelismos** (village to right); farther on is another village, **Sklaverokhorio** with its *Church of Presentation of the Virgin* containing especially notable frescoes of the fifteenth to sixteenth centuries: on the north wall is St Francis, holding a book – said to indicate the Venetian influence on the local Orthodox. These frescoes are cited, too, as typical examples of the 'Cretan school' of Byzantine painting. Proceeding on you come out on to the main east-west road from Ayies Paraskies to Kastelli: you turn right and come, in about 2 km., to **Kastelli**, named after a Genoan-Venetian castle erected here in the thirteenth century: nothing remains. Kastelli itself has little to offer, but there are two side-trips to be taken from here. One is to the *Church of Ayios Panteleimon* at **Pigi**, a village some 2 km. north of Kastelli on the road to Khersonissos: best is to ask directions to Pigi, and there enquire after the person who has the key to the church – which is itself not that easy to find. You will be rewarded for your efforts by an unusual structure in a lovely setting of shady oak trees. The name of this locale, *pigi*, means 'spring' and derives from the fact that in Greco-Roman times there was a spring here noted for its health-restoring waters. The first Byzantine church on this site dates from the tenth century. The present structure is a distinctive mottled grey brown-stone exterior and incorporates various ancient fragments in the south wall. The interior has two rows of columns – without capitals: meanwhile, one of the columns is made of ancient capitals decorated with acanthus leaves, all stacked one on top of another. There are frescoes and icons worth examining; the frescoes are said to be among the oldest on Crete and are not well preserved.

Back at Kastelli, you proceed some 3 km. to the east to the village of *Xidas* with its *Chapel of Ayios Georgios* and its important frescoes. Above the village lie the remains of the important Dorian-Greek city of *Lyttos*, or *Lyktos*, which flourished in the classical and Hellenistic periods, when it issued its own coins and had its own port down at Limin Khersonisou (p. 298). Lyttos played a role in many myths, legends, and historical episodes, but little remains at the site of general interest.

Returning to Kastelli once more, you must now decide where your time-table allows you to go. If it is back to Iraklion, you head straight west to Ayies Paraskies and then rejoin the road north. If you have the possibility of going on, there is a road at the edge of Kastelli that leads to Ano Viannos (sign-posted): taking this south you would be cutting along one side of a triangle and rejoining the Iraklion-Viannos road at about the 39 km. point. If you take this road, at about 2 km. from Kastelli you pass the village of **Liliano**, with its twelfth-to-thirteenth-century *Church of Ayios Ioannis*, built in a distinctive basilica style.

[31 km.] Assuming now that you did not bear off to the left at the 19·5 km. point along the main Iraklion–Viannos–Arvi road, you have been continuing on to the south-east until you come to **Arkalokhori.** In a nearby grotto there were valuable finds of bronze weapons and double axes. Some scholars suggest that this might well have been the cave where Zeus was either born or brought to be reared; in any case, the finds indicate that it was the site of a Curetes cult (p. 198).

[42 km.] After passing through **Panayia**, the road begins to climb around the edge of the Dhikti range. About 2 km. out of Panayia, a turn-off to the left leads to **Afrati**; on the hillside to the west of this village was the Dorian settlement of *Arkadhes* (or *Arkadhia*), where extensive finds were made in tombs from the ninth-to-the-eighth centuries B.C. – both ceramics and bronzes. A sanctuary of this period has also been discovered here, along with a fine bronze statuette of a youth. Continuing on the main road, you pass (left) the village of **Embaros**, which can be used as a base for climbing the peaks of the Dhikti Range.

[63 km.] After emerging from a pass, from which you can see the Libyan Sea to the south, and passing by Kato Viannos, you arrive at **Ano Viannos.** 'Upper' Viannos is the district's focal point, boasting a school and a fine plane tree. The village is delightfully situated on the mountain slopes, surrounded by vineyards and olive groves. The frescoes and icons of the fourteenth-century *Church of Ayia Pelayia* are worth investigating as are the frescoes of the fifteenth-century *Church of Ayios Georgios*. (Both are locked: enquire in town for keys.)

For Arvi, there are now two possibilities, the more scenic being the more difficult. Much depends on the available time, the state of the vehicle and individual appetite for rough overland roads. We describe the more difficult below in detail because it takes some careful navigating. But the alternative route is as follows: go on through Ano Viannos on its main street and proceed some 5 km. to the monument to hundreds of Cretans executed by the Germans in 1943; there you turn right on to a new road for **Amiras**; Arvi Beach is some 12 km. farther.

The other route from Ano Viannos requires you to turn right down the steep dirt track directly in front of the large modern church. You descend this road, ignoring various other tracks that lead off it (especially, at about 1 km., keeping right.)

[70 km.] The *Monastery of Ayia Moni* is on the left. As you continue, you will eventually see a huge rocky prominence rising ahead of you – and the Libyan Sea beyond: this rock, rising nearly 600 metres above the sea, is the *Keratokambos*; on its summit are the ruins of the *Keratokastello*; remains of a post-Minoan village were found at its base.

[72 km.] Keep left where the road branches and left again in 3 km.

[78 km.] Keep left (possibly sign-posted to Arvi) to get down to the south coast.

[85 km.] **Arvi.**

This tiny port-village lies on a small coastal plain, backed by high hills, and an almost tropical climate prevails; bananas grow here, as well as oranges (The bananas of Arvi, by the way, have played a role in the Greek diet and economy out of all proportion to their size and quantity. In order to protect this native banana crop, Greek governments for years put high import taxes on other lands' bananas. This may finally be changing under the EEC, but bananas remain surprisingly rare and expensive in Greece.) Behind the fruit groves is the gorge that has given Arvi its name and fame; legend has it that Zeus Arvios struck the rocky cliff, creating the cleft through which the irrigating waters flow. When the wind howls through the gorge or water rushes from the 300 metre-high fissure, the noise is said to be like titanic thunder. When Pashley came here in the nineteenth century he found remains of what he decided was the Temple of Zeus Arvios; it is claimed that the present village church is built on the platform of that ancient temple. On the hillside to the right of the cleft is the *Monastery of St Anthony*, where a few monks eke out a bare existence.

The village has a Class C hotel, the *Ariadne* (tel. 31.200), and modest meals are available. Arvi has been discovered by young people looking for a cheap place to stay, and in any case its attractions should not be exaggerated, but its beach, isolation, and general ambience make it a pleasant retreat.

When it is time to leave, there are two main alternatives. One, of course, is to retrace the route described (via Ano Viannos) all the way back to Iraklion, making any of the detours or side-trips that you have time for. The other possibility is to go on to Ierapetra, as indicated at the outset of this excursion. The route due north via Amiras brings you up on to the main road and the monument to the dead of the Second World War: there you turn right and pass through Pefkos. Shortly after this, a sign-posted turn-off to *Kato Sime* might be taken by those with extra time and energy: you can drive the first 2 km. up to the village, but the next 6 km. has such a bad road that you should be prepared to walk: it leads up (1,000 metres elevation) to a rustic sanctuary that has been excavated since the 1970s. Although some kind of cult activity occurred here continuously from Minoan times to the third century A.D., the main period was during the Geometric and Orientalizing periods when the sanctuary was dedicated to Hermes and Aphrodite. The excavation is by a spring and plane tree and the remains are not nearly as impressive as the many finds now on display in the Iraklion museum.

Back down on the road leading east, you continue past Kalami and arrive down on the coast at Myrtos (described, along with its nearby Minoan sites, on pp. 319–20). From Myrtos you drive another 15 km. to Ierapetra (p. 317).

Idha Range, Idha Cave, and Kamares Cave

Although no Alpine ascent, the climb to Psiloritis – the highest peak of the Idha range – and visits to the famous caves of Idha and Kamares involve more than the casual traveller will be able to manage. Only the most experienced climbers should undertake such excursions on their own – and even they might better go with a local guide who can show them the various trails and alternatives. Less-than-experienced climbers must go in at least small groups with an experienced guide. Such guides may be found in several of the villages used as starting-points (see below) but are better arranged for by starting with the National Tourist Organization offices. The Greek Mountain Club has branches in Iraklion, Khania, and Rethymnon, and occasionally they make these excursions; foreigners would be allowed to go, but you are dependent on their schedules.

Experienced or inexperienced, you must have the proper clothing and supplies. It can get cold at the higher elevations, even in mid-summer. You will want to bring your own food – and you definitely should bring your own water. Special footwear is necessary; sun-glasses will be appreciated. Even with a guide, you might want to have a fairly detailed map, and of course a camera and binoculars are optional.

This book cannot attempt to provide a detailed account of the actual climbs. Instead, it describes the goals and the various approaches, including the villages, sights, and attractions en route to the jumping-off points, so that the general traveller can at least enjoy some part of these excursions.

Although there are possibilities of approaching the Idha Range from various points, there are two main approaches: one is from the south and uses the village of Kamares as the jumping-off point; the other is from the north and uses the village of Anoyia as the starting-point. Obviously, true climbers and hikers may want to move on to quite different destinations from where they start out, but even the traveller with restricted resources should enjoy the excursions to these villages. And in the case of Anoyia, there is now a good road all the way to within a twenty-minute walk to the Idha Cave.

Incidentally, so that no one goes to all this trouble by mistake, the Mount Idha in question is not the classically famous one of Homer and Aeschylus – that is near Troy. Crete's Idha is, in fact, more widely known among the Cretans as Psiloritis, but it does have its own rich history.

Approach from the South

Route Follow the route from Iraklion to Phaestos (Route Exit A) as far as Ayia Varvara (p. 201), where you turn right along the mountain-slopes to Zaros and Kamares [55 km.]. If you make the climb to the Kamares Cave, you would then have several choices, while those who are simply driving through have several possibilities (described on p. 197).
Bus There is a daily bus service from the Khania Gate in Iraklion to Kamares.
Accommodation Simple overnight accommodation and meals may be had in Kamares.

[30 km.] Taking the Phaestos road out of Iraklion (p. 190), you come to Ayia Varvara; at the end of the village, take the right turn (sign-posted) towards Zaros and Kamares.

[40 km.] The road leads westwards along the southern slopes of the Idha Range and down into a lovely valley until you come to the village of **Yeryeri.** Its *Church of the Panayía* has fifteenth-century frescoes.

[45 km.] **Zaros** – actually two parts, Ano and Kato – seems cleaner and more prosperous than many Cretan villages, and many of its doorways have carved lintels. Ano Zaros is noted for its spring that once supplied water to ancient Gortyna, which lies south behind the mountains: some of the Roman aqueduct may still be viewed there (p. 203).

[47 km.] On the western edge of the village there is a turn-off right, (sign-posted) that leads (in 2 km.) to the entrance to a ravine where there is the *Monastery of Ayios Nikolaos*. It has fifteenth-century frescoes and icons, with altar panels in the early Renaissance style. Above this church, up the side of the ravine, may be seen two entrances to a cave where the hermit-ascetic St Efthimios lived for some years in the fifteenth century. The cave can be visited but it means a climb of $1\frac{1}{2}$ hours.

[50 km.] A right turn-off leads up a steep hillside to the *Monastery of Vrondisi*, well worth a detour. It stands high on the hill, with a fine view. There are two large plane trees in the clearing before the walls, and to the left of the entrance is a fifteenth-century Italianate fountain, one of the finest in the Cretan countryside and quite unascetic in its elegance: between the two pilasters are statues of Adam and Eve, while the water gushes out into the mouths of four men. The church is dedicated to St Anthony and the Apostle Thomas. Frescoes have been uncovered only in the late 1970s. The fine icons on display in the church are mostly from the nearby Church of Ayios Fanourios (see below) – moved here after the theft of a major icon from the church in 1975. The six famed icons by Damaskinos, however, that were once the property of this Vrondisi monastery, have been moved to the Church of St Katherine in Iraklion (p. 145).

[51 km.] Back on the main road, a kilometre or so along, you will note off to the left, across a gentle ravine, a small isolated chapel with a red roof: the *Church of Ayios Fanourios*. Although it is possible to park and walk down across the slopes to the church, most people will find it easier to drive on to the next village and turn back on to the dirt road that leads to the church. The village is **Voriza**, and you must enquire there after the key and a guide.

[53 km.] Having taken the dirt road out of Voriza, you arrive at the Church of Ayios Fanourios, all that remains of the Monastery of Valsamonero. The church reveals an Italian influence, with its small belltower, and its interior arches decorated with leaves and palmettes; but its form is unusual, with two parallel naves, a third at a right angle to these, and a narthex. The north nave is considered the original and is attributed to the fourteenth century; the other two naves are assigned, from the inscriptions of the donors, to the early fifteenth century. The iconostasis – its scallops indicating more Italian-Renaissance influence – became greatly damaged and its icons have been removed to the Vrondisi church (see above). The major attraction of this church is its frescoes, considered among the more valuable on Crete. Those in the north nave date from the early fifteenth century; those in the cross-nave are credited to Konstantinos Rikos in 1431 – one of the better-known Cretan artists. (You may be told that Damaskinos and/or El Greco painted some of these frescoes, but the authorities do not claim this.)

[55 km.] Proceeding on from Voriza, you arrive at the village of **Kamares**. Here you can get overnight accommodation and meals (but recent visitors complain of an unsatisfactory hostel); you can also hire a guide for the climb to the Kamares Cave and Psiloritis. (The route is marked by red dots, once you find the path at the edge of Kamares. Then, at a water trough, arrows point to Kamares Cave or Psiloritis summit.) The climb just to the cave takes about 4 hours, so you should probably stay overnight in Kamares – or get a very early start from Iraklion. If you were to go on to the summit of Psiloritis, you would either have to go equipped to stay overnight somewhere on the (cold!) mountain or else allow for a very long day.

Cave of Kamares

This is the cave viewed by hundreds of thousands of travellers – but from the comfort of the Palace of Phaestos (p. 208). It was discovered as a site in modern times by local shepherds in the early 1890s, and Italian archaeologists explored it shortly thereafter, but it was 1913 before the British fully excavated it. Used in Neolithic times as a shelter, the cave was regarded as a sacred locale by the Minoans from the Proto-palatial Period onwards (starting, that is, about 1900 B.C.). Here they brought various offerings to the gods, in particular the thin, polychrome, delicately decorated pottery that was first associated with this cave and still is known as 'Kamares ware'. (That on display in Iraklion's Museum remains among the most eloquent witnesses to the Minoans' subtle artistry.) The many remains of food found in the vases and dishes indicate that the Minoans brought offerings to the cave in order both to thank and beseech the gods for good crops.

The climb to Kamares Cave will have taken some $3\frac{1}{2}$–4 hours. From there it would be possible to climb the peaks above the cave. Or going back about half way down the trail, you would come to the point where a different route to the north would be the way to Psiloritis.

Summit of Psiloritis (Mt Idha)

This is a fairly ambitious climb of some 7 hours from Kamares village (or cave). Its highest point is some 2,456 metres elevation and provides a dramatic vista of both the north and south coasts as well as of the ranges to the east and west – assuming the peak is not 'fogged in'. At the peak are two adjacent structures: one is a shelter, while the other is the *Chapel of Timios Stavros* ('holy cross'). The nameday for this chapel is September 14th and a fair number of Cretans make their way up to the chapel on that occasion. There is a well at this locale, too, but the water must be boiled before drinking.

If you have made it this far, you now have several possibilities when you come to move on. You can obviously retrace the trail to Kamares village – and from there you could go almost due south via Grogoria and Kalochorafitis to Voroi, on the edge of the Messara and near

Phaestos (p. 235): alternatively, you could go west to Apodoulou and then south to Ayia Galini (p. 237). You could take a different trail off the mountain and come down more to the north-west of Kamares village, at the villages of Nithavris, Kouroutes, Fourfouras, or Visari – on the edge of Amari Province and the road to Rethymnon (p. 236). Or you could take a trail off Psiloritis to the east and come down on to the Nidha Plateau. But most people will approach Nidha from the north via Anoyia – as described below.

Idha Range and Cave from Anoyia

As with so many of the excursions described, this can be a single-goal trip – namely, to the mountains and the cave – or it can be a series of stops and side-trips, even while en route to a still farther destination. The description here will treat this excursion as probably most users of such a guide will – as a side-trip from the village of Anoyia (route details, pp. 242–3).

At the highpoint of the village a turn to the left leads to a 20 km. long road (asphalt) up along the edge of the Idha Range. En route you will note several chapels and shepherds' huts; it is in the latter that the shepherds make some of the tasty Cretan cheeses from fresh goat's milk. At some 1,500 metres elevation, you come to the last pass: the new road (left) goes off to the north-west to the tourist pavilion-restaurant, from which there is a 20-minute walk up to the cave itself. Below lies the Nidha Plateau – about 4 sq. km., enclosed by mountains and covered by grass that provides pasture for many herds.

Idha Cave

The Idha Cave sits above the western edge of the plateau; its entrance is some 9 metres high and 27 metres wide, and a zigzag way leads to the inner chambers – the largest of which is some 36 by 34 metres. The cave was discovered and explored in the 1880s (although one chamber was only discovered in 1955) and it has yielded many rich finds, from Minoan sealstones to Roman coins. But the most important finds have been the bronze shields, spears, cups, tripods, etc. dating from the ninth and eighth centuries B.C. Aside from showing Assyrian influence (and thus placing them in the Orientalizing phase of the Greek world), these finds have been taken to indicate that there was a post-Minoan cult of the Curetes who were worshipped in this cave. The Curetes were the warriors who danced around the cave where the baby Zeus was being nursed by Rhea; they covered his cries from his father Cronus by the clashing of their shields. (Robert Graves claims it was the son of Zeus, Zagreus, who was being protected at this cave.) One of the shields found here, displayed in Iraklion's Archaeological Museum, depicts Zeus and the Curetes. In 1982 Sakellarakis began intensive new excavations that have yielded literally thousands of new finds – primarily post-Minoan (Geometric) cult offerings but also many Neolithic tools and pots – and new insights into the people who visited the cave during many centuries.

If you have come up to the Nidha Plateau simply to visit this cave, you will want to return to Anoyia and then either go back to Iraklion or on to Rethymnon. Experienced climbers may want to ascend the peak of Psiloritis or even to proceed on to the Kamares Cave, but both of these are walks of some 4–5 hours and really require local guides (see p. 194).

ROUTE 1: IRAKLION TO PHAESTOS (VIA GORTYNA)

Here is one of those journeys through history so peculiar to Crete. It can be managed in a day, but could just as profitably take three or four, depending on how many detours and side-trips you make. Phaestos alone, as the second of the great Minoan palace-complexes, justifies a whole-day trip. Those with private transport will be able to set their own pace, but even those dependent on buses may find that the schedule allows Gortyna, Phaestos and Ayia Triadha to be included in a day's outing. Phaestos, with its Tourist Pavilion, is ideal for an overnight stay; careful planning with your transportation would allow you to see at least a couple of the other sites down along this section of the south coast.

Route Leave Iraklion by the Khania Gate along the Rethymnon road (Route Exit A), but about 2 km. from the centre of the town the road turns off to the left (sign-posted). You then climb up the hills to Ayia Varvara [28 km.] and descend to Ayii Dheka [44 km.], Gortyna and Phaestos [62 km.].
Bus The Iraklion–Timbaki bus, which leaves hourly from the Khania Gate, takes you all the way to Phaestos and will put you off at many points en route; the tourist agencies, of course, have many guided bus tours to these sites. There are also a couple of buses daily to and from Ayia Galini that will leave you off or pick you up on the main road below Phaestos.
Accommodation The Tourist Pavilion at Phaestos is, one might say, internationally famous for its hospitality: until the mid-1980s it did offer beds, but now only refreshments and meals are provided. And at places such as Timbaki, Kokhinos

Pyrgos or Matala there are now many beds available in Class C and E hotels or private homes. Ayia Galini itself has about nine C Class hotels, as well as some D and E, and rooms to let.

You leave Iraklion by the Khania Gate – passing the handsome *statue* of Captain Michael Korokas, one of Crete's nineteenth-century revolutionary leaders – and proceed along the Boulevard of 62 Martyrs, so named after sixty-two citizens of Iraklion murdered by the Germans in 1942, now sacrificed to the internal combustion engine and its offspring.

[2 km.] After crossing a little bridge, you follow the signs that lead you to turn left off the north-coast road to the west. From here you drive on for many kilometres through the fertile central basin of Crete; during the Middle Ages the prized *malvasia* wine came from here; today the celebrated *rosakí* grapes flourish. Then begins the long climb over the mountains.

[21 km.] After passing through the village of **Avyeniki**, you will see off on your right a rocky tableland (like a mesa) that is known today as Patela; it is the locale of the acropolis of ancient *Rhizenia* and the site known in the literature as *Prinias* (after a nearby village). There had been some settlement with structures here from Minoan times, but the site was not fully developed until the post-Minoan period when Dorian Greeks were running Crete. The Italians, excavating in the first decade of this century, discovered the remains of two archaic temples (roughly mid-seventh-century B.C.), including friezes depicting animals and warriors, and statues of two seated goddesses. The friezes are among the oldest Greek architectural sculptures and as such are considered an important example of the so-called Daedalic style (p. 110); they are now in Room XIX of the Iraklion Museum. More recent excavations of graves in the Prinias area have yielded finds of the Geometric Period (which are displayed in Room XI, Case 151). Most people will be satisfied to view the finds from Prinias in the museum, but anyone who wants to visit the site can do so by one of two approaches. Taking the road out of Iraklion as to the Messara (as described above), at the 3·5 km. point is a turn-off to the right to Voutes and Ayios Myron, and in this village – itself picturesquely located – you can get directions to Prinias, or Patela. Alternatively, this same road continues on through Ayios Myron south to Ayia Varvara, and so it could be approached from that village (see below).

[28 km.] **Ayia Varvara** is a sizeable village and serves as a centre for this region. As you enter the village, on the right you see a huge rock topped by a chapel: the latter is dedicated to Profitis Elias, while the former is called the *omphalos* – 'navel' – of Crete: popular lore claims that it is the island's geographical balancing-point. In the middle of the village a turn-off to the right would lead in some 4 km. to the village of Prinias (above), with a short walk then to the remains.

[30 km.] At the end of the village a road to the right leads in 27 km. to **Kamares**, a starting-point for the expedition to Kamares Cave and Mt Idha (as described in detail pp. 194–9).

[33 km.] Continuing on through Ayia Varvara you pass through the *Pass of Vourvoulitis* at an altitude of about 650 metres. At points you can enjoy a spectacular view, and as you begin the long, winding descent to the Messara, with the mountains all about, you will catch an occasional glimpse of the Libyan Sea off Crete's southern coast.

[43 km.] By a curving road, you come down on to the Messara, Crete's largest flat area with some 30 km. on the east-west axis and an average width of about 5 km. In previous centuries, this large, relatively fertile plain might have ensured the island's self-sufficiency in at least the basic cereal grains, but the land was so subdivided and there was so little application of the latest farming machinery and methods that it never fulfilled its promise. Now there has been considerable application of the latest techniques – a system of irrigation canals, co-operative sharing of large machinery, use of fertilizers – and the pace of life has definitely quickened in the villages around the Messara. But farm produce no longer sustains the full life that even twentieth-century Cretan farmers want, and it will be interesting to see what strains develop here, especially as such things as petrol and fertilizer become increasingly expensive. There is only one river that runs year-round here, the Yeropotamos, and even that is extremely low in the summer: an irrigation system is compensating somewhat, but water remains a problem on the Messara.

[43 km.] A sign-posted turn-off to the left is the road to the east that leads across the Messara and over the mountains to Ano Viannos and even to Ierapetra, a route described elsewhere (pp. 320–1). Increasing numbers of visitors to Crete now try this once remote route; it is asphalt most of the way but badly potholed in parts. Make sure you have a large map; pay close attention to signs, possible diversions (detours); and note that while the map leads you to think you are passing through certain towns, you are often passing *by* them.

[44 km.] You drive through the village of **Ayii Dheka**, a name meaning 'the holy ten', in reference to ten martyrs. In the third century A.D., ten of the inhabitants of this region refused to sacrifice to the gods of their Roman overlords and were beheaded. This was at a time when the Romans ruled in nearby Gortyna, and Ayii Dheka has had a revenge of sorts because many of its houses and other structures have been built out of the fragments of once-grand Gortyna.

In the village, on a turn-off to the left, there is a church dating from the Byzantine era but greatly restored; in it is an icon portraying the ten martyrs, and under this painting, in a glass case, is a stone on which they are said to have been decapitated. Just to the west of the village a track leads to the little *Chapel of Ayii Dheka*; it is a modern structure, but steps lead to a crypt (**10** on site plan) underneath it where some of the martyrs' tombs are displayed. Just opposite this has been a so-called museum, a courtyard with a haphazard collection of headless statues, columns, and inscriptions from Gortyna: this has long been promised a transfer to a new museum building by the Basilica of Ayios Titos (p. 205), but in any case the best finds from Gortyna are in the Iraklion Museum. A stroll through the village, however, reveals a different kind of museum: columns, statues, fragments of all kinds built into stairways, courtyards, walls, and other parts of Ayii Dheka over the centuries. It is nothing very dramatic, but it is illuminating to see how a once great imperial city like Gortyna has been absorbed by this placid village.

Striking across the fields from Ayii Dheka church and the museum, you come to one group of the remains of *Gortyna*: these are the somewhat more recent Roman ruins (**1** to **9** on Gortyna plan). A little farther on along the main road, the most interesting group of structures is on the right of the road, just behind the ruined Basilica of Ayios Titos: these are the older Roman, the Hellenistic and the Doric remains (**11** to **17** on Gortyna plan).

Hours 9.00–15.30
Entrance Drs 50

HISTORY OF GORTYNA

First a word about the various names of this site: in modern Greek it is called Gortys, but it is better known in literature by its Byzantine

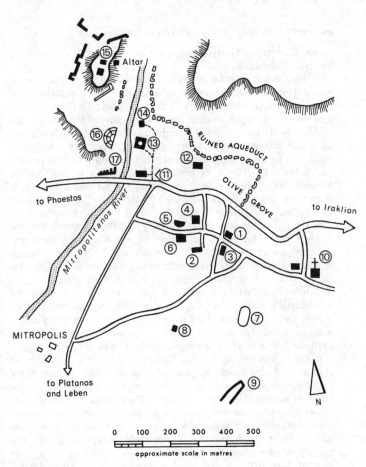

Gortyna

1 Nymphaion
2 Temple of Pythian Apollo
3 Praetorium
4 Sanctuary of Isis and Serapis
5 Theatre
6 Early Christian Basilica
7 Amphitheatre
8 Main Gate
9 Stadium
10 Crypt of 10 Martyrs
11 Basilica of Ayios Titos
12 Inactive Tourist Pavilion
13 Odeon and Law Code
14 Mill
15 Acropolis
16 Hellenistic Theatre
17 Storage Chambers

forms, Gortyna or Gortyn, and so we have chosen to use the form Gortyna throughout.

If there was any settlement at Gortyna during the Minoan era, it was completely overshadowed by Phaestos. Not until the great Minoan centres declined and the Dorians took over did Gortyna come into its own; it began to compete as a commercial power from the eighth century B.C., eventually controlling the ports of Matala and Leben. During the eighth to fifth centuries B.C. Gortyna was advanced enough to be working out the society that developed its famous laws (see below). By 300 B.C. it probably had control of most of the Messara. But there was never much time for peaceful exploitation; there were, instead, continual wars with the other Cretan city-states and Mediterranean powers, until Gortyna fell to the Romans along with the rest of the island about 67 B.C. As part of Rome's imperial vision, Gortyna became the seat of a praetor, the capital of Crete and the province of Cyrenaica. The Messara was to become a bread-basket for this empire, Gortyna to be turned into a splendid provincial city. Indeed, for a while, there was a period of prosperity and ambitious construction; irrigation helped the fields to flourish and brick-making allowed buildings to rise. When Byzantium replaced Rome, and Christianity the old idols, Gortyna managed to retain some of its prestige. But when it fell to the Moors in A.D. 824 it was partially destroyed and never again regained its stature.

Gortyna was among the first Cretan sites to be excavated – by Halbherr and the Italian mission, back in the 1880s. It took many decades, though, before all the ruins we see were exposed, and a new series of excavations, begun in the 1970s, continues to clarify and reveal the true extent and nature of this site. The total site is spread over a considerable area, and individual remains are sometimes difficult to single out, but that is what makes this such a fascinating spot: you walk through dry fields, across crumbling walls, past gnarled olive trees, discovering the sunken foundations, columns, statues, arches and fragments – slowly piecing together the once grand city of Gortyna.

DESCRIPTION OF SITE

Roman remains

The group of ruins on the left of the road mostly date from the second century A.D., although there had been some earlier structures in several cases and some were later adapted by the Byzantines. They include the Nymphaion (**1**), the Temple of Pythian Apollo (**2**), the Praetorium (**3**), the Sanctuary of Isis and Serapis (**4**), a theatre (**5**), an amphitheatre (**7**), a stadium (**9**) and the main gate (**8**). No one ruin is by itself very spectacular, but the total ensemble makes for an interesting stroll.

Basilica of Ayios Titos

Of the ruins farther along the main road and to the right, the first structure to catch your eye is the high apse of the Basilica of Ayios Titos (**11**) – the Titus said to have been commissioned by Paul in person to convert the Cretans, and the first bishop of Gortyna. It has been claimed that he was buried here, but there is no evidence for this. The basilica dates from the sixth century A.D., with alterations up to the tenth century; eventually it fell to pieces, but enough remains to show the extent of the structure. One of the small side-chapels is still used as a shrine by the local people, and fragments of the original frescoes adhere to the walls. Outside stands an odd miscellany of remains in various architectural styles.

Odeon and Law Code

Walking along a path that passes behind the basilica, you arrive at the ruins of the Roman Odeon (**13**). Originally there was a Hellenistic structure here; in the first to second centuries A.D. the Romans built this 'chamber theatre'. Enough has survived to give a good idea of its appearance. And behind the Odeon is the prize exhibit of Gortyna: the Law Code. Carved on stone blocks, it stands upright as it stood when the Romans came and incorporated it into their Odeon. It is now sheltered under a modern brick gallery that is fenced and locked but the characters carved in the stones are clearly visible through the fence; a caretaker is about during all normal hours. (A small tip is in order if you make use of the caretaker's explanation.)

The stones you see so clearly are the originals, although when first inscribed by the Dorian Cretans of Gortyna – some time between 500 and 450 B.C. – they stood elsewhere, most likely in a more public place. The Romans, who may not have truly understood its significance, probably used it to decorate their wall. And there the stones stayed for many centuries, gradually forgotten, and finally submerged under the mill stream. It was not until 1884 that Halbherr, the Italian archaeologist, happened to be on the site when the water was drawn off from the stream. Now it is true that fragments of inscriptions found near by in 1857 and 1879 had alerted archaeologists. But not one would ever have dared dream that, when the water went down, there would stand a whole code, virtually intact.

It should be said, by the way, that there were actually two codes found at Gortyna. The other, dating from roughly the same period, was found in only a few scattered sections. To scholars, of course, these fragments are valuable supplements. But the twelve columns preserved in the Odeon make up what is commonly referred to as the Gortyna Code.

More than 17,000 characters are carved in the stones. The language is an archaic Doric dialect of Greek and most of its eighteen letters are recognizably Greek. The script has been set down in what is called the 'ox plough' manner, according to which the eye travels from right to left in one line and then left to right in the next, alternating continuously as a field is ploughed.

What was set down in the fifth century B.C. is not actually a complete code. It is, rather, largely a number of regulations amending earlier laws. These earlier laws probably date from a century or two earlier and were, in turn, based on a still more ancient oral tradition of law. The laws deal essentially with civil matters such as marriage, divorce, adultery, property rights, adoption, inheritance and mortgage of property. There is also some reference to trial procedure and, in general, the Gortyna Code gives a glimpse into early forms of Greek law. But beyond that it affords a good impression of the social structure and general affairs of Dorian Crete.

Mill

Behind the Law Code gallery, by the way, is an abandoned mill (14) dating from the Venetian period; at least until the late 1960s it had been used for grinding flour.

Acropolis

On a hill to the right of the road and across a tributary of the Yeropotamos is the Acropolis (15) from the earlier post-Minoan period. (These remains, of interest only to a specialist, are approached from the nearby village of Ambelouzos with a guide.) Under the remains of the Hellenistic and Roman times were found an Archaic altar, several religious shrines and a fortress, with some remains going back to Mycenaean times. Sculptures, bronzes, terracottas and pottery have been found on the site, including some important works of the Daedalic style. Lower, towards the main road on a terrace, are the sparse remains of a *Hellenistic theatre* (**16**) that was later restored, while along the road itself are remains of *storage chambers* (**17**).

[46 km.] Back on the main road, opposite the ruins, there is a turning to the left off the main road that leads to Mitropolis and Platanos and then on to the tombs of the Messara (p. 233) or to Leben (p. 231).

After passing the ruins of the storage chambers of ancient Gortyna, you can see the *Agricultural School of the Messara*. Here young Cretans are taught up-to-date methods of agriculture on a self-supporting farm that has become an integral part of the Messara farming community.

[52 km.] At the largish village of **Mires**, a bus junction for the region (including some local buses to and from Matala), there are plenty of cafés for a refreshing pause. (There is also the Class D hotel, *Olympic*.) On Saturday mornings there is a lively market-bazaar. In the centre of town, a turn to the left (sign-posted) takes you by one route to Matala (p. 229) in 18 km.

[56 km.] A sign indicates the *Monastery of Panayia Kaliviani* off in the olive grove to the right; it now operates an orphanage, convalescent home and home for the aged.

About this time, you become aware of a low mountain ridge ahead and off to the left, breasting the Messara like the prow of a ship: on that spur is the site of Phaestos, some 65 metres above the plain.

[60 km.] The turn (sign-posted) to the left for Phaestos takes you across the Yeropotamos and winding up a steep ridge.

[62 km.] At the top of the hill is Phaestos, a spectacular combination of natural site and historic ruin.

PHAESTOS

Since Phaestos arouses as much enthusiasm by its situation as by its ruins, it is well to get oriented. As you stand looking down the long Messara Plain to the east, Mount Dhikti and the Lasithi range rise at the far end. To the right is the Asterousia range, bordering the south coast. To the north is the Idha range. If you look carefully you will see a dark hole, at the extreme right of the saddle between two peaks on the Idha slopes: this is the Kamares Cave (p. 197), where the famous pottery was found that has given its name to this type of delicate, black-based ceramics.

Hours Apt to vary, but essentially early morning to sunset in summer, with earlier closing in winter and on Sundays and holidays.
Entrance Drs 150.
Accommodation At the Tourist Pavilion, meals are available, and campers have been allowed to sleep on the roof. The atmosphere is more like a friendly inn than an official hostelry, and it makes a congenial starting-point for excursions to other sites in southern Crete.

HISTORY

The history of Phaestos is not so well known as that of Knossos, although recent excavations have brought much to light. It is said to have been founded by Minos, but it is traditionally associated with his brother Rhadamanthys – also a noted legislator. The weights and measures of Phaestos may have been accepted as standards throughout the Minoan 'empire'. Its people were known in classical Greece for their wit. The development of Phaestos, both political and architectural, seems to have paralleled that of Knossos, although it was never so extensive in power or so intricate in structure. The materials and workmanship at the palace of Phaestos were however at least as good as at Knossos. How closely Phaestos was linked to Knossos in its heyday is in dispute; certainly there is a similarity in the design and structure of the palaces as well as in many of the artefacts found at both sites. Some scholars place great emphasis on masons' marks on stones which, they say, show that the palaces were probably built by the same men. Without having been a mere dependency, it would seem that Phaestos was closely associated with the achievements of Knossos. Like Knossos, too, the palace passed through successive reconstructions and additions, and it fell to some natural disaster or invaders – or both. There is evidence of some reoccupation of the palace site in Mycenaean times, and the general area continued to be settled through Geometric and on into Roman times. The rise of nearby Gortyna, however, denied it any later glory, and there is even some suggestion that Gortyna destroyed what was left of Phaestos about the middle of the second century B.C.

Considering the height of the site, it is difficult now to understand how it ever came to be covered – but this happened. It was only after several trial digs in the area that Halbherr began full-scale excavations on the site in 1900 (the same year that Evans began to dig at Knossos). The great palace-complex was excavated over many years, largely by the Italians, and excavations continue periodically to this day. In particular the excavations between 1950 and 1970 revealed not only the actual remains of the first palace at Phaestos but helped to illuminate the whole first-palace, or Proto-palatial, period of Minoan Crete. (These excavations, directed by Doro Levi, have been published in his *Festos e la Civilta Minoica*, which, along with the previous Italian excavation reports by Pernier and Banti, takes its place on the shelf with Evans's work on Knossos.) These excavations, for instance, provide evidence of a quite rapid development of architectural style and building skills around 1900 B.C. and then further developments during the ensuing two centuries before the great second palace was erected on the site. They have also provided much of the solid evidence for the role of the palace as a centre of the economic life in this Proto-palatial period – ample storage facilities, crafts areas, even archives with clay sealings and tablets.

Phaestos has come to assume another important role as a result of the Italians' excavation procedures: they did not undertake as much restoration here as Evans did at Knossos. There has had to be some buttressing and patching; walls, walks, cisterns, chambers, urns and such have often been repaired *in situ*; otherwise, much of Phaestos has been left as found. Neolithic traces, pre-palatial structures, the first palace, the second palace, the private Minoan houses clustering around the palace, the Minoan town on the south side of the hill, the various post-Minoan remains on through the Roman period – all make Phaestos a particularly significant archaeological showcase.

DESCRIPTION OF SITE

With the aid of a plan, as provided here (pp. 210–11), the palace of Phaestos is a relatively easy site to explore on one's own – although there is often a guide who can be hired on the site. (The caretaker Alexandros, depicted by Henry Miller in his *Colossus of Maroussi*, for many years gave an inimitable tour: at the end, since he was officially prohibited from accepting payment, he would announce that he did, however, 'collect foreign coins'.) We shall single out the major points of interest (and assume that individuals with more specialized needs will have one of the more detailed guides such as those by Alexiou or Cadogan).

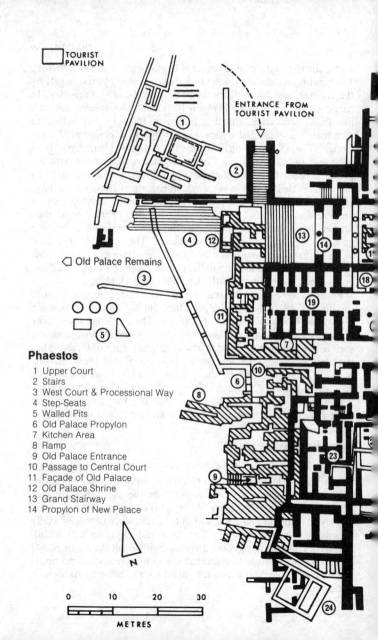

TOURIST PAVILION

ENTRANCE FROM
TOURIST PAVILION

◁ Old Palace Remains

Phaestos

1 Upper Court
2 Stairs
3 West Court & Processional Way
4 Step-Seats
5 Walled Pits
6 Old Palace Propylon
7 Kitchen Area
8 Ramp
9 Old Palace Entrance
10 Passage to Central Court
11 Façade of Old Palace
12 Old Palace Shrine
13 Grand Stairway
14 Propylon of New Palace

N

0   10   20   30
METRES

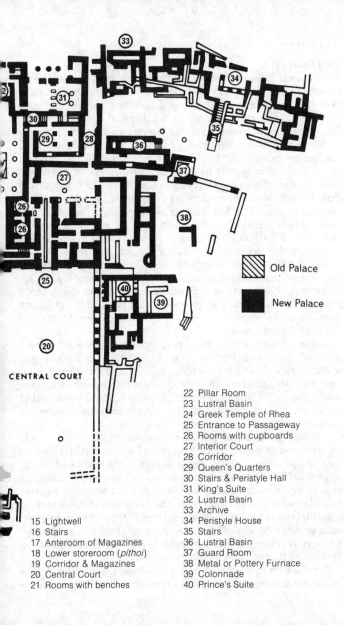

Old Palace

New Palace

CENTRAL COURT

15 Lightwell
16 Stairs
17 Anteroom of Magazines
18 Lower storeroom (*píthoi*)
19 Corridor & Magazines
20 Central Court
21 Rooms with benches

22 Pillar Room
23 Lustral Basin
24 Greek Temple of Rhea
25 Entrance to Passageway
26 Rooms with cupboards
27 Interior Court
28 Corridor
29 Queen's Quarters
30 Stairs & Peristyle Hall
31 King's Suite
32 Lustral Basin
33 Archive
34 Peristyle House
35 Stairs
36 Lustral Basin
37 Guard Room
38 Metal or Pottery Furnace
39 Colonnade
40 Prince's Suite

West Court (3)

You descend from the Tourist Pavilion down to the terraced area known as the Upper Court (**1**). Originally built in the Proto-palatial Period, it has traces of the Minoan processional way on its north-south axis as well as the row of 17 holes that held wooden posts that formed a colonnade (for market stalls?) along the west side. But most of the remains here date from houses of the much later Greek resettlement period; and just east of the processional way are slab graves that probably date to the early Christian era. You proceed down a narrow flight of stairs (**2**) – also first built in the Proto-palatial Period – and come down on to the West Court (**3**), with its raised processional way. This fine court, as now exposed, is that of the first palace and is presumed to have been used for various ceremonies and/or 'theatrical' occasions: these latter were most certainly dances and rituals for religious and state functions, not what we now understand by 'theatre' (even by classical Greek drama). But there is no ignoring that along the north side of this court are eight long, broad steps (**4**) – more than 20 metres long and seating as many as 500 people – and that these plus the raised walk that comes right down from the steps suggest a ceremonial space comparable to the Theatral Area at Knossos.

A side extension of the processional way goes westward along a group of walled pits (*koulouras*) (**5**). As with those at Knossos and Mallia, various functions have been proposed over the years, but it is now generally agreed that the 4 circular ones at least were silos – each holding up to 250 bushels of grain. Off to the west and south-west of the court (but off limits to the public) are numerous remains of Proto-palatial houses, streets, and other structures.

The main processional way leads southward and then turns into what remains of the old palace's propylon (or west porch) (**6**), with a base of one column still in place. Slightly to the north-east of this column base are two stones with a channel that was used to collect the juice of fruit pressed between the stones: this find has led to this area being known as the kitchen (**7**). To the south-west of the column, a ramp (**8**) led up a bastion to the second level of the old palace, while its main entrance (**9**) was off the small court south of this. An interior passageway (**10**) led from the propylon to the Central Court, but you are to enter the palace by a different approach.

Step back on to the West Court and you can get some perspective on the low-standing wall along its eastern side – all that survives of the façade of the old palace (**11**). When the second palace came to be built – as a result of the first palace's destruction, almost certainly from an earthquake – this façade was levelled and rubble was dumped over the whole courtyard, thus raising it about 1 metre to the level of the bottom step of the new Grand Stairway (**13**), and covering up the bottom stairs of the step-seats along the north side. It has been suggested that this new west court, since it was not paved, was used for the bull-leaping sport-ritual, but it seems a rather confined area for that.

As you approach the Grand Stairway, you will note a complex of rooms (**12**) from the old palace period, an area that has been identified as some sort of shrine because of the many ritual containers, benches, and other finds.

Grand Stairway and Entrance (13)

The new palace façade is set back about 8 metres from the first palace façade, and the entrance is a truly grand set of stairs (**13**) at the north corner. About $13\frac{1}{2}$ metres wide, they are slightly raised in the middle: explanations for this range from permitting water to drain off to making central figures in a procession appear taller. The side walls are ashlar masonry, but note that some of the stairs are actually carved from natural rock – a superb instance of how Minoan builders adapted their constructions to the natural environment. At the top of the stairway, you proceed straight ahead through the propylon (**14**), passing the base of a central column, then through two doorways and past three column-bases, to enter a smallish area with a facing wall. This last space was a light well (**15**), and when the adjacent areas were roofed, this dimly lit passageway must have created a sense of transition and anticipation for all who entered from the daylight of the stairway and were moving on to the Central Court.

West Wing

You leave the light well through a doorway at its south-east corner and go down a few stairs (**16**) to the anteroom (**17**) of the magazines, or storerooms. Before turning into the corridor of the magazines, it is worth stepping to the north edge of the anteroom and down to a lower storeroom (**18**) of the old palace with *píthoi* still in place. (Beyond this storeroom are remains of what was evidently a bathroom.) Back now to the anteroom, you will note the column bases and traces of gypsum paving in what must have been an important 'junction' in the palace.

You proceed (west) along the corridor with magazines on both sides (**19**) – not as big as the great west magazines at Knossos, nor do these have the cists set into the floors. In the middle of the corridor is the base of a column that supported the second floor. You will want to look into the storeroom at the far end, right side, which must have been used for storing olive oil: it contains *pithoi* (one with a Linear A inscription), a clay stool to stand on when drawing off oil, a raised platform in the centre to prevent slipping on a greasy floor, and even a slight slope to the floor towards a hole to collect spillage – all suggesting that the Minoans were economical.

Central Court (20)

You now step back through the anteroom (**17**) and proceed out on to the Central Court (**20**). Similar in size (51 metres by 22 metres), proportions, and orientation to the great court of Knossos, this court is in one respect even more impressive: its dramatic situation on a hilltop with a panoramic view. But in Minoan times, it should be realized, much of the view was blocked by two- or even three-storeyed structures. Still, it must have been a most impressive space. It was paved with limestone, and many of the original slabs survive. Along both the east and west sides were colonnades, and many of the bases of the columns or pillars survive. (Along the west side, there is a lower strip and the column bases there are from either the first palace or an early phase of the second palace.)

At the far north-west corner is a stepped stone: some have suggested this as an altar, but others propose that it was a mounting block for the bull-leapers to jump on to the bulls (but this asks us to accept that bulls were running around this flagstoned courtyard). At the north-east side are two cisterns with benches, and various suggestions have been made for these, too – from fish bowls to an athletes' resting corner.

Along the south-western edge of the court is a whole series of rooms, and many of the architectural details and finds from these strongly suggest they were used for religious functions. First come two small rooms with benches (**21**); in the middle of the first one is a low plaster table with cup-shaped hollows – presumably for offerings. Next comes the pillar room (**22**), with the bases of two piers suggesting it was used for a shrine. Behind this is a lustral basin (**23**) of the kind familiar from Knossos, with its descending steps and a parapet. And at the far south-western corner are the remains of a Greek temple (**24**), dedicated to Rhea many centuries after the Minoan Mother Goddess had passed on. The south-east section of the courtyard has fallen away down the hillside, along with probably other parts of the palace proper or adjacent structures.

North Wing

Now you turn back and approach the north end of the Central Court, what must have been, in its prime, an almost Renaissance façade in its studied formality. The central doorway (**25**) is flanked by half-columns (originally wooden, on stone bases); many experts have pointed out that such columns appear to be the direct ancestors of similar elements at the *tholos* tombs at Mycenae. Beside both columns are recesses that were probably used by guards; the interiors had geometric-figured frescoes.

As you proceed through this doorway, note the sockets on both sides of the threshold, pivot holes for some sort of double door. Just inside, on the left, was a guardroom to control access not only to the passage into the royal domestic quarters but also to the peristyle hall that was at the top of the stairs. You proceed along the north corridor, which was originally paved and had a central drain for rainwater, passing various rooms on both sides; note especially those on the right that had small cupboards in the walls (**26**). You then come into the Interior, or North, Court (**27**): it is walled in ashlar masonry and has a plaster floor; the round cistern in the centre is probably from a much later period. As you leave this court by its north-east corner, you go along another corridor (**28**) and pass, on your left, a suite of rooms at a slightly lower level. What has been determined to be the Queen's Quarters is at the left (**29**), now covered to protect it. The west section was paved with alabaster slabs with red plaster in the joints; the benches and dado were also veneered with alabaster (but what you now see is largely restoration). The four columns in the middle mark the corners of an open-air area, somewhat like the classical *atrium* or *impluvium*. In general, the details of this suite suggest a delicacy that led excavators to label it the Queen's Quarters.

Along the north side of the Queen's Quarters is a passage and stairs (**30**) that go up to the Peristyle Hall, an impressive area on the second storey. But you proceed on and around to the left to view the King's Suite (**31**), a complex of two rooms and a light well; its alabaster paving (partially restored) and fragments of wall paintings are now protected by a roof. This area, with its verandah on the north edge of the hillside, commanded an impressive view across to the north, with the Idha Range and the Kamares Cave as constant reminders of the Minoans' religious regard for nature. Off and around to the south-west is another lustral bath (32), with its steps, ledge, and alabaster facing.

North-east Extension

You leave the north-east corner of the main palace and go along what now appears to be a path and come to an oblong room (33). It was in this room that the famous Phaestos Disc was found (see Iraklion Museum, Room III, *Case* 41, p. 135). It was on the ground, but excavators believe it fell there from the floor above. Since Linear A tablets were found here, too, and because there is a row of compartments, this room came to be known as the archive, but it has since been suggested it was a storeroom for ritual objects.

Proceeding along the path, the next structure of interest is the peristyle house (34) entered via an L-shaped passage: its name comes from the pillars and columns that formed a peristyle, an open central space that once had a roofed colonnade around it. It is believed that this was a private house.

East Wing

Just south of this is a flight of stairs (35) that leads down to the palace level; coming off these, you proceed to the right to a low oblong room (36) that has been designated yet another lustral bath. Then you come back out of that and pass along a guard room (37), which must have been the checkpoint for entering the palace from the east. You then make your way on to the terraced area, the east courtyard, in the middle of which are the remains of a kiln (38). There have been two theories about this: one, that it was a potter's kiln (and potters' wheels were found near by); the other is that it was a bronzesmith's foundry. In either case, the artisans may have lived in the small rooms along the west side of the courtyard.

From here you make your way down past the colonnade (39) marked by bases of the columns; just west of that is a small set of rooms with several doorways that has been designated the Prince's Suite (40). From this you step back on to the Central Court – and are free to contemplate the vista, the palace, or any thoughts you may now have about the Minoans who once lived here. There are other remains – graves, houses, etc. – on the slopes around the palace but for most travellers the palace itself will suffice.

EXCURSIONS FROM PHAESTOS
Ayia Triadha

One excursion that can conveniently be made from Phaestos, even by those who have only the time between buses, is to the Villa of Ayia Triadha, one of the miniature gems of the Minoan civilization.

Route There are three possible routes. Those who have their own transport should continue west from the parking area and then take the right fork immediately after leaving the Phaestos site. Proceeding along the asphalt road from Phaestos for 3 km., you come out above the site, down on the left. Alternatively, you can drive (or the bus will drop you) along the main road from Iraklion 4 km. past the turn to Phaestos to another left turn; following this for about ½ km. you arrive at a river (sometimes not to be forded); the site is another few hundred metres along the path through orchards.

   The third route is for walkers. You pick up the trail by returning for 22 metres down from Phaestos towards the main road and then following a sign-posted foot-path to the left, which you take along the northern side of the Phaestos ridge. This path has become overgrown from lack of use, and it requires a persistent forty-five-minute walk to reach Ayia Triadha. And beware: women report being molested on this trail.

Entrance Drs 100. Ayia Triadha is open to visitors only during the same hours as Phaestos. There is a caretaker at the site who has quite a reputation as a 'naive' painter (and his works have been for sale).

HISTORY

The ruins of Ayia Triadha lie at the western end of the Phaestos ridge; they were excavated by the Italians early in the century, after the discovery of Phaestos. (A new round of excavations, begun in the 1980s, is revealing more details about the site and hopes that some of its questions may be answered.) The Idha range lies to the north; directly below, where the river meanders along the plain, is a lush, almost tropical region known as 'Paradise', where many fruit trees grow. (The asphalt runway you may notice from the terrace above the site is a Greek military airport.) Off to the west is the Bay of Messara.

   Exactly what Ayia Triadha was is not known. Some say it was a summer palace for the Phaestos royalty; others think it was a prince's residence; some see it as the home of a wealthy vassal-chieftain; still others think it was a royal annexe, used for special ceremonial occasions. Certainly it must have been dependent on, if not actually subservient to, Phaestos; the trail overland must have seen its share of messengers, functionaries and royal processions.

Just what this villa was called in Minoan times is also unknown. Its present name, which means 'Holy Trinity', comes from a village (since vanished) and its Byzantine chapel of this name, just beyond the site. There is a chapel on the site, though, the fifteenth-century *Church of Ayios Georgios Galatas* (**14** on site plan). This has fragments of frescoes and architectural elements from the Venetian period. ('Galatas', incidentally, means 'milky': one local legend is that the mortar for the church was mixed with milk.)

In post-Minoan times, the Mycenaeans imposed a megaron, a sanctuary and other structures on the site. Many Minoan tombs have also been excavated in the vicinity of Ayia Triadha; in one, about 100 metres to the north-east, was found one of the most significant remains of Minoan culture – the painted sarcophagus now in the Iraklion museum (Room XIV, p. 142). And, of course, there were still other remarkable finds here at Ayia Triadha. These include some frescoes as well as the three steatite vases – the Harvesters' Vase, the Chieftain's Cup and the Rhyton of the Athletes (all now in the Iraklion museum, p. 137); tablets inscribed with Linear A; and large 'talents' from the treasury of the sanctuary – weighing 29 kilos each, they must have served as an official standard. Ayia Triadha, if hardly as spectacular as the major palaces, nevertheless had a concentration of wealth and art that now figures among the great glories of Minoan times and makes it one of the important pre-classical sites in the Mediterranean world.

DESCRIPTION OF SITE

Whoever lived here and whatever its original function, Ayia Triadha was a sort of 'vest-pocket' version of the grand Minoan palaces. There are the usual chambers, stairways, courtyards, terraces and storage vaults. However, it has no ceremonial area and no central court – confirming the view that it was a 'pleasure palace' for the rulers of Phaestos. Instead of a grand stairway, there is a *ramp* (**1**) along the north front of the villa that leads round to the north-west side and eventually into the colonnaded *Men's Hall* (**2**). This was the main room of the villa, with its dimensions of 6 by 9 metres; it also had a *terrace area* (**3**), with a fine view of the sea and Mount Idha. The

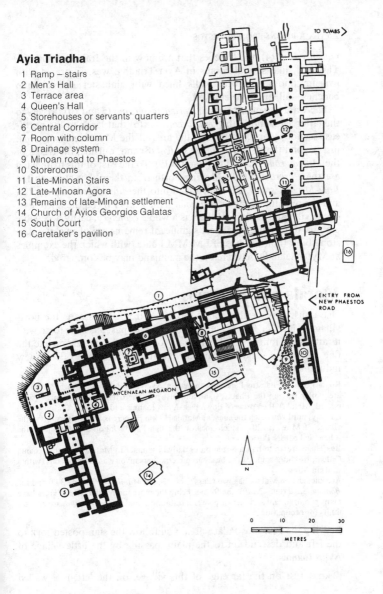

Ayia Triadha

1 Ramp – stairs
2 Men's Hall
3 Terrace area
4 Queen's Hall
5 Storehouses or servants' quarters
6 Central Corridor
7 Room with column
8 Drainage system
9 Minoan road to Phaestos
10 Storerooms
11 Late-Minoan Stairs
12 Late-Minoan Agora
13 Remains of late-Minoan settlement
14 Church of Ayios Georgios Galatas
15 South Court
16 Caretaker's pavilion

TO TOMBS

ENTRY FROM
NEW PHAESTOS
ROAD

MYCENAEAN MEGARON

N

0   10   20   30
METRES

Queen's Hall (**4**) had frescoes that are now in the Iraklion museum. This hall, like several rooms in Ayia Triadha, was decorated with gypsum floors and with walls lined with alabaster and gypsum benches – all still to be enjoyed.

There are two main series of *storage magazines* (**5** and **10**). Access to the latter set is along the *central corridor* (**6**) that leads to the north-east section; you pass through the area of the Mycenaean *megaron*; just beyond that is the *drainage system* (**8**) and, outside, the traces of the *Minoan road* that led to Phaestos (**9**). To the east of this main wing are the *storerooms* (**10**). Moving north from them you come to the *Late-Minoan stairs* (**11**) which lead into the *late-Minoan agora* (**12**), and the remains of the *late-Minoan settlement* (**13**). To the north-east of the villa and settlement there is a whole *cemetery*, easily accessible along a short path. The most significant remains are of two circular, stone-built tholos tombs of EM/MM I date, with which the examples at Mycenae and elsewhere on the mainland may be compared.

Matala and Kommos

One unusual place that might be visited from Phaestos is the port-village of Matala. Site of ancient Matallon, its past has little to do with its attraction for the people who now come to enjoy the terrain and the fine swimming. And the Minoan remains at Kommos offer a new inducement.

Route Leaving Phaestos Palace by the upper Ayia Triadha road, fork left immediately after leaving the Phaestos site and just past the Chapel of St George (sign-posted: Matala); then proceed down past Ayios Ioannis and Pitsidia (sign-posted all the way) until you reach the coast at Matala [12 km.]. There is also the turn-off in the village of Mires (p. 207) which goes on through Petrokefalion and then joins the other road before Pitsidia.

Bus There are up to half a dozen buses daily in summer to Matala from the Khania Gate in Iraklion; some of the buses go direct; others involve a change of bus (with a wait) in Mires.

Accommodation Matala has two Class C hotels, the *Matala Bay* (tel. 42.300) and the *Bamboo Sand* (tel. 42.370), the former being the more impressive. The villages have many rooms to rent and there are several restaurants and cafés. The caves are now off limits for occupation.

Leaving the Phaestos Palace area, you follow the sign-posted fork to the left and descend on to the plain, passing by the little village of **Ayios Ioannis**.

[2 km.] Just on the far edge of this village, on the left, is a walled enclosure within which stands one of the more unique architectural forms on Crete. It is the little early-fourteenth-century rough-stone *Chapel of Ayios Pavlos*. Burial plots lie round it; the charnel-house is at one side; within the chapel are a few old frescoes and icons. But it is the structure that is so remarkable: seemingly growing out of the ground, the chapel gives you the feeling you are witnessing the emergence of the Byzantine style out of some archaic kernel.

Immediately past the chapel, you bear left at the fork (a right turn here leads to **Kamilari**, a village with two pensions); proceed on, following the sign to the right when you come in about 2 km. to the road that comes in from Mires (see p. 207).

[7 km.] Having passed through the olive groves, you come to the edge of the village of **Pitsidia**; bear to the right (at the chapel) and by-pass the village (although a rough but drivable road leads to Kommos).

[7·5 km.] Barely 500 metres after passing the point where the old road out of Pitsidia rejoins the main road, you come to the crest of a hill with a dirt track on the right (usually sign-posted) that leads toward the site of **Kommos**. The track passes a sand quarry on the left; you can park here and make your way by foot down a rough track to the right (and then walk across to the site on the coast); alternatively, you can proceed in your vehicle on the track past the quarry about 1 km. until you come to the church of Ayios Pandeleimon, park there, and then walk down a precipitous path to the coast and the site. In any case, do not try to drive to the site from this locale.

N.B. The site is fenced in and not attended. Many of the houses, the larger structures, and such elements as the great Minoan court, the Minoan road, the Greek temple and altars can be seen as you walk around the fence. Those who want to examine the remains closer and in more detail must make arrangements in the village of Pitsidia with the part-time guard (who has been Georgios Beladakis) who holds the key and will accompany visitors during reasonable hours: make your arrangements and then perhaps go on to Matala until the time arrives. Professor Shaw is planning to write a detailed guide to the site but until that is available, the following description and site plan are the best aids to viewing Kommos.

Kommos

It was Arthur Evans, as so often, who first reported signs of a Minoan site here, but it remained for Joseph Shaw, of the University of

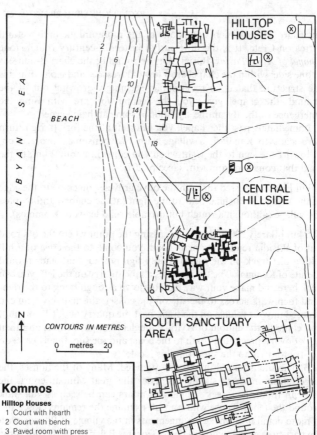

HILLTOP HOUSES

CENTRAL HILLSIDE

SOUTH SANCTUARY AREA

BEACH

LIBYAN SEA

N

CONTOURS IN METRES

0   metres   20

Kommos

Hilltop Houses
1 Court with hearth
2 Court with bench
3 Paved room with press
4 MM storerooms
5 Minoan road

Central Hillside
6 LM road
7 East room with hearths
8 Room for bathing
9 Slab-paved room
10 Storeroom (for pottery)

South Sanctuary Area
11 LM road
J LMI harbour building

N LMIII harbour building
P LMIIIA building with galleries
T LMI building with court and colonnade
A1 Temple room with hearth
A2 Temple room with columns and hearth

B Temple annexe
D Round structure
C, H, L, M Greek altars
E Hellenistic houses
Q Archaic Greek commercial building

X Trial digs: Minoan remains

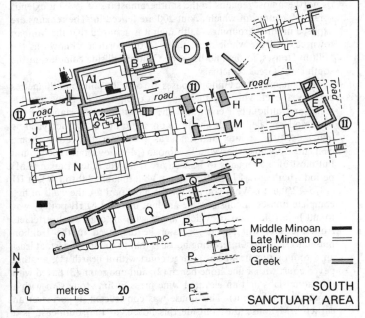

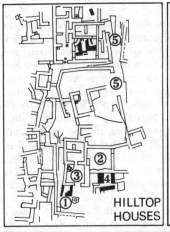

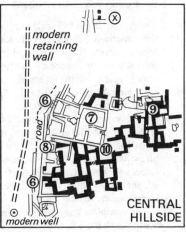

HILLTOP
HOUSES

*modern
retaining
wall*

CENTRAL
HILLSIDE

modern well

road

road

road

Middle Minoan ▬▬▬
Late Minoan or
earlier ═══
Greek ▨▨▨

N

0   metres   20

SOUTH
SANCTUARY AREA

Toronto, to begin full scale excavations in 1976. Under the auspices of the American School of Classical Studies and the Greek Archaeological Service, Shaw – assisted by his archaeologist-wife, Maria, and their team of professionals and the local workcrew – spent ten seasons removing the shifting layers of sand and earth to reveal this important and interesting addition to the Cretan canon. Shaw has established that Kommos was a well-developed town and port for the Minoans – almost certainly the main port for Phaestos, Ayia Triadha, and other centres of the Messara, and presumably the main port on the south coast for much of the traffic with all of central Crete. Beyond that, Shaw has revealed the unexpected remains of a fine, well-preserved, Greek sanctuary that was in use from about 900 B.C. to A.D. 150. All in all, the visitor to this site will be rewarded with some unusual, even some unique, remains.

The complete site extends along the coast that happens to have a north-south axis; facing the Libyan Sea, north is to your right. From its northernmost remains to the southernmost (as of 1988) it extends some 400 metres, of which about 200 are fenced in. The remains are exposed in three groupings – although it is assumed that the Minoan town covered the whole area; those to the north are known as the Hilltop Houses; in the middle is the Central Hillside complex; at the south is the Greek Sanctuary.

The remains of the Hilltop Houses are on a low hill some 20 metres above sea level. This was the first area completed by Shaw and his team, and although it confirmed the extent and importance of the town and revealed much about its domestic life, it did not yield as many exciting architectural finds as the other two areas. Some elements from an earlier Middle Minoan (MM) town have been found but most of the remains to be seen are from the Late Minoan (LM) period – built in LM I (1550–1450 B.C.) but inhabited through LM III (1375–1250 B.C.). What you see for the most part are the walls of five complete houses; a considerable amount of fine LM III pottery was found here (the finest of which, along with all other such artefacts from the site, will sooner or later be displayed in the Iraklion museum). The most interesting house is that to the south-east; at least an 8-room structure, it has a large court with a hearth (1); another paved court with a fine stone bench (2); and one room (3) paved with limestone slabs and an elevated wine press (a limestone slab with a depression and spout). This house was constructed in part over an earlier MM house. Just outside this house, to the south-east, is a group of MM storerooms (4); a large amount of pottery was found here. Along the north-eastern edge, on the north-south axis, runs a stretch of a paved road (5)

The Central Hillside complex is located about midway along the site and on the slopes leading down to the sea. Along the low cliff above the beach runs a LM road (6) that must have provided the Minoans with the same entrancing view over the Libyan Sea that we enjoy today. (A retaining wall has been built below this to help maintain the excavations from the wear-and-tear of the wind and sea.) The nature of excavating being as it is – with the last layers in time the first to be revealed – a large 7-room LM I-III building was the first major find here; its easternmost room (7) has two built hearths, a stone potstand, and a slab enclosure where a complete cooking pot was found. If this was apparently the kitchen, another room (8) proved to be a room for bathing. A LM dumpsite below this house yielded many interesting odds and ends that the Minoans discarded over the years, including amethyst and lapis lazuli beads, bronze fish hooks, and animal bones.

But of even more interest to the excavators was the relatively extensive series of MM rooms and structures found in this area – indicating that there was a sizeable and prosperous MM settlement at Kommos. Some of these MM rooms have walls preserved to over 2 metres high – and one wall still stands over 3 metres. One room in this MM complex (9) is lined with slabs; in its corner is a stone platform on which was set a spouted stone basin that could have been used to process wine or oil. Perhaps the most appealing finds from these MM rooms are the various artefacts – a stone slab kernos, an abrader of emery, some stone bowls, and many pieces of pottery, some intact, of the brilliant, polychromatic Kamares and post-Kamares styles. One room alone yielded 'an astounding amount of pottery', while below it a storeroom (10) contained many pieces of intact pottery of various types. Altogether, the MM pottery from Kommos is one of the richest deposits of intact MM pottery found anywhere in the Minoan realm. The fallen slabs and other remains in these rooms, by the way, indicate that the MM settlement was seriously damaged in an earthquake before being resettled in the early LM period.

It was in the southernmost section of the site, however, and during the second season of digging, that Shaw found the remains that will probably prove to be the most rewarding to most visitors. He had set out simply to investigate the area just east of the Minoan shoreline when he was, in his own words, 'temporarily confounded by a most unexpected discovery: a complex of unusual if not unique Classical and Hellenistic buildings'. The seasons that followed not only confirmed the unexpectedness of the first year but continued to yield a number of quite spectacular remains, including a most impressive Minoan highway (11). This road is itself, as the guidebooks say, 'worth the visit'. Some 2·85 metres wide, paved with limestone slabs (that show signs of considerable traffic), bordered along the north side by a drainage channel and retaining wall, this road leads directly from the shore and heads eastward, or inland; some 60 metres, at intervals, have been exposed, and it obviously went well beyond that – and probably branched off to lead to Ayia Triadha and/or Phaestos; as such it must have been the main link between central Crete and many points around the Mediterranean world.

Among the last remains to be found in this area of the site, and not as impressive to the non-specialist as are the later (historically) remains, are several large Minoan constructions. There are two quite large Minoan structures, (**J**) (LM I) and (**N**) (LM III), situated just south of the Minoan highway; of as yet undetermined use, they undoubtedly played some part in the trade and shipping that took place at harbourside. (There was a small offshore island at the port in Minoan times; in good weather, ships could have tied up there and been safe, but in general Minoan ships were pulled up on to beaches.) Proceeding eastward along the Minoan highway, you would come on the south side to a LM I building (**T**) – one of the more monumental buildings found at any Minoan site. Its ashlar (dressed) masonry wall runs at least 55 metres along the side of the road – the longest straight line of ashlar wall from Minoan Crete. Along the south-west corner of Building T was a colonnade, or stoa, that faced upon a large court (29 m. × 38 m.), paved with pebbles. (The colonnade is now largely hidden below later construction.) The exact function of Building T is not known but it seems to have served for storage and/or trading operations; its sheer size, however, like that of the other constructions here, suggests that Building T and its function represent the power and prosperity of the Minoans based in Phaestos, not that of local residents of Kommos. Whatever its function, Building T seems to have gone out of use at the end of the LM I period.

And then, if anything could have surpassed Building T, it was Building (**P**), erected just south of it in LM IIIA: Building P is the largest LM III building known from Crete. At least 35 metres long and 30 metres wide, on the west side it is divided into five great galleries that face west on to the same great court. As there are no signs of crosswalls within the galleries, they must have had un-interrupted roofed spaces as large as any known from Minoan structures. And since there was no apparent closure on the west side – that is, the galleries were completely open and facing the sea – it has been plausibly suggested that they were designed for storing ships during the winter months (when ships, throughout the ancient Mediterranean world, did not go to sea); the courtyard between the galleries and the shore seems to have been completely unobstructed and the ships could have been brought up on skids.

All this would surely be enough to satisfy true devotees of pre-historic sites, but the more familiar remains on this site – the ones the excavators did not expect to find – are those of a Greek sanctuary, one of the most complex and interesting of such sanctuaries found on Crete. It is known that as early as the 10th century B.C. – the so-called Proto-Geometric Period – there was a modest temple on this spot. Then, during the Late Geometric Period (approx. 800–600 B.C.), another temple was built over that one; this was during the time when Gortyna was a thriving Doric-Greek city. Within this temple, however, was a curious shrine consisting of three pillars: since its only model seems to be similar tripillar Phoenician shrines, the excavator suggests that Phoenician seafarers/merchants may have been resident here for an extended period.

But it was in the late 5th-early 4th centuries B.C. (say, 400–375 B.C.) that a sanctuary truly began to be developed on this site; it reached its acme – as judged by the artefacts recovered – in the Hellenistic Period (approx. 300–150 B.C.), then seems to have been burned about 50 B.C. The sanctuary, however, continued to be frequented by at least some people well through the 1st century A.D. There were other such sanctuaries around Crete during these centuries (one, for example, at Leben, just around the cape from Kommos – see pp. 230–2) but the unusual finds here at Kommos establish it as a site to be visited today as in the past.

The sanctuary was dominated by the 4th century by the temple currently designated as Building (**A**); it is still not known to which god(s) or goddess(es) the temple or sanctuary was dedicated, although an inscription mentioning Zeus and Athena was found, as well as a portable altar dedicated to Poseidon. This temple – which sits directly over the remains of the two earlier temples (the Proto-Geometric and the Geometric temples) – is formed of two rooms. Room A1 has a central hearth and benches around the interior. The room to the south, A2, was even more elaborate; it has not only a central hearth and benches but a floor paved with slabs; two large column bases are alongside the hearth; and along the west wall is a platform of fine masonry (note the base moulding) on which stood one or more cult statues. Finds from many centuries attest to the temples' attraction and include terracotta and bronze horse and bull figurines from the Geometric Period, Attic and Corinthian vases from the Archaic and Classic periods, and Hellenistic vessels and a delicate bronze wreath.

Abutting the north-east corner of Building A is Building (**B**); it faces south on to the altar courtyard, and its two rooms may be entered from that side; stairs in the western room indicate the building had an attic or second storey. Finds on the floors of the two rooms include goblets, plates, lamps, etc., dated to about 150–50 B.C.; obviously Building B played some supporting role to the temple of Building A. Then, directly to the east of Building B is Building (**D**) – a round structure, with its exterior diameter measuring about 5·5 metres and still preserved to five courses; built with obvious care, it seems an echo of other round structures at Greek sanctuaries (Epidaurus, Delphi) but its exact appearance and function are unknown.

All these buildings face on to the great altar courtyard that was dominated by four Greek altars – (**C, H, L, M**) – now little more than rectangular stone bases. Their symmetrical arrangement is perhaps unique among Cretan-Greek sanctuaries. A great deal of burnt animal bone was found upon and all around these altars; also suggestive is a terracotta bull (some 11 inches long) found upon one of them – an echo of Minoan religion of 1000 years before?

In addition to these buildings forming the sanctuary, there is Building (**Q**), a long narrow structure to the south (and lying across Minoan Building P); dated to the 7th century B.C., some 38 metres long and 5·8 metres wide, it is divided into at least four rooms; its exact function is also unknown, but it contained many fragments of transport amphorae, suggesting a thriving trade in oil and wine with the Eastern Aegean. And then, off to the east (and lying across the end of Minoan Building T) is Building (**E**), a house of the Hellenistic Period. It is assumed, too, that many other remains, Minoan and Greek, lie to the south and east of the present excavation site. At present they lie outside the land available to the excavators, but whether these or other remains at Kommos are brought to light, it seems that this site will continue to grow in significance as the excavators reveal their findings.

[12 km.] Matala

Until the mid 1960s, Matala was frequented only in the summer, and mainly by Cretans and the occasional foreigner; in the off-season, it was all but deserted. Certainly the village was unknown to most visitors to Crete, let alone to the world at large. Then, for a combination of reasons, Matala was 'adopted' by the international youth set conveniently labelled as 'hippies', and it has never been the same.

But to begin at the beginning, the really unique attraction of Matala is the great promontory that forms the right arm of the cove – a high, sheer cliff of parched yellow earth that time has packed into a sort of rock. Into this cliff, across the centuries, men have carved caves. Some are little more than pockmarks, warrens barely able to shelter a few people; others are regular rooms, complete with benches carved out of the walls; and a few are quite elaborate apartments, with steps, vestibules, framed doors and windows, and fireplaces. The beds are reminiscent of Etruscan tombs, with their platforms for the dead, carved out of the natural stone. The left arm of the harbour also has a few caves; some people, too, have built houses on its gentler slopes, back against the caves.

It is difficult to find an authoritative statement as to what caused this unusual terrain. One theory is that forces of water, millions of years ago, built up great sand barriers, and when a stream cut through the compressed mound the cliffs were left on both sides. Then, because Matala sits almost exactly on the hinge axis of the uplift, and because of the subsidence movements that have occurred on Crete over the centuries, these cliffs and their man-made caves may have been subjected to a fair amount of pressure.

No one seems to know for certain who first dug out these holes. During the Minoan period, the main port of the Messara was actually north of Matala at Kommos (see p. 236). Matala only came into its own in post-Minoan times, when Gortyna had assumed power. In any case, there is no evidence (or scholarly support) for suggesting that these caves were dug out or used by the Minoans, the Greeks or even by the Romans; the first known use, in fact, seems to have been as tombs by Christians between A.D. 500–1000. Many centuries later, during the Second World War, the Germans used the caves as military storerooms. Meanwhile, Matala had known its share of myths and legends. Here Zeus, disguised as a bull, came ashore bearing Europa (perhaps signifying the arrival of some Phoenician ship with the figurehead of a bull?); and here some of Menelaus' vessels were driven ashore on their return from the war at Troy (see *Odyssey*, Book III).

At least in the last few centuries, though, it seems safe to assume that local Cretans occasionally made use of the caves; after all, they are as comfortable as many peasant dwellings – and cost nothing. When, after the late 1960s, crowds of young people descended on Matala's caves in search of a free place in the sun, the Greek authorities cleared everyone out of the caves. But the young foreigners continued to come to Matala, in winter as well as in summer, living in rented rooms, in camping vehicles or wherever. Meanwhile, more ambitious sleeping and eating facilities have attracted conventional vacationers. But for the moment all parties seem to have achieved a congenial *modus vivendi*.

There are some underwater remains at the edge of the cliffs as well as grottoes – an invitation to skin-divers – and a Roman slipway on the south side, but most people who come to Matala are content to swim, to climb about or to enjoy the view. South from Matala, along the coast, are other more spectacular grottoes; you would have to get a local fisherman to take you in his boat; the trip takes about two hours. You could make a day of it by going on round Cape Lithinon to Kaloi Limines, the little fishing village on the south coast (p. 232), and even on to Leben (below). Another possibility for ambitious walkers is either to walk overland to Kaloi Limines (via the Monastery of Odhiyitrias) or to go north to Timbaki (p. 236) and from there to Phaestos (p. 207) or on to Ayia Galini (p. 237).

Leben

Another interesting excursion from Phaestos, although a fairly demanding drive, is the seldom-visited site of ancient Leben – now also known as Lendas, the name of a nearby village. It can also be combined with the trip to the Messara tombs (p. 233).

Route From Phaestos you go back through Mires on the Iraklion road nearly to Ayii Dheka; just about opposite the ruins of Gortyna (p. 207), turn right on to a small road for Mitropolis and Platanos. In Platanos turn left at the church for Plora, through which you will continue eastwards to Apesokarion. Then turn right (sign-posted) for Miamou and Krotos and the descent to the coast at Lendas [46 km.].

Bus There is one bus a day, in each direction, between Iraklion and Lendas; it leaves from outside the Khania Gate.
Accommodation Modest rooms and meals can be found at Lendas.

[10 km.] Going back from Phaestos, you pass through Mires (p. 207).

[16 km.] Opposite the ruins of Gortyna (p. 207), turn off to the right on to a road (sign-posted) for Mitropolis and Platanos.

[17 km.] **Mitropolis.**

[20 km.] **Koustouliana.**

[21 km.] **Platanos**: one starting-off place from which you can visit the tombs of the Messara (p. 233).

[23 km.] Follow the road round to the end of the village of **Plora**, and at the edge of the village bear left (sign-posted).

[24 km.] Just before the village of **Apesokarion**, turn right (sign-posted).

[34 km.] **Miamou**: in a nearby cave (first explored by the Italians in 1894), important remains were found indicating that it was inhabited in the Neolithic period and later used for burials.

[38 km.] **Krotos** via an asphalt road.

[46 km.] You descend to the village of **Lendas**, which sits at the end of the road above the sea. It is really only a cluster of houses and cafés, where you can find some rooms to rent and simple meals. The local people enjoy showing strangers about the ruins. The beach is decent enough.

Leben

The remains – first excavated in the nineteenth century by the ubiquitous Italians, who returned in 1910 to complete the work – are quite impressive for such an isolated spot. They are situated on the hillside some five minutes' walk east of the village, and command a fine view across the Libyan Sea.

Leben seems to be derived from a Phoenician-Semitic word for 'lion' – referring to the promontory that juts out into the sea here like a crouching animal. This helps to form and protect the small harbour, enclosed to the east by Cape Psamidomouri, which must have once witnessed a fair amount of traffic. It was in the post-Minoan period that Leben came into its own, especially during the sixth and fifth centuries B.C., when Gortyna used it as a port, and it attracted people from some distance, thanks to the curative powers of its spring. Until recently people came from as far away as the Greek mainland to drink the waters, which are especially recommended for ulcers. Leben is situated in such a favourable spot that tomatoes can be cultivated all the year round and swallows are said to winter there.

The major structure here was the *Temple of Asclepius* – as befits a site associated with curative waters. It dates from the third century B.C.; it may have been destroyed in an earthquake in A.D. 46 and then restored. Two columns are in place. Marble steps once led down to an elegant Roman *mosaic*, depicting a prancing sea-horse; this is above the subterranean *treasury-crypt*. To the north of this are the remains of a *portico*. The wonderful *well* with the curative powers that still attracts people lies to the south-east of the temple; a short distance to the south are large *baths*; and farther to the south-west are traces of structures that were probably the guest-houses for those who came to take the cure. Still farther to the east of these ancient remains is the eleventh-century *Church of Ayios Ioannis*. It stands in the ruins of the ninth-century basilica, which in turn was at least partly constructed out of ancient stones.

If you have a guide, you can go some 4 km. from the village to the remains of some Minoan circular tombs that were discovered in the late 1950s. It has long been known that there was some Minoan settlement at the base of the 'Lion Cape', and now these tombs have yielded pottery, Cycladic figurines, implements and jewellery – some of which confirms the early trade with Egypt. Dr Stylianos Alexiou employed the most advanced methods of stratigraphic excavation to learn still more about the Minoan era from this relatively obscure site.

Kaloi Limines

A possible excursion from Lendas is a drive west (some 10 km.) along the coast to the little fishing village of Kaloi Limines – the 'Fair Havens' mentioned in Acts xxvii 8. There is also a (poor) road to here from Mires (p. 207); you go down through Pombia and Pigaidakia – a total distance of about 23 km. Backed by *Cape Lithinon*, on the other side of which is Matala (p. 229), are a few houses; there *was* a nice beach here, but both it and the charm of the cove have been spoiled by the oil tanks erected here. Three rocky islets lie just off shore – one of which is called 'St Paul's Island'. There is a small *chapel* on the shore, said to mark the spot where St Paul is supposed to have preached when he put ashore in A.D. 60 on the way from Caesarea to Rome.

If you have driven to Kaloi Limines, you have several possibilities. Some kilometres to its east (you pass this when coming along the coast road from Lendas) is the site of *Lasaia* above the coast; once a port for Gortyna, it was a considerable Hellenistic and Roman settlement, but little of interest remains. You could also drive north to the *Monastery of Odhiyitrias*, famed for its role in the nineteenth-century struggles with the Turks (and indeed it looks more like a fort than a monastery); its chapel has fine icons and frescoes. Next to the monastery is a castle known as *Xopateras*, after the abbot who died fighting the Turks. From the monastery you can drive north to Sivas and then on to Pitsidia and Matala.

Tombs of the Messara

This rather specialized excursion would take at least a full day and is of interest only to quite serious students of the period. In any case, private transport and a good guide are essential; arrangements can be made before starting at the Tourist Information office in Iraklion. The excursion to Leben (p. 230) might be combined with this trip.

Route If you are based in Phaestos, you return along the Iraklion road through Mires to Gortyna and take the turn to the right that leads to Mitropolis and Platanos (described in the previous excursion to Leben). Platanos could be used as the starting-point for a visit to some of the tombs; others might better be approached from other directions (described below).

Bus There is a bus service to Platanos from the Khania Gate in Iraklion; it could be picked up in Ayii Dheka.

Accommodation We assume you will be using Phaestos, Matala, or even Mires as a base; at a pinch, you can find simple accommodation in the villages of the Messara.

[10 km.] You go back through Mires (p. 207).

[16 km.] Turn right on to the small road that leads through Mitropolis.

[21 km.] About $\frac{1}{2}$ km. beyond (sign-posted) the village of Platanos, you reach the first of the tombs of the Messara.

Tombs of the Messara

These tombs were among the earliest finds on Crete, as well as among the oldest remains of the Minoans. Some were excavated towards the end of the nineteenth century by local Cretan archaeologists and by the Italian mission. Then in the late 1950s there began a series of excavations in the more western 'fringes' of the Asterousia Mountains – at Leben (p. 230), at Kephali (near Odhiyitrias Monastery, p. 233) and elsewhere – that have suggested that the whole area was populated on a more extensive scale than had previously been thought; furthermore, some of the newly discovered tombs are even older than the Messara tombs.

But the basic ideas of the Messara tombs and their culture remain. The tombs were free-standing, stone-walled structures, usually circular; the roofs may have been anything from thatch or wooden beams to real stone vaults. Although hardly as dramatic as the great beehive tombs of Mycenae (and by no means as high), these Messara tombs were considerably earlier and may well have had some influence on the builders of the mainland tombs. They were regarded as homes for the afterworld, and it is from them and their contents that we have learned practically all we know of the people who used them for burial. It was a Pre-palatial culture, based on small tribes or clans. Existing well before the distinctive Minoan civilization, there were undoubtedly strong links with the Egyptian, Anatolian, Mesopotamian and Babylonian cultures, as the many finds testify. These finds – now in the Iraklion museum – include jewellery, amulets, pottery, idols, human and animal figurines, tools and weapons of all kinds. Some of the knives were from obsidian, a stone found on the islands of Milo and Yali (south of Kos), and in Anatolia, a fact that opens up wide speculation about the trade and communications of the age.

The most revealing finds have been the sealstones – small, flat and oval-shaped. At first these were made of soft materials like ivory and steatite; later, harder semi-precious stones were used. They were carved intaglio-fashion (often on several sides) with representations of various forms including animals and, less frequently, human figures. They seem to have been something like 'totems', expressing the personality or ideal of the owners with whom they were interred, although most sealstones were probably used for the more prosaic purpose of identifying and protecting property. In any case, many are gems of artistry and revelations of a whole way of life.

Of course none of this is to be seen *in situ*, which is why most people will limit their examination of the Messara tombs to the artefacts now in the Iraklion museum. One of the most impressive tombs is the one on the edge of Platanos (sign-posted to fenced-in area $\frac{1}{2}$ km. past church). Only its foundations remain, but these are enough to indicate its size – about 13 metres in diameter and nearly $2\frac{1}{2}$-metre-thick walls; the main tomb was surrounded by fifteen smaller chambers, in which were found many vases, tools, seals and other objects.

Some other interesting tombs were found some distance to the east between Loukia and Koumasa, along the northern slopes of the Asterousia Mountains. These are actually best approached from Ayii Dheka, by the road that leads south via Vayionia to Koumasa.

In addition to these – and, of course, the more accessible ones at Lendas (p. 232) and Ayia Triadha (p. 220) – there are many more scattered throughout the Messara: Kamilari, Kalathiana, Maratho-kephalo, Porti, Dhrakonas, Apesokarion and Ayia Ireni are among the places with tombs, but all these would definitely require a guide and a specialist's concern.

ROUTE 2:
PHAESTOS TO RETHYMNON

This is an alternative way back from Phaestos to the north coast for those who have their own transport and some time to spare – although you can make the trip by various buses. There is nothing of major import en route but it is a delightful trip through the heart of Crete.

Route Descending from Phaestos site on to the main road, turn left for Timbaki; from there proceed to the north-west past Ayia Galini and on via Spili to Rethymnon [79 km.]. Alternatively, you can turn north before Ayia Galini for Amari and then continue on to Rethymnon [77 km.].
Bus You can catch the bus from Phaestos to Timbaki and Ayia Galini; some buses even go to Rethymnon (enquire about schedules at the Tourist Information). There are also buses between Fourfouras and Rethymnon, and buses between Rethymnon and Lefkoyia (from which you can get down to the Monastery of Preveli – see below).
Accommodation In addition to the many hotels at Ayia Galini there are inns and rooms to rent at Timbaki, hotels at Spili, Timbaki and Kokhinos Pyrgos, and you could find a room to rent in some of the other larger villages en route.

[3 km.] Following the main road from below Phaestos westwards to Timbaki, you pass a fork to the right that would lead to **Voroi**.

[4 km.] Keeping on to Timbaki, you pass on the left a turn-off that leads in about $\frac{1}{2}$ km. to Ayia Triadha (p. 217).

[5 km.] On the left, as you approach the outskirts of Timbaki, is one of those incongruous features that crop up so often on Crete: several hundred metres of asphalt spread over the landscape to form an airstrip. Started by the Germans during their occupation in the Second World War, it was expanded for strategic emergencies after the war and is now maintained by the Greek Air Force.

[6 km.] You arrive at **Timbaki**, the terminus for the Iraklion bus. This developing village has nothing of importance to offer, but there is a Class C hotel, the *San Giorgio* (tel. 51.678) and a taxi can be hired for making other excursions.

[8 km.] On the left, 2 km. off the main road, is **Kokhinos Pyrgos**, with its tomato gardens, abandoned warehouses and Customs office – it was once a port for the African trade. In recent years it has become a popular beach 'resort' among Cretans of this region; there are several hotels, including one Class C, several inns and many cafés and restaurants. Off shore are two islets known as *Paximadhia*, which is the word for the hard-baked bread, or toast, that you get in Cretan villages; to be eaten it must first be dipped in water or milk. These islets get this name for obvious reasons.

A turn to the right at 14 km. (sign-posted Amari and Rethymnon) leads up into the hills to **Apodhoulou** in 6 km. and then left on to **Fourfouras** in another 12 km. These villages are in *Amari Province*, noted for the scenic attractions of its hills and valleys. It also has many churches and chapels, some with first-rate Byzantine icons and frescoes and including the *Church of St Anne* in Nefs-Amari with frescoes dated to 1225, among the oldest yet known on Crete. Wherever you choose to spend the night, you can be sure of finding some sort of accommodation. Fourfouras can also be used as a starting-point for the ascent of Mount Idha (p. 197). From Fourfouras you could go directly to Rethymnon, passing through the villages of **Apostoloi** and **Prasses** before striking the main Iraklion–Rethymnon road some 3 km. east of Rethymnon (the total journey from Phaestos to Rethymnon by this route is 77 km.). Incidentally, some 8 km. after Fourfouras you pass the *Monastery of Asomatos*. Founded in the tenth to eleventh centuries, its present structure dates from the Venetian period (as the architecture of the chapel suggests). The monastery served as an intellectual and resistance outpost during the Turkish occupation, and its Abbot Joseph (1833–60) established a school in the nearby village of **Monastiraki** that operated till 1913. In 1931 the monks donated much of their property to an agricultural school that still operates here. At Apostoli, a turn to the right leads in 2 km. to **Thronos**, with its *Church of the Panayia* built on the mosaic floor of an early Christian basilica; on a nearby hill are some walls and other remains of the ancient Greek site of *Syvrita*.

[19 km.] Having instead proceeded straight on at the 14 km. fork, you arrive at a left fork bringing you in 1½ km. to **Ayia Galini.** The name means 'holy serenity'. It was a small fishing port clinging to the south coast – a cross between a pirates' cove and the Italian Riviera.

Like several other villages on Crete, Ayia Galini was all but unknown until the late 1960s, when it was discovered by the young crowd looking for a cheap retreat; foreigners of all ages have since come in such numbers that they have overwhelmed, or at least altered the attractions of the village. There are numerous Class C, D and E hotels and many rooms to rent now, and meals are easily available. A path leads from the main bay eastwards to a wide beach where there is good swimming. The main attraction for sightseers has been the grottoes along the coast to the west, but these are only approached from the sea by hiring a boat. The fact is, Ayia Galini tends to be overloaded in the high season, and travellers who prefer their Crete more indigenous should avoid this place.

Climbing up from Ayia Galini back to the junction at the 19-km. point, you turn off to the left and head north-west along what is mapped as a major highway. You proceed past **Melambes** and **Akoumia**.

[49 km.] You pass through **Spili**, a village renowned for its cascades of water, shady trees, and its most unusual fountain: nineteen lions' heads spewing forth water into a trough. There is now a Class C hotel here, the *Green* (tel. 22.225), as well as two inns and several restaurants, so Spili could be used as a pleasant break or retreat.

[58 km.] A turning to the left to **Koxares** leads in another 16 km. to the *Monastery of Preveli*, down above the south coast and worth the detour for those with extra time. After passing through Koxares, you drive through the gorge of Kourtaliotiko – itself quite impressive – and pass, as you turn left at the fork, steps to the *Chapel of Ayios Nikolaos*, beside which springs the Megalopotamos, the river that comes out at the sea below Preveli. You proceed towards **Asomatos**, and immediately on entering this village turn left (the right fork leads on via Marjiou and Myrthios to **Plakias**, a wide beach with good swimming which is developing into a small resort); at the next junction, also take the left turn. You drive on, crossing the Megalopotamos on a Venetian bridge, and then pass by the long-abandoned old monastery of Preveli and proceed to the newer Monastery of Preveli.

The monastery actually consists of two parts, the upper one magnificently sited overlooking the Libyan Sea, and the lower one down on a fertile bank of the Megalopotamos. It is the upper one that most people will be content to visit. Its exact date of founding is unknown, but it has been claimed that it was founded in the seventeenth century by a prominent Rethymnon family. It is dedicated to St John the Theologian whose feast day is observed on May 8th. The present church dates only from the nineteenth century, and it claims no important frescoes or icons. However, it boasts a library and a small museum of religious articles, priests' costumes, and a fragment of the True Cross. But it is a pair of silver candlesticks, the gift of the British after the Second World War, that reveal the aspect of Preveli of interest to foreigners. The monastery, like so many others, had taken an active role in the resistance against the Turks. But it was after the defeat of the British forces in the battle for Crete at the end of May 1941 that Preveli Monastery became a 'waiting room' for many British and Commonwealth soldiers who hid here or in the adjoining hills until they could be picked up off-shore by motor launches and taken to Egypt. Eventually the Germans discovered this and put an end to such activities, but many owed their lives to these monks. (There is in south-west Australia a Prevally Park, named by one grateful Australian.)

Those with extra time might like to take the footpath down to the rocky shore below the monastery, a walk of some 25 minutes.

[69 km.] Back on the main road (beyond Koxares) you continue northwards across the mountains and pass through **Armeni**. Then, about 2 km. farther out of the village you will see a sign on the left indicating the Minoan necropolis, or cemetery, discovered here in 1969 by the Greek archaeologist Tzedakis. Over several years he has uncovered close to 200 tombs from the Late Minoan period. You can walk over and inspect several of them and note the approach channels, the *dromos* of the Mycenaean tomb, that leads to the tombs cut into the natural rock; many of the stones that covered the entrance are still there. The tombs have yielded not only the usual collection of vases, bronze-work, jewellery and seals but an especially fine set of painted sarcophagi (now displayed in Khania's Archaeological Museum, p. 260). What is perhaps most exciting about this discovery, however, is what is not yet to be seen: the Minoan settlement that required such an ambitious cemetery.

[79 km.] You descend to the coast to see Rethymnon (p. 245) spread out before you.

ROUTE 3: IRAKLION TO RETHYMNON

This can be a quick journey between two of Crete's major cities – especially if the new national highway is used; we describe instead the old route, which repays your mountainous, curving drive by lush landscapes and fine views. If even a couple of the side-excursions are made – Tylissos or Fodhele or the Melidhoni Cave – then it can become a full day's journey or longer. Also the preferred approach to the Idha Cave and Nidha Plain is now via Anoyia, as described as a side-trip on this route.

Route Follow the road to Khania that leaves Iraklion by the Khania Gate (Route Exit A) and proceed westwards along the coast; the road soon rises and skirts the Idha Range, and descends again to Perama and Rethymnon [79 km.].

Bus There are several buses daily in each direction; they leave from the bus terminal down by the harbour. There are also direct services to Fodhele, Tylissos and Anoyia; these leave from outside the Khania Gate. The Melidhoni Cave may be reached from Rethymnon by bus.

Accommodation There are resort hotels at Panormos and Stavromenos, while Platanias offers some choice.

[2 km.] Here the Phaestos road (p. 200) and new highway branch off to the left.

[8 km.] If you are travelling in your own car you can turn right here for a trip of 28 km. to Fodhele, birthplace of El Greco (see pp. 180–2). If you take this as a detour en route to Rethymnon, you will rejoin the main road at a point 20 km. from Iraklion (see below). As the roads may still be rough tracks this detour is only for enthusiasts.

[11 km.] Keeping on the main road, you come to a turning to the left that leads in another 3 km. to the village of **Tylissos**, where there is a Minoan site of the same name. To reach the excavations, turn left (marked) just as you come into the village, and then first left again (marked); proceed about 100 metres until you see, on the right, a sign: TYLISSOS, and gate. The site has been closing at 15.00 – enquire at the National Tourist Organization office in Iraklion; the caretakers are a village family; there is an entrance fee of Drs 100. There is a small pavilion with two or three beds available for archaeologists and students with some special concern with this site. (Enquiries must be directed to the Archaeological Museum in Iraklion.) In the village of Tylissos itself, rooms may be rented and meals obtained.

DESCRIPTION OF TYLISSOS

Tylissos hardly compares with the major Minoan sites, but it is still of some interest; as so often on Crete, it is the setting that satisfies. Three Minoan *villas* and a post-Minoan *megaron* were excavated here by Hadzidakis in the years before the First World War; Platon later did some valuable restoration work. The remains now offer a good glimpse into the architecture and living conditions of those Minoans one step removed from the great palaces. The discovery of more and more Minoan sites in the western part of Crete, meanwhile, suggests that Tylissos – and we must assume that these villas were merely part of a much larger settlement – derived whatever prosperity and importance it enjoyed from being on the route between Knossos and these western settlements.

Most of the surviving remains date from about 1600 to 1450 B.C. but, as with most Minoan buildings and sites, traces of both earlier and later structures also remain to complicate matters for the casual visitor. Tylissos was destroyed about the same time as the major palace centres, but new buildings arose on the site – themselves to be destroyed later. In the post-Minoan period, Dorian Greeks built on the site, issued their own coinage and worshipped Artemis.

Tylissos: Minoan Villas

House A
1 Entrance Hall
2 Stairs to upper floor
3 Corridor to South Wing
4 Room with storage jars
5 Lightwell
6 Storerooms
7 Site of staircases to upper floor
House C
8 Original threshold
9 Porter's Lodge

10 Corridor to South Wing
11 Staircase to upper floor
12 Rooms with original paving
13 Storerooms
14 Corridor to North Wing
15 Large room (Shrine?)
16 Room with Greek statue base
17 Room with open-air courtyard
18 N.E. Cistern and staircase
19 Filter basin for Cistern
20 Greek Altar

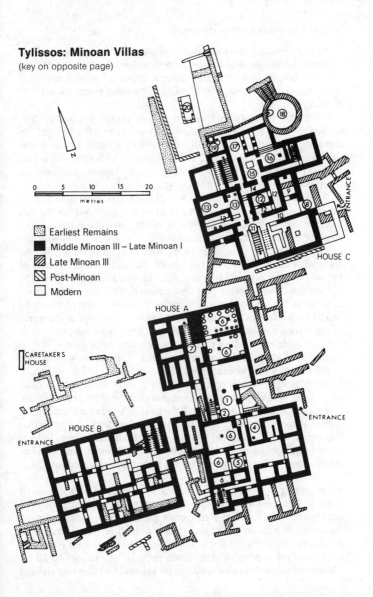

Tylissos: Minoan Villas
(key on opposite page)

N

0   5   10   15   20
          metres

▨ Earliest Remains
■ Middle Minoan III – Late Minoan I
▨ Late Minoan III
▧ Post-Minoan
□ Modern

CARETAKER'S HOUSE

HOUSE A

HOUSE B

HOUSE C

ENTRANCE

ENTRANCE

ENTRANCE

As you approach the ruins from a slight rise, *House B* lies to your right and below: this was smaller than the other two but carefully laid out and constructed. It is too poorly preserved to interest most visitors, but it has been important for providing traces of the first building period here.

Proceeding along (with House B still on your right, below), you come above the rear of *House A*, which extends to left and right. Its entrance was in the middle of the opposite (east) side. House A was the largest of the three villas; a walk through its rooms will reveal various remains – stairs (these were three-storey houses), large storage jars (*píthoi*), columns, original paving.

To the left (north) of House A was *House C*, the most luxurious of the three villas. Its entrance was also at about the middle of the east side: the threshold of this doorway is still in place and it leads into a corridor with a staircase, about midway, off to the left. Elsewhere in this house you may note some rooms with original paving, columns, walls with traces of painted plaster. At the north-eastern corner of House C, the large round structure with the stairway on one side is the *cistern*; this dates from the post-destruction period; the water – which came from the spring that still supplies Tylissos – entered via stone pipes that led from a filter basin, to the west. Above and to the north of this villa are some remains of the later Greek buildings.

Quite aside from walking about the remains, most people will be interested to know of the various finds from Tylissos, now to be seen in the museum in Iraklion. Bits of frescoes, vases, sealstones, tools, figurines (including a bronze worshipper), three large bronze cauldrons (one weighing some 50 kilos), and perhaps most crucial, some rare Linear A tablets – all testify to the level of Minoan culture even in such settlements as this. There was also a tomb excavated near by that had been used for a cremation burial; since this does not seem to have been the customary mode of burial for the late-Minoan period, it has been suggested that this was the tomb of some distinguished foreigner.

After visiting Tylissos – and assuming you are there on a detour en route to Rethymnon – you have an alternative to retracing the road back to the main Iraklion–Rethymnon road: you can continue on, by an asphalt but curving mountain road of about 35 kms. duration to rejoin that main road at about the 40-km. (from Iraklion) point and see several other points of interest en route. If you choose to do so, you continue on through the village of Tylissos and (bearing right at the edge) you continue on about 7 km.: on your left, at the roadside, is a late-Minoan villa known as *Sklavókambos*, discovered in 1930 during the making of this road and excavated just before the Second World War by Marinatos. In another 5 km. you pass through the village of **Gonies**, and then, in another 10 km., you arrive at **Anoyia**. If this village, with its choice location, has an unexpected raw-concrete look about it, there is a reason. During the last war, Anoyia was a centre of the resistance against the German occupation; after the partisans kidnapped the German commandant (see p. 102), it was discovered that Anoyia was one of several places used to hide him before he was removed from Crete. The Germans killed every male in the village and razed the buildings – except for the church. (Dedicated to John the Baptist, it sits below the main square and has a note-worthy set of frescoes.) Eventually the people rebuilt them, and today they live off their flocks and their handicrafts; Anoyia has long acted as a 'host' village to organized groups of tourists by offering meals, dances, and locally made wares, especially textiles.

Anoyia is the village now used to approach the Idha Cave, an excursion described in detail on p. 198.

But continuing on westward, you come in 8 km. to **Axos**, a village with one fine frescoed church: *Ayios Ioannis*. (A custodian in the village has a key.) Also, up a road to the left (sign) is the site of ancient *Axos*, first settled as the Minoans were abandoning their palace centres and later important in the Archaic period. On the summit of a spur end of the Idha Range, it is practically inaccessible; there are few remains except for the cyclopean walls, but the view is impressive.

Outside the village of Zoniana, 3 km. south of Axos, is the *Cave of Sedoni*, truly spectacular with its endless succession of chambers and passages, its dramatic stalagmites and stalactites, and incredible columns forming 'organ-pipes' and 'draperies'.

Continuing on as the road heads north-west, you pass in some 10 km. through the village of **Garazon** and then in another 2 km. rejoin the main road, with a left turn to Rethymnon.

But since this whole excursion has been a detour from our main route, we now go back to the point at 11 km. where you turned off to Tylissos. The road now climbs into some wooded and quite green terrain.

[19 km.] **Marathos.**

[20 km.] On the right is the turn leading in 7 km. by rough track to Fodhele (p. 182), past the abandoned *Monastery of Ayios Panteleimon*. From there you could return to Iraklion by reversing the route described on pp. 180–2.

[27 km.] **Dhamasta**, the last village in Iraklion Nome.

[34 km.] **Drosia.** This village was long noted for its roast suckling pigs but these have fallen victim – or rather, been saved by the diversion of most traffic to the National Road. As you drive on, the Idha Range dominates the surrounding landscape, with its drainage accounting for the fertility. The most prominent river is the *Mylopotamos*, which winds about the valley as it makes its way north-westwards to the sea.

[55 km.] You arrive at **Perama**, to be noted solely for the turning to the *Melidhoni Cave*, which attracts many visitors both as a natural phenomenon and as an event in Crete's history. (It can conveniently be visited by bus from Rethymnon.) The road to the Melidhoni Cave is a right turn out of Perama for **Panormos** – the site of a Hellenistic-Byzantine port on the north coast (and with ruins of a sixth-century A.D. Christian *basilica*, Ayia Sophia). But, after crossing a bridge on the Panormos road immediately outside Perama you fork right and reach, in 4 km., the village of **Melidhoni.** After driving through the village you take a road to the left, sign-posted Spileon, that curves for some 2 km. up to a chapel. Here you walk a few metres up to the left and then you immediately come to a small crater; the cave's entrance is down to the right.

The cave is quite large, with stalactites and chambers. At latest by the Hellenistic period there was a cult that worshipped Hermes here. The cave has also been claimed as the dwelling-place of Talos, the mythical bronze giant who went striding around Crete three times a day and hurled boulders at unwelcome strangers approaching the island. This story is part of the saga of the Argonauts; later Dante was to retell it in his vision of the *Inferno*. But it is its more recent historical associations that make the cave a shrine today. In 1824 several hundred Cretans from neighbouring villages had taken refuge here from a troop of Muslim soldiers ravaging the land. When the soldiers discovered that the Cretans were inside, they piled brushwood at the mouth of the cave and set fire to it. The Cretans within were suffocated. For decades afterwards, visitors to the cave reported seeing the bones and skulls in the crevices and corners where the people had scrambled for the last pockets of air. An altar in the first chamber commemorates this episode and, although not everyone will care to make such a pilgrimage, the cave and its surroundings serve to round out the story of Crete.

[58 km.] A turn to the left (sign-posted) leads southwards up into the hills and in 6 km. to the village of **Margarites**, noted for maintaining the age-old Cretan tradition of handmade ceramics. Several potters still practise their craft, and depending on the day and time you are there you can observe various stages of the processes. There are also three churches with frescoes and interesting architectural elements, but most people will settle for buying some handmade wares and then enjoying the vista and perhaps a simple meal on the terrace of the little taverna at the edge of the square. (Be sure to proceed on up to the upper square – don't stop only at the shops in the first square.)

[74 km.] Back on the coast road, at the village of Platanias are several hotels.

Hotels Class A: *El Greco* (tel. 71.281).
　　　　　　　Rithymna Beach (tel. 29.491).
　　　Class B: *Adele Beach* (tel. 71.081).
　　　　　　　Orion (tel. 71.471).
　　　Class C: *Golden Beach* (tel. 71.012).
　　　　　　　Rina (tel. 22.590).
　　　　　　　Seven Brothers (tel. 25.647).

A turn to the left at Platanias would lead to the historic Monastery of Arkadhi (p. 251), but, going straight on, you descend on to the flat and fertile coastal plain; to the left rises the Vrisinas range, source of Rethymnon's water. In 1972, a Minoan peak sanctuary was found on Mt Vrisinas, with many votive terracotta animal statuettes.

[79 km.] Rethymnon lies sprawled along the coast.

RETHYMNON

Rethymnon, an attractive provincial town, is the capital of Rethymnon Nome. It has a distinctive air, reminiscent of its Venetian and Turkish pasts; its minarets in particular give it a Middle Eastern flavour. It can be a restful place to pass a day or two while taking excursions into the countryside.

Population About 15,000
Information *Tourist Information*: E. Venizelos Ave. (*Map* **3**) (tel. 29.148).

Tourist Police: Arkadhio Street (by Loggia-Museum, *Map* **6**) (tel. 28.156).

Hotels Class B: *Braskos* (tel. 23.721).

        Hen (tel. 29.330).

        Ideon (tel. 28.667).

        Joan (tel. 24.241).

        Kriti Beach (tel. 22.353).

        Olympic (tel. 24.761).

        Xenia (tel. 29.111).

        Zania (tel. 28.169).

        Zorbas Beach (tel. 28.540).

    Class C: *Astali* (tel. 24.722).

        Ionia (tel. 22.902).

        Minos (tel. 24.173).

        Parc (tel. 29.558).

        Steris Beach (tel. 28.303).

        Valari (tel. 22.336).

In addition, there are several Class D and E hotels.

Camping Crete's oldest and most established camping site, 'Camping Elizabeth', is some 5 km. east of the town along the beach. Near by is the newer camp site, 'Arcadia'.

Restaurants Rethymnon has the usual variety of eating-places and cafés, clustered around the squares and along the harbour.

Night-life In the summer there are popular eating-places such as the *Romantzo* and *Trekhantiri* where there is also dancing. There is the usual selection of Greek cinemas. And near the end of July, there is the 'Wine Festival', observed with dancing, music and wine-sampling.

Clubs There is an active branch of the Greek Touring Club, making excursions to natural sites and antiquities of the nome. Foreigners are welcome to join in their activities; enquire at the Tourist Information office (*Map* **3**).

Swimming There are several good sandy beaches both west and east of the town. In addition, Rethymnon is fortunate to have a fine beach right along the central promenade of the town; there is a municipally operated facility, providing changing-rooms and snacks for modest fees. Eighteen km. west of Rethymnon along the new road is the 7 km. sandy Petres River beach. Access to this excellent beach has now become easy with the construction of the new road.

Buses The main terminal is close to the Gymnasion (*Map* **16**); here is where you would get buses to such places as Arkadhi Monastery, Eleftherna, Melidhoni Cave, Anoyia, Axos, Fourfouras, Amari, Lefkoyia (nearest village to Preveli Monastery), Spili and Ayia Galini. Through buses to and from Iraklion and Khania can also be picked up here.

HISTORY

Rethymnon is the third-largest city of Crete and enjoys the reputation of being the 'intellectual capital' of the island. But without getting too involved in this claim, one can say that it is at least a source of pride for its citizens. And as its share of the new University of Crete,

Rethymnon will get the humanistic and philology departments – already a new art school has opened on the slopes at the edge of the town. Travellers in Rethymnon – both the city and nome – have claimed to see a little more pride in appearances, a little more order and cleanliness. In any case, Rethymnon has its own modest charms, among which are the old crafts still being practised. One of the classics of contemporary Greek writing is *The Tale of a Town* (as it is known in its English translation) by Pandelis Prevelakis, a native of Rethymnon; in recapturing the Rethymnon of his youth – in the first decades of this century – Prevelakis has written not only a tribute to his home town but an elegy for all such communities, provincial and limited in many ways, but stimulating and cosmopolitan in others.

The city of Rethymnon is on the site of ancient Rethymnon, which seems to have developed in the late-Minoan period; but nothing of interest to the amateur remains and little of its history is known. In the medieval period, Rethymnon is mentioned only in passing, with its fort and towers sketched as seen from afar. The town received its distinctive imprint from the Venetian period of the sixteenth and seventeenth centuries, with a slightly Turkish veneer to give it that special air: Venetian arches back up against wooden, overhanging Turkish balconies, creating a unique impression for the visitor strolling through the narrow streets.

PRINCIPAL SIGHTS

Loggia and Archaeological Museum
Map 5
Hours Variable, but usual Greek hours prevail.
Entrance charge Drs 100.

The museum is now housed in the principal architectural survival of the Venetian period, the (potentially) elegant Loggia, dated at about 1600. There is a small collection of finds from the nome and it is in the process of growing, as a result of intensified archaeological activity in the region.

Among the displays that reward the visitor are: Minoan sealstones, jewellery, and ceramics from various sites; a case of Minoan bronze artefacts; sarcophagi and vases from the Armeni necropolis (p. 238); some Mycenaean and Archaic artefacts; ceramics and sculptures from the Classical, Hellenistic, and Roman periods; Roman bronze artefacts salvaged from a shipwreck off Ayia Galini; and coins from various periods.

There has been talk of moving the museum exhibits into a large building up by the Venetian Fort (see below) and greatly expanding the displays to include more of Rethymnon's historical spectrum; enquire at the Tourist Police if this new museum is yet open to the public.

Venetian Fort

Hours Daily 09.00–16.00 and 18.00–19.00 Tuesday to Friday in the summer.
Entrance charge Modest fee.

Map **1**

This is the most impressive structure left by the Venetians, a great fortress surmounting the rocky promontory on the coast. After earlier forts at this locale had been destroyed by marauders, the Venetians determined once and for all to build an impregnable citadel here, between 1573 and 1580. Within its confines they then proceeded to construct the Cathedral of St Nicholas (1585), the Rector's Palace and other public buildings. After 1646, when the Turks finally occupied the city and its fortress, the cathedral, the palace and the other buildings went to ruin, intentionally or otherwise (although the Mosque they built remains one of the chief attractions in the fort's grounds). The German bombardments of the Second World War finished the job. Its massive *walls*, though, are largely intact, its *main gate*, as entered from the town, is still impressive, and major renovations in the early 1970s have generally tidied up the place and made a walk through its structure quite rewarding. In addition to the outer ramparts, together with an inner 'cavalier' battery raised on massive vaulting for shooting far inland, and odds-and-ends of walls and arches, a large domed *mosque* dominates the slightly eerie scene; it is all wonderfully conducive to musing over the transience of impregnable fortresses.

By consulting the town map (p. 249), you will be able to approach the fort from almost any point you start out from; the only road for cars, though, is up Odhos Melissinou, and then turn up Odhos Kheimara.

Arimondi Fountain

Map **4.**

Another surviving example of the Venetian period is the Arimondi

Rethymnon

1 Venetian Fort
2 Old Harbour
3 City Bathing Facilities/Tourist Information
4 Arimondi Fountain
5 Loggia: Archaeological Museum (p. 247)
6 Tourist Police
7 Mosque-Minaret Nerantzes
8 Church of San Francesco
9 Minaret (behind City Gates)
10 Church of the Four Martyrs
11 Telephone/Telegraph Office
12 Post Office
13 Iroon Square
14 Mosque of Kara Pasha
15 Public Gardens
16 Gymnasion: Bus Terminal
17 Mosque and Minaret

A route to
  Khora Stakion
  Khania

B route to
  Armeni
  Monastery of Preveli
  Ayia Galini
  Phaestos
  Iraklion

C route to
  Monastery of Arkadhi
  Amari Province
  Melidhoni Cave
  Anoyia & Mt Idha
  Iraklion

N

0 100 200 300 400 500

metres

PORT

entrance

Paralia
Leoforos
Gavril
Dikastirion
Vyoulgaroutonou
Melissinou
Makri Steno
Ethniki Antistaseos
Venizelou
Arkadhiou
Gerakari St
Kountourotou
Ivron
Stoi

Fountain (to be found near the intersection of Thessaloniki and Paleologou Streets). Alvise Arimondi was a Venetian Rector and built several fountains around Rethymnon; this one, dating from 1623, has its four original Corinthian columns and lion-heads spouting water; the back wall was restored in the Turkish period.

Other sights

Rethymnon once had a clock tower from the Venetian period, but it fell into disrepair and had to be demolished after the Second World War. There are several churches in the city also from the Venetian period – *Church of the Madonna of the Angels*, *Church of San Francesco* (now partially restored and used as a civic hall for meetings, exhibitions, etc) and others – but none has anything that special to see. Perhaps the most interesting sights are the *minarets*. Most were simply attached to 'converted' Venetian churches. The *Mosque of Nerantzes* with its minaret (open 11.00 to 19.30 weekdays, 11.00 to 15.00 Saturday, *Map* 7) is well worth a visit; so, too, is the small *mosque of Kara Pasha* (now restored and to be a Botanical Museum, thanks to the Greek benefactor, Goulandris) (open 08.00–18.00 daily, *Map* 14); and off in the southern section of town is a *mosque* with minaret (*Map* 17), dating from the early eighteenth century, that has recently been restored. And wherever you walk through the old section of Rethymnon, your eye will fall on architectural fragments (e.g. the fine façade at 154 Arkadhiou Street).

EXCURSIONS FROM RETHYMNON

Rethymnon Nome lacks the extensive and spectacular sites of other parts of Crete; beyond that, recognizing that most tourists will be based in Iraklion, we have included several spots actually in Rethymnon Nome as trips from Iraklion or sites en route to Rethymnon – visit to Idha Cave and Nidha Plain (p. 198), Tylissos, Anoyia and Axos (pp. 239–43), Ayia Galini (p. 237), Melidhoni Cave (p. 244) or the attractions of Amari Province (p. 236). (See Chart of Excursions, pp. 12–13, for other places of interest described on routes to and from Rethymnon.) The new highway makes Rethymnon much more central for excursions to various parts of the island. As for Minoan remains in particular, and archaeological sites in general, these are only beginning to be discovered. During the occupation, the Germans turned up an ambitious Minoan compound at Monastiraki, which for some twenty years was considered the westernmost Minoan site. Then, during the 1960s, increasing archaeological activity in Rethymnon Nome began to turn up more and more Minoan remains: the cemetery at Armeni (p. 238) and the cave at Gerani Bridge (p. 253) are the most spectacular so far, but there have been other finds at sites such as Mixorrouma, Stavromenos, Apodoulou and elsewhere – and presumably there will be more by the time this book is being used. You would need a specialist's interest – and a guide – to find these sites; but if you are interested, you should start your enquiries at the Archaeological Museum in Rethymnon (or at Iraklion or Khania). Here we describe two points of interest – one greatly famous, the other little-known – that can be visited from Rethymnon.

Monastery of Arkadhi

A short but highly stimulating excursion from Rethymnon is that up into the mountains to the Monastery of Arkadhi, which of all Crete's religious foundations is the most famous for the part it has played in the island's history.

Route Follow the Iraklion road east out of Rethymnon (Route Exit C) for Platanies, where you turn right up into the hills. You pass through the village of Adhele (home of Giamboudakis, credited with having set fire to the powder magazine at Arkadhi, see below), Pigi and Kyriana before reaching the Monastery of Arkadhi [22 km.].
Bus Buses connect to the Monastery of Arkadhi (or to the village of Eleftherna, see below) from Gymnasion Terminal (*Map* 16) or from Iroon Square (*Map* 13).
Accommodation A café near the monastery can provide simple meals.

Monastery of Arkadhi
The Monastery of Arkadhi is the supreme symbol for Cretans of their ageless strife and dilemma: freedom or death. Like many other monasteries on the island – because of their isolated situations in the mountains – it has always served as a centre for resistance movements and revolts against foreign powers. Even under the German occupation, Arkadhi was used as a meeting-place for partisans.

It was during the revolution of 1866, however, that Arkadhi achieved its immortality. As usual, it had actively supported the uprising against the Turks; that autumn a sizeable group of Cretan fighters, as well as women and children, established themselves in the monastery. They were asked to surrender, but the abbot was the first to refuse. Thousands of troops were called in by the Turks, and when their overwhelming numbers made the fall of the monastery imminent the monastery's powder magazine blew up. Some said that the abbot himself gave the command to one Giamboudakis, and that is the story that has survived. Figures vary, too, but perhaps as many as 1,000 Cretans and 1,800 Turks perished. This was on November 9th, 1866, and the episode soon created reverberations around the world. The anniversary of the event attracts crowds and dignitaries from all over Crete and the mainland; it is marked by solemn ceremonies at Arkadhi, and in Rethymnon by athletic competitions, games, fireworks and dancing. But even if you cannot be there on that particular occasion, the monastery is something to see.

The *church* of the monastery, dedicated to Saints Constantine and Helen, although still bearing scars of the assault of 1866, has been greatly restored. Its *façade*, however, is of intrinsic architectural interest, being the most ornate of the Venetian structures on Crete. It dates from 1587, and is a mixture of styles: there are Corinthian columns, classical arches, Renaissance garlands and baroque scrolls. Its light, almost fantastic appearance is somewhat incongruous in the wilds of Crete.

The *stairs* and *portals* of the church date from the seventeenth century. The *main entrance* and *gallery* to the monastery itself, although rebuilt after 1866, are worth inspecting. You may be shown the site of the explosion – 'untouched'; also, some survivors were said to have been beheaded in the refectory, and the bloodstains may be displayed. There is also a small '*museum*', with mementoes of Arkadhi's history, in the great hall (modest entrance fee). On sale at the museum is a short guide in English of the monastery's history. Outside the monastery (to the left of the road, as you approach the last 50 metres) is a modern *monument* to those who died at Arkadhi; it contains busts of the principals (including the abbot, and Giamboudakis, who ignited the powder), as well as an ossuary with many skulls.

Eleftherna

About 6 km. north-east of Arkadhi is the post-Minoan site of Eleftherna. It can be reached by driving along a path that starts from the right of the monastery's Tourist Pavilion and continues round and then overland through the new village of Eleftherna to Prines. You can also get to the site from the village of Prines by taking the turning at Platanies to the Monastery of Arkadhi; then proceeding on eastward after Pigi (instead of turning up towards Kyriana) another 3 km.

to Viran Episkopi and from there some 10 km. to Prines. Although settled in the late Minoan period, Eleftherna became a prominent development in the eighth century B.C.; remains of a *bridge* from the classical era testify to its endurance. It is chiefly known, though, for the Archaic limestone *torso* found here; dating from the late seventh century B.C., this is one of the major specimens of Daedalic art (Archaeological Museum in Iraklion, Room XIX, Exhibit 7).

ROUTE 4: RETHYMNON TO KHANIA

This is a pleasant trip, notable more for its sights than its sites, but with a lovely landscape and several points of interest; it can be made in a fast run of $1\frac{1}{2}$ hours, or it can be made to fill half a day.

Route The new national highway can definitely be used to 'short-circuit' this journey – and there is one site, described below, now approached only on the new road; it also has its own attractions of an undeveloped landscape. But we continue to describe the old route in detail. For this, you follow the main road west out of Rethymnon (Route Exit A); this rises into the mountains and descends to the coast at Georgioupolis [33 km.], then rises and descends again, skirting Soudha Bay, and leads across the fertile plain to Khania [72 km.].

Bus There are frequent services between the two towns, starting from Gymnasion Terminal in Rethymnon (*Map* **16**) and from the bus terminal in Khania (*Map* **29**). There are also buses from Khania to points along Soudha Bay such as Aptera.

Leaving Rethymnon to the west, turn left on to the old main road at about the 4-km. point and climb up towards Prines [7 km.]. However, if you were to proceed along the coast on the new highway, you would come at about 7 km. to the *Gerani Bridge*: to the right and immediately below was discovered, as a result of the work for the new road, a large *cave* with dramatic stalactites. This cave was used as a cult sanctuary throughout the Neolithic period and human and animal bones, including those of elephants, have been found here. The cave formations are quite spectacular, and there have been plans to open it for visitors. For now, the cave remains locked, but arrangements to visit it can be made at the Information Office in Rethymnon (*Map* **3**).

[11 km.] Back on the old road, you pass through **Ghonia**.

[22 km.] **Episkopi** is the last village of any size in Rethymnon Nome.

[27 km.] The village of **Dhramia**, near which are fragmentary remains of the ancient Hellenistic site of *Idhramia*.

[32 km.] A turning to the left for **Kournas** leads in 3 km. to the only freshwater lake on Crete – *Lake Kournas* (the ancient Korion or Korisia). It is surprising to encounter such a lake on Crete, and travellers have long commented on its special atmosphere, tame and refreshing when compared with the island's usual rugged attractions. It covers some 65 hectares; local legend has it bottomless. Other legends have grown up about it: if you shoot across it, the bullet will never reach the opposite shore; it was once the site of a village; and the lake is haunted by the ghost of a young girl who was raped by her father. The real mystery is why such a body of water is found here and nowhere else on Crete; what also impresses at least the foreigner is that nothing has been erected on its shores. If you were to go on to the village of Kournas, you might visit the *Church of Ayia Irini*, with its fourteenth-century frescoes.

Hotels Class C: *Happy Holidays* (tel. 22.000).
    Manos Beach (tel. 22.221).

[33 km.] You pass over the new highway and enter **Georgioupolis** – on the coast – named after the Prince George who once served as High Commissioner of Crete (p. 100). Georgioupolis has some handsome eucalyptus trees and a fine beach with hotels and rooms. Nearby was the site of the Hellenistic *Amfimalla*. And as you leave the village you pass along a brackish *álmyros*, one of three such along the coast (p. 75). *Cape Dhrapanon* extends to the north as the road proceeds through well-wooded countryside, noted especially for its cypresses.

Hotel Class C: *Gorgona* (tel. 22.378).

[40 km.] **Vrises**, an attractive village with tavernas along the road under large plane trees – a popular spot for excursions; it is noted for its fine yoghurt and pork or lamb roasted on skewers (particularly at Easter time). There is a monument here to the Post-Constitutional Committee of 1897. The road to the left (sign-posted) leads south to Khora Sfakion (p. 272).

[55 km.] **Kalives**, the first large village on Soudha Bay.

[58 km.] Old road joins new road.

[59 km.] At **Kalamion**, sitting up above the road, is the old Turkish fort of *Izzedine*, which the Cretans have used as a prison. As you round the curve, stretching before you is a fine view of *Soudha Bay*, the largest and best-protected natural harbour of Crete, and among the most remarkable land-locked harbours of the entire Mediterranean. About 15 kilometres long and 3 to 6 kilometres wide, its deep waters can take even today's great ships. In fact, it is a Greek navy and NATO naval base, and you are likely to catch glimpses of ships and sailors from several nations if you drive along past the docks. This has also meant that much of Soudha Bay is off limits to random exploring and to photographs; the price of fame in an age of iron curtains.

More important than sheer size in ancient times was the fact that the entrance could be easily defended: the Akrotiri promontory protects the northern side, and there are three tiny islands – once known as the Lefkai ('white') Islands – at the narrows. The one that actually commands the bay is *Soudha Island*. (The Greek word *soudha* means 'trench' or 'passage' – in reference to the narrow entrance to the bay.) The Venetians built extensive *fortifications* on this island; these still exist, along with a *church*, and give a good idea of the importance of this outpost. It was one of the last three forts held by the Venetians on Crete, surrendering to the Turks only in 1715. Eventually British troops were quartered there at the turn of the century when the Great Powers were running Crete.

[61 km.] A left turn (sign-posted: Megala Khorafia/Aptera) leads up a hill in about 1 km. to the village of Megala Khorafia; there a fork to the left (sign-posted) leads in about another 2 km. to the ruins of ancient *Aptera*, an ambitious city excavated early in the twentieth century, spread across the flat-topped mountain.

'Aptera' means 'featherless'; it derived this name from a contest between the Muses and the Sirens at the Museion (a spot near the city). After the Muses triumphed with their music-making, the defeated Sirens plucked off their feathers and cast themselves into the sea, becoming the islands in the bay. From the fifth century B.C. onwards, Aptera was one of the chief commercial cities of Crete, and it was well known right into the early Christian era. There are fairly extensive remains, now in a ruinous condition, spreading over a large area to both sides of an abandoned *church*; cyclopean *walls* of an early settlement, a *theatre*, the *Temple of Demeter*, a Dorian *temple*, huge Roman *cisterns* (the best of which lie north of the church) and other Roman and Byzantine remains including *bas-reliefs* and *inscriptions*. The view across Soudha Bay is one of the chief attractions of the spot; the best vantage-point is reached by taking a side-road to the left before moving along the last 50 metres towards the large church; at the end of this side-turning is an old Turkish *fort*, and going around in front of this gives you a spectacular view down on to the Izzedine fort (p. 254) and out across Soudha Bay.

[62 km.] You can turn off right, sign-posted to Soudha, and rejoin the old route.

If you go on the old road, you descend to the water's edge at **Soudha**, with its modern harbour installations. Soudha has long served as the port of call for Khania, and since the Second World War has grown at its own pace, what with the great walls surrounding the naval facilities, the housing developments, the headquarters structures and all the other paraphernalia of the contemporary situation. The main square of Soudha is watched over by a *statue* of Prince George of Greece, who came ashore here in 1898 to take over as High Commissioner. There are two Class D hotels here, the *Knossos* and *Parthenon*, and numerous cafés and restaurants.

[67 km.] After proceeding high above Soudha on the new road, you descend to join the old road. Although the New Road continues on at this point, it leaves you at the wrong edge of Khania in a maze of streets; it is better to leave the New Road here and enter Khania by the old route from Soudha. (There is a turning indicated off to the right that leads towards a large *cemetery* on the slopes for the Allied Forces – mostly British and Commonwealth troops – who lost their lives on Crete during the Second World War.) The road now crosses a fertile plain, with olive trees, vines, plane trees and orange trees making the landscape unusually green and lush. The west is the chief orange-growing region of Crete, by the way, and Khania is the centre for export. (The orange is called *portokáli* in Greek, as it was introduced here from Portugal.)

[71 km.] A left turn sign-posted to Malaxa would bring you, after taking a right fork, in 4 km. to Mournies (p. 272).

[72 km.] The approach to the centre of Khania is down a street that turns from provincial-suburban to bustling-commercial.

KHANIA

Khania is not only the capital of the Nome but the commercial centre of western Crete too, and it has all the activity befitting such a status. At the same time, it has a more indigenous appearance and provincial air than Iraklion – due in part to the fact that it has only recently begun to experience the pressures and prosperity of international tourism. Khania's faded glories and understated attractions may not be to everyone's taste, but anyone who can enjoy an afternoon watching a man make a wooden barrel will appreciate Khania.

Population About 53,000.

Air and sea connections See pp. 18–21. Khania airport is near Sternes on the Akrotiri peninsula (p. 269); the Olympic Airways terminal is at 88 Tzanakaki Street (*Map* **24**). The port of Khania is Soudha (p. 256), where the regular mainland-Crete ships put in. For information or tickets apply to the Minoan Lines office at 4 Khalidon Street or at the ANEK office, Sophocles Venizelos Square. (If you are planning to approach Crete by coming ashore at Khania, we remind you that the ANEK lines has offered a daily sailing between Piraeus and Khania.) In addition, there now seems to be a year-round boat service linking Kastelli-Kissamou, only 45 km. west of Khania (see excursion, pp. 287–91), to the Peloponnesos, various Aegean ports and islands, Piraeus, and even other Cretan ports.

Information *National Tourist Organization of Greece*: Janissaries' Mosque, on the harbour (*Map* **3**) (tel. 26.426).

Tourist Police: 44 Karaiskaki Street (*Map* **28**) (tel. 24.477).

Hotels Class A: *Contessa* (tel. 23.966).

        Kydon, 1897 Square (tel. 26.190).

  Class B: *Ariadni* (tel. 50.987).

        Doma, Venizelou Street in the Khalepa Quarter (tel. 21.772).

        Domenico (tel. 53.262).

        El Greco (tel. 22.411).

        Lagonikakos (tel. 22.161).

        Lissos, Dimokratias Street (tel. 24.671).

        Pasiphae (tel. 23.187).

        Porto Veneziano, Akti Enosseos (tel. 29.311).

        Samaria, Katastimaton Street (tel. 51.551).

        Xenia, *Map* **2** (restaurant) (tel. 24.561).

  Class C: *Afroditi* (tel. 57.602).

        Amphitriti, Lithinon Street (tel. 22.980).

        Astor (tel. 55.557).

        Chania, 1866 Square (tel. 24.673).

        Diktina, Christou Episkou (tel. 21.101).

        Elyros, Mylonyianni Street (tel. 22.462).

        Kriti, Nikiphoros Phokas Street (tel. 21.881).

        Kypros (tel. 22.761).

        Lukia (on the old harbour) (tel. 21.821).

        Manos (tel. 29.493).

        Mary Poppins (tel. 23.357).

        Omalos (tel. 57.171).

        Plaza, on the harbour (tel. 22.540).

        Theophilos (tel. 53.294).

There are also many D and E hotels, several quite convenient and atmospheric.

Beach Hotels At Ayii Apostoli, 5 km. to the west, an ambitious new beach development is planned, but so far there is only a camping site here (tel. 48.555).

At Galatas, 3 km. west of Khania, are:

Hotels Class A: *Panorama* (tel. 54.200).

Class B: *Ariadni* (tel. 21.084).

Class C: *Delfini* (tel. 48.467).

A modest resort 3 km. west of the centre with bungalows and a restaurant is *Aptera Beach* (Class C) (tel. 22.636). Maleme lies 14 km. further west where there is a large beach resort, *Chandris Crete* (Class A) (tel. 91.221), see p. 288.

Camping *Camping Khania*, a few km. west of the town, open in the summer only (tel. 51.090).

Youth hostel The latest known youth hostel is at 33 Drakonianou Street (over near Dexameni Square in the south-east section of town) (tel. 53.565).

Restaurants Apart from the hotels with restaurants, there are numerous restaurants and cafés in Khania; some of the most atmospheric are those around the old harbour, where everyone gathers on summer evenings. There is a large café in the Public Gardens. But walk about and look around; new restaurants are opening (and closing) constantly, and you may be the first to discover the next fashionable place.

Dining and dancing Some eating-places that feature music and dancing are: *Prasini Paparouna* ('Green Poppy'), King George Street, and *Honolulu*, Venizelou Street. Outside the town, on the coast road west towards Platanias (p. 288), are a number of such places along the beaches. On the Akrotiri is the *Neraida*, the *Nykterida* and the *Asteria* – with fine views along with the music and food.

Cinemas There are several cinemas around town, some open-air in summer.

Consulates Only France, Germany and Sweden maintain consulates in Khania.

Churches Roman Catholic services are held at the Catholic Church just inside the arch at 46 Khalidon Street (*Map* 13).

Clubs and Institutes There is a library, a music conservatory and a broadcasting station. The French Institute of Athens and the Goethe Institute of Germany support institutes where the languages are taught and other programmes are offered to advance the cultural contacts between their lands and Greece. The local Greek-American institutes are private organizations that teach English. There are several intellectual and artistic organizations in Khania, as well as professional associations for everyone from doctors to grape-growers. Anyone desiring to contact any of these groups could get help at the Tourist Office. For clubs concerned with excursions and mountain-climbing, see under Sport and swimming (below).

Hospital The Government Hospital, where foreigners can be treated, is located in Dragoumi Street (tel. 27.231). There are many specialized clinics, too.

Shops and souvenirs The shops of Khania offer a complete line of goods and services, and can handle all normal needs of the tourist; if they lack any of the chic of Iraklion's shops, they are that much more authentically Greek.

Khania offers a fine selection of native handicrafts in many shops: textiles, jewellery, costumes, needlework, embroidery and such. Khania is especially noted for its wood-carving: you can see a couple of shops on Khalidon Street where men and boys work away in the old tradition. There is also one narrow street – Skridlof Street – where a whole string of shoemakers make and display their products. (And anyone who is so minded can go to the east edge of the city, down along the coast, and see – and smell – the tanneries.) There are also several potters who make interesting ceramics, both functional and decorative.

Sport and swimming For information about special sporting events in Khania, contact the office of the National Stadium on Dimokratias Street.

There is good hunting – hares and partridges – and fishing in the region; enquire at the Tourist Police about seasons and regulations (and see p. 66–7) and for information about local associations devoted to these sports.

Khania is the centre of much activity in the field of mountain-climbing and excursions. In particular, the Khania branch of the Hellenic Mountain-Climbing Association operates an impressive series of excursions and maintains several shelters. Foreigners would be welcome, and for more information enquire at the Tourist Information office.

Khania has a modern city swimming-pool on the coast, just west of the Xenia Hotel (*Map* **20**). There are several fine beaches to the west of Khania, too – at about 5 km. is the impressive new beach complex of Ayii Apostoli: and at about 11 km. along the coast road is the beach at Platanias. The most convenient public beach, however, is just about 1 km. west of the Xenia Hotel (*Map* **20**).

Buses Khania is the terminal for all buses within the nome as well as those for Rethymnon and Iraklion. The bus station for all major routes is now near the south-west corner of Katastimaton Square (*Map* **29**). Some local buses (to Soudha, Akrotiri, etc.) may be boarded in front of the Market (*Map* **21**).

Taxis and car hire Taxis are round all the major public squares. (For charges, etc., see pp. 32–3). Cars may be hired at several agencies; enquire at the Tourist Information office (and see pp. 33–4).

Tourist agencies and guided tours There are several tourist agencies that arrange group tours or private excursions; enquire at the National Tourist Organization.

HISTORY

Khania is the descendant of ancient Kydonia, home of the Kydonians, one of the early pre-Greek peoples of Crete; they took their name from King Kydon, son of Apollo. (The Greek word – and scientific name – for the quince is also derived from the name, and Crete is credited with being the homeland of this fruit.) Kydonia and the Kydonians had figured in ancient literature, and occasional finds during the twentieth century had hinted at a Minoan presence in and around Khania, but it was not until the 1960s that systematic excavations in Khania – particularly in the Kastelli quarter (p. 263) – revealed that the city has been inhabited continuously from the Neolithic through the Minoan and post-Minoan times, making Khania one of the oldest continuously inhabited cities in the world. During the post-Minoan periods – Mycenaean, Geometric, Archaic, Classic, and Hellenistic – Kydonia assumed a prominent role in the various intra-island wars and alliances, even taking the lead in the resistance against the Romans. Under the Romans, Khania was important enough to have its own theatre (no remains); in the early Byzantine-Christian era it was the seat of a bishop, but after the Arabs took over in the ninth century, it lost whatever importance it had enjoyed and became noted for little else than its cheese. When the

Venetians took over in the thirteenth century, they named it La Canea, an Italian version of Khania, which had for several centuries been the town's name (scholars cannot agree on its derivation). The Genoese seized it from 1267 to 1290, but the Venetians took it back and turned it into a centre for the western end of Crete. During the next 350 years the Venetians built so many fine private and public structures that La Canea enjoyed the reputation of being 'the Venice of the East', but its ambitious fortifications proved far less effective than Iraklion's and it fell to the Turks in 1645 after only a two-month siege. The Turks settled in, repairing the fortifications and converting the churches into mosques; in the nineteenth century they made the former Venetian Kastelli the capital of the whole island. The Pasha's seraglio was also here, and travellers in the nineteenth century report a community of Africans and Arabs at the edge of Khania, which must have had a generally exotic atmosphere. In 1898 the Turkish troops had to withdraw, and international forces moved in under the aegis of the Great Powers. Prince George came as the High Commissioner, and Khania retained the honour of being the capital of Crete when the island was united with Greece in 1913. It lost this distinction to Iraklion in 1971, but whatever it lost in official status it has maintained in its private charms.

MUSEUMS

Archaeological Museum
Map **14**
Hours Variable, but observes usual Greek times (see p. 59). Closed Tuesdays.
Entrance charge Drs 100.
Fee for taking photographs Drs 50.

The museum is installed in the former Church of St Francis, itself of some historical interest (p. 266). Because of the major restoration completed only recently, there has also been a quite thorough change of the exhibits' numbering and location, so no effort is made here to refer to these. But the major exhibits remain the same. Although it can hardly rival the great Minoan collection of Iraklion, the Khania museum has an interesting collection of art and artefacts from western Crete, including vases, terracottas, sealstones, mosaics, glassware, jewellery, coins, utensils, armaments, inscriptions and sculpture. An intensified series of excavations in recent years is adding considerably to the museum's collection, which is also in a continuing process of being reorganized and displayed. Among the new exhibits are finds from the excavations of ancient Kydonia in Khania itself; these include some Neolithic and Minoan pottery, imported Cypriot pottery of the late Minoan period, pottery inscribed with Linear B, and a Roman mosaic. There is also a collection of early Minoan stone and pottery vases from Platyvola Cave (some 25 km. east of Khania), including 'sauceboats' and a large incised vase. From Kastelli there are Minoan vases and fragments of late Minoan frescoes; from Modi and Kavoussi Proto-geometric vases, and from Tarrha Greek and Roman jewellery. To walk through the museum – beginning with the cases on the left as you enter – is to experience a 'compressed course' in Mediterranean civilization, from Neolithic through Roman times; what is more, to the extent that it is not selected works from some unique palace or two, you are getting a more representative impression of what the mass of people actually knew. In the side-court garden there is a fine old Turkish fountain and a collection of architectural fragments from Venetian Khania. One of the most recent and most unexpected exhibits is photographs of a quite impressive early Christian tomb found in 1980 at the edge of Khania. Finally, the museum structure itself, now restored to its classic Italian lines, make the whole visit a pleasure.

Historical Museum
Map 26
Hours 08.00–13.00. Closed on weekends and public holidays.
Entrance free.

This is considered one of the major archives of all Greece, with its many rare documents and books from the late-Byzantine, Venetian and Turkish periods as well as from modern Crete. There are also other items of historical interest – armaments, flags and documents relating to Crete's resistance to invaders up to and including the Germans in 1941–45, historical pictures and icons, and some genuine Venizelos relics, including his writing desk.

Naval Museum
Map 17
Hours Open 10.00–14.00, and 19.00–21.00 on Saturday. Closed Monday.
Entrance charge Modest fee.

This was opened in 1973 in the renovated Firkas structure (p. 267) on the old harbour; it has an interesting collection of items and mementoes associated with the maritime history of Crete.

During the summer, performances of classic Greek and Cretan-renaissance dramas are occasionally given in the courtyard: enquire at the National Tourist Organization in any major city for further details.

PRINCIPAL SIGHTS

Khania may be thought of as two cities – the old and the new. New Khania has grown up along the plain behind the harbour, gradually absorbing the suburbs such as Khalepa (p. 268), and it has some of the facilities needed by visitors, although the cafés and restaurants by the old harbour remain the most popular. The new town has the bus terminals, however, and the Public Market (*Map* **21**); this is a large structure in the shape of a cross, modelled after the great market at Marseilles and dating from 1911. Here is brought the produce of the region, and it can be quite a heady experience to stroll through the crowded aisles. More restful are the Public Gardens (*Map* **25**), originally laid out here in 1870 by a Turkish pasha; a bandstand, small zoo, playground, cinema, and café add to the attractions – at least for the native Khaniots.

Old Khania: Within the Walls

It is old Khania that attracts the traveller and deserves the account. This city is clustered around the harbour and spreads back through narrow streets; it is essentially the area embraced by the great fortified walls erected under the Venetians in the sixteenth century, after they found the fourteenth-century walls on this perimeter inadequate. The walls were designed by the same Sammicheli who designed the great walls of Candia-Iraklion (p. 147). Khania's walls had a total perimeter of some 3 km.; alongside them was a moat, 50 metres wide and 10 metres deep in places; there were four great bastions (of which the Schiavo-Lando, or San Dimitrio, complex is the best preserved, *Map* **11**); much of the wall along the western side is still intact and well worth a viewing.

Old Khania is now divided into five quarters (in Greek, *synoikia*); Kastelli, centre, above the harbour; Chiones, to the east; Splanzia, south-east; Evraiki, south-west; and Topanas, to the west. The once magnificent Venetian structures of La Canea have largely disappeared, of course. But what still makes a walk through Khania so suggestive is to be able to stand on a contemporary Cretan street and see on one side the Neolithic and Minoan remains, and on another the fragments of a Venetian structure, with a Byzantine church in the middle distance and a Turkish minaret rising in the background. The following account describes the principal points of interest that might be viewed on a quarter-by-quarter tour of this old city and its fringes.

Kastelli Quarter

This was probably the site of the original Neolithic settlement as well as the centre of the Minoan town, but its name seems to be derived from some Byzantine fortress. When the Venetians moved in, they centred their city here for the same reason that motivated the previous peoples – namely, the high ground – and they erected a wall on old Byzantine foundations around the base of the hill: a few remains may still be seen, especially along the southern edge, parallel to Karoli Dimitrio Street. Within this wall, above the harbour, the Venetians built their fine *palazzi* and many public structures such as the palace and cathedral (probably using some stone from Minoan ruins), but nothing of these remain. The most notable Venetian remains in Kastelli now are the *portal of the archive* at the end of Lithinon Street (*Map* 4), with an inscription dated 1624; and the *Arcade of St Mark* (*Map* 6), along modern Kanevaro Street, once the Corso of the Venetians.

At the west base of the hill, and on the harbour itself, stands the *Mosque of Djamissi* (Janissaries' Mosque), or *Mosque of Hassan Pasha* (*Map* 3), erected in 1645 immediately after the Turks conquered the city; the original domes survive, although the arches are of a later period. Its pure form has now been spoiled by the addition of the restaurant. It now houses the Information Office of the National Tourist Organization and is well worth a visit. Also there has been a room set aside for an exhibit of works by local artisans (with the intention of interesting visitors in buying such work, but it is not for sale here).

Meanwhile, the remains of the Minoan Kydonia, which Greek and Swedish archaeologists have been excavating since the 1960s, lie mainly in the Kastelli Quarter. The most notable are those on Kanevaro Street, on the left as you pass Lithinon Street (*Map* 5) – a late Minoan *megaron* with paved floors and parts of storage rooms. Elsewhere, in vacant lots and construction sites, other digs are revealing various structures and evidence of occupation in this locale from Minoan through Geometric to Hellenistic times. Some of the most interesting finds are on display in the museum (p. 260), but among the most significant finds are tablets inscribed in Linear A, still being worked on by the specialists.

Chiones Quarter

This is the area to the east of Kastelli and down around the harbour. The Venetians had great plans for La Canea but, no matter how much they dredged, the harbour was never really successful. The Venetians built the breakwater (*Map* 1) by dumping rocks, and at about the halfway point they erected a small fort and a church dedicated to St Nicholas (no remains worth viewing); the Venetians and Turks used this spot to execute criminals. At the end of the breakwater, the Venetians erected a lighthouse, although the fine tower now there (which can be entered and climbed, to provide a superb view of Khania) seems to be largely a nineteenth-century structure. A large iron chain once ran from the lighthouse to the point opposite below the Firkas (p. 267) and served to keep out unwanted ships. Along the eastern edge of the harbour the Venetians constructed great *arsenali* (*Map* 2), large domed dockyards for shipbuilding and repairs. These were built in two major projects, one in the fifteenth and one in the seventeenth century, but of the two dozen *arsenali*, only nine remain.

Khania

Khania

Ave of the Polytechnic Heroes

Dragoumi

Dhikastirion Square

Is. Mitsotaki St

Hadzidaki

Dimitrakaki St

Stakianaki St

Stadium

Nikiphorou Phoka St

Dimokratias Street

Venizelou St

N. Episkopou

Tzanakaki Street

Solomou St

Apokoronou St

Karaiskaki

Markou Botsari

Mylonoyianni

Zymvrakaki

Smyrnis

Kydonias

Skalidi Street

Hadzimikhali Dialeti

Hadzimikhali

Giannari

Daskaloyiannari

Sq

1866 Sq

1897

Kouderon

Khalidon

Dimitriou

Skridlof

SPLANTZIA

Ayii Anaryiri St

SINTRIVANI

HALEPA

Minoos

Moschon

Kanevaro

TOPANAS

Theotokopoulou St

Kountourioti

Zambeli

Lambraki

Isodion

Betolo

Portou

outer wall

metres

0   100   200   300   400   500

N

KISSAMOU

1 2 2 3 4 5 6 7 8 9 10 11 12 13 14 15 16 17 18 19 20 21 22 23 24 25 26 27 28 29

A B C D

Splanzia Quarter

Situated just south of the Chiones Quarter, the centre of this quarter is 1821 Square, a delightful place to sit and enjoy a cool drink under the shade of a large plane tree – just as the Turks did in bygone years, for they chose this square as their centre. (They also hanged an Orthodox bishop here in 1821, providing the square with its name and a plaque.) The square is dominated by the *Church of St Nicholas* (*Map* **8**); built as part of a Dominican monastery, it was converted by the Turks into the Imperial Mosque of Sultan Ibrahim. It did not become an Orthodox church until 1912. As a result of its various conversions, it now possesses a beautiful *minaret* to balance its *campanile*. On the north corner of the square is the small Venetian *Church of San Rocco* (*Map* **7**), with a Latin inscription from 1630. It has long been closed and out of use.

A few streets behind the square, to the south-east, is the *Church of Ayii Anargyri* (*Map* **9**), dedicated to the martyrs Kosmas and Damianos. This was a Greek Orthodox church in Khania allowed to hold services under the Venetians and the Turks. Its icons are of considerable age and artistry.

The other main attraction of this quarter are the picturesque narrow lanes, and at 23 Hadzimikhali Daliani Street there is a fine *minaret* (*Map* **10**).

Evraiki Quarter

Extending from the centre of the harbour, this quarter is also the centre of most visitors' activities. It includes the square at the south-east corner of the harbour, known as Santrivani Square (from the Turkish word for fountain) or by its more recent name, Venizelos Square. Leading south, and away from this harbour square, is Khalidon Street, and on the right is the *Church of St Francis* (*Map* **14**), now housing the Archaeological Museum (p. 260). Dating from the sixteenth century, it was one of the finest of the Venetian buildings on Crete and the largest of the twenty-three Venetian churches in Khania. It had three vaulted naves, with Gothic-style windows; its façade is disfigured and its campanile gone, but it still repays a close look. (By 1981, a major restoration of the interior had attempted to restore as much of the original as possible.) The Turks converted it into a mosque, named after the Youssouf Pasha who had conquered Khania; they left a minaret (only the base remains) and a lovely *fountain* in the side-court garden.

Several metres along Khalidon Street, on the opposite side, is a plaza with the *Orthodox Cathedral of Khania*, the Church of Tri-martyre, or the Three Martyrs (*Map* 12). Dating only from the 1860s, it is architecturally undistinguished but enjoys a stirring history: it was built here by a grateful Turk whose son's life had been saved by the intervention of the Virgin Mary, the subject of a famous icon that once belonged to an old Byzantine Church on this spot (used since Venetian days as a soap factory). At the north-west corner of the plaza, facing Khalidon Street, the old domed structure was a Turkish bath.

Back on Santrivani Square, Zambeliou Street (one block back from the harbour road) leads off to the west and to the fifth and final quarter of the old city. There are numerous old structures and side streets to explore, but among the most notable sites is No. 43, the remains of a *Venetian palazzo* (*Map* 15), with a crest and Latin inscription. Of more specialized interest would be the abandoned and largely ruined old synagogue of the Jewish community of Khania who lived here from the Middle Ages until the Germans rounded them up in the Second World War (and sent them off to their death). The synagogue is clearly recognizable from the Star of David in its surviving window-grill; to see it, proceed up Kondolaki Street from the middle of the harbour, then turn right on to Parados Kondolaki, and then turn left.

Topanas Quarter

Zambeliou Street leads on into the Topanas Quarter, and as the street begins a slight incline, a right turn into Moskhon Street leads to the *Renieri Gate* (*Map* 16), bearing the escutcheon of the Renieri family and an inscription dated 1608. Passing through this gate, to the left is an elegant doorway, all that is left of a Venetian chapel; further along, on the left, are Venetian structures that served as the powder magazines and armoury headquarters. At the corner of Theophanos Street, a right turn leads down to the harbour; proceeding on to the far end of the curve brings one to the Venetian building (*Map* 17), restored in the early 1970s and housing the Naval Museum (p. 261). This locale is known as the *Firkas* (from a word referring to an army unit that was stationed here) and incorporates parts of the bastion at the north-west corner of the Venetian walls; many of the original elements are still to be seen. It was at the Firkas in 1913 that the Greek flag was first officially hoisted on Crete to signify that island's uniting with Greece. This flagpole is the focal point of many holidays and festivities.

Leading up from the front of the Naval Museum is Angelou Street, with some of the finest Venetian mansions and architectural elements still surviving. Proceeding up this street, you come out on to Theoto-kopoulous Street, perhaps the most Venetian in its atmosphere of all the old Khania streets. A right turn leads towards the sea; at the corner, on the mound to the right, is the abandoned Venetian *Church of San Salvatore* (*Map* **18**), which the Turks used as a mosque. Off to the left is the *Xenia Hotel* (*Map* **19**). The sea road leads around the Firkas and back to the old harbour.

Khalepa Quarter

This is a modern quarter of Khania, to the east, a pleasant, hilly suburb that repays a visit on its own or as a stop en route to the Akrotiri (p. 269). When Prince George moved to Crete in 1898 (p. 100), he settled in Khalepa, making the area a magnet for many Khaniots of any pretension as well as for the foreign diplomatic community; as a result, numerous villas were built here in the early years of this century, and these, together with certain historical and public structures, lend an unexpected air of grandeur to this part. There are frequent buses to Khalepa, and strong walkers might even enjoy going on foot. You can head east on almost any of the major avenues out of Khania, and aim for the Avenue of the Polytechnic Heroes (at the far right of the map, p. 265). This impressive boule-vard leads from the sea back to Dhikastirion, or George I, Square, which has a statue of Venizelos (p. 101) and is dominated by a large building that served as Prince George's administrative headquarters and now houses the law courts at Khania. Above and behind this building is a large new Orthodox church that, at least until the late 1980s, was unfinished.

Proceeding eastwards on Eleftherios Venizelou Street, as it bears right away from the sea (near the 2 km. marker), you pass a walled estate that is the *French Convent School*; just beyond, on the left, is the mansion where Prince George lived; and beyond this, also on the left, is a *house of Eleftherios Venizelos* (and still in the Venizelos family). Facing this, in a small square, is a *statue of Venizelos*. And in the walled garden off to the side of the square is the *Church of St Mary Magdalene*, built by Prince George's mother and sister as a private chapel but presented to the city of Khania in 1909; it is more Russian than Greek in style, and as a curiosity makes a fine climax to a tour of Khania.

EXCURSIONS FROM KHANIA

The main points of interest are described in some detail here; for a few other places that might be reached from Khania see the Chart of Excursions, pp. 12–13.

The Akrotiri

Akrotiri means 'the promontory', and a glance at the map reveals how it acquired this name. It is a region rich in history, from earliest times to contemporary Crete, and is visited every year by thousands of people, from native Cretans to international travellers. There are two main destinations for most visitors: the Hill of the Prophet Elias (only a few kilometres outside Khania) and the Monastery of Ayia Triadha (some 17 km. into the hills). Buses take you to both places, as well as to one or two other sites on the Akrotiri; only feet will take you to some parts. And many people will get a glimpse of the Akrotiri en route to or from Khania's airport, which is located near Sternes on the south-east corner.

Route Leave Khania by Venizelou Street (Route Exit C), passing through the suburb of Khalepa (p. 268). Continue until in about 6 km. you come to a left turn (sign-posted: Venizelos Graves); if you follow this all the way around to the left and then (following the sign) turn right, you enter the park-site of the Hill of the Prophet Elias; if you follow a sign to the right (Kounoupidiana), you go on to the Monastery of Ayia Triadha [17 km.]. If you stay on the main road and keep to the right, you go on via Korakies [8 km.] to the airport.
Bus Buses for points on the Akrotiri leave from the main terminal (*Map* 29). They go as far as Ayia Triadha Monastery, but not to Gouverneto.

[6 km.] After leaving Khania by Venizelou Street and climbing up through Khalepa, you come to a sign: Venizelos Graves; you turn to the left and follow the approach road through the park to the handsome monumental site of the *Hill of the Prophet Elias*, with its superb view across the water and down on to Khania. This hill is a symbolic peak of Crete's long struggle for freedom; until 1967 a statue of Athena, goddess of wisdom and war, stood at the edge of the terrace, but it was damaged in a storm and no longer stands here. The reason why the statue was here is that it was on this point in 1897 that

Cretan insurgents raised the flag of Greece, despite the injunctions of all the Great Powers and the presence of the Turks. When the flagpole was broken by the subsequent bombardment from the fleet off shore, a Cretan stood up and held the flag in his own hands. Many legends have since accrued to this incident: one is that the sailors of the fleet stopped firing and cheered the valiant Cretans; another claims that an explosion occurred in one of the Russian ships taking part in the shelling – and this was attributed to divine anger, because the shells were destroying the little *Church of Elias* (still standing on the wooded slopes). If any further associations with Cretan aspirations are needed, there are the *graves* of Eleftherios Venizelos and his son Sophocles on the site.

Back on the main road, if you proceed straight on (following the signs to the airport), you turn left off the main road after 2 km. to reach **Korakies**; there are several restaurants here, with fine views over Soudha Bay – a favourite gathering-place for Khaniots in the evening. There is also the *Convent of John the Baptist* here, noted for its embroidery. Then if you proceed for several kilometres, you pass a NATO school and come to Khania airport.

Back at the turn-off to the Venizelos Graves, however, if, instead of turning into the Hill of the Prophet Elias, you take a right turn (sign-posted: Kounoupidiana), you go on towards the Monastery of Ayia Triadha. (Do not be confused by signs indicating 'Airport' on this route: this is merely an alternative approach to the airport.)

[8 km.] As you come to **Kounoupidiana**, keep straight and then bear right and curve through the little village; at the other side of the village, follow the sign indicating 'Airport' (*not* 'Khorafakia').

[12½ km.] Bear left at sign indicating Ayia Triadha.

[14 km.] Turn left at sign indicating Ayia Triadha and proceed down a narrow, tree-lined track through cultivated fields.

[17 km.] *Monastery of Ayia Triadha.* (Closed 14.00–17.00)
   This is one of the most important monasteries of Crete, although like all of them it has declined since the old days. It is situated in a sheltered position at the foot of limestone hills. Founded in the seventeenth century by Jeremiah Zangarola, a Venetian convert to Greek Orthodoxy (and thus the monastery is sometimes referred to as Zangarola Monastery), it shows a strong Venetian influence in its

architecture (and the buildings have recently been greatly restored). A monumental *entrance* in the classic style dates from 1632; its *campanile* dates from 1650. It has an especially rich *treasury*, *library*, an ornate iconostasis – and a water-cooler in its spacious courtyard!

Gouverneto Monastery, St John's Cave and Katholiko Monastery

There is a somewhat more ambitious excursion for those who have the extra time and energy. The first part, to Gouverneto Monastery, can now be driven. The road leads to the left past the Monastery of Ayia Triadha and takes you up to the northern edge of the Akrotiri to the *Monastery of St John of Gouverneto*, a local hermit-saint who lived and died in a cave near Katholiko. The monastery, situated in its isolated mountain landscape, dates from 1548 and shows Venetian influence. Note especially its circular chapel with rich gilded furnishings. About 45 minutes' walk is required to reach Katholiko. You set off behind Gouverneto Monastery and the path leads eventually down to a narrow gorge; there, wedged between rocky precipices, are the remains of the deserted *Monastery of Katholiko*, cave-dwellings of early Christian hermits, and a quite unexpected bridge. It was one of the older monasteries on Crete, but in the late sixteenth century it was pillaged by pirates from Africa; the monks began to abandon it, moving to Gouverneto. In a nearby *cave*, which you pass on the right before reaching the ruined monastery, St John the hermit died. Inside is a large chamber – about 150 metres at its longest, and up to 20 metres high, and with many stalactites. It is all quite spectacular but can be dangerous: don't go alone or without light.

The saint's day is observed every October 7th, when many pilgrims and visitors converge on Gouverneto and Katholiko. A 20-minute walk leads to a rocky inlet, once the harbour for Katholiko.

Other remains

The Akrotiri has other remains, usually ignored except by those with exceptional interests or free time. At **Sternes**, the village near the airport, are remains of the old *Church of Ayii Pantes* (on the right as you enter the village); in the centre of the village, next to the *Church of the Annunciation*, are remains of structures and catacombs from the early Christian era; remains of a Late-Minoan country house were found here in the 1970s.

The Akrotiri is also especially rich in caves, many of which have yielded important finds to archaeologists and anthropologists during the twentieth century. To name only a few: in the *Koumarospilion*, the German Jantzen discovered human skulls at least 5,000 years old and excavations in the 1970s produced later finds. Above the beach at **Stavros** is the *Cave of Lera*, where was found a sanctuary dedicated to Acacallis, mother of Kydon. (It was on the steep coast here below Stavros that they filmed the scenes for the film of *Zorba the Greek* depicting the cable-transport of the wood.) Stavros and **Kalithas** are now popular in summer and offer tavernas.

Theriso and Mournies

These two villages are of interest only to those intent on pursuing the career of Eleftherios Venizelos. **Theriso** is his mother's home village. Having formed a party in 1901 with the pledge to seek union with Greece, he convened a Revolutionary Assembly at Theriso in 1905 and ended up by resorting to armed rebellion. The village is some 17 km. south of Khania and can be reached by taking a left turn off the road from Khania to Kastelli-Kissamou at about 1 km. on the outskirts of Khania. The road goes through an impressive ravine; 2 km. outside Theriso, located in this ravine, is *Sarakina Cave*, where finds from the Neolithic, Minoan and Geometric periods have been made.

Mournies, meanwhile, contains what is called 'the house where Venizelos was born'. In any case, it is a pleasant enough village, with its plane trees and spring water. It can be reached by taking the Khania road back towards Rethymnon, and just on the edge of town following the sign (Malaxa) to the right; Mournies lies some 4 km. down this road.

Khora Sfakion and Sfakia Province

On an island where nature and history have conspired to create a tangle of legends and myths, perhaps no part of Crete has quite such a fabulous aura as the province of Sfakia of which Khora Sfakion is the centre. Among those who know, the very word 'Sfakia' conjures up visions of almost superhuman mountain-men – staunch fighters for their independence, marauding brigands clambering over stark gorges, tending their flocks, hunting the wild goat, striking down their enemies. Inevitably, too, Sfakia prompts visitors and writers to superlatives: the land is the most rugged, the people are the most fearless (or lawless!), the flora and fauna are unique. In brief, it is a region that will attract some and repel many.

How much time is required for a trip through these parts? Well, the village of Khora Sfakion can be reached in two hours by bus or car. But to explore the region thoroughly – going from site to site and taking things as they come – would require many days. Most of the possibilities are described below.

Route Follow the main Rethymnon road (Route Exit B) east out of Khania (pp. 254–6), in reverse, turning right at Vrises [32 km.] to cross the island to Khora Sfakion [74 km.].

NOTE: The road from Vrises to Khora Sfakion is often blocked by snow in winter.

As an alternative return trip you could drive overland from Khora Sfakion to Rethymnon via Komitadhes, Patsianos, Skaloti, Rodakino, Selia and Ayios Ioannis, joining the Timbaki–Rethymnon road above the turning to the Monastery of Preveli (p. 237). This drive through some wild but spectacular terrain would allow you to take in excursions to Frangokastello (p. 276) and the Monastery of Preveli (p. 237) – the latter by turning right after Selia at 43 km. for Myrthios, Marjiou and Lefkoyia; after Lefkoyia you turn left (north) and then after about 1 km. turn right to join the previously described road (p. 237) to the monastery. You could then come back to join the Timbaki–Rethymnon road via Asomati and Koxares and continue either to Rethymnon or to Phaestos (pp. 235–9).

Bus There are regular services to Khora Sfakion and the surrounding region from the main bus terminal in Khania (*Map 29*).

Accommodation Vrises, en route, has an inn and several other eating-places. Khora Sfakion has a Tourist Pavilion, the *Xenia* (Class B) (tel. 91.202), which provides beds and meals throughout the year, and several other small hotels. Plakias (on the coast below Selia) has several new hotels that indicate its increasing popularity.

Hotels Class A: *Calypso* (tel. 31.210).

        Class B: *Alianthos Beach* (tel. 31.227).

                Lamon (tel. 31.205).

        Class C: *Alianthos* (tel. 31.227).

                Livykon (tel. 31.216).

                Sofia (tel. 31.226).

For the reverse route from Khania to Vrises see pp. 254–6.

[32 km.] **Vrises** (p. 254) is where you turn right and head inland. Climbing up into the mountains you pass the ravine of *Katrai*, named after a son of Minos and the scene of two bloody massacres: in 1821 thousands of Turks were trapped and slain here; and some forty-five years later the troops that had occupied Arkadhi were destroyed here.

[39 km.] A turn-off to the left leads in 1 km. to **Alikambos**. Before the upper village, to the left, sits the *Church of the Panayia*, in a cemetery.

It has superb frescoes from 1315–16 by Ioannis Pagomenos, one of the celebrated artists who worked in western Crete.

[52 km.] The *Plain of Askifou* opens up before you with the remains of an old fortress at its head; situated about 730 metres above sea level, it is surrounded by hills and villages, of which **Askifou** is the most important.

[58 km.] Continuing south on the main road you pass through the village of **Imbros.** Then you wind through a lovely cypress forest and descend through a ravine with a dramatic view of the barren landscape and the rugged coast of the Libyan Sea.

[71 km.] A turning on the left leads in 1 km. to **Komitadhes** and **Frangokastello** (p. 276).

[74 km.] You come down to the coast at Khora Sfakion, with its imposing cliffs giving it the air of a pirates' nest.

Khora Sfakion and Sfakia Province

In its heyday, during the sixteenth century, Khora Sfakion was the largest town on the southern coast, with some three thousand inhabitants, a thriving commercial life and – it is claimed – one hundred chapels and churches. These were built by individual benefactors and neighbouring villages; most of them are now gone or in ruins. Although it does attract many tourists (and serves as a junction for the thousands who now go through the Samaria Gorge) Khora Sfakion today is a village with only a few hundred permanent inhabitants.

Nevertheless, it is still the centre of Sfakia Province, home of the Sfakians. It is hard to say whether the land made the men, or the men chose the land. Now they are inseparable in their rugged isolation. Although the population has declined drastically, this cannot really be blamed on the terrain. One theory has it that the Sfakians are pure descendants of the Dorians who moved into Crete after the break-up of the Minoan–Mycenaean empire; other theories claim them as Achaeans, as the Eteocretans – as Saracens, even! Whatever their origin, the Sfakians were left to their own resources, and over the centuries came to be feared by native Cretans as well as by invading foreigners. The Venetians had the intention of subduing the Sfakians and built the impressive Frangokastello on the coast (p. 276), but little came of this. When the Turks divided up the island among the Pashas at the end of the seventeenth century, the Sfakians still held their own.

They not only continued their autonomous affairs, but actively harassed the Turks – often to the great discomfort of their less belligerent fellow-Cretans, who lay exposed to the vengeance of the Turks after the Sfakians withdrew to their mountain stronghold. By the end of the nineteenth century there was hardly a patch of Sfakian soil that was not coloured by the blood of some incident. During the German occupation this region once more became the centre of resistance. It is fair to say that Sfakians have remained a law unto themselves throughout their history.

Then, too, they have this not entirely undeserved reputation of being lawless – pirates, smugglers, brigands, revolutionaries, brawlers, what you will. That day is largely past, except for a bit of sheep-stealing or petty smuggling. And to give them their due, they have always fought and killed as much among themselves as against outsiders; vendettas have taken the lives of many Sfakians. As with those other island outposts, Sicily and Corsica, family blood ran thick, passions ran high and quarters were close. But none of this involves the visitor to Sfakia. What the visitor notes, rather, is a land inhabited by mere hundreds, where once thousands lived and worked and fought. Ports lie idle. Flocks and trade have dwindled. Decimated by rebellions and vendettas, bypassed by history, many Sfakians have emigrated in search of a livelihood. The people remaining still hold to the old ways – in fact, Sfakia is noted for the pure tradition of its handicrafts. There are the ruins and sites of its past that may yet draw tourists. There will always be the spectacle of the land. But Sfakia's energy is slipping. Perhaps it is because there is no longer any serious challenge to their existence, no tension in their lives; Sfakia thrived on resistance. A bastion of independence, Sfakia is now independent – and ignored.

Churches and caves

As Khora Sfakion has always been a rallying-point for revolutionaries, the whole area has many sites associated with various historical episodes. In Khora Sfakion itself – up on the hill to the right as you descend into the village – is the *Church of the Twelve Apostles*; several others have frescoes of the Byzantine period. Nearby, on the left after you have taken the turning to Komitadhes village (below), is the *Thymniani Panayia Church*, where the self-governing Sfakians held their assemblies during the years before 1821.

There are also several caves in the region, the most famous one being the *Cave of Daskaloyiannis* – 'John the Clerk' or 'John the Educated'. It is reached by sea, some ten minutes to the west. Daskaloyiannis is one of the best known of the many revolutionary leaders of Crete, thanks largely to the ballad, *The Song of Daskaloyiannis*, set down some sixteen years after his death and recounting his bloody fate. He had taken the lead in the uprising of 1770 and, when he finally delivered himself over to the Turks to discuss surrender terms, they disagreed and he was seized, tortured in the fort at Iraklion and then skinned alive. (His bust is at the edge of the square in Iraklion named after him.) It was in this cave that the revolutionaries of 1770 established their own mint.

Frangokastello

An interesting excursion from Khora Sfakion is to Frangokastello, about 12 km. to the east; you can pick up a bus from Khora Sfakion which will drop you at Patsianos within walking distance of the castle. To get there by car you return along the main road out of Khora Sfakion; after 2 km. turn right and continue a further 1 km. into **Komitadhes**. There is a *Church of St George* about ten minutes' walk down from this village which dates from the early fourteenth century and has some fine frescoes by one of the most admired Cretan painters, Ioannis Pagomenos (see p. 274).

Then you pass on through the villages of **Vraskas** and **Vouvas** towards **Patsianos**. Just before this village a right turn, sign-posted Frangokastello, leads down to the coast in about 2 km. to the castle. Alternatively, if you continue about 4 km. beyond Patsianos, a track (which will take a car) leads across to the isolated point on the coast where this old Venetian fort is situated.

The Venetians thought they could subdue the Sfakians, and so in the fourteenth century they erected this impressive fort, using, in part, stone from some ancient site. It is a sizeable, square fortress, with four corner towers – and still fairly well preserved, with the Lion of St Mark on guard. But the Venetians never really succeeded in taming the Sfakians, despite the many bloody battles fought in this area. It is said that the Cretans used to dance on the flat land by the castle – doing the *pyrrikhios*, the soldiers' dance of war, as taught by Rhea to the *Curétes* who had protected the young Zeus. Nowadays, in place of battles and dances, the Cretans claim to see the ghosts of the hundreds of Sfakians who died defending the fort against the Turks in 1828; a monument now commemorates their deaths. Only in early May, at dawn, do these *drossoulítes* – 'dew shades' – appear; evidently a mirage of some sort, due to peculiar weather conditions.

A small 'resort' is now developing around the fine, sandy beach below the fortress; there are several restaurants and rooms for renting. The swimming from here is particularly good. Returning to the Patsianos road, you could continue on eastwards and northwards to Rethymnon by the route described on p. 237. This will take you via Selia, from where you can drive down to Plakias, another resort in the making with small hotels and rooms.

From Khora Sfakion to Ayia Roumeli

It is possible to take a small boat from Khora Sfakion to Ayia Roumeli, the village on the coast to the west and at the end of the Gorge of Samaria (p. 282). There are several boats a day to Ayia Roumeli (via Loutro). The demands made by hiking overland above the south coast are too much for most people; however, we describe major 'way stations' below. But even experienced hikers are advised to make use of local guides for at least some of the stretches: at best it is a walk of many hours, and a wrong turn could lead you into some truly formidable terrain. As for the boat trip, almost everyone who makes the trip through the Gorge will come down through from the north and take the boat *to* Khora Sfakion, and so this possibility is described on p. 284.

One possibility is to break the boat trip between Ayia Roumeli and Khora Sfakion and spend several hours or a day at **Loutro** (overnight in a pension), a village near the site of *Phoenix*, a port mentioned by Strabo. Loutro is a relatively unspoiled village on its own little cove; to the west is a promontory shaped like a spade, with shelter on both sides. Phoenix was on the west side and served as the port for Anopolis (p. 278). There are scattered remains from the Roman period, as well as some early Byzantine ruins (when Phoenix was the seat of a bishop). But there are vaults from the Venetian period, indicating that the port functioned even that late. On the promontory is the *Church of Christ the Saviour*, with frescoes from later Byzantine times. There is also a building in a fair state of preservation, where the first 'government' of the Cretan revolution of 1821 met: it is called the *Kangelia Kivernion*, 'the chancellery'.

From Loutro, an ambitious hike to Ayia Roumeli takes you up via **Anopolis** (see below) and across the ravine of Aradena to the village of **Aradena**. Its *Church of the Archangel Michael* dates from the Byzantine period, although it was probably built with material from ancient ruins; the frescoes are worth examining. Near by is the site of ancient *Aradin*; its name is Phoenician, and it is mentioned in an ancient military alliance with the King of Pergamon in Asia Minor. The ruins include a structure called 'the dance of the Hellenes', as well as some ancient man-made caves in the rocks.

From Aradena, the path leads on to the village of **Ayios Ioannis** (by which time you will have been walking at least five hours from Loutro). The *Church of the Panayia* in Ayios Ioannis has some fairly well-preserved Byzantine *frescoes*. Near by, too, is the *Dhrakolakoi*, or 'dragon cave'; it is quite large, with water and sandy ground, and should be explored only by those with the proper experience and gear.

From Ayios Ioannis, the trail descends to the coast and passes the *Chapel of St Paul* (p. 284) and then goes on to Ayia Roumeli; but this trail down from Ayios Ioannis is not easy to find, and a guide is called for.

Anopolis

A less ambitious excursion from Khora Sfakion is to the village of Anopolis, some 12 km. to the west. There is one bus a day from Khora Sfakion, but then you would have to wait till the next day to get it back – or walk back. (Alternatively, you could walk down to Loutro, p. 277, and there get the boat to Khora Sfakion.) In its protected position, and with its harbour at Phoenix (p. 277), Anopolis flourished under the Romans and on into the Byzantine period. With its various dependent villages it may have numbered many thousands of inhabitants at its peak; it is said to have had its own mint. There are only a few ruins to be seen, including cyclopean walls. There are also remains of a house said to have once been the residence of Daska-loyiannis (p. 276) who is honoured by a statue in the square. Anopolis can be used as the base for climbing or hiking expeditions into the White Mountains, but, again, a local guide should be employed.

Gorge of Samaria

Probably the most spectacular adventure that Crete offers is a trip through the Gorge of Samaria. Until the late 1960s, relatively few people each year made the trip, but now many thousands make the passage each year. On certain days during high season, at least 2,000 people may pass through in one day: at best it can be said a holiday spirit prevails. On such days the boat service may run so late that you have to spend the night at Khora Sfakion if you are not with a group. (The best advice for crowded days during high season: as soon as you arrive at Ayia Roumeli, no matter how tired you are, go straight to the boat ticket booth and make your reservation. Then relax and enjoy your cool drink and swim.)

To do it properly, you should allow two days, starting from Khania, not because it takes that long to walk through the gorge – you can get through in five hours – but because the whole excursion (the trip from Khania to the top of the gorge, the passage through and the return via Khora Sfakion) takes up the time. If you were to combine several of the sites along the south coast, as side-trips from Ayia Roumeli and/or Khora Sfakion, then still more time could be profitably spent. There are various ways of making the passage. Many tourist agencies make it easiest by offering a (long) one-day tour, basically only a bus that leaves Khania early in the morning and then meets you at Khora Sfakion. Another possibility is to arrange for a guide through the National Tourist office. But this is not necessary; all that is advised is that no one go alone, since it is rocky terrain and there are usually patches of water to be crossed. If you twisted your ankle, it might be awkward, to say the least, to depend on strangers to get you out. Otherwise, there is no risk involved. There are several piped springs along the way, as well as the gorge stream itself, for water. But be prepared to feed yourself.

Not so incidentally, the gorge is now officially closed during the winter months. Furthermore, there are no tour buses and few scheduled boat connections from about October 1st to the end of April. So the excursion is something to undertake only from May to September and even then, depending on the rainfall, the gorge may be impassable at either end of the season.

Route Follow the Kastelli road westwards out of Khania (Route Exit A) and at 2 km. turn south at a junction marked to Omalos, for Alikianos and Lakkoi. Continue on to the Omalos Plain, at the far edge of which is the Xyloskalon ('wooden steps') that leads down to the gorge [42 km.]. The actual walk through the gorge is described in the text that follows (and see the sketch map, p. 283). If you have driven to Xyloskalon, you will either have to walk back up through the gorge, or go all the way round via Khania by one of the ways suggested under Bus and boat (below).

Bus and boat Regular buses go from the main bus terminal (*Map* 29) in Khania. At least during the high season, there are several buses daily, the first leaving Khania at about 05.00, that go all the way to the entrance to the gorge; enquire at the National

Tourist Information offices about this schedule. (And, as mentioned, private tourist agencies organize complete tours through the gorge.)

Once you have arrived at the south end of the gorge, at Ayia Roumeli, you have several possibilities. Most people will take one of the regularly scheduled small boats departing three to four times daily between 09.00 and 17.00 (in summertime, that is) to Khora Sfakion, where they may want to spend the night in the Tourist Pavilion. It is possible to spend the night in Ayia Roumeli's own rooms and pensions, and then set out the next day in one direction or another. There is the possibility of walking overland to the east and Khora Sfakion – an ambitious hike described on pp. 277–8. Or some might want to walk back up through the gorge; this is rather harder going than the trip down, and you must be careful to bear to the left after the village of Samaria (p. 282) to avoid getting side-tracked and on to the mountain of Melindaou.

For those who find the idea of a walk either up or down the gorge alarming, a sensible alternative would be to take a boat from Khora Sfakion to Ayia Roumeli and then walk only as far into the gorge as the Sidheroportes. This is the most dramatic part of the whole walk anyhow, and gives the less energetic traveller a fair idea of what he might otherwise have completely missed.

Accommodation There is the Tourist Pavilion (tel. 93.237), which can accommodate about eight persons, at the top of the gorge, as well as cheap beds on the Omalos Plain (at the bus stop by the restaurants). There are pensions and rooms at Ayia Roumeli, and more ambitious accommodation at Khora Sfakion.

[2 km.] Turn left for Alikianos, after leaving Khania (Exit A) to the west.

[12 km.] After driving through fertile, almost lush scenery, with many orange groves, you come to a fork with a *war memorial* to people of the surrounding villages killed in the Second World War. The right-hand turn leads in 1 km. to **Alikianos**, where there is a nice little restored Byzantine church, but you keep straight on for Fournes.

[15 km.] At the end of the village of **Fournes**, you have to fork right to Lakkoi. If you were to take the left fork, however, you would come in another 6 km. of largely non-tarmac but driveable road to **Meskla**, known as Crete's 'Garden of Green'. (There is a direct bus connection from Khania to Meskla.) Thanks to its well-watered orange groves, Meskla is a prosperous as well as a green village with fountains and a fast-flowing river even in August. The Venetians used Meskla as an administrative centre; it was also the headquarters of Kantanoleon, a native leader in the struggle against the Venetians. Meskla has other little points of interest. The *Church of the Transfiguration* – just off the road and up to the left before you enter the village – has early fourteenth-century *frescoes* (but now repainted). At the far end of the village a *chapel* is built over the *mosaic* of a temple to Venus; this is now kept locked most of the time, as is the new church in whose shadow it nestles. Near Meskla, too, is the site of what scholars have decided was ancient *Rizenia*; little is known about it, but judging from its cyclopean walls and rock-carved chambers, it must have been settled fairly early.

[20 km.] Most people will have taken the right fork at Fournes, and now, some 5 km. farther, you follow the road round to the left.

[25 km.] **Lakkoi**, another of those idyllic mountain villages of Crete, surrounded by green slopes and fields.

[37 km.] Driving through a pass, you note, on the right, a subterranean water escape which starts at 1,040 metres and drops to 281 metres in just over 2 kilometres. A notice-board commemorates a Birmingham University expedition of 1967. The *Omalos Plain* lies spread out ahead. At over 1,000 metres' elevation, and covering some 25 square kilometres, the Omalos is one of the most impressive of the Cretan upland plains; it almost seems to be a great drained lake – and indeed becomes quite marshy in the centre at certain seasons. It is not nearly so populated as the Lasithi Plain, but people from villages in the region do cultivate potatoes and cereals. All there is by way of a village on the road is a couple of houses and cafés near the chapel (and where the bus stops) but they can provide modest meals and beds.

[38 km.] Soon after reaching the plain, you see on a rocky outcrop a *chapel* and the *house* and *grave* of Hadzimikhali Yiannàri, one of the leaders of the nineteenth-century rebellions against the Turks; he later wrote his memoirs.

[42 km.] At the far end of the plain, you arrive at the entrance to the gorge, the *Xyloskalon*, or 'wooden steps'. There is a Tourist Pavilion here to provide basic beds and meals in the season; there is also a most impressive view out across the mountains.

Gorge of Samaria

The Gorge of Samaria, one of the largest in Europe, and now designated a National Park, is 18 kilometres long and varies in width from 3 to 40 metres. The steep walls rise from 300 to 600 metres, at some points so sheer that there is barely any sunlight, and at the *sidheroportes* ('iron gates') you walk through a narrow pass of steep rock. Thousands of years of torrents have eaten away the rocks, creating such a gorge. Even now there is a sizeable stream during the rainy season and after the thaw; in 1955 Ayia Roumeli was inundated, owing to unusually heavy rains in the White Mountains. Throughout the trip you will see flowers, herbs and shrubs clinging to the crevices; dittany and cypress are especially notable. The famous Cretan wild goat – the *agrími* – is so elusive that it is unlikely that the casual visitor will ever see one here in the wild, but those who have confirm the tales of its prodigious leaps and agility.

You set out, zigzagging down the Xyloskalon, descending into the gorge. After descending about 5 km., you pass, standing in a lovely grove of pines and cypresses, the little *Chapel of St Nicholas*. Continuing down, you pass on your left the village (now deserted) of *Samaria* with its stone huts; its Venetian *Church of Ossia Maria* (1379) has given its name to the gorge. (This Mary is not the mother of Jesus but an Egyptian whore who repented when an icon of the Virgin appeared before her. She then retired to Jordan and when she died she was buried by a lion. The icon is now preserved on Mt Athos. The little church's fourteenth-century frescoes are worth viewing if you have the time.) Pashley, the famous nineteenth-century classicist-traveller, placed the site of the ancient Dorian city of *Kaino* near Samaria. There was an oracle of Apollo; here, too, according to myth, was born the nymph Britomartis, daughter of Zeus – the Cretan Artemis or Dictynna. And the nereid Acacallis, wife of Apollo, was said to have been worshipped in this region. All in all, it is most atmospheric; it is easy to believe in the gods and goddesses of nature as you pass through such a gorge.

The gorge begins in earnest after Samaria, and you will do best to follow the river; it will be dried out in the summer, and you can make your way along the rocky river-bed, along the upper trails, and back and forth over the rock-fords. After passing below the *Church of Aphendis Christos* (on the left), you pass through the narrowest section, the *sidheroportes* (or 'iron gates'); you then proceed on to the small village of Ayia Roumeli; moving through this almost deserted village, you continue another 2 km. to arrive at the coast itself. This is a small alluvial plain, and since there is a sudden drop at the shore, no delta forms where the river enters the sea.

Ayia Roumeli

The hamlet of Ayia Roumeli offers nothing spectacular; it was noted largely for its inhabitants, Sfakians who made their living tending flocks, hunting game and otherwise subsisting off the sea and the land.

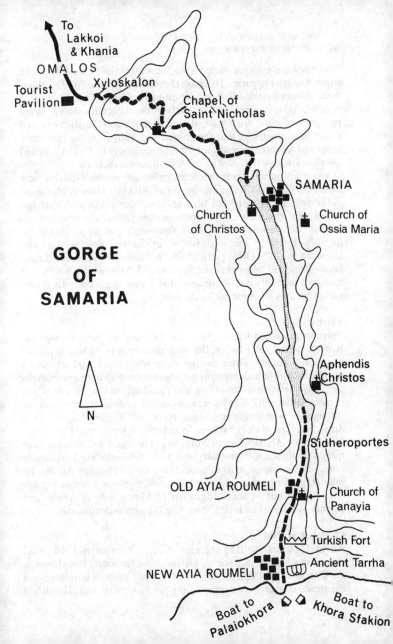

To Lakkoi
& Khania

OMALOS

Xyloskalon

Tourist
Pavilion

Chapel of
Saint Nicholas

SAMARIA

Church of
Christos

Church of
Ossia Maria

**GORGE
OF
SAMARIA**

N

Aphendis
Christos

Sidheroportes

OLD AYIA ROUMELI

Church of
Panayia

Turkish Fort

Ancient Tarrha

NEW AYIA ROUMELI

Boat to
Palaiokhora

Boat to
Khora Sfakion

Now they are engaged in servicing the thousands of travellers who come through the gorge. There are the remains of a *Turkish fort* above Ayia Roumeli. And there is one church of note: *Our Lady of St Roumeli*, built by the Venetians early in the sixteenth century. In the pavement round it are *mosaics* dating from the pre-Christian era, and it has been suggested that the church was built over the ruins of a temple to Apollo, a sacred spot for the ancient city of Tarrha, situated on what are now the outskirts of Ayia Roumeli (below).

There are now several pensions, cafés and rooms available here including the Class B *Ayia Roumeli* (tel. 91.293). There is also good swimming. Boats to Khora Sfakion have been making at least five round trips daily during the main season (unless the seas are too rough); it takes about $1\frac{1}{2}$ hours (one-way) and stops at Loutro (p. 277). Boats to the west put in at Souyia, Palaiokhora, and Gavdhos (p. 287). Other possibilities for leaving Ayia Roumeli have been mentioned under Bus and boat, p. 280. Meanwhile, there are at least two relatively easy excursions that people might consider if they stayed on in Ayia Roumeli for the odd day.

Tarrha

Tarrha was settled from at least the fifth century B.C., through the Roman period, and on to the fifth century A.D. It was probably abandoned because of the decline of the trade routes and attacks by pirates. A few Hellenic remains have been turned up in recent years, as well as some Roman structures and fortifications (to the east of the present settlement). Tarrha was important enough to have its own coinage; it is also surmised that there was a glass factory, as a distinctive type of glass has been found only in this part of Crete (now in Khania's Archaeological Museum). The latest excavations have turned up tombs with jewellery and pottery. Tarrha was particularly noted as the site of a temple-sanctuary of Tarrhanean Apollo. Its inhabitants had a flourishing religion and mythology, involving not only Apollo but Acacallis (daughter of Minos, wife of Apollo and mother of Kydon) and the Cretan virgin-goddess Britomartis.

Chapel of St Paul

About $1\frac{1}{2}$ hours' walk to the east of Ayia Roumeli is a delightful chapel on a little terrace some 3 metres above the shore. It is known as the Chapel of St Paul, for he is said to have come ashore here and christened converts in a nearby spring (now only a trickle). The chapel is in the free cross form; its façade has an arcade of the Byzantine style from the twelfth century. It is not particularly spectacular, but it is well worth a detour from Ayia Roumeli, and could be taken in on a hike along the coast to the east – a trip referred to when starting from Khora Sfakion (p. 277).

Palaiokhora and Selinos Province

Tucked away in the south-west corner of Crete is the province of Selinos, probably the least visited area of the island. Today it is noted for its fine olives and oil, but it has many ancient sites and historical monuments that deserve to be better known. None of them is very spectacular in itself, but taken as a whole they provide an interesting glimpse into the post-Minoan, Byzantine and Venetian periods of Crete. It is difficult to imagine that such isolated settlements could ever have 'made' history, but in their time they were involved in the power struggles of the Mediterranean. In the third century B.C., for instance, several of them – Elyros, Lissos, Hyrtakina, Syia and Poikilassos – formed the Confederation of Oreioi, allying with Gortyna and Cyrenaica under King Magus (p. 96). Under the Romans, some of these prospered; in the early Christian centuries, still others – Syia, in particular – came into their own. Later, many Byzantine churches and frescoes flowered, and the Venetians saw fit to develop some of the sites. What remains today is fragmentary and only partially explored; the definitive excavations and identifications have yet to be made. For the average traveller these remains will be too specialized; but anyone wishing to explore the area will find one generally available source to be *The Tourist's Guide to Khania* by Anestis Makdridakis, which gives an impression of the history and remains of the regions.

Route Taking the Kastelli road westwards out of Khania (Route Exit A), you follow that route for 20 km. to Tavronitis (p. 288); there you turn left and continue to Kandanos [59 km.] and on to Palaiokhora [76 km.].
Bus The buses for Kandanos, Palaiokhora and other places in Selinos Province leave the main bus terminal (*Map 29*) in Khania.
Accommodation There is a hotel, the *Lissos* (Class C) (tel. 41.226), numerous rooms, and restaurants at Palaiokhora, with the possibility of light refreshments en route.

Follow the road westwards out of Khania as described on the excursion to Kastelli-Kissamou (p. 287–8).

[20 km.] At **Tavronitis**, turn left and south, passing slowly along by the river through cultivated land and starting to climb slowly through orange groves.

[28 km.] **Voukolies**, a clean, prosperous town, is notable for its Byzantine *Church of Ayios Konstantinos in Nembros*, on the left just before reaching the village, and for the market, or bazaar that draws many visitors on Saturday. You climb through green, wooded land.

[42 km.] Soon after **Kakopetros** you enter the province of Selinos.

[50 km.] **Floria** has two fifteenth-century Byzantine churches with frescoes: the *Church of Ayii Pateres* in Epano (Higher) Floria and the *Church of Ayios Georgios* in Kato (Lower) Floria.

[58 km.] **Kandanos**, the prosperous centre of this olive-growing region. During the Second World War this village won such a reputation as a centre of resistance against the Germans that they destroyed it, but today it has largely been rebuilt. This whole region is noted for its Byzantine churches and their frescoes. In the hamlet of **Anisaraki**, a few kilometres to the north-east of Kandanos, are the *Churches of Ayia Ana, Panayia, Ayia Paraskevi*, and *Ayios Georgios*, all with fine wall-paintings.

[64 km.] **Kakodiki** is also known for its Byzantine remains, including fine frescoes in the nearby *Churches of Panayia* and *Ayios Issidhoros*.

[66 km.] Before the village of **Kadhros**, the *Churches of St John and the Nativity of the Virgin* have noteworthy frescoes.

[76 km.] At the cross-roads on the edge of Palaiokhora a left turn leads down into the harbour; the right turn takes you into the town.

Palaiokhora
Palaiokhora is a small town, once known locally as 'the bride of the Libyan Sea'. It is also known as Kastelli Selinou, after the Venetian fort on its promontory. As it has hotels and several eating-places, it makes a convenient spot to spend some days while making excursions in the region. In recent years it has become a sometimes noisy hangout for the young. There is good bathing from a long sandy beach on the west side of the peninsula, where windsurf boards and paddle boats can be rented.

It would be possible to hike overland to visit some of the sites in this area – *Hyrtakina* and *Elyros* inland to the north-east of Palaiokhora and *Lissos* and *Syia* on the coast. There is a bus from Khania to the modern village of **Souyia** where the site of Syia is located; in recent years Souyia has become popular with those looking for a cheap and basic beach holiday. Lissos is a fifteen-minute boat trip from Souyia to the west and has remains of a temple and *Asklepieion* with mosaics.

Gavdhos Island

A more interesting possibility for most tourists would be an excursion to the island of Gavdhos, some 50 km. off shore from Palaiokhora. It has the distinction of being the southernmost territory of Europe – once you concede that Crete belongs to Greece and Greece belongs to Europe. A boat leaves twice a week from Palaiokhora (weather permitting) and in summer you may be able to get a boat from one of the other ports along the south coast – Ayia Roumeli, Khora Sfakion or Ayia Galini.

Little is known about the island's exact history. There are some ruins to be seen, but although surface finds from Neolithic times have been claimed, it was most probably not settled until post-Minoan times. Some have claimed it as Calypso's island; if so, it is not hard to see why Odysseus kept moving. In Acts xxvii 16 it is mentioned by its Roman name, Clauda. It was also known as Kaudos. By the Middle Ages, it was actually the see of a bishop and boasted 8,000 inhabitants. It has probably seen its share of pirates come and go, too. Today less than one hundred people live there, supporting themselves by the flocks of sheep. The village of **Kastri** passes as its capital, but the general impression of the island is of a desolate landscape and deserted houses. There is no electricity and no motor vehicles. A few kilometres north-west of Gavdhos is the islet of *Gavdhopoula*, a deserted spot used for pasturing sheep.

Kastelli-Kissamou and north-west Crete

This region of Crete reveals still another practically unknown island: rough terrain; a primitive landscape of valleys, mountains and isolated villages; unexplored ruins. For the traveller with two or three days to spare, an excursion into this region can be a unique experience. And starting in the mid-1970s, a boat service between Kastelli and the Greek mainland (see p. 21) introduced many new possibilities, both for the town and its visitors.

Route Take the road west out of Khania (Route Exit A) and drive along the coast to Kastelli-Kissamou [43 km.].

Bus Buses from the main bus terminal (*Map* 29) in Khania run regularly to Kastelli-Kissamou.

Accommodation There are hotels in Kastelli-Kissamou and several possible eating places. There are also hotels along the way, such as the *Panorama* (about 5 km. west) and the *Chandris* at Maleme. Accommodation can be found along the beaches between Ayia Marina and Platanias.

[2½ km.] On the left is an imposing *eagle*. It had been erected by the Germans as a memorial to their parachute assault on Crete in the Second World War; the Cretans have chosen to leave it there – as their own memorial.

[8 km.] The village of **Ayia Marina** marks the beginning of the beach resorts on this stretch of coast.

[11 km.] The village of **Platanias** straggles along the road surrounded by bamboo and banana groves – picturesque Platanias is above, on the turn-off. At several restaurants here you can eat delicious *dolma-dhákia* and *souvlákia* (p. 51); one of them, the *Milos*, is enhanced by its situation – beside the mill stream that supports ducks. Fine sandy beaches run along the coast. Off shore you should note the *Ayii Theodhori Island*, the ancient Akytos. It has a cave that seems to have been used as a place of worship around 2000 B.C.; its mouth looks like the gaping jaws of some beast, and legend has it that the island was once a wild animal that tried to devour Crete but was petrified by the gods. The Venetians and Turks used the island as a fortress, and for many years it has been a sanctuary for the *agrími*. There are two or three dozen of these wild goats there at present.

[17 km.] A large beach-resort, the *Crete Chandris*, is prominent on the shore (see p. 258). (At a sign-posted turn-off, left, a road leads to the cemetery for the Germans who died in the assault on Crete.)

[19 km.] **Maleme** is the site of the airport where the decisive battle for Crete was fought by the invading German airborne forces (p. 101). It is now maintained by the Greek Air Force.

[20 km.] Driving along through the valley of the Tavronitis river (from *távros* = 'bull') you come to the village of **Tavronitis.** This is where a turn to the south inland would take you to Kandanos and Palaio-khora in Selinos Province (p. 286).

[23 km.] Keeping along the coast road, a right fork marked to the

Monastery of Ghonia would bring you almost immediately into the village of **Kolymvarion**, situated just within the curve of the Rodhopou Peninsula. Kolymvarion has an inn and a restaurant and is noted for its wines. It also has a sheltered bathing beach.

Rodhopou Peninsula was known in ancient times as Cape Tityros; today it is sometimes called Cape Spatha, after its outermost point. It is one of two peninsulas that crown this end of Crete like bulls' horns; the western peninsula is *Cape Vouxa*, and between them lies the Gulf of Kissamos. At its widest part, Rodhopou Peninsula is only some 8 kilometres across, but its central ridge rises to 750 metres.

If you proceed on to the peninsula, about 1 km. past Kolymvarion you will come to the *Monastery of Ghonia*, overlooking the coast and the Gulf of Khania. Also known as Odhyitrias, the monastery was founded in 1618, burnt down by the Turks in 1645, re-erected in 1662, restored in 1798 and raised by another storey in 1874–84. Although it has a fort-like appearance, the Venetian influence is evident, especially with the baroque decoration of the refectory door. It counts among its attractions a handsome main gate, a rich treasury and several fine icons of the sixteenth and seventeenth centuries – particularly a crucifixion by Paleokapas. The monastery observes its main feast-day on August 15th. A modern Orthodox Academy was built in the late 1960s just beyond the monastery for international theological conferences. (It owes its existence to the progressive Bishop Ireneus, who in 1980 became the centre of a controversy when his former Cretan parishioners 'kidnapped' him to force the Orthodox hierarchy to reassign him to this episcopacy.)

Some distance by boat along the coast is the *Cave of Hellenospillos*. The cave is quite long, with many corridors and pools, stalactites and stalagmites; many archaeological finds, including some from Neolithic times, have been made here.

Farther up towards the tip of the peninsula is located the site of *Dhiktinaia*, named after the goddess Dictynna. The site can be reached by boat or by a long, arduous walk from Rodhopou (below) and a guide is essential. It was from this spot that the nymph Dictynna (alias Britomartis, alias Artemis) threw herself to escape from the lustful Minos. She was saved by the nets of fishermen – her name is derived from 'net' – and has since been venerated in western Crete as everything from a goddess of nets to a moon-goddess. At times the whole peninsula was called after her – Dhiktinaion. There was a Hellenistic temple to her on the site; this was replaced by a Roman temple in the second century A.D., and it is mainly the remains of this that are to be seen.

Back on the main road to Kastelli-Kissamou, and opposite the turn-off (at 23 km.) to the Monastery of Ghonia and the Rodhopou peninsula, a road would bring you in 2 km. to **Spilia**. Through the village is the *Church of Our Lady*, fourteenth-century frescoes, superb examples of the Cretan school (head south 1 km. along the road leading off the square behind the café with the Venetian fountain). Above the village is a cave with a man-made interior amphitheatre; here, on October 7th, is observed the death day of the St John the Hermit from Akrotiri (p. 271). (This amphitheatre-cave is hard to find; best approach is via turn *before* Spilia, sign-posted Maratho-kephala-Spilia Ayios Ioannis; proceed about 1 km. to village centre and turn left; go another 1 km. till road widens for parking, a small sign in Greek points to path on left that leads in 50 metres to the cave.)

Another 6 km. brings you to one of the oldest (if now restored) churches on Crete, *St Michael the Archangel at Episkopi*. Dating from the tenth century originally, it was enlarged in the eleventh and has some noteworthy architectural elements. About half-way, at Drakona, is a little white chapel to St Stephen with superb fourteenth-century frescoes, along a path sign-posted from the road 'St Stephen'.

[27 km.] Continuing westwards along the main road, you come to a right turn that leads on to the Rodhopou peninsula again and arrive in 5 km. at the village of **Rodhoupou**. A difficult walk of some $2\frac{1}{2}$ hours leads to the *Church of St John Giona*, where a festival is held each August 28th and 29th. It is probably the largest religious festival in the entire nome of Khania, and crowds from the whole western part of Crete gather here to celebrate and baptize the babies of Crete named John.

Back on the main road, you continue driving through a distinctive landscape of dry earth, limestone slopes, olive trees, and vines. After emerging from a mountain pass you enjoy a spectacular view of the sea.

[43 km.] As you come to the edge of Kastelli-Kissamou, you bear right off the main road (which otherwise takes you along the southern edge of the town) and move on into the little square.

Kastelli-Kissamou

Present-day Kastelli is quite subdued, but it is the centre for the production and trade of the wines of the district; there are three hotels and *tavérnas*; a delicious garlic roast pork has traditionally been available on Sundays.

Today's town is on the site of ancient Kissamos, port for Polyrhinia (see below). Kissamos was an autonomous post-Minoan settlement; the Romans took it over; and excavations from the 1960s to the 1980s have revealed various structures – baths, aqueducts – the remains of which may be seen. The finest find so far, the mosaic floors of a second-century A.D. house, had to give way to the new road; enquire at the little *museum* in the town square if anything is now to be seen. (If the museum is closed, ask for information at the Castron Hotel opposite.) This collection is expanding, by the way, with the increased archaeological activity in this region. In the early Christian era Kissamos served as an episcopal seat. The Venetians continued to develop the community, making it the see of a Catholic bishop, encouraging trade and constructing walls (of which vestiges remain); a Venetian *church* also survives.

The quay for the new boat service to the Peloponnesos, Piraeus and points to the east is well outside the town, to the west. What with this new impetus and increasing numbers of tourists who make their way here, Kastelli may yet experience its own little 'boom'.

Hotels Class B: *Helena Beach* (tel. 23.300).
       Class C: *Castron* (tel. 22.140).
           Kissamos (tel. 22.086).

Polyrhinia

On the main road leading along the southern edge of Kastelli, just before the 42 km. marker (on right, as measured from Khania), a sign on the left (recently, at least, marked with blue paint and arrow on white wall) points to Polyrhinia; this road leads in about 7·5 km. to the modern village of **Ano Palaikostro.** (On the way there you pass the *Convent of Parthenonas*, noted for its woven fabrics.) You must leave your vehicle in the village and then make a fairly rugged climb up a rocky path (fifteen to twenty minutes, depending on how fast and how far you choose to go) to the scattered remains of ancient Polyrhinia – 'town of many flocks'. The path twists and turns up the hillside through backyards but villagers will point the way. At some 275 metres above sea level, it enjoys an excellent view over the Gulf of Kissamos. Founded during the eighth century B.C., Polyrhinia was one of the chief settlements of Archaic Crete. Statues, bas-reliefs and coins contribute to the image of a once influential city that probably dominated much of the area because of its strategic position. The worship of such familiar gods as Apollo, Hermes, Dionysus, Dictynna-Artemis and Zeus is indicated by the coins. The foundations of cyclopean walls, aqueducts, reservoirs, temples and some graves carved in rock-caves are to be seen, but the inhabitants of the area have used much of the material over the centuries. The nearby *Church of the Ninety-nine Holy Fathers*, for instance, has probably utilized parts of older temples.

Phalasarna

If you proceed westwards along the main coast road from Kastelli, the road turns to the south after 3 km., and then after another 7 km. reaches **Platanos**. In this village, a right fork takes you along a road (the last 2 km. of which are very bad), bearing left in **Kavousion** over the hill and down to the sea. Turn right after 2 km. Continuing northwards along the coast you come after another 4 km. to the fragmentary remains of the post-Minoan city of Phalasarna [16 km. from Kastelli].

The site of Phalasarna was noticed by those indefatigable travellers, Pashley and Spratt, but it was not investigated, and then only superficially, until early in this century. Then in 1986 a team of Greek archaeologists began a thorough series of excavations that should eventually clarify the full extent, function, and age of the remains. For now, the general outlines are clear. Most of the remains – walls, reservoirs, houses, storage chambers, tombs, etc. – date from the Classical and Hellenistic periods – Phalasarna was not a Minoan site. The inhabitants at some point built two, possibly three, temples on the slopes of the town acropolis. But there was no 'palace' here, and the so-called throne that many early visitors commented on is probably nothing more than an up-ended sarcophagus. What Phalasarna was was a harbour town – probably serving as the port for Polyrhinia, up in the hills, and other inland settlements of this region. Its once ambitious harbour installations – great stone walls and quays – are now, however, some 200 metres in from the shore, because at some time this end of Crete was raised up (about 7 metres). Whether this happened gradually and by stages – due to the inexorable movement of the African plate that is still moving under the Aegean plate – or whether it happened rather suddenly due to a cataclysmic earthquake (which at least one geologist has dated to the early 6th century A.D.), is still being argued. Also, the excavators have found large stone blocks that seem to have been deliberately thrown across the old harbour entrance – perhaps by Romans seeking to isolate some Cretan 'pirate' and his band. In the later years of the Roman Empire a settlement grew up across the bay, where today's fishing harbour is located.

But much yet remains to be spelled out. For now, Phalasarna sits on the promontory in all its megalithic, isolated splendour, looking out across the Mediterranean to the west. Some of the finds from this site, by the way, are on display in the Khania Museum. There are tavernas, simple hotels, rooms to rent, and – unauthorized – camping on the adjacent coast.

Above Phalasarna protrudes *Cape Vouxa*, the ancient peninsula of Korykia, now virtually deserted. Off the tip of the peninsula are two islets: the one to the north is *Agria* ('wild') *Gramvousa* and the one to the west is *Imeri* ('tame') *Gramvousa*. The latter is a precipitous, almost inaccessible islet that is probably one of the oldest Mediterranean pirate lairs. The Venetians constructed a fortress here and it was one of the last three holdouts against the Turks, capitulating only in 1692. Eventually the Christian Cretans managed to get it back, and marauders operating from there became a nuisance to all parties. The fort is in fair condition and offers a dramatic view to anyone who takes the trouble to hire a boat in Kastelli to visit it. If you did hire a boat, you should investigate a couple of the other sites on the peninsula that would otherwise require many hours of hiking. At the north-eastern side of the peninsula is the Doric site of *Agneion*, with its shrine to Apollo. And on the north-western side is the coral-red beach of Tigani-Balos.

Nunnery of Khrysoskalitisa

This is an excursion that should appeal to those who want to get away from the main routes and popular attractions of Crete. Its ostensible goal is a nunnery down on the south-west corner of the island, but the real appeal of the trip – and it can easily be done in a day – is in the various sidelights and diversions. Much of the road has been very rough, but a sound vehicle and strong will can get you through.

You set out eastwards from Kastelli, towards Khania, but at about 4 km. you turn right at the village of **Kaloudiana** (with its giant eucalyptus tree). The road passes through **Potamida** and **Topolia** and then begins to wind through a narrow pass. About ½ km. after Topolia you will see up on the right a white chapel sitting at the mouth of a cave: this is the *Cave of Ayia Sophia*, and a path leads up (about five minutes) if you care to investigate it. (This little known cave is actually quite dramatic, with numerous large stalagmites, an interior lake, and a huge circular inner chamber. Frequented since Neolithic times, today the Orthodox gather here on St Sophia's day: tradition claims that the ikon of Ayia Sophia of Constantinople was hidden here after the Turks took that city in 1453.) You push on through **Elos** and **Kephalion** (always taking care to observe the signs for Moni Khrysoskalitisa) where you turn left and go through **Vathi**: in a vineyard on the left sits the *Chapel of Michael the Archangel* with frescoes worth examining. All this while you have been winding and climbing and descending through almost lush terrain, and as you push on through **Stomion** you come out above the coast. Finally, after only some 39 km. from Kastelli, you arrive at the nunnery, perched on a rocky promontory above the sea. It is not known exactly when it was founded, but the present structure is built over an older one. It is dedicated to the Assumption of the Virgin Mary, which means that it attracts large numbers of Cretans on August 15th. By 1990, however, only two nuns were in residence, and it is questionable how much longer it can remain active. Its name, by the way, means 'golden stairway' and refers to the legend that one of the ninety steps to the top of the rock is made of gold – but only those who have committed no sins can see it!

There are a couple of modest cafés just before the nunnery and you can usually get cold drinks and snacks at them; the beach here, however, is neither that attractive nor accessible. So if you have come this far, you should go on another 5 km. to the south-west where there is a fine sandy beach and the offshore islet of *Elaphonisi*. The road is rough going, but you simply have to drive slowly. You will be rewarded by an almost tropical lagoon – spoiled only by the litter left by campers or washed ashore. On the islet is a monument erected to Australian sailors who lost their lives here in the wreck of the *Imperatrice* in 1907. It all makes for a delightful picnic spot.

You return via the nunnery – and note beyond that the gypsum works on the coast – but rather than retrace the route all the way back to Kastelli, go only back to Kephalion; there turn left and go on to Papadiana, Amygdalokephali, and Keramoti. As you push on (and this road may now be totally asphalt) you are driving through landscape that has gained this region the name of the 'Switzerland of Crete'. You pass through Sfinari (with easy access to a beach where there are cafés) and on to Platanos (the turn-off towards Phalasarna, p. 292); from there it is an easy 11 km. to Kastelli.

ROUTE 5: IRAKLION TO AYIOS NIKOLAOS (VIA MALLIA)

This is another of those unique excursions through time that Crete offers; to take advantage of the many points of interest en route, you should have your own transport and a long day. The palace of Mallia – contemporary with those at Knossos and Phaestos – is merely the best-known attraction of the trip; the other sights will come more as surprises, despite the burgeoning beach resorts and hotels bulging with sun-loving tourists all along this coast.

Route As usual, the route described here does not use the new highway except where necessary as this would by-pass at least some of the sights. Leaving Iraklion by the St George Gate (Route Exit C), you descend sharply round a corner and then pass through the suburb of Poros; continuing along the coast road for Mallia [33 km.] and Neapolis [52 km.], you arrive at Ayios Nikolaos [67 km.].

Bus There are frequent buses to Ayios Nikolaos via Mallia; they depart from the terminal at the harbour (*Iraklion Map* **29**) and the trip takes about one and a half hours. Careful planning should allow a person to get an early bus, visit Mallia and pick up a later bus to go on from there. Some of the sites nearer Iraklion can, of course, be visited by buses from and back to Iraklion.

Accommodation There are now so many hotels and other types of accommodation along the coast between these two cities – at Poros, Karterou, Gournes, Gouves, Limin Khersonisou, Stalis, Mallia, Neapolis – that everyone can organize a trip to his own needs.

[1 km.] As you pass through Poros – your mind on the Minoans, your eye avoiding this modern suburb – it is appropriate to know that one of the building sites in recent years exposed an important rock-cut Minoan tomb with valuable artefacts.

[2 km.] You come down to sea level at **Katsamba**, at the mouth of the Kairatos river (now usually dried up), once a harbour town serving Knossos. Excavations have turned up remains of tombs and houses, testifying to the continuous habitation of the site from Neolithic through Minoan times. Among the more valuable finds in the tombs have been a vase inscribed with the cartouche of Pharaoh Tuthmosis III (and thus invaluable for the chronology of Crete) and a lovely ivory pyxis (these objects to be seen in *Cases* 82 and 79A of the Iraklion Archaeological Museum).

[2·9 km.] At this point – unless there has been yet another change, as there is apt to be – a sign on the right indicates a turn off the coast road to Ayios Nikolaos and points to the eastern part of Crete. To continue straight along the coast would bring you to the airport (and no further). So you will turn right and proceed a few hundred metres; unless you are in a hurry and want to get on to the New Road (posted), you will turn to the left and proceed along a road that runs parallel to (and somewhat below) the New Road and along the edge of a Greek military base; proceeding along this road, you are essentially going around the airport (which is on the coast, to your left) and you will come down on to the coast road, passing a small wayside chapel built into a cliff, on your right. On your left, as you head east along the coast, is Karteros Beach, known locally as 'Florida Beach', a popular swimming area, with facilities (showers, changing rooms, snacks) operated by the Tourist Organization.

[8 km.] A sign indicates a turn to the right to Episkopi, but the reason you will want to make this sidetrip is the **Cave of Eileithyia**, which is located about 1·4 km. from this turn-off. However, to really visit this important cave, you must plan ahead: it is now gated and locked, and to gain entrance you must be accompanied by a caretaker; he has been located at the Megaron Nirou at Kokini Hani (see at 13 km., below) and has been available from 9.00 to 15.00 daily except Mondays. The cave is worth the arrangements, but you must allow the time; if you do not have the need to enter the cave, you could at least stand at the gated entrance and peer in. You drive under the overpass (of the New Road) and wind up the steep and curved road until you see, on the left, a small sign indicating 'Cave' (sometimes it is only in German, *Höhle*). Park as best you can off to the side (making sure your car can be seen by drivers making the curves) and then carefully make your way down the slope several metres; a fig tree marks the cave's entrance, a deliberate sign for this 'womb of the earth', the fig being an ancient symbol of fertility. It was first explored by Hadzidakis and Halbherr in the 1880s, though local people had never really lost it (and if you can't locate it today, they will know it as *Neraidhospilios*). It is known that the cave was a burial site and shrine in the Neolithic era, well before 3000 B.C. and the later Minoan civilization. Through Minoan times it was revered as a sacred spot, dedicated to manifestations of the Nature Goddess and to Eileithyia the 'liberator' – goddess of childbirth in particular and protector of women in general.

(Hera is said to have given birth to Eileithyia here.) It retained its prestige throughout Crete's history, and is mentioned in the *Odyssey* (Book XIX), when Odysseus, disguised as a beggar, lies to Penelope and claims that Odysseus put in at Amnisos, 'where the cave of Eileithyia is'.

You can walk about 50 metres into the cave; a flashlight or some means of illumination is necessary, however, if you go back this far. The ground can be slippery, too. About midway you will see two stalagmites, walled at their base, indicating they were regarded as sacred (like lingams?).

Back on the coast road, and almost immediately opposite the turn-off to Episkopi and the Cave of Eileithyia, you will see another sign (pointing toward coast) to 'Amnisos Antiquities'. Down this turning, before you reach the beach, just off to the left are the remains of *Amnisos*, surrounded by a metal fence. Amnisos was a Minoan settlement, sometimes referred to as the port or 'naval headquarters' of Knossos. It was from here that Idomeneus and his ships left for the Trojan War. Vestiges of several buildings have been discovered here, including the circular *Altar of Zeus Thenatas* and the *Villa of the Lilies*. It has been suggested that this villa was the home of the port commander. In the 1960s, Alexiou established that the Minoan settlement here extended to the west of the hill, while still farther west of that were Mycenaean houses. This site is also famous because it was here that Marinatos, excavating in the 1930s, found pumice-stone that led him to propose that the explosion of volcanic Santorini had brought disaster to the Minoan centres on Crete (p. 94).

Continuing on the coast road again, heading east, you pass Tombrouk Beach on the left, a popular gathering place for Irakliots, and then follow the road as it curves around the flank of *Kakon Oros*, the mountains that descend sharply to the sea here – a delightful drive. Offshore is the islet of *Dia*, the principal island refuge for the wild goats of Crete (p. 81).

[13 km.] At the village of Kokini Hani, on the right hand side as you enter, are the remains of the Minoan *megaron* of *Nirou Khani*. (There is a sign-post for this site.) The site is locked but there is a caretaker with a key, the same man who keeps the key of the Cave of Eileithyia (above). (He keeps regular hours – usually 08.00–12.00 and 16.00–18.00.) The remains are not spectacular, but important finds were made there: great bronze double axes, oil lamps, vases, tripod altars –

all to be seen now in the Iraklion museum. They were found in such concentration that it is thought that this was the dwelling of some high functionary of the Minoan state religion, who may have acted as a distributor of these religious objects through the small port at this spot. Evans reported sighting a submerged quarry and column bases in the harbour of the settlement for which Nirou Khani's structure must have served as the centre; this harbour is about 1 km. west, at a spot known locally as Ayii Theodhori.

[16 km.] Just past the little village of **Gournes** on the slopes to the right, you come across (on the left) one of the most unexpected sights in Crete – an *American Air Force Station*. It is virtually a pocket of the twentieth century, and, although it has acted as a great stimulus to the local economy, it is surely one of the strangest labyrinths ever erected on this island. The *America Hotel* (Class B) you pass on your right can be used by anyone, but it has obviously been placed here to accommodate people connected with the American base.

[17 km.] The old road joins (and becomes) the new National Road.

[18 km.] Several large, new hotels cluster along this stretch. A turn-off to the right leads via **Gouves** in 6 km. to **Skotino**. (The sign-post only indicates Gouves.) A half-hour's overland walk (get a local guide) would bring you to the large *Skotino Cave* which was evidently an important sacred shrine in Minoan times, judging from the many pieces of pottery, bronze and other materials found here; and it remained a goal of worshippers at least through Greek and Roman times. It is one of the most spectacular caves on Crete, with four levels, its largest chamber being 90 by 36 metres and some 12 metres high.

[22 km.] To the right is the turn-off (sign-posted) that leads up into the mountains to the Lasithi Plain and the Dhiktaion Cave (p. 183).

[27 km.] As you drive into the village of **Limin Khersonisou**, you will note a turn to the left (sign-posted Plage – 'beach'); if you take that you will come down to a waterfront lined by touristic souvenir shops. Along this waterfront you will note (fenced in) a curious pyramidal Roman fountain with its fragmentary mosaics and gutters for the water to run through. But although Khersonisou was a thriving seaport and town in Hellenistic, Roman and early Byzantine times, this fountain is about all that survives to appeal to the average visitor. The traces of theatres and other structures in the environs are disappointing, while the many coins and inscriptions are in museums. For some visitors, however, there is the special attraction of submerged remains; Evans himself reported seeing some along the shore here, and remains of the harbour works can still be seen in the waters around the promontory at the west side of the modern community. The area was settled even back in Minoan times, but it was not until Greece's classical period that Khersonisou seems to have been colonized from the Peloponnesos; from this time, too, its fortunes became linked with Lyttos (p. 191), for which it served as the port town. Under the Christians, Khersonisou became the seat of an archbishop; little of interest has survived from that era, either, although above the little *Church of Ayios Nikolaos* (on the promontory to the west) are traces of a sizeable fifth-century Christian basilica with a mosaic floor; remains of another basilica were found at a nearby locale known as Kastri, to the east, with a tomb cut into the rock south of the church.

But there is no denying that what has drawn people to Limin Khersonisou are its beaches; it has become a popular resort for many Europeans as well as a favourite vacation spot for people from Iraklion. Along with its various pensions and rooms to rent, Khersonisou now provides quite a choice of accommodation; there is the *King Minos Palace*, Class A (tel. 22.781) with its bungalows; up on the slope across from the shore is the *Belvedere*, Class A (tel. 22.010); to the east is the *Nora*, Class B (tel. 22.271), while to the west is one of the largest, most spectacular resort complexes on Crete, the *Creta Maris*, Luxury Class (tel. 22.115). There are also numerous Class C hotels, guest houses and apartments.

[31 km.] Proceeding along the main road, you reach the village of **Stalis**, noted for its fine beach and palm trees. There is comfortable accommodation at the *Anthousa Beach* (Class A) and *Blue Sea Motel*, Class B (tel. 31.371), apartments, villas, and cheaper rooms to rent along the road, and *tavérnas* to provide simple meals.

As you continue along the road you find yourself entering the bay and plain of Mallia, spread out at the foot of the Lasithi Mountains. Many windmills are to be seen here, pumping water for the farming; bananas are also grown here.

[33 km.] You arrive in the village of **Mallia**; with its beach reputed to be one of the finest on Crete, it has been drastically transformed in recent years, what with the various cafés and tourist shops on its 'main street' and the several large beach hotels along the shore – *Ikaros*

Village, *Sirines Beach*, *Kernos Beach*, *Mallia Beach* (all Class A), and still others by now. There is also the less pretentious but no less sympathetic *Pension Grammatikakis*, Class B (tel. 31.366), which still commands one of the loveliest sections of the beach, with its fine white sand and the tiny off-shore islet and its chapel. In the village itself, there are also cheaper pensions and rooms to rent, a youth hostel and a selection of eating-places.

[37 km.] Proceeding eastwards on the main road out of Mallia village, you come to a side-road to the left, sign-posted 'Mallia Antiquities'. You take this road and head towards the sea; on both the left and the right are remains of Minoan houses and other structures of interest mainly to specialists. (For those who are so inclined, there is a small book available in Iraklion, in French only: *Guide des Fouilles Françaises en Crète*, by Claire Tiré and Henri van Effenterre (Ecole Française d'Athènes, 1966); it devotes most of its space to Mallia.) A short way farther on you arrive at the parking area by the small house used by the caretaker; behind this are new buildings used by the French archaeological mission. Hadzidakis made the initial excavations here during the First World War, but the French eventually took over and have continued to make important finds here up to the present, revealing a most ambitious settlement in addition to the palace. The ongoing excavations at Mallia, in fact, each year yield finds – both fixed structures and portable artefacts – that are beginning to raise questions as to which is more ambitious: ancient Minoan society or modern archaeology.

MALLIA PALACE

Hours The usual admission times for major sites (see p. 59).
Entrance Drs 100.

Although not as dramatic as those of Knossos or Phaestos, the remains of the palace of Mallia are relatively well preserved, with a minimum of restoration. There is no better way to feel the authenticity and delights of a Minoan palace than to stroll through this site on a good day, when Mallia seems to hover between the mountains and the sea. Although the original name of the settlement is still unknown, the history of the palace is generally analogous to those of Knossos and Phaestos. After the first Neolithic settlement on the site, which was relatively small and short-lived, the first palace was begun about 2000 B.C.; a new and more splendid palace was built in its place

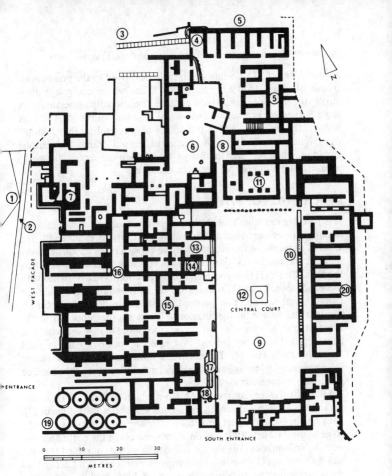

Mallia: Main Palace

1 West Court
2 Procession Road
3 Flagstoned Street
4 North Entrance Hall
5 Storage Magazines
6 Tower Courtyard
7 Lustral Basin
8 Corridor
9 Central Court
10 Colonnade

11 Pillared Hall
12 Sacrificial Pit
13 Throne room or Loggia
14 Staircase
15 Pillar Crypt
16 West Corridor
17 Ceremonial Staircase
18 Kernos
19 Storage Silos
20 Storage Magazines (enclosed)

around 1700–1650 B.C.: this was largely destroyed in the great catastrophe of about 1450 B.C. (see p. 94). What we see today are principally the remains of this second palace, traditionally associated with
King Sarpedon, brother of Minos and Rhadamanthys. And like its
history, the basic lay-out of the palace here resembles that familiar
from Knossos and Phaestos: the large central court, the various
corridors, chambers and stairways, the storage magazines, the royal
quarters, the room for religious occasions, etc.

DESCRIPTION OF SITE

It is possible to walk through the palace in about an hour, seeing the
major features described in the following tour; to examine all the
various elements of the site takes more time. You enter through the
fence at the south-west corner and approach the palace from across
the West Court (1) (not completely cleared until the early 1960s) with
the Procession Road (2) running on the north-south axis before the
palace's west façade. You proceed to the north, however, and turn
towards the palace on the flagstoned street (3) that once led to the
Minoan town and the sea (and again, much more of this 'sea road' has
been exposed since the 1960s). You enter the palace by the original
North Entrance Hall (4). The north and north-east sides of the palace
were enclosed by storage magazines (5); notable now are the *píthoi*, or
giant urns, some decorated in relief.

Enter the Tower Courtyard (6), from which you can go on to the
north-west section with the King's Quarters and a lustral basin (7).
Back at the Tower Courtyard (6), a corridor (8) leads you into the
large Central Court (9). It was once enclosed along the north and east
sides by colonnades (10); on the north side of the courtyard is a fine
hall with pillars (11). Various clues suggest that this was a kitchen and
the pillars supported the dining room above. In the middle of the main
courtyard is a sacrificial pit (12), the only such one found in a Minoan
palace.

Moving down the west side of the courtyard, you come first to a
loggia, or 'throne room' (13), overlooking the courtyard; then to the
staircase to the second storey (14); and then into an area from which
you go into the Pillar Crypt (15), a flagstoned room with two pillars
marked with double-axe signs. The west wing of the palace contained
living quarters and the West Corridor storage rooms (16).

At the south-west corner of the main courtyard is the ceremonial staircase (**17**), which led to the upper storey. Beside this staircase, still *in situ*, is a *kernos*, or offering table (**18**). It is a circular stone nearly a metre in diameter, with a depression in the centre and thirty-four tiny concave circles carved round the rim. It is believed that the stone was a sort of altar for offering thanks and prayers for continuing fertility and that each of these hollows was for one of the different seeds or crops produced on Crete.

Just outside the palace at the extreme south-west corner are eight sunken, stone-walled pits (**19**) – now conceded to be storage silos. The central pillars supported the roof. Along the east side of the main courtyard are storage magazines (**20**) with rebuilt walls, now entirely enclosed by a stone shed. They once served as a museum for the various artefacts found on the site, but these are now in the Iraklion museum, and the magazines are kept locked at all times.

OUTLYING REMAINS

Excavations carried on since the 1960s have revealed a significant series of remains outside the palace, particularly to the north and west. Thus, just to the west of the northern end of the palace, the roofed-over area is the *Hypostyle Crypt*, a complex of rooms, benches and storage magazines: its exact function is not known. Then, to the north of this was revealed the *North Court*, a vast flat, open area of 29 by 40 metres (larger than any Minoan courtyard except the Central Court of Knossos); the surrounding structures and the finds from this area suggest that it was used by the 'general public' (as opposed to the palace set) – more like an *agora* associated with later Greeks: as such, the North Court stimulates certain speculations about Minoan civic life. A short walk along a path around the south side of the French excavators' workshop brings you to what is being called Area Mu – an extensive complex of Old Palace structures (now covered and off limits). The full significance of this area is not yet known, but one building has been identified by sealstone fragments, tools, etc. as a seal-cutter's workshop. In addition to these remains, various houses, tombs, a sanctuary and roads have been revealed. But perhaps the most interesting of the outlying structures is still the one found in the early excavations at Mallia – the *Khrysolakkos*, or 'pit of gold', about 500 metres north-east of the palace, close to the sea. About 40 metres long and 30 metres wide, it contained many burial chambers, a columned hall and a sanctuary with an altar. It must have served as a communal tomb for the royal family. It has been plundered long ago, but random surface finds of gold gained it its name; and when it finally was excavated, it did yield several treasures (now in the Iraklion museum), including the exquisite honeybee pendant (*Case* 101).

[42 km.] Having returned to the main road to Ayios Nikolaos, you climb up from the coastal plain and continue driving through a dramatic ravine. Where the road widens, high on the right sits the *Monastery of Selinaris* – now a home for the elderly. Its *chapel* is dedicated to St George, and it has been customary for travellers – including buses – to stop here and say a few prayers for a safe journey. Fresh spring water is to be had here, and outside the chapel is a mimosa tree that has lovely flowers in the early summer. In the chapel is a rather incongruous, if typically Greek, scene: an impressive modern safe to hold the offerings and, alongside, the little silver simulacra – *taxímata* in Greek – of the various parts of the human anatomy that people want cured or blessed – arms, heads, eyes, torsos – moulded in metal and crowding round the altar. This monastery attracts one of the largest gatherings on the name-day of St George, April 23rd.

After this, most people will undoubtedly stay on the new national highway, which makes the trip to Ayios Nikolaos so fast and easy. But since nothing is to be seen on this road – except, of course, some typical scenery – the old road will be described. You get over on to the old road by a (sign-posted) turn to the left just after leaving the monastery-chapel of Selinaris.

[45 km.] Climbing along the curved road, you come to the mountain town of **Vrakhasi.** From here you go on through a pass and start the descent.

[49 km.] A turn-off to the left (sign-posted) to **Milatos** leads along a good road to the village and cave of that name. Inside the village, a turn-off to the left (sign-posted: Spilion) would lead you to within a couple of hundred metres of the *cave* where in 1823 (in a tragedy reminiscent of that at Melidhoni Cave, p. 244) a large number of Cretan men, women and children were trapped by the Turks until forced to surrender – the men to be killed, the elderly trampled by the cavalry, the women and children enslaved. If you have come this far, you might enjoy going the extra kilometre down to the shore for a snack or swim. (There was a Mycenaean settlement in the area, but nothing of any interest has been found.)

[52 km.] Back on the main (old) road, you wind down until you come into **Neapolis**, the central town for this region, with its leisurely, provincial air, yet just enough bustle of buses and markets. As the judicial capital of Lasithi Nome, it also gets the court traffic. The people of Neapolis pride themselves on their intellectual traditions: their schools (you pass the handsome new *Technical School* as you enter the town), library and even a small collection of antiquities from the region. The latter are displayed in a little *museum* off the central square, but you must obtain the key from a teacher at the local high school. (Any policeman would be able to assist your search.) It was in the village of Kares, on the site of present-day Neapolis, that Peter Philargos was born in 1340 – the man who went on to become Pope Alexander V (see p. 113).

Neapolis has one hotel, the *Neapolis* (Class D), but the Tourist Police could help to make other arrangements. There are several eating-places. The local speciality is *soumádha*, a milky drink made from pressed almonds – drunk warm in winter and cold in summer.

In addition to proceeding on to Ayios Nikolaos, two other major excursions might be taken from Neapolis.

One is to the Lasithi Plain and the Dhiktaion Cave: this is by a good road that climbs south from the town square and goes on via Vrises to Drasi, where you join another road coming from outside Ayios Nikolaos and then climb up to Lasithi (a route described from the other direction on p. 186).

The other is to the site of *Dreros*, for which you drive along the main square of Neapolis, the route to Ayios Nikolaos and the east; just as you come to leave the town, that route curves right, but for Dreros you take a sharp left instead and drive a few metres to a road that turns off to the right; it is sign-posted: Kourounes/Nofalia/Skinias; you take this right and, following various curves and the signs, (Pros Dreron) you wind uphill until the well-surfaced road comes to an abrupt stop; here you must leave your vehicle and climb by foot up a small path to the summit above the parking place. You are advised to get someone from one of the villages to guide you, as the site needs some searching out – and a bit of climbing. Dreros was an Archaic settlement, with an acropolis that dominated the passes and plains of the vicinity. Its harbour was Olous (p. 314) and together these two cities were said to have counted many thousands of inhabitants. The French, excavating here in the 1930s, found the remains of a small temple of Apollo Delphinios; they also found some small bronze idols, made by hammering the metal over a wooden core – a technique for which the Cretans were famed. In addition, they found two bilingual Eteocretan – Greek inscriptions that will undoubtedly prove crucial in the final decipherment of the Eteocretan language (p. 328).

[54 km.] Proceeding eastwards out of Neapolis on the old road, you approach a row of turret-like structures on the left that turn out to be old windmills placed so as to catch the winds. In the village of **Nikithiano**, by these mills, there is a side-road to the left (sign-posted: Fourni/Elounda). If you take this turn, you wind up a good asphalt road until in about 4 km. you come to the outskirts of the village of **Kastelli**. For **Elounda**, a village on the coast which can more easily be reached from Ayios Nikolaos (p. 313), you continue through Kastelli and on through **Fourni**, situated on the edge of an upland plateau, and on again through **Pines**; except for the obvious poverty, you could begin to feel you have stumbled on some Cretan Shangri-La. Then again, you may wonder how anyone makes any kind of living from such rocky land. But such thoughts are easily dispelled from the casual tourist's mind by the wonderful view over the gulf of Merabello and the Sitia Mountains – which you may enjoy as you descend to Elounda (p. 313). From Elounda there is a good asphalt road into Ayios Nikolaos.

[67 km.] Most people will have stayed on the main road to Ayios Nikolaos, and after some hairpin bends and a fine view of the Gulf of Merabello and the mountains of Sitia in the distance, you descend to Ayios Nikolaos. For the harbour keep left at a fork as you enter the town.

AYIOS NIKOLAOS

Until the late 1960s it was enough to describe this town as a quiet little port-town, noted for its pleasant climate and clean beaches. It is still that, but something new has pretty much overpowered the old Ayios Nikolaos: tourism on the grand scale. Ayios Nikolaos is now more of an international resort than a Cretan town. In any case, beside its own attractions it is the point from which one can visit the sites of eastern Crete.

Population About 6,000.

Sea connections See pp. 21–4.

Information The Tourist Information office is run from the office of the Tourist Police, alongside the 'bottomless pool' (*Map* **4**) (tel. 22.321).

Hotels There are half a dozen Luxury and Class A hotels, numerous Class B and C establishments, as well as a few Class D and E hotels. There are still cheaper and simpler pensions and rooms to be had (including the pleasantly situated *Dolphin* on its own beach); and then there are the other possibilities of Elounda (p. 313).

Youth hostel There is a youth hostel (*Map* **2**) (tel. 22.823).

Restaurants There is the usual choice of restaurants, *tavérnas* and cafés. An old favourite, the *Rififi*, is in a new building; the *Limni* has gained a following with a somewhat more varied menu.

Night-life There are now any number of discotheques, bars and dance places that operate during the high season and attract a mainly younger crowd. During the summer Ayios Nikolaos has been sponsoring usually weekly programmes of dancing, choral and other musical groups, who perform by the 'bottomless pool'.

Shops and souvenirs Ayios Nikolaos has become a haven for a selection of tourist-gift shops; specialities of Ayios Nikolaos are leather goods – sandals, boots, shoes, belts, bags, etc. – and hand-loomed rugs and wall hangings.

Sport and swimming Ayios Nikolaos has several beaches on its outskirts – the nearest a stony beach near the bus station – and the new resorts have not yet 'occupied' them all. There is good fishing off Ayios Nikolaos, too, and boats can be rented through a tourist agency such as Knossos Tours. The luxury hotels, of course, offer such things as tennis and water-skiing; these are usually restricted to their clients, but you could always enquire.

Excursions There are now numerous excursions operating out of Ayios Nikolaos – by boat to Spinalonga (p. 314) and other sites around the Gulf of Merabello, and by bus to Kritsa (p. 311), Gournia (p. 322) and other places in eastern Crete. You can also be taken close to the islet of Ayii Pantes, just outside the harbour, to get a good look at the wild goats there.

Buses There are services to Iraklion (and places en route, including Mallia); to Sitia (and places en route, including Gournia); to Ierapetra (also via Gournia); to Kritsa and Elounda (see below); and to Psykhro (for the Dhiktaion Cave). The schedule may be seen at the bus station (*Map* **6**) or at the Tourist Police (*Map* **4**).

Ships Ayios Nikolaos is a port of call for ships going between Piraeus, Santorini, Sitia and Rhodes and return. (See pp. 21–4.)

HISTORY

Although there was a Hellenistic and, centuries later, a Venetian port on this site, the town of Ayios Nikolaos is comparatively new – largely built up since 1870 – and somewhat artificial; a small creek was developed into a harbour when it was decided to establish the town on the hillside. (Excavations since the 1970s have begun to reveal such remains as Hellenistic and Roman tombs, but these soon become built over by new structures.) During the late nineteenth century, many Sfakians seeking employment and a new lease of life (see p. 275) settled here. Officially it is now the capital of Lasithi Nome, but neither the town nor its citizens have ever seemed too impressed by this. On the promontory that forms the southern side of the harbour, and up near the modern Prefecture, was the site of the Genoese-Venetian Castle of Merabello, but there are no remains to speak of. But there is no pretending that people come here to see archaeological remains (although the new museum (*Map* 1) has a fine little collection). The chief attraction of the town has always been the harbour with its nonchalant activity: an occasional fishing-boat puts in, a naval patrol keeps guard, once in a while a large tourist cruise sails in, but mostly the cafés and strollers create their own slightly narcissistic excitement. Ayios Nikolaos had long appealed to visitors as an especially neat and clean town: shady trees, whitewashed kerbs, everything well tended – down by the harbour you could almost believe you were in a Dutch or Scandinavian village. So many visitors have become impressed by this that, since the early 1970s, Ayios Nikolaos has been turned into just that: another international resort town. But some of the old quiet charms are still to be enjoyed, especially if you can arrange to visit Ayios Nikolaos in the off-season.

PRINCIPAL SIGHTS

Archaeological Museum
Map 1.
Hours The usual Greek admission times (p. 59) but enquire immediately upon arriving in town.
Entrance charge Drs 100.

Although relatively small and modest, this collection has its own new building and is still growing with finds from Lasithi Nome. In addition to the Minoan artefacts (Vasiliki flameware vases, sealstones, bronze-work, statuettes, etc.), the collection includes works from post-Minoan times up into the Middle Ages. Be sure to notice the unique ceramic of the woman clutching the water jug, the so-called 'goddess of Myrtos' (in the first, central hall). The modern building and selective displays make a visit well worthwhile.

'Bottomless Pool'
Map 3.
Perhaps the most spectacular natural attraction of the town is the dark, so-called 'bottomless pool', Lake Voulismeni, situated a few

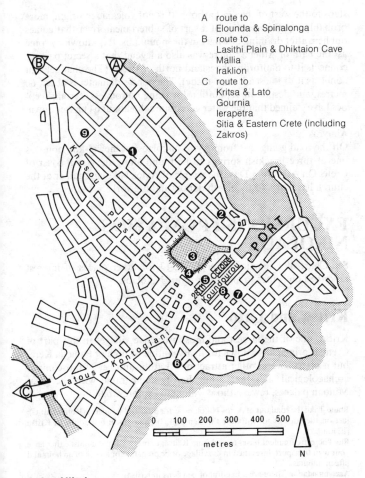

A   route to
    Elounda & Spinalonga
B   route to
    Lasithi Plain & Dhiktaion Cave
    Mallia
    Iraklion
C   route to
    Kritsa & Lato
    Gournia
    Ierapetra
    Sitia & Eastern Crete (including
    Zakros)

Ayios Nikolaos

1 Museum
2 Youth Hostel
3 'Bottomless Pool'
4 Tourist Police and Information
   Office
5 Post Office
6 Bus Station
7 Telephone/Telegraph Office
8 Olympic Airways
9 Hospital

steps to the west of the sea harbour. It is not volcanic in origin; more probably it is the aperture of a sort of subterranean river that comes out here after draining down from the mountains. It is known by some as 'the bath of Athena'; there was also a legend that a secret passage connects it to Santorini, the island north of Crete. (The channel that connects it to the sea is man-made). The pond's diameter is about 60 metres, and despite its reputation for being bottomless, certain sceptics have claimed that the water gets quite solid about 64 metres down.

Almyros

Off the road going east from Ayios Nikolaos (at the 2·5-km. point) is one of three brackish springs to be found along the north coast of Crete. On Ascension Day, the people of Ayios Nikolaos gather at the church here for a festival with dances and fireworks.

EXCURSIONS FROM AYIOS NIKOLAOS

See Chart of Excursions, on pp. 12–13 for other places of interest described on routes to and from Ayios Nikolaos.

Kritsa and Lato

Kritsa, one of the largest and most attractive villages in this part of Crete, is principally known for its Byzantine Church of Panayia Kera, but it offers several other attractions. Lato is another of those minor archaeological sites that, while hardly comparable with the great Minoan palaces, reward those willing to explore Crete.

Route Take the road out of Ayios Nikolaos as for Sitia and Ierapetra (Route Exit C); just on the edge of town follow the sign and continue up into the hills to Kritsa [12 km.].

Bus There are frequent buses to and from Kritsa; to reach Lato you must either have your own transport, hire a taxi in the village or be prepared for a walk of an hour and fifteen minutes.

Accommodation There are a handful of pensions in Kritsa.

[1 km.] Following the signs in Ayios Nikolaos for Sitia and Ierapetra, at the edge of the town, you do *not* turn left on to the new road but follow the sign for Kritsa, basically straight ahead, and climb the asphalt road up through the olive groves.

[10 km.] Before the village of Kritsa, a sign-post *Panagia Kera* indicates, on the right, a white church standing in the middle of an olive grove and surrounded by white walls. This is the chief glory of Kritsa and one of the jewels of Byzantine art: the *Church of Panayia Kera* (All-Holy Lady). There are three naves, with corresponding apses, of which the centre nave is now considered to be the oldest, dating from the fourteenth century; tambour and buttresses were added considerably later. The frescoes, dating from the fourteenth and fifteenth centuries, are accepted as one of the major ensembles of Byzantine painting; they have been heavily restored, but their strength and artistry derive from the originals. There has been a custodian assigned to keep regular Greek hours, and he can identify the subject of the frescoes (a tip is in order), but here we call your attention to the major points of interest. The central nave is dedicated to the Mother of Christ and has scenes from the life of Jesus including His birth, the slaughter of the innocents, the banquet of Herod with the beheading of John the Baptist, the dance of Salome, the Last Supper, and the crucifixion; there are also depictions of various Church fathers and saints. The north nave (left as you face the apses) is dedicated to St Anthony and shows episodes from the Second Coming of the Lord, the weighing of souls, Paradise, and many saints. The south nave is dedicated to St Ann, the mother of Mary, and shows scenes from their lives as recounted in the Bible; from the angel's announcement to Joachim, the husband of Ann, through the birth of Mary, Mary's appearance before the High Priests, and the journey to Bethlehem; various Church fathers and saints are also depicted.

The church can be overcrowded at certain times during the high season, but usually it will clear out and reward your waiting. Besides the pleasure in recognizing the familiar Biblical scenes, you will find that the saints and evangelists portrayed around the walls, with their rich gowns, muscular lineaments, and intense eyes, make an irresistible impact whether you have any interest in Cretan-Byzantine art or not.

Hours Variable, but closed on Tuesday and Wednesday.
Entrance charge Drs 100.

[12 km.] **Kritsa.**

The main asphalt road leads on to become the narrow, winding main street of Kritsa and eventually opens up to become its main square. The village has a spectacular position, clinging to the steep mountain-side and with a superb view over the Gulf of Merabello – especially from all those balconied houses that crowd the slopes. The people of this region have kept up the traditional handicrafts, particularly in textiles, and the villagers are very willing to show their work to anyone who may be interested in buying. It was in Kritsa, incidentally, that the film version of the Kazantzakis novel *The Greek Passion* (or *Christ Recrucified*) was made; it was called *He Who Must Die*. The director was the American Jules Dassin (later known for his *Never on Sunday*); the principal actors were French and Greek, and many of the local people appeared. Although the setting of the novel was Anatolia, both history and the film make the Cretan setting quite legitimate.

There are several other attractive small churches with frescoes in the neighbourhood of Kritsa, the finest being the *Church of Ayios Georgios Kavousiotis*, with its fourteenth-century frescoes, and the *Church of Ayios Ioannis* which also has frescoes. Enquire in the town as to the exact location of these churches and who has the keys.

Lato

Just before entering Kritsa, a sign-post to the right directs you along a road that passes the cemetery; after some 4 km. the road ends at the lower group of remains.

Lato was originally explored by Evans, but the French took charge of the excavations there early in the twentieth century and have returned in the 1960s and 1970s to uncover still more ambitious remains. Founded in the post-Minoan period, probably as a Doric settlement, most of the remains date from Classic to Hellenistic times – mainly fifth to third centuries B.C. In its day, Lato must have been a fairly impressive and prosperous city. The extensive remains rise in banks or tiers as in an amphitheatre, with two acropolises, fortifications, houses, shops, cisterns and roads. The marketplace, or *agora*, the so-called magistrate's house and other structures have been identified. And south of the market-place is the small *Temple of Apollo*, with its pronaos and cella, that is dated to about the second century B.C. Among the curiosities of the site is a circle of stones now considered to be a threshing area. But it is the setting of Lato that is its principal charm; it is worth the climb to the north acropolis to enjoy the fine view down across the almond and olive trees to the coast and the Gulf of Merabello.

Elounda, Olous and Spinalonga

The little fishing village of Elounda has profited – some might say suffered – from the tourism radiating from Ayios Nikolaos. Until the end of the 1960s it was visited only by occasional tourists. Then came the tour parties from the hotels of Ayios Nikolaos as well as the luxurious Elounda Beach resort on the edge of the village itself – although as a virtually self-contained complex the latter has in some ways made a less obvious impact on Elounda than all the new houses and apartments to accommodate those who come seeking more simple pleasures. But Elounda and its inlet have seen the comings and goings of many peoples: Olous was originally a Minoan settlement, and after the Minoans came the Greeks, Romans, Venetians, Turks, English, Italians and Germans. So, perhaps it will survive the tourists. In any case, it is still possible to sit down along the old harbour and feel you are on a remote, calm fjord, if that is what you are seeking.

Route A good asphalt road leads from Ayios Nikolaos (Route Exit A) to Elounda [11 km.]. It is also possible to drive to Elounda from the Neapolis–Ayios Nikolaos road (p. 306).
Bus There is a regular bus service from Ayios Nikolaos to Elounda.
Sea You could hire a boat in Ayios Nikolaos to take you to Elounda and its adjacent sites; the tourist agencies arrange for regular group trips by boat.
Accommodation The *Elounda Beach*, *Elounda Mare* and *Astir Palace* are truly luxurious resorts offering every possible diversion; they are, of course, Luxury Class in price. Elounda has, too, many other hotels, pensions and rooms to let.

[9 km.] About this point you begin to enjoy a quite dramatic view of Spinalonga and the inlet, as you wind down to the coast (and past the Elounda Beach resort).

[11 km.] As you drive into the village of **Elounda**, a track – sign-posted: Olous – forks sharply backwards to the right. You go along the coast and then turn left on to a built-up causeway across the salt flats; this leads over a small bridge across the channel between the large peninsula of Spinalonga and the isthmus linking it to the mainland. The French are credited with these constructions during the occupation by the Great Powers at the end of the nineteenth century. There are also abandoned windmills to be seen. The salt flats – which were operated until quite recent years – were first filled with sea water; the dykes were then blocked and the water evaporated, leaving the salt. Under the Venetians, Elounda was an important trading port; during the 1930s English hydroplanes used the bay; and even now largish merchant ships lie off shore.

Olous

To visit the remains of ancient Olous (it once extended on to the isthmus here) you continue on across the little bridge (above) on foot and make your way around the shore of the peninsula to the right. Since there are no longer any visible remains to aim for, you stay along the shore until you come about opposite the white church standing in a field. Here, along the shallows, you should be able to make out some remains of what are thought to be *ship-berths* of ancient Olous, the port of Dreros (p. 305), sunk due to local sub-sidence (p. 76). What you see is not all that impressive, but skin-divers may find it worth exploring. Olous was a city important enough in post-Minoan times to make treaties with Rhodes and other minor powers. There were once structures on the site, including temples to Zeus and Britomartis (Artemis), but the stone was carried off to be used in walls and other buildings. The most interesting survival now is the *mosaic floor*, within the remains of an early Christian basilica, Ayios Nikolaos. It is situated in the field about 100 metres from the shore, and its fenced enclosure can be seen as you cross the bridge. The mosaic depicts some lively dolphins, and is worth crossing the fields to see. Excavations are continuing on other parts of the peninsula and have turned up various other finds.

Spinalonga Island

Just to the north of the peninsula of Spinalonga is an islet of the same name; it can be seen across the bay from Elounda. The Venetians constructed a most impressive fortress here in 1579, and it became one of their last outposts on Crete; it was 1715 before the Venetians finally surrendered this fort to the Turks. The Turks held it until 1903 when, under the administration of Prince George, it was converted into a leper colony. This has long since been dispersed and now the island is abandoned except for caretakers and tourists. (The Greek ship tycoon Onassis once had plans to convert it into a casino.) Many boats from Ayios Nikolaos or Elounda take groups to the island; if you want to go ashore, there is no risk of getting leprosy. Hardly a major historical site, but appealing to those who enjoy imaginary peopling of old castles.

Psira and Mokhlos Islands

At least during the main season there are daily excursion boats from

Ayios Nikolaos to take you to both these islands in the eastern reaches of the Gulf of Merabello; or it is possible to arrange a trip from the village of Mokhlos (p. 327), farther along the coast. The ideal way would be to cruise around the entire gulf, to visit Elounda, Gournia and even Sitia.

The islands, which were excavated by Seager (p. 325) during 1906–7, are barren now and without water, yet they were among the earliest of the active Minoan communities. Psira, about 3 km. off shore, obviously had a good spring; one well with eight steps leading down into it is still to be seen. Houses contemporary with and reminiscent of Gournia were found, yielding stone and pottery vases and fragments of painted stucco relief. Psira's east coast has three sheltered coves and these must have made it an attractive port; some of the finds from Psira indicate close relations with Egypt, Syria and Palestine.

The Minoan remains at Psira are hardly major but they are among the few on Crete where you can stand in an ordinary Minoan room with walls up to 2 metres high still in place. New excavations since 1985 have made several important discoveries including the location of the Minoan 'town square', the identification of a Byzantine church, and the unearthing of buildings from the 6th–8th centuries A.D., a period of which little is known in this part of Crete.

Mokhlos is not really an island but a circular mass of land, now some 200 metres from shore, cut off by the subsidence of a much later age (see p. 76). The town remains on the south side that slopes into the sea are similar to those on the north coast of the island, opposite; possibly the submerged peninsula formed the harbour. The major finds on Mokhlos were the tombs and their contents: vases of alabaster, marble, breccia and steatite, some as thin as porcelain; some of the earliest sealstones known from Crete; and volcanic ash that may have come from Santorini. The modern village of Mokhlos, facing the ancient site, offers a Class B hotel, the *Aldiana Club* (tel. 94.211).

Ierapetra and Myrtos

This is the largest town on the south coast of Crete, but until the late 1960s that in itself hardly attracted foreigners, as the area lacked antiquities or historical sites. By the beginning of the 1970s, a rather sudden coincidence of commerce, tourism and antiquities that appeared on Ierapetra's doorstep conspired to change things: new buildings and services and other signs of prosperity began to change the face of the rather sleepy little port. Whatever your interests, it now offers at least a pleasant excursion from Ayios Nikolaos.

Route Follow the Sitia road (Route Exit C) out of Ayios Nikolaos; after passing Gournia (pp. 322–5), turn right just past Pakhia Ammos [22 km.] to cross the island to Ierapetra [38 km.].

From Ierapetra you have several choices. You can re-cross the island north to the main coast road and then go either east to Sitia or west and back to Ayios Nikolaos. It is also possible to take the improved road west via Myrtos up to Ano Viannos, with a detour south to Arvi (p. 320) and then over the mountains via Martha and Skinias to the Messara and Ayii Dheka (p. 202). There is also a route to the north-east, via Koutsouras to Lithines from which point you could either go on direct north to Sitia or cut over (very poor road!) via Armeni and Chandras to Ano Zakros for Kato Zakros (p. 329).

Bus There are regular services from Ayios Nikolaos to Ierapetra; you can get these buses to drop you off and pick you up at Gournia.

Accommodation In Ierapetra itself there is one Class A hotel, the *Petra-Mare* (tel. 23.341) and numerous Class C and D hotels as well as various pensions and rooms. But for those who prefer to stay out of this bustling town, there are numerous possibilities all along the coast both east and west of town. There is the Tourist Village of traditional cottages at Koutsounari (p. 43) (tel. 61.291), some 6 km. to the east; at Ferma, 16 km. to the east, there is the Class A *Ferma Beach* hotel with bungalows (tel. 61.341); and many others too numerous to mention. Enquire at travel agents.

For the route as far as Gournia and Pakhia Ammos [22 km.], where you turn south and inland, see pp. 321–6.

[25 km.] Continuing southward across the island – on what is the narrowest 'waist' of Crete – on your right is a knoll where the early Minoan settlement known as *Vasiliki* was first excavated by the American Seager, in 1903. The site is about 1 km. to the right of the main road; it is best reached direct from the village of Pakhia Ammos by a track to the village of **Vasiliki**, which is near the excavations. Dating from as early as 2500 B.C., the remains are of little interest to most people. What does concern us, though, is the extraordinary pottery found in graves around Vasiliki: this mottled red-and-black pottery is found elsewhere around the Mediterranean, but nowhere with such a brilliant quality as here. And because this was one of the first places where such pottery was found it has given its name to a basic pottery type, the 'Vasiliki flameware' (and may be seen in *Case* 6 in the Iraklion Museum). New excavations begun in 1972–3 have revealed structures that indicate more extensive habitation from Early

Minoan to Mycenaean times than was previously thought; they have also found the first Roman structures at this site.

[30 km.] Proceeding along the road to Ierapetra, you come to the village of **Episkopi**. Just to the left and below the road opposite the church square is a tiny *Byzantine church*, with an especially fine fifteenth-century wood-carved *iconostasis*. (Sadly the church is now locked.)

[33 km.] The new road bypasses **Kato Khorio** but it is worth a detour to inspect its handsome *fountain* from the Turkish period.

[38 km.] **Ierapetra.**

Until the late 1960s, Ierapetra seemed like a town at the end of the line. It had long ago lost whatever importance it enjoyed as a port of trade with Africa or Asia Minor. For some decades it attracted occasional individuals who made their way there to partake of its sandy beaches, good wine and relaxed hospitality. Then several phenomena began to change this. One was the discovery of Minoan remains at nearby Myrtos (described below, p. 319). A more direct effect on the local economy was the introduction of a new method of growing winter crops of tomatoes, cucumbers and other vegetables along the coastal plain outside Ierapetra. Using new varieties of plants, cheaply constructed plastic-covered hot-houses and a highly organized transport system, the people have been shipping their crops to the markets of western and northern Europe; Ierapetra, as the junction of this activity, has been the gainer in bustle and prosperity (although the surrounding countryside has paid dearly with all the plastic and traffic). Meanwhile, as the local people were finally entering into the twentieth century, the international youth set popu-larly known as hippies were discovering the Ierapetra region as a refuge from the twentieth century. Attracted by its relatively mild winters, its cheap prices and the very absence of traditional tourist goals, they began to come in the late 1960s, often spending many months or more, camping in their vehicles or renting the simplest accommodation. By the 1970s, more traditional vacationers began to replace the hippies. Their most apparent impact on Ierapetra – beside the hotels – has been the several discotheques and the profusion of cafés and eating-places.

Whatever the next development – and whether the tomatoes, the Minoans, the tourists or the Ierapetrans of old win out – the town has greatly prospered and barely retains its basic appearance along the gently curved quay. Modern Ierapetra is on an alluvial plain, with the town protruding in to the sea. It is situated on the site of ancient Ierapytna, a harbour-town that gained some importance as a junction for trade between Crete and the African and the Asian ports to the south and east. It must have been linked with Gournia as part of an overland route, but as of now nothing has been found commensurate with that site. The post-Minoan peoples kept up the port, and it is said to have been the last Cretan city to fall to the Romans under the conquering consul, Metellus. It once had fine Roman buildings, including theatres, but little remains from that period except fragments (although excavations begun in the late 1970s have revealed some new structures). Later came the Venetians and the Turks. From their times survives the *Venetian Fort*, at the western end of the quay; four of its square towers are well preserved. Also in the western part of the town are a *Turkish minaret* and *fountain*. You may also be shown a house where it is claimed Napoleon spent a night on his way either to or from Egypt; there is no evidence to support such a claim, but it adds to the charm of the town.

Aside from such sights, Ierapetra has a small collection of antiquities in the *Town Library*, in particular a collection of Late Minoan sarcophagi. (The prize is a sarcophagus, found at Vasiliki, painted on all sides with hunting scenes.) It is also known for its local wine, which has been compared to everything from sparkling Burgundy to sweet port. There are the hotels and other accommodation (see p. 316), and several decent eating-places, particularly around the central square and all along the quay.

There are also a number of side-trips that might be taken using Ierapetra as a base. Mountain-climbers might make their way to **Males** to the north-west or to **Orinon** to the north-east, and then use these villages as bases to climb the peaks of the Dhikti or Sitia ranges. An ambitious excursion would be east along the coast road to *Moni Kapsas*, a fascinating old monastery on a terrace above the coast. A less demanding excursion would be to take one of the excursion boats (daily, weather permitting) to the small island of *Gaidhouronissi*, just south of Ierapetra with its unusual coloured beach.

Another islet, off to the east, is *Kouphonisi*, where in the late 1970s was found a theatre with 10 rows of seats, an elaborate stage structure, and many architectural fragments. Other finds include an ambitious 8-room house with 2 rooms floored with pebble mosaics; quantities of purple shells suggesting the islet was a centre of dye production; water conduits; temple remains; etc. Although possibly settled by Minoans, the major remains are from Hellenistic-Roman periods when the islet was known as Lefki.

We describe in some detail a side-trip that probably lies within the range of more users of this volume.

Myrtos, Pyrgos and Fournou Korifi (Trouli)

Some 15 km. to the west of Ierapetra, a pleasant drive along the narrow coastal plain (lined with plastic-covered hot-houses) lies the little village of **Myrtos.** In 1943, the Germans destroyed its houses and killed its menfolk, and Myrtos languished until the late 1960s, by which time the hot-house crops and the hippies had brought an unforeseen revival. It now boasts two Class C hotels, the *Esperides* (tel. 51.298) and the *Myrtos* (tel. 51.226), several cafés (some with rooms) and a restaurant (also with rooms). The pebble and sand beach is good for bathing.

Meanwhile British archaeologists had been busy at two sites in the neighbourhood. One is known as *Pyrgos*. It lies on the hills just east of the Myrtos River (or Kriopotamos) on the opposite side of the bridge from the village. Coming from Ierapetra it is a right turn, directly before the bridge; you must park your vehicle, however, somewhere along the river's edge and make the climb on foot; you start up the rough track, which soon gives out, but if you sight on the very summit you will make out the ancient terrace wall, and by proceeding along the edge of the ridge, you will arrive at the top – the whole walk requiring only ten to fifteen minutes. There, with a spectacular view north up the valley to the Dhikti range and south to the sea, sat a fine country villa, presumably the 'lord of the manor' over the settlement on the surrounding slopes. The settlement itself goes back to at least 2200 B.C.; its most notable remains are the *terrace wall* to the north, and a large plastered *cistern* (3 metres deep and 5 metres in diameter), a major engineering feat for the day (although it did break). The *villa* was built about 1600 B.C.; it was some 20 metres long, had possibly two storeys above the ground floor, and with its courtyard and other features it seems like a miniature of the palace of Knossos. The casual visitor may note the cobbled street that passes along the façade of the villa and then crosses the courtyard by a raised walk; the scarcely worn gypsum staircase (now covered) near the south-west corner; the beautifully preserved gypsum bench (also covered) opposite the staircase; and the use of local purple limestone in floor paving. What the visitor will not see are such finds as the Linear A tablet, the carbonized grains from the giant urns, all the pottery found on the site, and, perhaps most suggestive of all, the volcanic material mixed with the building rubble. Since various evidence indicates that this villa was destroyed about 1450 B.C., this might be fall-out from the Santorini explosion, suggestive of that disaster's role in the destruction of the Minoan palaces.

Some 3 km. east (and thus only about 12 km. from Ierapetra) is another Minoan site, known in the literature as *Fournou Korifi*, but known locally as Trouli. The best landmark is a new chapel on a slight elevation on the coast side of the road, 100 metres east of the Trouli site; coming from Ierapetra, then, Trouli is on the first prominent peak and to the right (across from the coast side) of the chapel. The peak can be climbed from either the east or west side – on foot – in about a ten- to fifteen-minute walk up to the very summit. Fournou Korifi was a still earlier settlement than that at Pyrgos, and dates from about 2600 to 2200 B.C. Although its complex of ninety-odd rooms is not that impressive for the casual visitor, the site was excavated and studied with such care that it has yielded a great deal of information about the way these early Minoans lived. Among other things, the hundred or so inhabitants seem not to have made much of their living from the nearby sea but to have depended rather on mixed farming and a textile 'industry'. They used sealstones (carved with obsidian from Melos); they had contacts with settlements on the northern coast; and they seem to have been preoccupied with obtaining water. Well they might have been, since the site was destroyed by fire and not resettled; possibly the survivors moved to nearby Pyrgos with its better water supply.

On the very edge (west side) of the village of Myrtos, by the way, are some remains of a *Roman bath*, possibly part of a villa. They are along the right side of the old dirt coast track and are recognizable by the distinctive flat Roman bricks. There is even the trace of a mosaic pavement to be seen if you climb about.

After Myrtos, it is possible to continue driving west on over the mountains to the Messara (p. 201) and such sites as Phaestos. (See advice about this route, p. 201.) The route is as follows (with distances from Myrtos): good new road past Mournies [6 km.], Kalamion [12 km.], Kato Sime [15·5 km., see p. 193], Arvi turn-off [20 km., see

p. 193] to Ano Viannos [25 km.]. Pass through the centre of Ano Viannos and continue on the good new road; at about 29·2 km., at the sign, bear right to Iraklion; *ignore maps* that indicate that route is via Messi (a turn to the left at 31·4 km.) and continue on the good new road to the Martha turn-off [35 km.]; take this turn to the left and proceed via the dirt road to Skinias [42 km.]; from here the road is as indicated on maps, via Pyrgos, Pretoria, Gagates, most of it now surfaced, until you join the main road from Iraklion to Phaestos a little before Ayii Dheka (p. 201) – a total of some 85 km. from Myrtos. Although not an especially difficult drive, it is also not especially scenic; its appeal is that it allows for a non-backtracking round trip through some typical pre-touristic parts of Crete.

Alternatively you can drive eastwards from Ierapetra along the coast road past the Koutsounari tourist village (p. 43), Ferma and Koutsouras. About 20 km. from Ierapetra you arrive at **Makriyialos**, a straggling village with a splendid sandy beach, several rooms to let and, round the corner, a new hotel, the *Sunwing*. (A Late Minoan villa with some interesting artefacts was excavated nearby in 1972.) Beyond are deserted beaches for a more solitary swim. After Makriyialos the road turns north to cross the island to Sitia (p. 327).

ROUTE 6: AYIOS NIKLAOS TO SITIA (VIA GOURNIA)

The drive to Sitia starts along a pleasant, although extremely winding, road, with the Gulf of Merabello off to the left, the sheer vertical rise of the Monasteraki ravine in the middle distance and the Sitia range in the far distance. There are a few straggling villages en route – and, of course, the impressive site of Gournia – but it is the dramatic landscape of Crete's 'Riviera' that makes the trip – inlets, promonto- ries, beaches and green slopes. You could also make a detour across the island to Ierapetra on the south coast (p. 316).

Route The new national road has essentially taken over the previous road on this stretch, but it is greatly widened and improved. Follow the road out of Ayios Nikolaos (Route Exit C), and continue eastwards along the coast to Sitia [72 km.].
Bus Bus services from Ayios Nikolaos to Sitia (about 2½ hours); also to Ierapetra (about 1 hour); both these buses will drop or pick up passengers at Gournia or Pakhia Ammos.
Accommodation Between the two main towns, there is the Luxury hotel *Istron Bay* (tel. 22.189) and the Class C *Elpida* (tel. 22.854) at Kalo Khorio (13 km.) and a Class C hotel, the *Golden Beach* (tel. 93.278), at Pakhia Ammos. In fact, there is so

little chance to eat along the way that you should time your trip to be at Ayios Nikolaos, Ierapetra, or Sitia at mealtime.

[13 km.] A turn to the right leads to **Kalo Khorio** and then down along the Dhikti range to the south; a bus takes this route as far as **Males.**

[18 km.] A track to the right leads up to the *Convent of Faneromeni,* perched on a steep hill with its grotto church and dramatic view of the Gulf of Merabello.

[19 km.] As the new road curves along the flat land beside a small bay, a small sign to the right points to 'Gournia Antiquities', just beside the old road. Gournia deserves to be better known as one of the wonders of the archaeological world: here was uncovered not another Minoan palace but the almost complete remains of a Minoan town. It is a sort of poor man's Pompeii, and, although lacking the glamour of some of the great Mediterranean sites, should be visited by anyone who intends to go home feeling that he has seen Minoan civilization. There is a helpful, competent caretaker on the site throughout all normal visiting hours (the site itself is never closed); his English is adequate and, with the aid of the site plan, p. 324, you will get a good impression of the site. (A tip is not out of place if you enjoy his services.) And there is a pavilion on the site – open at least during the main season's normal visiting hours – that provides at least water and public toilets.

HISTORY OF GOURNIA

The name of this site is derived from *gourní,* the small troughs from which barnyard animals drink and which were found here in considerable quantity. At this little bay on the narrowest section of Crete, sailors and traders of old probably beached their craft in order to take their cargo overland, thus avoiding the rough passage round the eastern end of the island. Ierapetra (p. 315) was at the other end of this commercial route. An early Minoan settlement grew up and prospered, and by 1600 B.C. it must have been a flourishing town, self-supporting if not self-governing. Little is known of its exact relationship with the great Minoan powers to the west; certainly Gournia had some sort of ruler, whether an independent prince or a dependent governor. Undoubtedly its prosperity was linked with the wealth and influence of the great Minoan palace centres. But Gournia grew and functioned on its own terms, as a self-contained town with many of the features that we see in Greek towns today. It made no impact on the times, and when Minoan power declined, Gournia declined. Probably it fell to the marauders, was destroyed in a conflagration and then practically abandoned; this would have happened around 1500–1450 B.C. It was forgotten, and eventually disappeared from men's sight and minds. When the great age of Cretan excavation began, Gournia's whereabouts were not only unknown, its very existence was unsuspected. There were no traditions, no classic references, no remains.

Evans may be credited with arousing interest in this area, for it was his early surface explorations that established that there had been Minoan settlements in this part of Crete. A young American student in Athens, Miss Harriet Boyd, inspired by Evans's reports, began to dig in nearby Kavousi (p. 326) in 1900; the next year, a 'peasant antiquarian' indicated a spot where he knew that pottery and walls were to be found: this was Gournia. Digging began in 1901 and by 1904 virtually the whole town had been unearthed – the answer to an archaeologist's dream. Miss Boyd (who married the English scholar Hawes and so is often referred to as Boyd-Hawes) was assisted by her American colleagues, Miss Hall and Richard Seager – not to mention the local people who did the actual digging.

DESCRIPTION OF SITE

The site is a limestone ridge, and the town – its streets and structures – was built to conform to the lie of the land, so that Gournia sprawls comfortably over the hillside. It was never fortified, and it was quite exposed except for what protection the sea afforded. On top of the hill – one hesitates to call such an unclassical place the 'acropolis' – was the 'palace': a miniature Minoan palace, even less ambitious than Ayia Triadha. The palace rose in three storeys on the rocky terraces; there were stairways, pillars, courtyards, a banqueting hall, the usual apartments, but nothing is particularly grand in comparison with the rest of the town, nor is the palace particularly isolated from the community – its occupant must have seemed more like a governor than a king. Adjacent to the palace was the public courtyard, or *agora*. Down the road was a small sanctuary or shrine where cult objects were found, showing that the Mother Goddess was worshipped here: terracotta images twined with snakes, doves, tripods, the double axe.

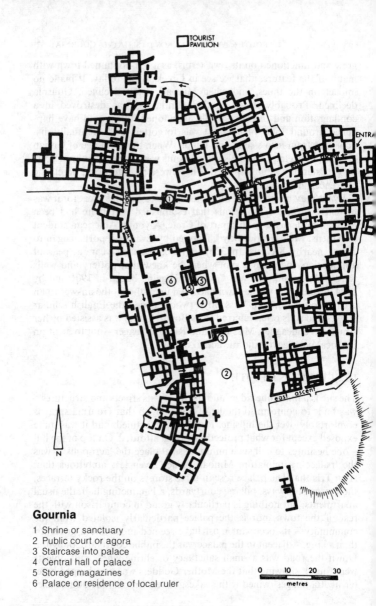

ENTRA

ridge

road

road

① ⑥ ⑤
⑤
④
③
②

east ascent

Gournia

1 Shrine or sanctuary
2 Public court or agora
3 Staircase into palace
4 Central hall of palace
5 Storage magazines
6 Palace or residence of local ruler

N

0 10 20 30
metres

But none of this really advances our knowledge of Minoan civilization. It is, rather, as a revelation of domestic economy that Gournia is unique, for within and around the houses and shops were found objects invaluable for the study of the life of the 'middle' and 'lower' classes: vats and implements for producing olive oil; a forge with a mould for casting chisels, awls and nails; loom weights; a carpenter's kit, including saws, files, axes, chisels and nails; razors, tweezers, knives; mortars and pestles; and many other artefacts (now in the Archaeological Museum in Iraklion).

Up and down the streets you may walk, stepping in and out of the houses. You can still see some of the sea-worn stones carefully laid to make the streets; you can still step over thresholds and through doorways and observe the stairways to the second storeys. Stones were used for first storeys, sun-dried bricks for second storeys and partition walls; walls were often plastered; ceilings were reeds daubed with plaster. It is all very familiar to anyone who has strolled through a contemporary Greek mountain village; some of these houses at Gournia would need little except roofs to be habitable as modern peasants' homes.

More than one visitor to Gournia has commented on how small the houses are; but think of other primitive settlements of this era, and then look at Gournia as a whole. Here are block after block of dwellings where people lived and worked, roads and steps they climbed, urns and tools that they used, a square where they gathered to conduct their affairs, altars where they worshipped. True, it is all rather crude and cramped. But it is basically recognizable: Gournia is the prototype of European civic life. Three thousand years later, a Siena is nothing but Gournia writ large.

For the last striking impression of Gournia, continue along the main road to the east some few hundred metres, as the road climbs up to a pass. If you halt about halfway up and look back, you will see Gournia spread out like a great spider's web or fisherman's net across the slopes.

[21 km.] After going through a small pass you emerge to look down at the harbour of the little port of Pakhia Ammos. High on the right as you descend is a large stone *villa*. This was constructed early in this century by Richard Seager, when he was excavating in eastern Crete. A young American of independent means, he is reputed to have given grand parties in his villa, with dozens of distinguished guests.

Although he has no major discovery to his credit, he made important basic digs and was a perceptive interpreter of Minoan affairs. After volunteer duty with the Red Cross in the First World War, he went off to Egypt in 1923 to be present at the uncovering of Tutankhamun's tomb; long in poor health, he took ill on his way back to Crete in 1925 and died in Iraklion at the age of forty-three. The Germans occupied the villa during the Second World War; you may still see signs of their occupation although these have probably been erased during the renovations of recent years.

[22 km.] **Pakhia Ammos** is a port of call for local coastal shipping. Tomatoes and olives are cultivated on the rich plain behind the harbour. Seager excavated Minoan tombs along the beach (with trussed bodies jammed into burial jars), and a chamber tomb has recently been excavated up near his villa, but there is nothing of interest to the non-specialist. In the town is a Class C hotel, *Golden Beach*, and several pensions as well as several eating-places; on the edge of the town a large hotel has been going up for some years and it may now be open.

Just outside Pakhia Ammos (at the large hotel that was never finished) you could take the road south across the island for 16 km. to Ierapetra (p. 316).

[28 km.] Continuing along the Sitia road you come to the village of **Kavousi.** On the mountainous slopes at the edge of Kavousi are two adjacent sites, Kastro and Vronda, initially explored by Harriet Boyd in 1900 but since the late 1980s being thoroughly excavated under the auspices of the American School of Classical Studies. Most of the remains date from the post-Minoan Geometric period, although a pottery kiln in the area is Late Minoan (c. 1200 B.C.). Although the site itself does not offer much of interest to casual travellers, the Kastro-Vronda finds are casting more light on the dim lives of Cretans who followed the end of the Minoan civilization. And the town itself boasts three *Byzantine churches*. Kavousi may be used as the base for a climb up to the peak of Aphendis Stavromenos.

The next stretch of road – from Kavousi to Sitia – has been called the 'Riviera of Crete', with its slopes and tiers of orchards and olive trees, and the villages clinging to the slopes, and the sea below. The road, too, certainly reminds one of a corniche with its everlasting twists and turns. At one point, about the 35-km. point, known as

Platanos, you can stop and enjoy a snack and some fresh spring water as you look out on the island of Psira (p. 315).

[40 km.] Just before the village of **Sfaka** there is a side-road to the left leading down in 7 km. to the village of **Mokhlos** on the coast; directly off shore is the islet of Mokhlos (p. 315), and a boat can usually be hired in the village to take you out to it and over to Psira.

[57 km.] **Exo Mouliana.** This area is famous for its red wine. There are also some *beehive tombs* where finds were made of swords and bronze objects.

[63 km.] At **Khamezi** were found the remains of an oval structure from the Proto-palatial period. As this is the only known oval-shaped Minoan structure, some scholars think it may have been some sort of sanctuary rather than a house. Khamezi is also the village where it has been claimed that the seventeenth-century poet Cornaros (p. 112) was born, since his family are known to have lived there. (Others nominate Piskokephalo, p. 339, as his birth-place.)

[67 km.] After passing through **Skopi**, you see the *Bay of Sitia* spread out before you; in the distance stretches the north-east extremity of Crete – *Cape Sidheros* – with the islands known as the *Dionysiadhes* to the north-west of the cape.

[72 km.] You descend to the coast and arrive at Sitia.

SITIA

Sitia retains something of the travel-poster version of a little Mediterranean port, with its cafés along the harbour and an air of awaiting ships that never come in. But although it has yet to experience the surge of tourism that has transformed Ayios Nikolaos, Sitia is also losing some of its undeveloped charms. It is a port of call for ships that pass weekly between Rhodes and Santorini-Piraeus; it is also a jumping-off point for several interesting excursions into the easternmost reaches of Crete. (And plans for an airport have been discussed.)

Population About 6,200.
Sea connections See pp. 21–4.
Hotels Class A: *Sitia Beach* (tel. 28.821).
　　　　 Class B: *Denis* (tel. 28.356).
　　　　 Class C: *Alice* (tel. 28.450).

Castello (tel. 23.763).
Crystal (tel. 22.284).
Elena (tel. 22.681).
Itanos (tel. 22.900).
Mariana (tel. 22.088).
Vai (tel. 22.528).

Several Class D hotels, a youth hostel (tel. 22.693) and various other pensions and rooms are available.

Restaurants The usual collection of eating-places all along the quay.

Swimming There is a sandy beach, with cabins, just east of the town. Waterskiing, windsurfing, and paddleboating available.

Buses There are regular services westwards to Iraklion via Gournia and Ayios Nikolaos. There are also buses to Ierapetra and to villages in the district, including Palaikastro, Ano Zakros and Ziros (for Praisos). There is also a summer service to Toplou Monastery, Vai and Itanos.

PRINCIPAL SIGHTS

Gently sloping to the sea, crowned by a few remains of the *Venetian fort*, Sitia has little of the glory that the Venetians projected for it: Sitia was to be the fourth of the great coastal cities but never quite became one. The Venetians themselves recognized its failings and dismantled much of the fort, carrying the cannons off to other cities. There was a small castle and a rector's palace, but when the Turks took over these fell into decay along with the fort. Two *churches* remain, one in the form of a Greek cross and the other in the Venetian style, with three naves.

Today the chief source of income for the region is the *sultanina* – the raisin. The people are mild and genial – a far cry from their brawling relatives in Sfakia. Incidentally, this part of Crete was occupied by the Italians during the Second World War.

Sitia has provided the name of this region and nome: 'Lasithi' is a corruption of La Sitia, the Venetians' name for their settlement. Before the coming of the Venetians, this eastern region had the reputation of being the home of the 'Eteocretans' – the 'true' or indigenous Cretans. It is claimed that with the arrival of the Dorians after the break-up of the Minoan–Mycenaean civilization, some native Cretans retired to these eastern hills where they preserved their language and culture in some 'pure' form. As we shall see when we discuss some of these eastern sites, some traditional modes survived; but in general no modern scholars really believe that the 'pure Minoans' – whoever they would be – linger on in Lasithi.

Most visitors to Sitia will probably settle for strolling along the waterfront and the adjacent streets to pass the time between eating and swimming. In fact, Sitia offers two interesting little museums, both worth a short visit.

Archaeological Museum
Hours Weekdays except Tuesdays, 9.00 to 15.00; Sundays 10.00 to 15.00.
Entrance charge Drs 100.

Opened only in 1984, in a modern building at the eastern edge of town (in a jumble of commercial activities, but unmistakably a modern museum), this modest collection will probably grow in interest as more and more sites in this part of Crete yield more and more finds. The present finds extend from the Proto-Minoan through to the Roman period; many are from cemeteries and sanctuaries of eastern Crete; there are some Linear A tablets, rare anywhere in the world's great museums; there are finds from the new site on Kouphonisi Islet (p. 318). Labels are in Greek, English, French, German, and Italian, so most visitors can learn something.

Folklore Museum
Hours Most days 10.00 to 13.00, 17.00 to 20.00.
Entrance charge Drs 100.

Precisely because it is so 'typical' in its setting and collection, this little museum might be of more interest to many people who do not ordinarily go out of their way to visit such museums. It is in a small formerly private house up on the hill that rises from the harbour; there has been a sign at harbourside on the street called Patriarchio Metathaki directing you up the hill; you turn left on G. Maryrikaki. The materials have been donated by local Cretans to show something of the culture and life of eastern Crete; they include tools, kitchenware, ceramics, basketry, textiles, weavings, clothing, furniture, and musical instruments. Labels are in English and French as well as Greek. Well worth an hour's visit if you have come this far. And there are some handsome items – textiles, etc. – for sale.

EXCURSIONS FROM SITIA
Kato Zakros

The discovery of a Minoan palace at Kato Zakros has been one of the most exciting archaeological developments in recent decades. It is now an easy day excursion from Sitia (and, indeed, those with a limited time can make it in a full day and return to Iraklion, from which it is about a five-hour drive). You can stay at Ano Zakros throughout the year, at Kato Zakros in the summer only. And, of course, by staying in Sitia you can combine a visit to Kato Zakros with visits to other places in this eastern corner of Crete.

Route Following the coast road eastwards out of Sitia, after 19 km., you arrive at the modern village of Palaikastro (p. 337); here you turn south, winding up through a pass and through several villages until you come to Ano Zakros [39 km.]. The road continues descending to the coast at Kato Zakros [46 km.] where the site is located.
Bus There is a bus from Sitia to Ano Zakros, which would still leave a 7-km. walk down to the site; but especially during the main season, you can probably count on someone giving you a ride in both directions.
Accommodation Ano Zakros has a small Class C hotel, the *Zakros* (tel. 28.479); you can also get other rooms there, as well as simple meals. During the summer, you can get rooms and simple meals along the beach at Kato Zakros. There is a Class B hotel, *Mare Sol*, at Ayia Fotia (tel. 28.950).

[7 km.] Here at **Ayia Fotia**, in 1971, was discovered an extensive early Minoan *cemetery* (over 250 tombs). Among the earliest reported finds were such objects as copper daggers, a lead box containing thin sheets of gold, amulets with deities represented as animals and hundreds of vases. As with most such sites, the things of interest to the layman will be on view in a museum (in this instance, in Ayios Nikolaos).

[14 km.] A turning to the left leads up in 4 km. to the *Monastery of Toplou* (p. 336).

[19 km.] **Palaikastro**, the modern village (p. 337). A sign in the centre of the town indicates straight ahead to Zakros (with Vai and Itanos (p. 337) off to the left); some metres after that sign, you bear sharply to the right and curve back and down out of the town on an asphalt road.

[23 km.] The village of **Langada.** You proceed on through the mountains.

[39 km.] **Ano Zakros** (*áno* = 'upper'; *káto* = 'lower'). Due to the increased traffic to the nearby site, this village now supports a decent Class C hotel, the *Zakros*, as well as other rooms to rent. It also prides itself on its fine spring water. At the end of the village 'square', the road turns right (signed). As you leave the village, note (right) the few remains of a Minoan villa beside the road. The road that descends to the coast is now tarmac all the way. (Watch for the turn to the left at about 41 km.) The road passes through fertile fields and olive groves and then along a mountain ridge. To the left you see the dramatic rocky cliffs forming a deep gorge that has become known as the 'Valley of the Dead' because of the Minoan tombs and burials discovered there. The road descends in curves to the sea, with the little bay of Kato Zakros in the distance.

[46 km.] You arrive at the sign announcing the little village of **Kato Zakros**, but continue, winding through the luxuriant groves of bananas and olive trees; just before the last stretch to the sea, you come out in a clearing. You park near the beach and follow a (sign-posted) path over to the site. Down on the sea, rooms and meals are available during the summer season; and there is a fine beach for bathing. The excavations may be visited throughout the year.

HISTORY OF KATO ZAKROS

Kato Zakros was first excavated in 1901 under the direction of the British archaeologist D. G. Hogarth. He turned up some small houses, with finds of potsherds and seal impressions, but concluded that it had been little more than a Minoan port of call for ships between Crete and Africa and Asia Minor. That seemed to dispose of the site. Then, just before the Second World War, some gold objects found their way into the collection of Dr Giamalakis; they were said to have been hoarded by a peasant who had worked on the original dig under Hogarth. In 1945 the Greeks supported an archaeological survey of the sites in eastern Crete, and Nicholas Platon took a special interest in Kato Zakros. In subsequent years several finds of stone and other objects convinced Dr Platon that there must have been more than a little port here. In 1961 he sank a trial trench and turned up still more evidence of an ambitious settlement. Meanwhile, Mr and Mrs Leon Pomerance, Americans with an active interest in ancient art and archaeology, came across Platon's statement in the Museum guide that there were still important Minoan remains to be dug on Crete. They confronted Platon, who countered with Kato Zakros; the Pomerances offered to help finance the project, and digging began in the autumn of 1962. Excavations have continued ever since then, financed by the Greek government as well as by donations by the Pomerances, and the result has been the unearthing of the fourth great Minoan centre.

In addition to the palace, of course, there have been other finds in the immediate and nearby areas. Among the first were the burials in the caves (going back to 2600 B.C.) in the 'Valley of the Dead' (p. 331). They also found a large Minoan villa, up near Ano Zakros, with fresco fragments, a wine press and a *pithos* inscribed with twenty-five signs of Linear A. Other villas, other cemeteries and a hill sanctuary have been found near by. In 1968 they began to unearth the structures on the terraced slope north-east of the palace proper, revealing an extensive complex; some were Pre-palatial and Proto-palatial remains including roads, structures, and numerous domestic artefacts such as tools, loom weights, and hearths. And then, on the ridges and slopes flanking the depression around the bay, there have been unearthed increasing indications of a well-planned harbour-town, with its network of roads, large homes for the upper classes and blocks of dwellings for the lower classes. They also have revealed quite an extensive section of the paved road to the harbour – some 2·6 metres wide – with a number of houses lining the road. The harbour installations seem to have disappeared – possibly due to the subsidence of this part of the coast? With so much still to be discovered and published, scholars remain guarded in their interpretations. But certainly among the tangible results of the discoveries at Kato Zakros has been the stimulus for further explorations and excavations in the eastern part of Crete.

DESCRIPTION OF SITE

Burials in the caves and other cemeteries, remains of houses and other signs indicate that this site was inhabited at least as far back as 2600 B.C. Although the palace ruins visible date from the period between 1600 and 1450 B.C., excavations have revealed remains of an earlier palace underneath this one – just as at the other great palaces. Probably at some point, the chieftains at Knossos realized the settlement here could be a crucial link in the Minoan trading 'empire': not only as a refuge for ships in trouble in these remote waters but as the 'outermost' harbour for ships making the voyage across the Mediterranean to the east. But whether the initiative came from Knossos or from the local people, this site – whatever its name at the time – became a prosperous outpost of Minoan culture as well as an important trading centre. As the former, it must have been a major transmitter and sustainer of the 'high' Minoan civilization in eastern Crete; this is supported by such matters as the presence of Linear A tablets and the close similarity of the palace's design to Knossos palace. And like Knossos, it had especially strong connections with Egypt and the Levant, as evidenced by such finds as copper from Cyprus, ivory from Syria and gold, alabaster, basalt and diorite from Egypt. Kato Zakros itself probably exported both manufactured goods and local produce – oil, wine, resin, honey, aromatic oils, and wood.

By about 1600 B.C. it must have been almost the peer of Mallia if we may judge from the palace that began to go up at this time. This palace eventually covered a hectare, and had some 250 to 300 rooms in its two – possibly three – storeys. In general, its features conform to the other Minoan palaces: the large main court, and grouped around it the cult and religious rooms, the royal ceremonial areas, the light-wells, the stairways, the work-rooms, the storage rooms, the domestic quarters, etc. One feature of this palace, however, seems to have been quite unique: a large cistern and a fountain-well (see 23 and 24 on site plan) were inside the palace and tapped spring water that was directly distributed to the palace's water supply.

About 1500 B.C. this palace experienced a major disaster – possibly an earthquake, possibly a seismic wave – necessitating considerable rebuilding, although the basic lay-out of the palace remained the same. And then, perhaps about 1450 B.C., it experienced a relatively sudden and even more drastic catastrophe: an earthquake and fire were certainly involved, and there are some who claim that it may have been directly related to the great eruption of Santorini (Thera), with the resultant tidal wave and fall-out of ash (see p. 94). Whatever happened, the people in the palace at Kato Zakros must have had just enough warning to cause them to drop whatever they were doing and flee. The result was an almost completely destroyed structure but almost intact contents; and not only was this the only one of the great Minoan palaces not reconstructed, it remained unplundered.

This has meant that treasures were uncovered at Kato Zakros in an unusual number, condition and value. In the storerooms thirty-four large *píthoi* were found; in the 'archives' were found clay tablets with Linear A script (one of the few such finds outside Ayia Triadha); and in the treasure room, or cult repository, some fifty-five stone vessels – quite incredible in the diversity of their forms and decorations – were found, along with an equal number of ceramic pieces. Also found here were many metal artefacts, including a large saw used for cutting stone, cast-iron tools and some fine swords; a dark stone capital of a

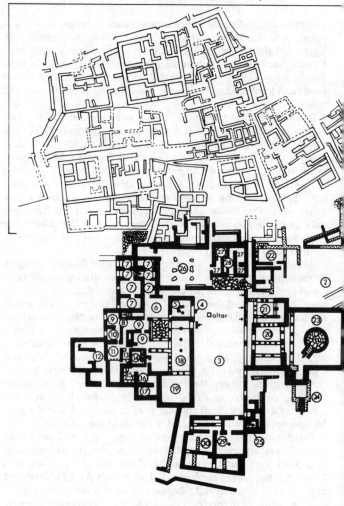

Palace at Kato Zakros

1 N.E. Gate
2 Courtyard for service operations
3 Central Courtyard
WEST WING
4 Chief Entrance
5 Anteroom
6 Lobby
7 Storerooms
8 Main staircase to upper W. Wing
9 Rooms for Priests
10 Room (Pantry?)
11 Archive room
12 Workshop extension with
   dye-house
13 Shrine
14 Lustral basin
15 Treasury
16 Workshop
17 Storeroom
18 Hall of Ceremonies
19 Banquet Hall
EAST WING
20 King's room
21 Queen's room
22 Bathroom
23 Hall of the Cistern
24 Well of the Fountain
25 Second Well
NORTH WING
26 Kitchen
27 Storerooms
28 Site of large staircase to
   dining-room
SOUTH WING
29 Sitting-room
30 Workshops

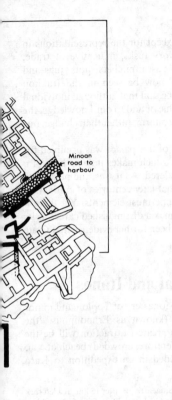

Minoan
road to
harbour

0 5 10 20 30
metres

N

column, the first such to be found except for the representations in frescoes; large copper ingots and ivory tusks, indicative of trade; traces of frescoes; and thousands of vases, pitchers, pots, jugs and other vessels. All these things may now be seen in the Iraklion museum (p. 138). In general, it might be said that, although individual pieces have their intrinsic aesthetic value or add to our knowledge, the site and finds at Kato Zakros serve to confirm, rather than change, our previous image of Minoan Crete.

Interestingly, the surrounding area of this palace was occupied for many centuries after the catastrophe, which makes it something of a mystery why the palace was not plundered. As it was, the palace lay under such a shallow cover of earth that later centuries of cultivation on the site did destroy some of the uppermost elements. Yet there it sat, until Dr Platon came along to climax a distinguished career as its excavator. All in all, Kato Zakros has been further evidence that Crete is a place where legends are born.

Toplou, Palaikastro, Vai and Itanos

This expedition takes in the isolated Monastery of Toplou and minor remains at Palaikastro and Itanos (known as Erimoupolis, 'the deserted city'). For many people the greatest attraction will be the beautiful palm-fringed (sometimes, therefore, crowded) beach at Vai. Some of these places could be included in an expedition to Kato Zakros (p. 329).

Route Follow the coast road eastwards out of Sitia, arriving after 15 km. at a left fork for the Monastery of Toplou. If instead you proceed straight on for a further 4 km. you arrive at Palaikastro, from where a road leads north in about 10 km. to Itanos and Vai.
Bus There is a bus service to Palaikastro from Sitia; you could get off at the turning to Toplou (4-km. walk). There is a summer bus service to Toplou, Vai and Itanos.
Sea Another way to get round to these sites would be to hire a boat at Sitia and put in at various coves, from which you would then have to make some overland treks.
Accommodation You can stay at Palaikastro or at Ano Zakros (p. 330).

[14 km.] Following the coast road eastwards out of Sitia, you arrive at a fork to the left which takes you up a track in about 4 km. to the *Monastery of Toplou*.

Originally an old church stood here, long before the monastery was founded some time in the fourteenth to fifteenth centuries. The first monastery was destroyed by an earthquake in 1612 and reconstructed that same century; at this time, too, was built its distinctive *bell-tower* (restored in the nineteenth century). It was named Toplou by the Turks – derived from their word *top*, 'cannonball', since the monastery was armed with a cannon. It has the appearance of a fortified castle and has indeed been an important centre for resistance and refugees from the occupation of the Turks to the Second World War. The Panayia Akrotiriani – 'Virgin of the Cape' – is worshipped here. On the façade of the chapel is an ancient *plaque* commemorating a treaty between the Cretan realms of Itanos and Ierapytna (second century B.C.). Within are some valuable *icons*: one by Ioannis Cornaros, dating from the eighteenth century, depicts the greatness of the Lord and scenes from the Bible – a masterpiece crowded with figures and scenes.

What makes a visit to Toplou really worth while, besides the distinctive architecture of the monastery showing Venetian influence (greatly restored in recent years) is the primitive isolation of its situation. The monastery is also reputed to be one of the richest monasteries in Greece as it owns much land in the region.

From Toplou a paved road leads overland north-eastwards towards the sea and after about 8 km. joins the road from Palaikastro to Itanos and Vai (see below).

[19 km.] Having returned to the main road from Sitia, however, from the Toplou fork you proceed another 5 km. eastwards to arrive at the modern village of **Palaikastro**. (There are a Class B hotel, the *Hellas* (tel. 61.240), the *Marina Village* (tel. 61.284), which is Class C, and rooms to rent.) A sign indicates the left turn to Vai and Itanos (see below), straight ahead to (Kato) Zakros. As described on p. 330 for Zakros you make a sharp curve to the right some metres later; for the Minoan site of Palaikastro, instead of turning right you continue straight along a narrow street that soon turns into a dirt track that winds down through olive groves; bear right on this dirt track until you come to a bridge foundation; turn left here and then always bear to the right as you proceed toward the coast, a settlement off to the right and the large flat-topped hill (known as Kastri) rising ahead of you; at about 1·9 km. from the edge of town you come to a sign pointing to the archaeological site. You now have a short walk across the fields to your right to find yourself near one edge of the remains. (A good beach and a café-restaurant reward your efforts in the summer.)

And after all this, only the most dedicated ruin-haunter will feel rewarded. The British excavated here back in 1902–6 and turned up a quite extensive Minoan harbour-town, as well as remains of later settlements from the Geometric to Hellenistic periods. Over the decades, though, the site became overgrown, and although the British returned in the 1960s for a bit of cleaning up and further excavations in the 1980s, the site has nothing very dramatic to recommend it to the casual visitor. Indeed, it is often difficult to separate the ancient remains from more recent farm-lot walls, since over the years the local people have used some of the ancient stones for their own purposes. Still, there is a most impressive well-paved main street, lined by houses and shops (in one of which were found weights, jars, a sink and a drain) and various side streets with their houses. There was also a many-roomed palace of large stones, the seat of some local prince. But Palaikastro's importance was not as a palace centre but as a commercial-port settlement, whose heyday was in the late Minoan times – comparable to, and perhaps larger than, Gournia. Lying close to the shore, with its acropolis rising behind it and the lofty bluff before it, Palaikastro must have been imposing in its way. And it was one of the few places on Crete to be rebuilt after the great catastrophe of about 1450 B.C. – unlike Gournia to its west and Kato Zakros to its south. (A 1983 survey revealed a much larger Minoan site than suspected.)

In addition to the town itself, Minoan cemeteries were found dotted over the plain; and an important Minoan sanctuary was discovered in 1903 in a rock shelter in the nearby hill of *Petsofa*. Among the more important finds of the later periods were remains of an Archaic-Hellenic temple, with a fragment of a frieze, and a stele – memorial column – inscribed with a hymn to Dhiktaian Zeus (now in room XIX of the Iraklion museum). The carving on the stele dates from the third century A.D. but the hymn itself is centuries older and reveals the religious sentiments of an earlier age. Other valuable finds were bronze tripods, shields, terracotta figurines, ivory plaques and a great quantity of pottery and vases. Further excavations in the 1970s yielded more finds, including bronze artefacts, terracotta statuettes, and stone offering tables with Linear A inscriptions.

Back in the modern village of Palaikastro, you may now take the turn to the north – indicated by the sign to Vai-Itanos.

[27 km.] After some 8 km. along a new road, you arrive at a fork. The right branch brings you in about another 1½ km. – as you pass through the rather spectacular palm grove of *Vai* – to a fine tropical-looking beach, itself ringed with palm trees. Simple meals and refreshments may be had there throughout the summer, but like so many such places, as word of its seclusion has spread, it can now be quite crowded during the summer with campers and sun-worshippers.

Back at the 27 km. fork, you may take the left branch and proceed north for about $1\frac{1}{2}$ km. to reach the site of ancient *Itanos* – known to local people as *Erimoupolis*, 'the deserted city'. Originally a Minoan settlement, it did not come into its own until the post-Minoan period, when its importance is evidenced by records of its quarrels with other city-states in eastern Crete (see the inscription at Toplou, p. 337); it flourished through the Roman period and on into Byzantine times. But of all this, only fragmentary remains are to be seen – the walls of the Hellenistic acropolis, parts of an early Christian church, the base of a Roman statue, tombs, etc. As so often on Crete, it is the setting that justifies the trip: the nearby sea, the dark headland beyond and Cape Sidheros reaching out to the north (although the seclusion has been spoiled by the heavy military development of this locale).

Praisos

This important post-Minoan site, and a few other places en route, might make a day's excursion from Sitia, although it will interest mainly specialists. And now that the new highway is completed, you could continue all the way via Lithines to the south coast and then on to Ierapetra.

Route Follow the signs out of Sitia south towards Lithines, but at 10 km., after Epano Episkopi, turn left for Nea Praisos [14 km.]
Bus There is a bus service from Sitia to Ziros, which passes through Nea Praisos.

[1·5 km.] Scant remains of a Minoan villa are sign-posted immediately to the right of the road. Known in the literature as the Manares country house, it must have enjoyed a view over the valley – and it is possible that a river allowed boats to come right up to the bottom of a set of stairs still to be seen.

[3 km.] You pass through the village of **Piskokephalo**, a leading candidate for the birthplace of Vincenzo Cornaros, the seventeenth-century Cretan credited with several major literary works (p. 112). Many Minoan votive statuettes have been found on a nearby hill, suggesting it was the site of a peak sanctuary.

If you turn off to the left, you would come to **Zou**, near which are remains of a Minoan farmhouse of about 1600 B.C.; the road proceeds for about 1 km. to **Kato Episkopi**, where you turn right at a fork and continue for about another 2 km. to Zou. The remains are beside the road (sign-posted) about 300 metres north of the village. The house is in good condition and must have enjoyed a fine view over the valley.

A right turn back in the village of Piskokephalo would bring you in about 5 km. to **Akhladia**, a small Minoan settlement: a good specimen of a domed tomb was excavated here.

Although few will want to make the trip, it is possible to go on from Akhladia west and south through the Sitia Range, heading for **Stavrokhorion** and going down to the south coast at **Koutsouras**, and then along the south coast to Ierapetra (below). It is a scenic ride of about 65 km., and the road is rough but passable; a map would be advisable.

[10·5 km.] Continuing on the main road south from Sitia, you arrive just before the village of **Epano Episkopi** at a track to the left (the road to the right goes on down to Lithines) that winds its way up in about 4 km. to **Nea Praisos** (also known as Vaveloi); outside the village (to the east) lies the site of ancient Praisos.

Praisos

The ancient city of Praisos, which spread across three small hills, is considered to be one of the chief post-Minoan settlements; as such, it was the centre of the so-called Eteocretans – Minoans who retreated from the Dorians. Only jumbled stones remain: a Minoan farm, tombs, the Hellenistic acropolis and a late Hellenistic house of some size hint at the fairly continuous settlement and prosperity of the site from Minoan through Hellenistic times. Here also were found three inscriptions with Greek characters but recording a non-Hellenic language. The inscriptions date from somewhere between 600 and 300 B.C. and have been attributed to the Eteocretans. The American scholar Cyrus Gordon has proposed that the language is of the Semitic family – and, what is more, a direct descendant of the Semitic language that he claims to have deciphered as the language of Linear A. Not all scholars accept such claims.

Praisos was first explored in the late nineteenth and early twentieth centuries, but in the 1960s other remains have been found in the environs: a Minoan villa at **Tourtoula** (the summit of Profitis Elias) has some frescoes; and **Fotoulas** had a rectangular vaulted tomb. At **Sklavi**, some kilometres over the hills to the south-west, other tombs have been found. And these are only some of the many remains that testify to an extensive and millennia-long habitation of this area.

Back at Epano Episkopi (at the 10·5 km. point) you could continue south through quite spectacular mountain terrain, although on a first-class road to Ierapetra. The route passes by Lithines [22 km.]; at about 25·5 km., a bend in the road reveals the Libyan Sea and Crete's southern coast down in the distance; at 30 km. you arrive at the southern coast and pass through Makriyialos [30·5 km.] where there are beaches with good swimming and accommodation (p. 321). Continuing west, you pass through Koutsouras [33 km.]; Ferma [41 km.] with its hotels; Koutsounari [51 km.], the Tourist Village high on the right (p. 43), and arrive at Ierapetra [57 km.].

SELECT BIBLIOGRAPHY

This is only the cream of the books about Crete. The latest editions (often revised and enlarged) are listed; several have also been published in paperback and some are once more available in facsimile hard-cover editions.

GENERAL

Leland Allbaugh, *Crete: A Case Study of an Underdeveloped Area* (Princeton University Press, 1953): now dated in its statistics and descriptions, but a reminder of how many Cretans lived until recent years.

Franz Altherr and Hanni Guanella, *Crete as seen today* (NZN, Zurich, 1971): striking photographs of the whole spectrum of Crete today.

Clutton and Kenny, *Crete* (David & Charles, 1976): a readable survey – strong on history – in The Islands series.

Adam Hopkins, *Crete – Its Past, Present and People* (Faber, 1977): as title suggests, a fine mix of history, contemporary conditions, and personal contacts.

Nikos Kazantzakis, *Zorba the Greek, Freedom and Death, Christ Recrucified* (or *The Greek Passion*), *The Odyssey: A Modern Sequel* and *Report to Greco*: five of the more striking works by perhaps the strongest 'voice' of modern Crete. (All are widely available in paperback editions.)

Raymond Matton, *La Crète au cours des siècles* (Institut Français d'Athènes, 1957): a good survey of Crete's complete history. The first section has been published as a separate book, *La Crète antique* (Athens, 1960).

Mary Renault, *The King Must Die* (Longmans, 1971; New English Library) and *The Bull from the Sea* (Longmans, 1976; Penguin); imaginative reconstructions of the Theseus legend and Minoan Crete. (Available in paperback.)

Michael Smith, *The Great Island* (Longmans, 1965): an interesting mixture of personal travel, folk-lore and history.

MINOAN CRETE: HISTORY AND ARCHAEOLOGY

Stylianos Alexiou, *Minoan Civilization* (Iraklion, 1973): a sound survey drawing on the latest scholarly information.

Gerald Cadogan, *Palaces of Minoan Crete* (Methuen, 1980): a detailed guide, by an archaeologist, to more than the title suggests.

John Chadwick, *The Mycenaean World* (Cambridge University Press, 1976): an excellent account of this society as revealed by Linear B tablets, by one who worked with Ventris in the original decipherment.

Leonard Cottrell, *The Bull of Minos* (Evans, 1971; Holt Rinehart, 1958; Pan; Grosset): a readable account of the lives, work and worlds of Schliemann and Evans.

Arthur Evans, *The Palace of Minos* (Macmillan, 1921–36; Biblo & Tanner): despite all that has happened since, still the seminal work; fascinating to browse through.

James W. Graham, *The Palaces of Crete* (Princeton University Press, 1962): a solid analysis of the Minoan palaces.

Charles Herberger, *The Thread of Ariadne* (Philosophical Library, 1972): an ingenious decipherment of the famed bull-leapers fresco that encompasses much of the Minoan mythology.

L. R. Palmer, *Mycenaeans and Minoans* (Faber, Knopf, 1964): controversial, but one of several reappraisals of the Minoan materials.

J. D. S. Pendlebury, *The Archaeology of Crete* (Methuen, 1939; Biblo & Tannen; Norton, 1965): a good objective survey of sites and finds up through the Roman period.

Nicholas Platon, *Crete* (Frederick Muller, 1966; World, 1966): especially valuable for its account of the Kato Zakros site by the discoverer and excavator.

CRETE SINCE THE MINOANS

Alan Clark, *The Fall of Crete* (Anthony Blond, 1962; Morrow, 1962): a solid account of the battle of Crete in the Second World War.

Richard Clogg, *A Short History of Modern Greece* (Cambridge University Press, 1979): Crete plays its part in this story.

Deno J. Geanakoplos, *Greek Scholars in Venice* (Oxford University Press, 1962; Harvard University Press, 1962): some curious sidelights on late-medieval and Renaissance Crete.

William Miller, *Essays on the Latin Orient* (Cambridge University Press, 1921): still more curious sidelights on medieval Crete.

Pandelis Prevelakis, *The Tale of a Town* (Doric Publications, Athens, 1977): an English translation (by Kenneth Johnstone) of this Cretan author's affectionate portrait of Rethymnon.

George Psychoundakis, *The Cretan Runner* (Murray, 1955; Transatlantic, 1955): a fine account of the Cretan–British resistance operations by one of the participants.

Sterghios Spanakis, *Crete* (Iraklion, 1968): organized as a guide, this is especially valuable on the Byzantine, Venetian and Turkish aspects of the island's history and remains.

R. F. Willetts, *Ancient Crete: A Social History* (Routledge, 1965; University of Toronto, 1965): Post-Minoan to Roman Crete by the authority on the period.

CRETE AND THE ARTS

Alexiou, Platon, Guanella and Von Matt, *Ancient Crete* (Thames & Hudson, 1967; Praeger, 1968): a fine survey in words and pictures.

Giuseppe Gerola, *Monumenti veneti nell'isola di Creta* (Venice, 1905–32): the definitive work on the Venetian structures on Crete.

Konstantin Kalokyris, *The Byzantine Wall Paintings of Crete* (Red Dust Inc., New York, 1973): a fully illustrated translation of a work that, for all its limitations, remains the best general introduction.

M. J. Manoussakas, 'La littérature crétoise à l'époque vénitienne' in *L'Hellénisme Contemporain* (mars-juin 1955): the most complete survey of Cretan literature under the Venetians.

F. H. Marshall, *Three Cretan Plays* (Oxford University Press, 1929): translations of three of the Cretan–Venetian dramas.

James A. Notopoulos, 'Homer and Cretan Dramatic Poetry: A Study in Comparative Oral Poetry' in *American Journal of Philology* (July 1952): a glimpse into the oral folk culture of Crete.

CRETE AND RELIGION

Robert Graves, *The Greek Myths* (Penguin, 1969): a vital source for understanding the essence of Crete.

John C. Lawson, *Modern Greek Folklore and Ancient Greek Religion* (Cambridge University Press, 1910; University Books): a minor classic that traces the relationships between the two traditions.

Martin Nilsson, *The Minoan–Mycenaean Religion and Its Survival in Greek Religion* (Gleerup, 1950): the standard work on the subject.

—— *Greek Folk Religion* (Harper, 1961; Torchbooks).

R. F. Willetts, *Cretan Cults and Festivals* (Barnes and Noble, 1962; Routledge, 1962): a complete survey of the mainly post-Minoan religious world before Christianity.

TRAVELS ON CRETE

David Doren, *Winds of Crete* (Murray, 1974): an American–Swedish couple living on Crete and learning of themselves.

Xan Fielding, *The Stronghold* (Secker & Warburg, 1953): an ex-resistance fighter returns to live on Crete.

Edward Lear, *The Cretan Journal* (Denise Harvey, 1984): a beautifully produced edition of an eccentric experience – a delight to read and own.

Henry Miller, *The Colossus of Maroussi* (Heinemann, 1960; Penguin, New Directions): Miller and Crete make a surprisingly good match.

Robert Pashley, *Travels in Crete* (Murray, 1837; reprinted in 1970): still stands up as the pioneer traveller on Crete.

Dilys Powell, *The Villa Ariadne* (Hodder & Stoughton, 1973): an unusual quest that combines history, archaeology, and the personal.

Capt. T. A. B. Spratt, *Travels and Researches in Crete* (J. van Voorst, 1865; reprinted in 1965): another good encounter with nineteenth-century Crete.

Joseph de Tournefort, *A Voyage into the Levant* (London, 1718): the English translation of the French (Paris, 1717) classic.

Aubyn Trevor-Battye, *Camping in Crete* (Witherby & Co., 1913): a naturalist's adventures on Crete.

PRACTICAL

B. Bruun, *Hamlyn Guide to the Birds of Britain and Europe* (Hamlyn, 1970; McGraw-Hill).

Huxley and Taylor, *Flowers of Greece and the Aegean* (Chatto and Windus, 1976).

Map of Crete (1:250,000) (Efstathiadis Group, Athens). Updated for roads. City plans. Large and clear.

Landscapes of Western and *Eastern Crete* (Sunflower Books, London, 1987): two small but thorough guides to the natural delights and routes to be experienced on car tours, walks (of varying difficulty), and excursions.

INDEX